An Approach to the
Book of Mormon

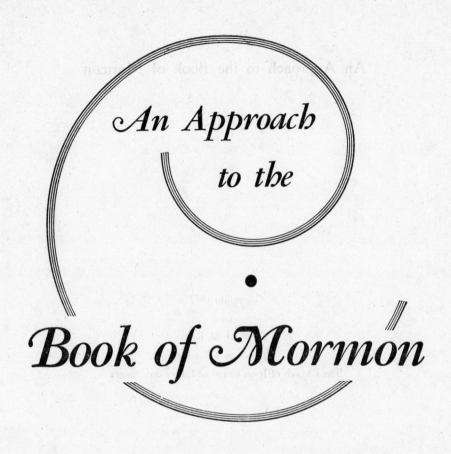

An Approach
to the

Book of Mormon

HUGH NIBLEY

Course of Study for the
MELCHIZEDEK PRIESTHOOD QUORUMS OF
THE CHURCH OF JESUS CHRIST OF LATTER-DAY SAINTS
1957

Published by
THE COUNCIL OF THE TWELVE APOSTLES
of
THE CHURCH OF JESUS CHRIST OF LATTER-DAY SAINTS

An Approach to the Book of Mormon

DESERET NEWS PRESS

Salt Lake City, Utah

PRINTED IN THE UNITED STATES OF AMERICA

PREFACE

The Book of Mormon is one of the most marvelous records ever revealed to the world. Many members of the Church do not seem to realize that when this record was revealed to Joseph Smith he was but a lad in his teens and that when it was translated and the Church organized he was but twenty-four years of age. Because of family circumstances his privilege to attend school was extremely limited and it is absolutely beyond comprehension how any youth, by his own initiative and ability, could have produced such a record. In fact, we may defy all the learned men in the world to produce such a work and present it to the world as an authentic document giving the history of an ancient, but lost people. Should they attempt it their effort would be filled with glaring errors and their work could not endure.

No book ever published has passed through the intense criticism and the most bitter opposition of the learned as well as the ignorant, yet it has triumphed over them all. Had it been a work of fiction it would have been forgotten, notwithstanding the divine claims which it contains. The truth has met with severe opposition all through the ages, yet it goes on. The thousands who have come into the Church can testify that the words of Moroni are true. Every man who seeks to know the truth will come to the light if there has been a sincere and prayerful desire to know the truth. It is only natural that a record of this kind which is true, would have to face the most intense and bitter opposition.

In these lessons Dr. Nibley has approached the study of the Book of Mormon from a rather unique, but very interesting point of view. It will appeal to every sincere student and should be studied by every member of the Church. It is to be hoped that all the brethren holding the Melchizedek Priesthood will show their gratitude to Dr. Nibley by taking a deep interest in these lessons, which sustain the record of the Book of Mormon from this new and interesting approach.

JOSEPH FIELDING SMITH

FOREWORD

Everyone who reads this manual will find new material in it—material that has not appeared in print before and is, therefore, of vital importance. The work is a new approach to the Book of Mormon and for that reason demands careful reading and study of every member of the priesthood classes using it.

In this work the Book of Mormon is seen in a new perspective; we see it in a world setting, not in a mere local one. It takes its place naturally alongside the Bible and other great works of antiquity and becomes one of them. As we study the manual, the mystery that some writers have tried to throw around the Book of Mormon disappears and the book and its characters become real and natural. False arguments which in the past have prospered against it are shattered by the material of this course. The author has thrown up such a background for the study of the Book of Mormon, and has fitted it into such a framework of world history as to make it one of the great books of all time. The success or failure of the study of the course depends upon seeing and clearly grasping this point of view and one will be rewarded according to the energy expended in gaining such an important vision.

Some of the lessons of the manual are too long for one recitation period. This should disturb neither the instructor nor the class members—two or even more recitation periods, in some cases, can be profitably spent on one lesson.

Every member should be constantly encouraged to carefully and earnestly read every lesson that he may contribute to the mastery of such vital material.

The captions, and notes at the back of the book, if carefully used, can be made to enrich the text. These notes should not be neglected.

While many of the references cited will not be available to all, others may be. These will also help to enrich the study of the manual.

The questions at the close of each lesson may well be assigned to members of the class for brief discussion in order to bring boldly to the front significant points in the lesson.

This is a course that needs diligent and prayerful study.

AN APPROACH TO THE BOOK OF MORMON

CONTENTS

(Numbers refer to pages)

AN APPROACH TO THE BOOK OF MORMON

Lesson 1

INTRODUCTION

Prospectus of Lesson 1: This is a general introduction to the lessons. It declares the purpose of the course as being to illustrate and explain the Book of Mormon, rather than to prove it. In many ways the Book of Mormon remains an unknown book, and the justification for these lessons lies in their use of neglected written materials, including ancient sources, which heretofore have not been consulted in the study of the Book of Mormon. In spite of the nature of the evidence to be presented, the average reader is qualified to pursue this course of study, though he is warned to avoid the practice common among the more sophisticated critics of the Book of Mormon of judging that book not in the light of the ancient times in which it purports to have been written, but in that of whatever period the critic himself arbitrarily chooses as the time of its production. The Book of Mormon must be read as an ancient, not as a modern book. Its mission, as described by the book itself, depends in great measure for its efficacy on its genuine antiquity. After stating this purpose, the present lesson ends with discussion of the "Great Retreat" from the Bible which is in full swing in our day and can only be checked in the end by the Book of Mormon.

Purpose of the Lessons: These lessons are dedicated to the proposition that no one can know too much about the Book of Mormon. To believe in a holy writing is just the beginning of wisdom and the first step to understanding. In these lessons on the Book of Mormon we intend to get a closer view of the mighty structure through the mists of time, and to size it up from new positions and angles. Our purpose is to illustrate, explain, suggest and investigate. We are going to consider the Book of Mormon as a possible product not of Ancient America (for that is totally beyond our competence) but of the Ancient East (which is only slightly less so). The book itself claims its origin in both these worlds, and the logical starting point for an investigation is in the older of the two.

"Proving" the Book of Mormon is another matter.

You cannot prove the genuineness of *any* document to one who has decided not to accept it. The scribes and Pharisees of old constantly asked Jesus for *proof*, and when it was set before them in overwhelming abundance they continued to disbelieve: "...O ye hypocrites, ye can discern the face of the sky; but can ye not discern the signs of the times?" (Matt. 16:3.) When a man asks for proof we can be pretty sure that proof is the last thing in the world he really wants. His request is thrown out as a challenge, and the chances are that he has no intention of being shown up. After all these years the Bible itself is still not proven to those who do not choose to believe it, and the eminent Harry Torczyner now declares that the main problem of Bible study today is to determine whether or not "the Biblical speeches, songs and laws are forgeries."[1] So the Book of Mormon as an "unproven" book finds itself in good company.

The Forgotten Evidence: The Book of Mormon can be approached and examined by specialists in many fields. In exploring the past, a leading archaeologist reminds us, "no tool may be ignored," and the findings in one field of research even when they seem perfectly clear and unequivocal, may not override contradictory findings in other fields. For example, when the experts went about dating the recently discovered Dead Sea Scrolls, the specialists in each field, the textile experts, literary historians, linguists, paleographers, theologians, pottery experts, chemists, and numismatologists all came up with different answers, sometimes many centuries apart. Only by comparing notes could they come to an agreement, and those who refused to compare, in the conviction that as authorities in their fields honestly pursuing rational methods they *could* not be wrong, still maintain that their dating is the only correct one and all the other equally competent people are wrong![2] The moral of this is that the Book of Mormon must be examined by experts in many fields, but may not be judged by the verdict of any one of them.

But if all types of research are important for understanding this book, all are not *equally* important, and the reason for writing these lessons is the author's conviction that some of the most important evidence of all has heretofore been completely ignored. A competent biologist has considered the problem of bees in the Book of Mormon, a mathematician has studied the ingenious Nephite monetary system, a great many people have dug among the ruins or taken due note of native American customs and traditions. All that is essential, but in the zeal to conduct scientific research the investigators have entirely overlooked the most telling evidence of all — that of the written documents.

For centuries it was maintained that all knowledge, scientific or otherwise, was contained in the writings of the Ancients. Oddly enough, when that claim was made, it was very nearly true, for ancient science was actually far ahead of Medieval. But with the rise of modern science it was no longer true, and the reaction against the documents was carried to the opposite extreme, which taught that science alone could teach us all there is to know about the world. That was a mistake. If the documents do not tell us everything, it does not follow that they tell us nothing. They are in fact the diary of the human race, that alone can tell us what men have been doing and thinking all these years. Running into millions of pages and going back thousands of years, they are the lab-notes and field-notes from which the ways of mankind may best be studied. There is no substitute for these documents. There are no natural laws by which the social scientist can tell whether events and situations described in the Book of Mormon were real or not; all we have is a huge heap of ancient records which will indicate more or less whether such things were possible or plausible.

The total neglect of these documents, the most powerful and effective instrument for testing and examining our revealed scriptures, has cost a heavy price in misdirected effort and useless wrangling. The only realm in which every page of the Book of Mormon may be examined has become a lost and deserted world, for our modern education regards the reading of ancient texts as pre-eminently impractical, and those areas of basic research which used to make up the subject and object of university education have yielded to the more ingratiating disciplines of "education for success."

Who is Qualified?   The real cause of the neglect of those studies which alone make possible a critical investigation of the Book of Mormon is the tremendous language barrier they present.   As we have fully demonstrated elsewhere, no document can be studied critically in translation.[3]   The ancients communicated with each other by language, as we do.   They also communicate with *us* by language—but it is their language, not ours.   Who, then, is qualified to receive their message? Neither the writer of these lessons nor, in all probability, the reader.

The one is merely a filing-clerk, who has been told to look something up and does it—the other is a person of normal intelligence who in the light of what he knows about the Book of Mormon (the only ancient text in a modern language) can decide for himself when anything significant is being conveyed.

By far the most important area in which the Book of Mormon is to be tested is in the reader's own heart. The challenge of Moroni 10:4 is by no means unscientific; every man must build his own structure of the universe but in so doing must forego the prerogative, reserved by God alone, of calling his own work good.

Anyone who attempts to read a historical source with an eye to being critical will naturally refer everything in it to his own experience. In so doing he will quickly discover in the document the most obvious parallels to the world in which he lives. This stuff, he decides, could have been written yesterday, and therefore must have been. If the document is an ancient one, however, he will also run into absurd and unfamiliar things so foreign to his experience or that of his fellows as to prove beyond a doubt that the document is a wild fabrication. This is the normal method and result of Book of Mormon criticism, which always finds proof for fraud in two kinds of matter: (1) that which is obvious and commonplace and therefore shows that Joseph Smith was simply writing from his own experience, and (2) that which is NOT obvious and commonplace and therefore shows that Joseph Smith was making it up. The critics, putting their trust in the easy generalizations of our shallow modern education, are apparently unaware that *any* authentic history of human beings is bound to contain much that is common and familiar, while on the other hand any genuine ancient record of any length is bound to contain much that is strange and unfamiliar to modern readers.

The Only Valid Approach: According to Blass, the first thing to do in examining any ancient text is to consider it in the light of the origin and background that is claimed for it. If it fits into that background there is no need to look farther, since historical forgery is virtually impossible.[4] Five hundred years of textual criticism have shown the futility of trying to judge ancient writings by the standards of modern taste, or of assuming that any ancient document is a forgery before it has been tested. Yet today the literary condemn the Book of Mormon as not being up to the standards of English literature that appeal to them, social scientists condemn it because it fails to display an evolutionary pattern of history, and the exponents of Pure Thought are disgusted with it because it entirely ignores the heritage of Medieval Scholaticism and fails to display the Victorian meliorism which should be the mark of any 19th century history of humanity.

Today some critics are fond of pointing out that the Book of Mormon is written in the very language of Joseph Smith's own society. That is as if a professor of French literature were to prove Champollion a fraud by

showing after patient years of study that his translation of the Rosetta Stone was not in Egyptian at all but
in the very type of French that Champollion and his
friends were wont to use! The discovery is totally without significance, of course, because Champollion never
claimed to be writing Egyptian, but to be rendering it
into his own language. To test his *Egyptian* claims we
would have to go back not to Grenoble but to Egypt;
and for the same reason to test the claims of the Book of
Mormon to antiquity we do not go back to the town of
Manchester but to the world from which it purports to
come. There is only one direction from which any
ancient writing may be profitably approached. *It must
be considered in its original ancient setting and in no
other.* Only there, if it is a forgery, will its weakness be
revealed, and only there, if it is true, can its claims be
vindicated.

Yet this is the one test to which the Book of Mormon has never been subjected. The usual thing today is
to regard the problem of the origin of the Book of Mormon as solved if one can only show, as Alexander
Campbell did a century and a quarter ago, that the Book
deals with matters of doctrine commonly discussed in
the world of Joseph Smith. One of the latest studies of
the subject finds decisive proof for the origin of the Book
of Mormon in the fact that it treats "the very doctrines
which thirty years of revivalism had made most intensely
interesting to the folk of western New York."[5] But it
can be shown that those very same doctrines have been
a subject of intense interest to the folk of every land and
every century in which the Bible has been seriously read,
and one might argue most convincingly that the Book of
Mormon had its real origin in any one of those times and
places,—but it would be a waste of time. This obvious
point has been completely missed in the case of the Book
of Mormon.

Why the Book of Mormon? The 27th and 29th
chapters of the Book of II Nephi explain the conditions

under which the Lord has brought forth the Book of Mormon in modern times and his purpose in doing so:

To show the human race the vanity of their wisdom and to show them ". . . that I know all their works." (2 Ne. 27:26-27.)

To teach the meek and correct ancient misunderstandings. (2 Ne. 27:25, 30.)

To serve as a great central rallying point for the work of the last days: ". . . a standard unto my people," recalling them to their covenants. (2 Ne. 29:1-2.)

To stand beside the Bible as ". . . the testimony of two nations . . . a witness unto you that I am God, that I remember one nation like unto another." (2 Ne. 29:8.)

". . . that I may prove unto many that I am the same yesterday, today, and forever . . . for my work is not yet finished. . . ." (2 Ne. 29:9.)

It is ". . . written to the Lamanites . . . and also to Jew and Gentile . . . Which is to show unto the remnant of the House of Israel what great things the Lord hath done for their fathers; and that they may know the covenants of the Lord, that they are not cast off forever—And also to the convincing of the Jew and Gentile that Jesus is the Christ, the Eternal God, manifesting himself unto all nations." (Preface to the Book of Mormon)

At a time when men ". . . cast many things away which are written and esteem them as things of naught" (2 Ne. 33:2), the Book of Mormon, containing ". . . the fullness of the gospel of Jesus Christ to the Gentiles and to the Jews also; . . . was given by inspiration, and is confirmed to others by the ministering of angels, and is declared unto the world by them—Proving to the world that the holy scriptures are true, and that God does inspire men and call them to his holy work in this age and generation, as well as in generations of old; Thereby showing that he is the same God yesterday, today, and forever. Amen." (D & C 20:9-12.)

But does the world really need more than the Bible to do these things? Nephi predicted what the reaction of the world would be to the claims of the Book of Mormon: ". . . many of the Gentiles shall say: A Bible! A Bible! We have got a Bible, and there cannot be any more Bible." (2 Ne. 29:3.) The moment the book was presented for sale this prophecy began to be fulfilled, when the most eminent newspaper of the region, "The Rochester Daily Advertiser of Rochester," New York . . . published . . . the following opinion:

BLASPHEMY

Book of Mormon—Alias the 'Golden Bible'

The Book of Mormon has been placed in our hands. A viler imposition was never practiced. It is an evidence of fraud, blasphemy, and credulity, shocking to both Christians and moralists . . .[6]

The Great Retreat: For a century the Book of Mormon continued to be regarded as an unspeakable affront to the claims and the very existence of the Bible. But in our own day a strange thing has happened: A large influential number of diligent Bible students have declared that the Bible itself is nothing but mythology, and that in order to mean anything to modern man it must be "demythologized" or "deeschatologized," that is, everything of a miraculous, prophetic, or supernatural nature must be removed from it! That is tantamount to putting the Book of Mormon and the Bible on the same footing, not by accepting the one, but by rejecting the other—and the men who do this are clergymen.

When the rest of the clergy have risen in indignation and charged these "existentialists" with taking out of the Bible all that gives it power and removing from Christianity all that is uniquely Christian, the others have rightly retorted that the clergy itself have always taken the lead in discrediting supernatural demonstrations of God's power.[7] When Bultmann says that no one who makes use of electric light, radio, or modern medical science can possibly believe in the miracles of the New Testament, even the liberal clergy protest that he is going too far; yet for a whole century *their* strongest charge against the Mormons has been that they have been guilty of "seeing visions in an age of railways."[8]

So now the Christian world has reached a point of decision; it must either believe what the Bible says or reject it—it is no longer possible to have it both ways by the clever use of scholarly jargon and sanctimonious double-talk. The show-down has been forced by what one scholar calls "the breakthrough of the eschatological interpretation," which he compares to a strategic military breakthrough that throws a whole army into panic and disorder.[9] Conventional and long-established views of the nature of the Christian religion, whether liberal or fundamentalist, are so completely out of line with new discoveries that the "existentialist" school now proposes to ignore history altogether. This decision is, we are told,

witness to the increasing embarrassment felt by Christian thinkers about the assumed historicity of their faith. Such a suggestion of embarrassment in this connection may possibly cause surprise and provoke an instant denial that such a situation exists in any significant academic circle. However . . . the historical character of Christianity, which was once proclaimed apologetically as the greatest argument for the validity of that faith, has gradually been found to be a source of great perplexity if not of weakness.

Until now, according to this authority, Christian scholars have willingly accepted

the claim that . . . Christianity . . . must be investigated by the most austere standards of historical judgment. For many decades, under the aegis of the liberal tradition of scholarship, this task was undertaken with fervent conviction, and great was the knowledge amassed by such methods of research about Primitive Christianity. But in time this process of investigation into Christian origins has gradually revealed itself to be a journey ever deeper into a morass of conjecture about the imponderables which lie behind or beyond the extant literary documents.[10]

In all this what is found wanting is not the Bible but men's interpretations of it, the root of the trouble being that they simply don't have enough evidence to go on one way or the other. The noisy protests brought against the Book of Mormon, that the Bible contains a fulness of knowledge to add to which is only blasphemy, are now seen to have been unjustified and premature. And now the learned hold the Bible responsible for their own shortcomings and denounce it as a fraud, whose historical claims Bultmann and his school, like the Jew Torczyner attack with "truly vehement repudiation."[11]

To the hopeless inadequacy of man's knowledge

may be attributed what now goes by the name of "the Modern Predicament," which is, "that man seems to be faced with an unbridgeable gulf between . . . knowledge and faith. . . . Religion was born in a world different from ours—a tiny, comfortable world. . . . That ancient world has been nibbled away by science and the question arises whether against a new and scientific background religion in any form will find it possible to survive."[12] It was just that "tiny, comfortable world" of conventional Christianity that was so mortally offended by the coming forth of latter-day prophecy; the mighty revelations of the Book of Mormon, Doctrine and Covenants, and Pearl of Great Price were an unpardonable affront to the established Christian framework of time, place, and custom. The Christian world is now for the first time learning how wrong it was, and the experience is not a pleasant one. In countless journals, Catholic and Protestant alike, a cry of distress goes up "What is left to us," they ask, "if the things we have always been taught are not so?"[13] If they only knew it, the Book of Mormon is the one way out of their dilemma. And how does it fare?

The Unwelcome Deliverance: "In such an age as ours," a modern churchman writes, "critical of all claims that run counter to what may be scientifically proven, the Mormon has a heavy burden of proof upon him."[14] He is speaking of the Book of Mormon, and fulfilling the prophecy of Mormon 8:26: "And it shall come in a day when it shall be said that miracles are done away." The same scepticism that has systematically dismantled the Bible would reject the Book of Mormon out of hand. But that is not so easy. Dr. Braden may not directly declare that the Book of Mormon "runs counter to what may be scientifically proven" and then skip lightly out leaving the "heavy burden of proof" on those that believe it. He should know that in textual criticism or law or even by that scientific reasoning to which he is so devoted anyone who challenges the authenticity of a document put forth in good faith has taken upon himself the *whole* burden of proving it false. I am not obliged to prove to you that the dollar bill I offer you in good faith is genuine; you may believe it is counterfeit and refuse to accept it, but if you do, it is entirely up to you to prove your case or perhaps face a libel suit.

We offer the Book of Mormon to the world in good faith, convinced that it is the truest of books. To those who may say it is counterfeit, actually "running counter to what may be scientifically proven," its defects should be at once apparent, and would be. But what do we find? "Naturally," says Braden, speaking of the Prophet's story of the coming forth of the book, "it has been doubted by those outside the faith and *every effort has been made* to find a more plausible explanation of the sources of this scripture."[15] (Italics ours) In view of this it is strange that this writer cannot present a single telling argument against Joseph Smith's story, but not strange that he avoids responsibility by seeking to drop the whole problem in the laps of the Mormons.[16]

In the following lessons we have attempted to give full consideration to the principal arguments against the Book of Mormon as well as those for it. But it must be admitted that we do not look upon both sides with equal favor. No fruitful work of science or scholarship was ever written that did not attempt to prove one thing and in so doing disprove another. It is impossible to impart new information or explore new areas without treading on controversial ground, since by that very act one is passing beyond accepted bounds. Anyone defending the Copernican system may be legitimately charged with bias against the Ptolemaic system, and if, as some have noted with disapproval, there is little in our writing to *dis*prove the Book of Mormon, it is because we honestly believe that the arguments against it are few and feeble —the case of Dr. Braden shows that. We leave it to others to show that we are wrong.

Questions

1. How is it possible for specialists in different fields to reach conflicting conclusions regarding the same object of study?

2. When two such investigators disagree, which is to be believed?

3. Why must the Book of Mormon be tested first of all in the light of its purported background?

4. Friedrich Blass says every ancient text must be assumed to be genuine until it is proven otherwise. Is that a prejudiced approach?

5. Can the Book of Mormon be judged in the light of common sense and everyday experience alone?

6. What is the principal threat to the authority of the Bible today?

7. Why can it no longer be claimed that the Bible itself contains all that it is necessary to know about it?

8. Why do the "existentialists" reject historical evidence as a support of the Christian faith?

9. What is the "Modern Predicament"? Is it strictly modern?

10. Why have the written documents been neglected as a source of information on the Book of Mormon?

11. Why does the Christian world need the Book of Mormon today?

12. Why is a completely unbiased study of the Book of Mormon impossible?

Lesson 2

A TIME FOR RE-EXAMINATION

Prospectus of Lesson 2: The Book of Mormon can and should be tested. It invites criticism, and the best possible test for its authenticity is provided by its own oft-proclaimed provenance in the Old World. Since the Nephites are really a branch broken off from the main cultural, racial, and religious stock, that provenance can be readily examined.

In case one thinks the Book of Mormon has been adequately examined in the past, it is well to know that today all ancient records are being read anew in the light of new discoveries. In this lesson we discuss some of the overthrows of the last decades that make it necessary to undertake the thoroughgoing re-evaluation of ancient records, including the Bible. The old evolutionary interpretation is being re-examined, while in its place is coming the realization that all ancient records can best be understood if they are read as a single book.

Claims of Book of Mormon Can Be Tested: A century and a quarter ago a young man shocked the world by bringing out a large book which he had set up right beside the Bible not as a commentary or Key to the Scriptures, but as original scripture—the revealed word of God to man: "And the Book of Mormon and the holy scriptures are given of me for your instruction," says the Lord. (D. & C. 33:16) Likewise the book was given out as genuine history: "Which contains a record of a fallen people, and the fulness of the gospel of Jesus Christ to the Gentile and to the Jews also." (D. & C. 20:9)

How can one "control" such a claim? In the Primitive Church it was taught that no one had a right to question a prophet on "intellectual" grounds. History, however, is another thing. If the Book of Mormon is to convert the honest in heart it must provide convincing tests for them. For the righteous, Moroni 10:4 offers adequate conviction; for the others, who must either convict the Book of Mormon of fraud or be convicted by it, the best and most immediate of many checks upon it are to be found in its Old World background. The "fallen people" that it tells us about are described by one of their prophets as a "branch of the tree of Israel, and has been lost from its body in a strange land." (Alma 26:36) Another says they are a "lonesome and a solemn people, wanderers, cast out from Jerusalem . . . ." (Jac. 7:26) These two statements, written purportedly 410 years apart, show that our Book of Mormon people never think of themselves as an indigenous or autochthonous culture in the New World, but always and only as the heirs of Old World civilization. The very metal plates on which the book was preserved from generation to generation were made in imitation of older records brought from Palestine (1 Ne. 19:1-6); its language and style from the first were consciously modeled after the literary and linguistic usage of the Old World. (1 Ne. 1-2) The Book of Mormon in many ways declares itself to be an authentic product of the Near East; it gives a full and circumstantial account of its own production, declaring that it is but one of many such books to have been produced in the course of history and placing itself in about the middle of a long list of sacred writings, beginning with the first Patriarchs and continuing down to the end of human history; it cites lost prophetic writings of prime importance, giving the names of their authors; it traces its own cultural roots in all directions, emphasizing the immense breadth and complexity of such connections in the world; it belongs to the same class of literature as the Bible, but along with a sharper and clearer statement of Biblical teachings contains a formidable mass of historical material unknown to Biblical writers but well within the range of modern comparative study, since it insists on deriving its whole cultural tradition, even in details directly from a specific time and place in the Old World.

The Rediscovery of the Ancients: In the light of these claims recent developments in the study of scriptures take on an intense interest for students of the Book of Mormon.

We are living in a time of the re-examination and re-evaluation of all ancient records. It is not only in the field of religion but in all ancient studies that preconceived ideas are being uprooted on all sides. New discoveries should be received with joy, for though they bring into question the *forms* in which the labors of scholarship have molded the past, they bring a new *substance* and reality to things which the learned of another age had never thought possible. The same discoveries which, it appears, may alter the theories of the doctors, are at the same time vindicating that Bible world which they had consigned to the realm of myth.[1] Years ago the celebrated Niebuhr observed that Ancient History is always treated "as if it had never really happened" — it is a thesis, a demonstration, an intellectual exercise, but not a real account of real people.[2] "Ingrained in our subconscious," says a recent study of ancient Egypt, "is a disbelief in the actual existence of those times and persons, which haunts us through the schools and in the theaters and libraries and dominates the whole concept of 'Antiquity'."[3]

From this mood of academic complacency the learned ones are now aroused to face another world entirely. Among other things that must be viewed in the new cold light of day is the Book of Mormon. If this seems a late date to be asking, "What is the Book of Mormon?" it should seem far stranger to ask "What is the Iliad?" "What are the apocrypha?" "What is the Book of the Dead?" or "What is the Bible?" Yet these questions are being more seriously considered today than at any other time. Up until the present scholars have thought they had a pretty good idea of what the historical, literary, philosophical or religious writings of the past were all about. Not so today! The whole question of ancient records is now undergoing a thorough re-investigation.

Significant Changes: How this state of things has come about may best be illustrated by considering the

case of the famous Eduard Meyer. In 1884 the first
volume of his great *History of the Ancient World*
(*Geschichte des Alertums*) appeared, presenting to the
world "for the first time a history of the Ancient East
in a scientifically satisfying form, a work which at the
time produced a veritable sensation."[4] Hardly was the
first edition completed, however, when the author was
hard at work revising the whole thing, for the history of
the Ancient World must be constantly rewritten. By
considering a few of the things that happened between
Meyer's two editions one may gain some idea of the
tempo of discovery in our times. As Walter Otto summarizes the developments:

> . . . the History of the Ancient East had taken on a totally
> different aspect . . . Times and areas which formerly had been al-
> most or completely unknown were brought to light; we have become
> acquainted with completely new languages and learned to use them
> as sources; people known formerly only by name now stand
> before us as concrete realities; the Indo-Germanic element, which
> serious scholarship had long concluded was of no significance
> for the Ancient East . . . now shows more clearly every day as
> an important historical element even in the more ancient periods;
> empires, such as the Mitanni and especially the Hittite, of whose
> history and structure not long ago only a few scattered details
> were known, have recently emerged as worthy rivals of the great
> traditional empires of the East, who actually recognized the Hit-
> tites as their equal . . .[5]

In the two decades since those words were written,
things have gone faster than ever. To mention only a few
of the developments, there is afoot today a general re-
evaluation of the oldest Egyptian texts and a far-reach-
ing reinterpretation of the very essentials of Egyptian
religion; the origin and background of Sumero-Baby-
lonian civilization is being reconsidered completely in
the light of excavations made along the periphery of
that area and of epic texts whose real significance has
just begun to dawn on the experts; the unearthing of
the oldest known villages gives us a new and unexpected picture of a civilization that "seems to have
come into being with relative (even revolutionary) sud-

denness," instead of with that evolutionary gradualness with which all such things were once supposed to have happened.[6] The involvement of the Hebrew Patriarchs, especially Abraham, with our own Indo-European rela-tives has called for a wholly new picture of Old Testa-ment times and peoples. The application of new methods of dating has cut down the conventional time scale, es-pecially for the earlier periods (e.g. as at Jericho) abruptly and drastically. The discovery of a new date for Hammurabi has called for a thoroughgoing re-vamping of ancient chronology. "The Hurrians have emerged from total obscurity and have come to occupy a stellar role. . . . A new planet has appeared on the historical horizon and an area that was formerly dark has been flooded with a new and strange light."[7]

Within the last five years with the discovery of a single inscription a whole world of Greek myth and legend has been transmuted into the category of flesh and blood reality. Within the same short period the decipherment of the Minoan Script B has with a single sweep rubbed out two hundred years of the Homeric problem, and shown us the Greeks writing good Greek a thousand years before anyone had credited them with literacy. At the same time the mystery of Etruscan has been solved, and the true nature of the mysterious Runic writing of our Norse ancestors explained. Today nearly all scholars accept the original identity of the Hamitic, Semitic and Indo-European languages—a thing that the less informed and more opinionated gentlemen of a few years ago laughed at as a Fundamentalist dream.

The Discovery of the Israelites: In all this fever and ferment of discovery and re-evaluation no documents have been more conspicuously involved than those re-lating to Israel's past and that of the earliest Christian Church. Since World War II the greatest discoveries ever made in these fields have come to light. In the great days of "scientific" scholarship, the only safe and respectable position for any man of stature to take was to

say "no" to any suggestion that the Bible might contain
real history, not the least sensational of Eduard Meyer's
many ingenious pronouncements was the startling declaration that the Old Testament was not only history
but very good history—by far the most accurate, reliable, and complete history ever produced by an ancient
people, with the possible exception of the Greeks, who
came much, much later.[8] Time and research have strikingly vindicated this claim.[9] It is hard now to realize that
as recently as 1908 Eduard Meyer could announce to
the Berlin Academy: "Twenty-five years ago there existed *not a single historical document"* to confirm the
early history of Israel as given in the Bible.[10] It was,
however, quite suddenly in the 1880's that such documents began to appear, and then like the coming of
spring floods, great collections of material began pour-
ing out year after year in a breathtaking sequence that
appears not yet to have reached its crest.[10]

Golden Plates: The main obstacle to a fair and
unbiased testing of the Book of Mormon in the past
has been the story of the golden plates. Scholars have
found it hard to be impartial or even serious in the face
of such a tale, and as recently as 1954 a learned critic
wrote: "To expect anyone to believe in the existence
of the 'gold plates' . . . is in spite of the witnesses simply
preposterous (*unerhört*)."[11] Critics of the Book of Mormon often remark sarcastically that it is a great pity
that the golden plates have disappeared, since they
would very conveniently prove Joseph Smith's story.
They would do nothing of the sort. The presence of
the plates would only prove that there were plates, no
more: it would not prove that Nephites wrote them, or
that an angel brought them, or that they had been translated by the gift and power of God, and we can be sure
that scholars would quarrel about the writing on them
for generations without coming to any agreement, exactly as they did about the writings of Homer and parts
of the Bible. The possession of the plates would have

a very disruptive effect and it would prove nothing. On
the other hand a far more impressive claim is put forth
when the whole work is given to the world in what is
claimed to be a divinely inspired translation—in such a
text any cause or pretext for disagreement and speculation about the text is reduced to an absolute minimum:
it is a text which all the world can read and understand,
and is a far more miraculous object than any gold
plates would be.

But still the story of the plates deserve more examination than our "learned critic" above was willing
to give it. We learn from the Book of Mormon itself
that gold plates were indeed a rarity, and that the rule
was to keep records on plates of copper ("ore") or
bronze ("brass"), and that the practice of keeping records on metal plates was of great antiquity in Palestine,
and by no means an invention of the Nephites. We
know that the ancient Hebrews, like the Egyptians,
wrote on leather,[12] and from the Lachish seals, discovered in 1938, for the first time "we now know for certain
that round about 600 B.C. papyrus was being commonly used as writing material in Judah."[13] A private
letter written in Hebrew on a copper plate has turned
up and been dated to the 12th century B.C.[14] No doubt
the highly literate and educated Lehi had all sorts of
writing materials.

This is illustrated in the account of how a certain
Book of Mormon king when a royal speech, given at
the great national assembly, could not be heard by all
the people, "caused that the words which he spake
should be written and sent forth among those that were
not under the sound of his voice." (Mos. 2:8.) The
same king interpreted the engravings on an ancient
stone (Omni 20), and at great public meetings read to
his people from the ancient plates (Mos. 25:1ff), which,
as his son Heleman says, "enlarged the memory of this
people." (Alma 37:8.) Exactly so "Darius the Median"
who was to liberate the Jews of Lehi's own generation,

since a public proclamation of his written on stone could
not be seen by all the people, had copies of it made and
circulated on papyrus throughout the empire, and some
of these have actually turned up in the Jewish colony at
Elephantine, where the Jews of Lehi's day fled when
Jerusalem fell.[15]   The same ruler had his royal proclamation put on plates of pure gold and silver and buried in a
carefully made stone box, which was discovered in 1938.[16]
Thus we find parallel practices between Book of Mormon
kings and the kings of the East who ruled in Lehi's time,
and all this is of recent discovery.

Another pair of gold and silver plates has been
found since the Darius plates, and of these the golden
tablet begins: "Palace of Assurnasirpal . . . on tablets
of silver and gold I have established my foundations
. . ." This has been held to illustrate a general belief
in the East that a building should be founded on plates
of gold and silver recounting the name and the deeds
of the royal builder.[17]   The great antiquity of the practice may be seen in the discovery in 1937 of such a gold
tablet in Sumerian Umma,[18] and its persistence through
the ages is apparent from the report that the wise Arab
King No'man of Hira ordered a copy of the Book of
Origins, that told the whole history of the world, to be
buried in his White Palace.[19]   Such foundation tablets
are actually histories, and recall Eusebius' report that
Noah inscribed a "history of everything" and then buried
it in the city of Sippar.[20]

The duplication of the records on a precious metal
is as much a sign of their importance as a device for long
preservation.   Certainly lead would have done as well
as silver and a lead tablet recently found in Egypt bears,
with some important exceptions, the same inscription as
is found on a royal stele of stone.   It is a mysterious
writing in a peculiar type of Egyptian that has never
been deciphered, and its age is not known.[21]

Within the past decade some silver plates from the
time of Lehi have turned up not far from his home.   They
were found in the "Bertiz" valley, carefully laid away

in a bronze vessel. The plates measured 4.5 by 5 centimeters, were quite thin, and entirely covered with writing, twenty-two lines of Semitic characters "pressed into the metal with a hard sharp object."[22] Almost at the same time small plates made of gold and silver foil and covered with Hebrew and Aramaic inscriptions were found: they seem to have been carried about as talismans, and the writing on them included magic words and names of power, along with the name of the God of Israel.[23] In form and function they closely resemble the Golden Tablets of the Orphic mysteries which protected and guided the bearer in his ways and on which devotees might also inscribe an account of their wanderings.[24] One of these plates, recently found in Thurii and dated to the 4th century B.C., ends with the words, "Hail, hail to thee, journeying the right-hand road by holy meadows and the groves of Persephone."[25] This immediately suggested to scholars Plato's description of Minos sitting in judgment "in the meadow at the dividing of the road, where are Two Ways, the one leading to the Isle of the Blest and the other to Tartarus (hell)."[26] Now there is no more prominent doctrine in Early Christian or Jewish teaching than this very doctrine of the Two Ways, which we treat below in connection with the Book of Mormon.[27] Here it is enough to note that the carrying of scrolls and plates of scriptures for protection and guidance on a journey was a widespread practice in the ancient world. This was especially prominent among the Jews.[28] Lehi himself refused to undertake his wanderings without "the record of the Jews . . . engraven upon plates of brass." (1 Ne. 3:3) And these plates were closely associated with the Liahona "which led our fathers through the wilderness," and together with the sword of Laban comprised the national treasure and symbolized the survival and preservation of the people in their wanderings and their journey through life. (Mos. 1:16-17) The celebrated Demotic Chronicle of Egypt, a document of great importance in the study both of Jewish and Christian beliefs regarding the coming of the Messiah, was copied from a text originally written on 13 plates.[29]

In India and the Far East some very interesting plates have turned up. To those mentioned in *Lehi in the Desert,* etc., (pp. 119ff) may be added the Kalawan copper-plate inscription of the year 134, which records the depositing of relics in a shrine, and is "about contemporary with the Taxila silver scroll inscription of the year 136."[30] In 1956 the two copper rolls from the Qumran Cave on the Dead Sea were unrolled and found to contain, like the Kalawan copper plate, a record of the depositing of relics.[31] If it seems strange that we should find identical practices going on at the same time so far apart, it should be remembered that the Sanskrit writing of India is itself derived from the Aramaic script of Lehi's world, and also that an ancient Phoenician alphabet has been found in Sumatra.[32] If it was possible for the Phoenicians, that is the men of Lehi's Sidon, to cross the Indian Ocean and reach the Pacific, we must admit at least that the same way was open to Lehi!

Such metal rolls as described above actually go back to Lehi's day, for the seven lead rolls from a private house in Assur found in 1905 and engraved in Hittite hieroglyphics are dated "from the end of the 7th century B.C." They were private business letters written apparently by the owner of the house.[33] It is most interesting to find writing on metal practiced even in everyday affairs by Lehi's fellow merchants. Of course other types of writing material were used. "The Hittites also wrote on wooden boards . . . often covered with wax," while the common word for wax-tablet used in Palestine and Syria in Lehi's day was an Old Babylonian loan-word, showing the custom to be very old.[34] Very recently, there were discovered in Assyria some waxed writing-boards which "take the history of the 'album' or book back to the 8th century B.C. . . ."[35] The significant thing about this is that while the folding boards were often made of wood or ivory they could also be of *metal*. It is still "uncertain whether the boards made of precious metals were votive gifts (since they must have been very expensive) or plaques inscribed with a short dedicatory inscription, or whether they were 'writing-boards,' for the same term denotes a *word* or *metal plate* used in overlay-work."[36] The continued use of metal plates in Assyria (no actual plates have been found from the earlier period) is seen in the recent discovery of a copper plate in Maghreb, beautifully written on both sides with a continuing text in Arabic.[37]

We told in *Lehi in the Desert*, etc., of a Karen inscription plate which cannot be read but which to judge by practices found in the neighboring regions probably contained the account of the founding of the nation and/or its ruler's claim to the throne. We also noted that visitors to the Karens have often been struck by what seem to be unusually close affinities to the Jews.[38] Now as late as the 19th century the people "were accustomed to assemble once a year from all parts of the nation, to propitiate it (the plate) with offerings. The gathering of the people takes place in the month of March, and is with them the great feast day."[39] One cannot help thinking of how King Mosiah called all his people together in a great national assembly in order to read to them out of holy plates and to discourse to them on the history of the nation and his own claim to the throne.[40]

The general concern and anxious attention to the keeping of records in ancient Israel was entirely unknown to scholars until the work of Eduard Meyer and the discovery of the Ugartic library in 1929. The eminent Orientalist A. H. Sayce describes the surprising result of that find:

There is no longer any difficulty in believing that there were abundant literary documents for compiling the earlier books of the Old Testament. . . . Consequently there is no longer any need of our believing as I formerly did that cuneiform tablets lie behind the text of the earlier Biblical books. . . . In the Mosaic period the Oriental world was so well stocked with books and what we should call public libraries as it was in the Greek epoch. . . . The royal library of David and Solomon would have preceded the temple libraries in the age of the judges . . . Samuel as a lawgiver or *mehoqeq* would have been accompanied by his scribe (Jud. 5:14; Gen. 49:10), and at Shiloh there would have been a temple library. . . . It is significant that as late as the reign of Solomon the 'prophecies' of Ahijah the Shilonite were still being committed to writing.[41]

All this, brought forth since 1930, is a remarkable vindication not only of the great concern of the Book of Mormon people with the keeping of books and records, but of the peculiar manner in which those records were kept and the ways in which they were disseminated. The Book of Mormon writers leave us in no doubt that the engraving of plates was a hard and laborious business which they did not relish. They would much have preferred writing in ink, as we can surmise from the state of the Kasia plate:

An interesting fact revealed by this plate is the way in which copperplates were inscribed. The matter was first written out in ink on the plate, and when the ink dried the engraver cut the written letters into the metal. . . . Here the engraver was manifestly incapable, for only the first line has been carved and most of the letters in it are bungled. There can be little doubt that, as his work was so unsatisfactory, the incision of the rest was given up and the plate was accepted as it was, written only in ink.[42]

So we can sympathize with Jacob when he says, "I cannot write but a little of my words, because of the difficulty of engraving our words upon plates." (Jac. 4:1.)

The Book of Mormon bids us look at the larger background before we judge it. As soon as we attempt to do so we meet everywhere with striking hints and suggestions, odd coincidences, and astonishing parallels. If it is too early to work these into a single consistent picture, it is not too early to show that they are actually there. If heavenly books brought by angels and writings on gold plates seem fantastic to modern man, they were perfectly familiar to the ancients. A realization of that is the beginning of wisdom in any examination of the Book of Mormon. Plainly we are dealing not with a modern book but with an ancient one. That must be the point of departure for any fruitful criticism.

Questions

1. Why must the Book of Mormon be subject to testing by objective methods? Is it not enough that the honest in heart believe it?

2. How does the Book of Mormon provoke questions and investigation? Is that intentional?

3. What has brought about the re-evaluation of ancient documents at the present time?

4. How does the newly established "oneness of all ancient literature" affect Bible study?

5. Why has Joseph Smith's story of the gold plates always excited derision?

6. Are inscriptions on metal plates a rarity in history? Why should metal be used as a writing material at all?

7. Dougherty has shown that papyrus rolls are mentioned in Cappadocian texts which are dated at 2300 B.C. (*Jnl. Roy. As. Soc.* 1931, p. 786.) What does this imply as to the "development" of writing materials through the centuries? Did the ancients use only one kind of writing material at any one time?

8. Why did scholars once think that writing on stone and clay was the only type of writing employed? What made them change their minds?

Lesson 3

AN AUSPICIOUS BEGINNING

Prospectus of Lesson 3: The note of universalism is very strong in the Book of Mormon, while the conventional views of tribal and national loyalties are conspicuously lacking. This peculiar state of things is an authentic reflection of actual conditions in Lehi's world. Lehi like Abraham was the child of a cosmopolitan age. No other time or place could have been more peculiarly auspicious for the launching of a new civilization than the time and place in which he lived. It was a wonderful age of discovery, an age of adventurous undertakings in all fields of human endeavor, of great economic and colonial projects. At the same time the great and brilliant world civilization of Lehi's day was on the very verge of complete collapse, and men of God like Lehi could see the hollowness of the loudly proclaimed slogans of peace (Jer. 6:14, 8:11) and prosperity. (2 Ne. 28:21.) Lehi's expedition from Jerusalem in aim and method was entirely in keeping with the accepted practices of his day.

Lehi's World was "one world": The most conspicuous feature of the Near East of Lehi's day was the general and pervasive cultural unity brought about by an unusual if not unparalleled activity in international trade and travel. This will be the subject of the next three lessons, but since it will be our practice to begin each study with the Book of Mormon itself, it is in order now to point out how that text anticipates the discoveries of the last decades in this regard.

The most strongly emphasized as well as the most arresting aspect of history in the Book of Mormon is the all-pervading universality of its point of view. This is the more interesting since it is the complete antithesis of the view universally taken of ancient history up until the last few decades. Ancient societies were believed by one and all to have been tribal, exclusive, suspicious, mutually hostile on principle, super-nationalistic. This established misconception was inherited by modern scholarship not from modern science but from the ancient intellectuals who in their compilations of universal history were as obsessed by the evolutionary concept as the moderns have been.[1] The whole trend of contemporary study is away from this idea of ancient tribalism to the awareness of a oneness of world-civilizations that go back far beyond those Hellenistic times in which world civilization was so long thought to have had its origin.[2]

Rushing rapidly through the Book of Mormon one may point out some of the more striking statements of its universal point of view:

Behold, the Lord esteemeth all flesh in one; he that is righteous is favored of God. . . . (1 Ne. 17:35.)

For I, Nephi, have not taught them many things concerning the manner of the Jews; . . . Wherefore, I write unto my people . . . that they may know the judgments of God, that they come upon all nations. . . . (2 Ne. 25:2-3.)

. . . (Christ) manifesteth himself unto all those who believe in him, by the power of the Holy Ghost; yea, unto every nation, kindred, tongue, and people, working mighty miracles, signs, and wonders, among the children of men according to their faith. (2 Ne. 26:13.) . . . All men are privileged the one like unto the other, and none are forbidden. (2 Ne. 26:28.) . . . and he denieth none that come unto him, black and white, bond and free, male and female; and he remembereth the heathen; and all are alike unto God, both Jew and Gentile. (2 Ne. 26:33.)

Know ye not that there are more nations than one? Know ye not that I, the Lord your God, have created all men . . . and I bring forth my word unto the children of men, yea, even upon all the nations of the earth? . . . I speak the same words unto one nation like unto another . . . For I command all men, both in the east and in the west, and in the north and in the south, and in the islands of the sea, that they shall write the words which I speak unto them. . . . (2 Ne. 29:7-11.)

For behold, I say unto you that as many of the Gentiles as will repent are the covenant people of the Lord; and as many of the Jews as will not repent shall be cast off; for the Lord covenanteth with none save it be with them that repent and believe in His Son. . . . (2 Ne. 30:2.)

For my soul delighteth in plainness; for after this manner doth the Lord God work among the children of men. . . . for he speaketh unto men according to their language, unto their understanding. (2 Ne. 31:3.)

Do ye not suppose that such things are abominable unto him who created all flesh? And the one being is as precious in his sight as the other. And all flesh is of the dust; and for the

self same end hath he created them, that they should keep his
commandments and glorify him forever. (Jac. 2:21.)

. . . for thus saith the Lord: Ye shall not esteem one flesh
above another, or one man shall not think himself above another. . . . (Mos. 23:7.)

Now my brethren, we see that God is mindful of every people, whatsoever land they may be in; yea, he numbereth his people, and his bowels of mercy are over all the earth. (Alma 26:37.)

For behold, the Lord doth grant unto all nations, of their
own nation and tongue, to teach his word, yea, in wisdom, all
that he seeth fit that they should have; therefore we see that the
Lord doth counsel in wisdom, according to that which is just
and true. (Alma 29:8.)

. . . I have other sheep which are not of this land, neither of
the land of Jerusalem, neither in any parts of that land round
about whither I have been to minister. (3 Ne. 16:1.) . . . But I
have received a commandment of the Father that I shall go unto
them, and that they shall hear my voice, and shall be numbered
among my sheep. . . . (3 Ne. 16:3.)

. . . ye must all stand before the judgment seat of Christ, yea,
every soul who belongs to the whole human family of Adam. . . .
(Mormon 3:20.)

. . . For the power of redemption cometh on all them that have
no law. . . . (Moroni 8:22.) . . . if not so, God is a partial God,
and also a changeable God, and a respecter of persons. . . .
(Mormon 8:12.)

The Ancient Near East—A Single Community: But it
is not so much by precept as by example that the Book
of Mormon people display their remarkable freedom
from racial and national prejudice. They simply do not
think in terms of nationalism which is the very essence
of history and history-writing in modern times. Even
Moroni's "Title of Liberty" campaign is strictly a religious undertaking. The complete absence of the nation as a factor in Book of Mormon history can only be
explained by a type of social organization in which the
state did not figure conspicuously.[3] Such a condition of
civilized society has been quite unthinkable to historians
since the Middle Ages. It was first pointed out by the
great Orientalist, Hugo Winckler when he was describing the peculiar state of things in Jerusalem in the
days of Zedekiah, that is, of Lehi. By way of explain-

ing Jeremiah's intimate knowledge of affairs at the court
of Babylon and throughout the Near East generally,
Winckler wrote:

It has been customary to depict conditions in the Ancient
East as those of isolated societies each living its own life. Precisely the opposite was the case. The Oriental was better acquainted with the situation of other peoples in his cultural area
than the average man is today . . . Before all, the Oriental was
totally unaware of national or language differences as forming an
effective barrier between peoples. Just as Islam united an enormous geographical expanse of races and nations in a single unity
that surmounted political and racial bounds, so in ancient times
. . . commerce brought people into much closer contact with
each other than our modern means of communication do.[4]

At the beginning of the present century anyone
wishing to find out about the world of Lehi would have
begun by reading some standard work such as Rawlinson's *Ancient History*. There he would have discovered
that Lehi, assuming he lived at all, must have moved in
a world peopled by puppets and shadows, the exotic
half-world of the Ancient East as our grandfather knew
it. For Rawlinson's sources were Greek writers whose
first tangible contacts with the past went back but a little beyond 600 B.C.; for them as for him, Cyrus, Psam-
metichus, and Nebuchadnezzar—contemporaries of
Nephi—were the kings of old, and beyond lay only
legend. To try to fit a real Lehi into such a make-
believe world could only lead to trouble.

Things are quite different today. Lehi now finds
himself not at the beginning of ancient times, but almost
at the end of them. His century some have claimed to
be the greatest of all centuries, producing from beginning to end more innovating geniuses and more epoch-
making "firsts" than any other century, not excluding
the nineteenth. The overall picture of that marvellously
dynamic age cannot be overlooked in the study of the
Book of Mormon, for Lehi was a child of his century
and steeped in its culture. When they crossed the waters
he and his people took with them a specific cultural baggage—that of the early sixth century and the Near East.

Never did they forget that they were "a lonesome and a solemn people," cut off from the main stream of world civilization, and never did they cease to cherish and remember their cultural origins. Not merely the opening pages but every page of the Book of Mormon bears the stamp of its ultimate origin.

Lehi's World Background: No other time or place could have been more auspiciously chosen for the launching of a new venture in civilization. At no other time in history and from no other spot on earth could the colonizers have set forth more richly equipped. If the Book of Mormon people lived for a thousand years on a single cultural endowment, that endowment itself represents the cumulated and concentrated heritage of all the great civilizations of the earth. As a matter of fact, our own twentieth century is scarcely less beholden to the men of Lehi's day than the Nephites and Lamanites were. Recently Cyrus Gordon has made such a claim as this for the age and heritage of Abraham. Thus he concludes his significant study:

> Palestine happened to be the point of maximum synthesis, where Mesopotamian, Egyptian, and Mediterranean influences fused with the native Canaanite culture. A picture of what was happening is clearly reflected in the Narratives. Abraham was of Mesopotamian origin, and his son and grandson married girls from their kin in Mitanni. At the same time, Egyptian blood was in the Patriarchal household; Hagar was Egyptian as was also her son Ishmael's wife. Moreover, famine repeatedly drove the Patriarchs to Egypt from Abraham's time on. Canaan itself was a melting pot of Semite, Hurrian, Caphtorian, and other groups. The Patriarchal Hebrews enjoyed the ideal spot and the ideal time to fall heir to the rich and varied heritage of the entire ancient Near East, when Egypt and Babylonia were nearly spent. Furthermore, the pastoral and semi-nomadic purity of Patriarchal life saved the Hebrews from the decadence of that cosmopolitan age.[5]

All this applies with equal force to the age of Lehi as described in the Book of Mormon, not omitting Lehi's flight to the "semi-nomadic purity of Patriarchal life," which was so resented by his elder sons, the spoiled children of "that cosmopolitan age." Every year new finds are revealing some new and heretofore unsuspected phase of the astoundingly cosmopolitan world in which Lehi lived.

A Wonderful Age: It was an unsettled age of big ideas and big projects, a time of individual enterprise and great private fortunes flourishing precariously under the protection of great rival world-powers, everlastingly intriguing and competing for markets and bases.[6] A strange, tense, exciting and very brief moment of history when everything was "big with the future." No other moment of history was so favorable for the transplanting of civilization, so heavily burdened with the heritage of the past or so rich in promise. For a brief moment the world was wide open. "The Saitic epoch was a period of great prosperity which was not limited to the ruling classes but was extended to the working populace as well."[7] Everyone was making money in the new economic paradises of the XXVI Dynasty and the revitalized Babylon. After a generation of war the Assyrian troublemakers had disappeared, like Nazi Germany, literally overnight, and the nations revelled in an unparalleled post-war boom backed by a phenomenal upsurge of population.[8] Wise men and prophets were worried,[9] but who would believe that within a few short years all the glory and dominion of the East as the Old World knew it would suddenly vanish forever? There was nothing on the political or economic horizon to indicate that the peace and prosperity achieved by the shrewd and experienced leaders of Egypt and Babylon could not be permanent, or that the undreamed-of riches that were being amassed on all sides actually represented the burst and glitter of a rocket that would in an instant vanish into utter darkness. The key to the future was not in population or business statistics, but where Lehi saw it, in the moral picture: ". . . for their works were works of darkness, and their doings were doings of abominations." (2 Ne. 25:2.)

World Trade in Lehi's Day: The population squeeze accelerated a world-wide activity in exploration and colonization that had been going on for some time but that reached its peak almost exactly in 600 B.C., in which year the two greatest Greek colonies, Massilia (Marseilles) in the west, and Olbia in the east, were founded. Everyone was taking part in new settlement projects or forming companies to finance them. The search for new resources and new horizons was everybody's business. A newly found papyrus from the 4th century B.C., Wilcken has shown, illustrates conditions in Lehi's day as well, and deserves to be quoted here because it has survived as an original document and in considerable detail. It is a legal text in which certain merchants living as far apart as Carthage in Africa, Massilia in France and Elea in Greece pool their resources to form a company for importing oil and aromatics from South Arabia and Central Africa to Alexandria! The raw product had to be sold to the King of Egypt for 46 drachmas per metrete, and he in turn immediately resold it to manufacturers for 52 drachmas, and continued to exercise nominal control over every stage of the manufacture of the cosmetics. Yet from first to last the actual operations were carried on by private individuals and companies, to whom the king allowed a fair profit, likewise guaranteeing protection from pirates and caravan raiders. Thanks to the peculiar willingness of the merchants to be content with the huge profits they were getting, this arrangement proved amazingly stable and workable: the system was going full blast in the time of Hatsheput, a thousand years before this particular document, and in the 3rd century A.D.—600 years later! In Lehi's day, the most secure and prosperous of all, it was at its height.[10]

Colonization—The Search for Promised Lands: Methods of colonization and exploitation of new lands were the same, whether followed by Greeks or Orientals. For a long time the Near East had been getting crowded, the pinch being first felt in Syria and Phoenicia—due perhaps as much to deforestation and over-grazing as to population increase.[11]   Of this area Ebers writes: "Their small country could not contain its numerous population; accordingly there sailed out of the Phoenician harbors many a richly laden vessel to search out favorable places of settlement for emigrants bound for the coasts of Africa, Crete, Cyprus and Sicily."[12]   Such colonies would continue to enrich the Mother city (hence our word "metropolis") by furnishing her with markets and raw materials. The Greeks were playing the same game.[13] We read already in the *Odyssey* (VI 7 ff.) how Father Nausithous led his people on a new colonial venture after their failure to find rest in the Cyclops country:

They had first settled down in the wide valleys of Hypereia,
Hard by the Cyclopes, those savage inhospitable men,
Who constantly molested them, being stronger than they were.
Leaving that place, they were led by the godlike Nausithous
To Scheria, a place far removed from any civilized settlement,
Where they built a walled city, erected houses and temples, and
    began to cultivate the land . . .

Every schoolboy should know of the wanderings of "Father Aeneas" who led his people through many toils by land and sea that he might reach his promised land. Thus he encourages his people:

Rally your spirits and get rid of this disgraceful fear.
Some day you will be glad to remember these things:
Through all these vicissitudes and dangers
We are making our way to Latium, where Destiny hath
Promised us rest and security; there it is decreed that the
Rule of Troy (the mother city) shall be revived.
Hang on, and look forward to better times! (Virgil, *Aen.* I, 202
    ff.)

These are no mere literary inventions. Almost every important literary figure of the 7th and 6th centuries participated in such projects, which are often dramatically described. Thus among the Greeks Hesiod (*Works and Days,* 631 ff.) writes of an earlier period:

Even as my father and yours, foolish brother Perses,
Used to sail around, trying to make a living,
And so landed here, after having journeyed much on the waters,
Having put forth in a black ship from Cyme in Aeolis,
Not running away from prosperity or wealth or success,
But from grinding poverty, such as Zeus gives to men.
So he came here and settled in the Mount Helicon country
In a miserable little community,
Askra—a vile place in wintertime, a hard place in summer, a nice
    place never!

In the seventh century Tyrtaeus reminds the Spartans:

Zeus himself gave this place to the children of Herakles,
In the days when they left windy Erineus
And came to the broad island of Pelops.

                    (*Eunomia*, cit. Strabo, *Geog*. VIII, p. 362)

He is urging them as Aeneas did the Romans, to fight for their homeland as a *promised* land, granted by God to the wandering Herakles and all his descendants in the days of migration. About 600 B.C. Mimnermus wrote embittered lines on unsuccessful colonizing projects in which he participated. Thus a fragment cited in Strabo, *Geog*. XIV, p. 634:

We left our village on the cliff, Neleius in Pylos,
To come sailing full of hope to Asia Minor,
Where we settled in delightful Colophon by force,
Taking everything over as if we owned it.
But the river rose and flooded us out,
And so by the will of the gods we moved to Smyrna. . . .

The great poet Archilochus, who wrote in the seventh century, has left many vivid fragments recalling the hardships and disappointments of unsuccessful colonizing ventures in which he participated. Simonides of Amorgos himself led a colony from Samos, and is full of tedious practical wisdom. Alceus sought employment in Egypt in the days of Lehi, while his brother hired out as a mercenary in Babylon.

An Age of Adventure: From these and many other sources we can see what was going on. Small bands of people, usually friends and relatives, would go forth under the direction of an able and daring leader, a *patriarch* (for that may well be the origin of the word "Father-leader"), from the "mother city" (for that is definitely the origin of the word *metropolis*), to try their luck in some chosen or eagerly-quested spot, a "promised land" where they could escape the hardships of their old life. These settlements always remained colonies, however. The purpose in sending them out was not only to relieve economic and population pressure at home but to provide "factories" of raw materials and markets for finished goods to the mother city. The control of the mother city depended not on military force but on cultural and sentimentalities which were carefully nurtured through the centuries, as we learn so movingly in Thucydides. By the sixth century hopeful parties of Greeks were everywhere being turned back by the discovery that other settlers—usually Phoenicians but often other races as well—had already occupied the best spots.[14] As the pickings became poorer, explorations became more daring and settlement projects more ambitious. Merchants and settlers in Lehi's day were already moving along the Atlantic seaboard and into the heart of Asia and even the Far East![15] In the year Lehi left Jerusalem the Egyptian government sent an expedition consisting largely of Syrian and Phoenician personnel sailing clear around Africa from east to west.[16] Shortly after, the Phoenicians reacted to the challenge by sending Hanno on the same mission of circumnavigation in the opposite direction.[17] In the middle of the 6th century Scylas reconnoitered the coasts of the Red Sea and the Indian Ocean from the Euphrates to the Indus, while in the west Carthage "reconnoitered the Atlantic Ocean to north and south with mighty fleets."[18] The Phoenicians ended a long phase of fierce mercantile competition in the Mediterranean by burning the great trading city of Tartessus—Isaiah's Tarshish of the proud ships—and closing the whole western Mediterranean and Atlantic areas to all trade but their own in 530 B.C.[19]

"The very spirit of the age," writes Paul Herrmann, "seems to have been at work in the Punic voyage into the immense distances of the ocean, announcing the dawn of a new epoch. . . ."[20] The ancients always chafed at the limitations of their geographical knowledge (though we are beginning to realize how much greater that knowledge was than we have ever given them credit for), but never until modern times was that knowledge as great as it was in the 6th century.[21]

When Father Lehi led his little clan into the wilderness in search for a promised land he was not engaging in a fantastic enterprise at all. He was only doing what hundreds of idealistic and courageous men had done before him. If he had visions of a bountiful land in some far place (1 Ne. 5:5), so did they. If his followers never forgot their homeland and wept to remember it in the desert places, so did theirs, and if he had to rebuke and encourage them with strong words, so did they. The Book of Mormon opens on a note of complete authenticity. But to Lehi there is much beside, as the next lesson will show.

Questions

1. How does the attitude of the Book of Mormon towards nation and tribe differ from that of the Bible? From that of conventional history?

2. What considerations now make it appear that the attitude depicted in the Book of Mormon is historically a correct one; i.e., the attitude actually prevalent in the Near East of 600 B.C.?

3. In what ways was Lehi's time favorable to the project in which he was called to undertake?

4. What historical considerations enhance the plausibility of the whole story of Lehi's migration?

5. How did Lehi's education and business activities prepare him for his great task?

6. How did the age of Abraham resemble that of Lehi? Of Moses?

7. Compare the characters, mission, and activities of these men.

8. In what ways does Lehi's age resemble our own?

9. What warning is there for us in the story of Lehi? What comfort?

10. Does the fact that Lehi was a typical leader of his age detract from the claim that he was guided by the Lord?

11. Does the story of the Nephites appear at first glance to have had an auspicious beginning? Did the Restored Church of this dispensation have an auspicious beginning?

Lesson 4

LEHI AS A REPRESENTATIVE MAN

Prospectus of Lesson 4: There are many indications in the book of First Nephi that Lehi was a merchant. That title meant a great deal in Lehi's day; there is ample evidence that the greatest men of the ages engaged in the type of business activities in which Lehi himself was occupied. But along with that these same men were great colonizers, seekers after wisdom, political reformers, and often religious founders. Here we see that Lehi was a typical great man of one of the most remarkable centuries in human history, and we also learn how he was delivered from the bitterness and frustration that beset all the other great men of his time.

Portrait of Lehi: Lehi does not belong in the fantastic world that passed as the Ancient East a few years ago. He is at home in a very different kind of world, and a very real one. In the brief compass of Nephi's account, which is an abridgment of his father's own journal, whose type it imitates and continues (1 Ne. 1:2, 15-16), we are given an amazing amount of information, both general and particular, regarding conditions in Lehi's day. From this it can be shown that Lehi has an excellent claim to being a thoroughly representative man of his time and place. First consider what the Book of Mormon says.

Lehi was a man possessed of exceeding great wealth in the form of ". . . gold and silver, and all manner of riches. . . ." (1 Ne. 3:16, 2:4.) He had ". . . his own house at Jerusalem;" (1 Ne. 1:7), yet he was accustomed to "go forth" from the city from time to time (1 Ne. 1:5-7), and his paternal estate, the land of his inheritance, where the bulk of his fortune reposed, was some distance from the town. (1 Ne. 3:16, 3:22, 2:4.) He came of an old, distinguished, and cultured family. (1 Ne. 5:14-16.) The opening verse of the Book of Mormon explains the expression "goodly parents" not so much in a moral sense as in a social one: Nephi tells us he came of a good family and "therefore" received a good traditional education: "I was taught somewhat in all the learning of my father." (1 Ne. 1:1.) He was of the tribe of Manasseh which of all the tribes retained the old desert ways and was most active in the caravan trade.[1] He seems to have had particularly close ties with Sidon (for the name appears repeatedly in the Book of Mormon, both in its Hebrew and Egyptian forms),[2] which at that time was one of the two harbors through which the Israelites carried on an extremely active trade with Egypt and the West. He was proud of his knowledge of Egyptian and insisted on his sons learning it. (Mosiah 1:4.) He was a meticulous record keeper, conscientious to a fault, and given to addressing long moral tirades to youth. (1 Ne. 1:16-17 and elsewhere.) From his sons Nephi and Jacob one gathers that Lehi must have been something of an expert in vine, olive, and fig and honey culture.

He and his sons were connoisseurs of fine metal work (gold, silver, "precious things," weapons, armor, plates, engravings, "curious workmanship," "fine brass," etc.), though they had to acquire the skill of making them after they left Jerusalem (1 Ne. 17:9-10, 19:1, 2; Ne. 5:14-15); that is, their relationship to fine workmanship and precious materials had been that of handlers and owners but not of artisans and craftsmen.[3] As we shall see, Lehi's behavior was a remarkable combination of courtesy and firmness, gentleness and toughness, caution and daring. Put all these things together, and you have a perfectly consistent and convincing picture of Lehi the merchant.

Merchants and Supermen: But being a merchant in Lehi's day entailed far more than sitting in a counting-house or bazaar. The ancient merchant blazed his own trails and made his own markets: ". . . he became patient, unflinching. . . . Only the bravest men, the most intrepid, the best swordsmen and fighters, became traders."[4] On this subject we can do no better than to quote at some length an essay by Hugo Winckler:

The merchant went forth in person, and personally sought out the places and people that would receive his wares. . . . The caravan visits each place on the route and mingles with the inhabitants of each, while the modern transport employee knows only the overnight quarters at terminals and harbor towns . . . the traveling merchant of the caravans conveys his goods personally to the buyer, whose taste and temperament he must understand if he is to do business with him. . . . The person-to-person system of trade fostered a lively intellectual and cultural intercourse, as in our own Middle Ages, which was far more effective in spreading ideas than the modern method of the printed word. No temple, no center of culture, was ever out of contact with the great world-centers. . . . The student was obliged far more than he is today, to seek knowledge at the actual sources. . . . In Israel no one could be an educated man whose knowledge did not have ties with the temples of Babylon or Egypt, or whose degree of education was not judged in terms of how closely it matched both the theoretical and practical teachings of the great centers.

Intellectual intercourse was further promoted by the passion for traveling which is inborn in the Oriental. . . . He is not bound to the furrow, as the European is. The Islamic pilgrimage to Meccah is a necessary outlet for this vagrant urge, and the Orient has at all times known the wandering scholar . . . the man who was driven from land to land by wanderlust and the thirst for knowledge, and who covered distances that appear tremendous even to our modern means of communication, and did so with means and equipment so limited as to be beyond our comprehension. . . . Cultural conditions in the East threw men together and mixed them up in a brisk give and take of trade and craftsmanship . . . that took no account of language or racial differences and connection.[5]

Winckler, as we noted in the preceding lesson, wrote these words by way of explaining conditions in Israel in the time of Zedekiah. They say a good deal for the spirit and background of the Book of Mormon. The Oriental universalism here described is, as we have said, one of the most strongly marked characteristics of the Book of Mormon.

Lehi like his great contemporaries in the East and West, was a strange combination of man of action and dreamer. He was greatly worried about the future of Jerusalem, (1 Ne. 1:5) and his prayers and studies were rewarded by an apocalyptic vision. (1 Ne. 1:6-14.) His

attempts to make this public met with a violently negative
reaction which put his life in danger. (1 Ne. 1:20.) After
being severely rebuffed, Lehi was ordered in a dream to
". . . take his family and depart into the wilderness."
(1 Ne. 2:2.) From then on he shows himself as the
great leader and colonizer—daring, resourceful, patient,
and strong-minded.

Some Great Contemporaries; Solon: And so he takes
his place among the titans of the early sixth century; a
seeker after righteousness, a prophet, a poet, a scholar,
a man of the world, a great leader, and a founder of
nations. A thoroughly typical product, we might add,
of 600 B.C. and of no other period in history. Let us
explain this assertion. The Greeks always regarded
Solon of Athens as the wisest and best representative of
their race. He was a gifted poet, an able soldier, an in-
curable idealist, a great political theorist and practical
politician (the real founder of Greek democracy). He
was also a first-rate businessman, who never made much
money but thoroughly enjoyed traveling all over the
world. He built up a reputation for sagacity and honesty
that has made his name proverbial to this day.[6] His life
span exactly matches that of Lehi.[7] He spent a good deal
of time traveling as a merchant in Egypt and the East,
visiting the same important centers as those frequented
by the importers and manufacturers of Jerusalem—including Lehi.[8]

"Solon must have carried many a cargo of oil or
pottery from his own rocky Attica to the wealthy cities
across the Aegean," writes Professor Linforth, "and in
spite of his love for his own native land he must have
been charmed by the brilliant society which he found in
Asia. . . . He may have been tempted into luxury and
prodigality, as Plutarch supposed when he offered in
excuse for such habits the trials and dangers of his
mercantile career."[9] Certainly Lehi's sons were so tempted, and it was to get them away from such "prodigality
and luxury" that the Lord led his family into the wilder-

ness. Solon's words to the people of Athens bear astonishing resemblance to those being spoken at the very same time by the prophets at Jerusalem, for he was before all else a preacher of righteousness. No one would be surprised to discover such statements as the following in Jewish or Christian apocrypha, or even in the scriptures:

Behold the inhabitants of the city are minded to bring about the destruction thereof through their love of gain. They who lead them are of treacherous minds, but verily great sorrow and lamentation are about to fall upon them in their pride. Behold, they know not how to contain their lust. . . . They heed not the holy foundations of righteousness (the word *dike* here used may actually cognate with the Hebrew *tzedek*), which in silence lets things take their course until the latter-end, when surely comes the time of retribution. Behold a dire destruction cometh upon all the city and there is none who shall escape. The people have been quick to do iniquity and bring themselves into bondage. . . . As if it had fallen to a foreign enemy our cherished city is wasted away and consumed by those secret combinations which are the delight of evil men. . . . Thus evil worketh its way among the people, and many of the poor and needy are loaded with shameful chains and sold into bondage in foreign lands. . . . No man findeth security within his own gates, for evil leapeth over the high wall and finds him out even though he hideth himself in the secret recesses of his inmost chamber. . . .

These lines, quoted by Demosthenes in his oration on the False Embassy, were written by Solon about the year 600 B.C. How like some of the prophets they sound! So might Lehi have spoken to Jerusalem. And just as Lehi when ". . . he went forth among the people and began to prophesy, . . ." was greeted with mockery that was a prelude of worse things to follow, (1 Ne. 1:18-20), so when Solon went forth to preach to the Athenians in the market place at that time, he had to feign insanity so that the people might mock him rather than put him to death.[10] It should never be forgotten that it was this man, standing absolutely alone "like a wolf holding his own against a great pack of dogs closing in from every side," who gave Athens her constitution and later single-handedly preserved it from destruction, and thus did perhaps more than any other one man for the cause of popular government in the world.[11] We are still in his debt.

Thales: Another who visited the East on business in Lehi's day was Thales of Miletus, recognized to this day as the Father of Western philosophy and science. His mother was a Phoenician and he received most of his education in Egypt, which gives him much the same cultural background as Lehi himself.[12] Aristotle says that Thales, being laughed at as an impractical dreamer, taught his critics a lesson when he turned his remarkable intelligence to business and in a short time succeeded in cornering an important market in olive-oil; thereby qualifying as the first man to achieve a monopoly by playing the stock market.[13] After that he returned to a life of thought, but it was by no means thought devoid of action. Like Solon, he remained all his days a traveler and a man of the world, going from city to city and land to land imparting freely of his great scientific and political knowledge, which were in world-wide demand, to all who asked for it. Among other things he drafted a constitution for a United States of Greece.[14]

The Seven Wise Men: Like Solon, Thales would seem to be ages ahead of his time. But was he? Not at all: these men were no freaks or misfits in their day, but thoroughly representative. They were contemporary with, and usually numbered among, the Seven Wise Men, for example—a fictitious society of the wisest men then living, who left behind enduring reputations as the wisest of all time. The imagination of succeeding ages endowed the Seven Sages with supernatural wisdom and powers, and told how they used to meet from time to time to sup together and exchange among themselves the choicest wisdom of the East and West.[15] All the seven, who captivated the imagination of succeeding ages, were thought to combine great powers of imagination with sound, disinterested political sense and unshakeable moral integrity, and though indifferent to

wealth all had possessed at some time great private fortunes.[16] Their historical importance rested on the role
they played as political teachers and advisers in a time
of political world crisis.

The century that saw the fall of Jerusalem also saw
the collapse of the old sacral kingship throughout the
ancient world, and into the vacuum it left behind rushed
all sorts of political parties and theories; almost every
city in the world was torn between oligarchical, dicta-
torial, and democratic factions in a desperate struggle
to establish a new principle of authority in government.[17]
Even in the East where monarchy continued its sway,
it was on a new liberal footing established by Cyrus the
Great, the ideal philosopher king whom Jews and Greeks
vied in honoring as a saint and model ruler forever after.[18]
It is against this background of political ferment that the
Seven Wise Men played their principal role, which was
that of wise and disinterested counselors to a perplexed
and leaderless humanity.[19]

The Great Religious Founders: It is not without significance that Lehi counted among his contemporaries
not only the greatest first names in science, politics, and
business, but also the most illustrious religious founders
known to history: Gautama Buddha, Confucius, Lao-
tze, Vardhaman Mahavira (the founder of Jainism),
Zarathustra, and Pythagoras were all of Lehi's day.[20]
All these men were seeking for light, and whatever degree of success they may have enjoyed, their lives are
an eloquent commentary on the unparalleled display of
physical, mental, and spiritual energy that renders the
century of Lehi unique among all others. If it seems
asking a lot for the culture of a great nation to derive
its whole substance for a thousand years from a single
moment in history, let us remember that our own civilization of the twentieth century is hardly less deeply indebted to the century of Lehi. The political, economic and
religious traditions of the world still bear clearly and un-

mistakably the stamp of the great Greek and Oriental innovators of that wonderful age.

But Lehi Was Different: But in one thing Lehi stands quite apart from all the others save his fellow prophets in Israel. He actually *found* what the rest were only looking for. Solon summarized his life's experience in a single famous line: "No mortal ever knows real joy: all upon whom the sun shines are but miserable wretches."[21] The same sad conclusion epitomized the wisdom of all the Seven Wise Men, East and West. One hears the wise humanity of Solon the merchant behind this sad but sympathetic conclusion:

> Like gaping fools we amuse ourselves with empty dreams. . . . Do not doubt it, insecurity follows all the works of men, and no one knows when he begins an enterprise, how it will turn out. One man, trying his best to do the right thing, steps right into ruin and disaster, because he cannot see what is ahead; while another behaves like a rascal and not only escapes the penalty of his own folly but finds himself blessed with all kinds of success.

In the end, he says, no one can look forward to anything but "death or dire disease or the creeping evil of old age."[22] Disillusionment and a wise resignation are the sum and substance of the teaching of the wisest men who ever lived (read Socrates' *Apology* if you doubt it)—they did not have the answer, and the essence of their great wisdom was that they were honest enough to recognize it and admit the fact.

Now Lehi too was of this sober persuasion; he found neither happiness nor security in his wealth and success. And then something happened that changed everything: he had a revelation, and as a result ". . . his soul did rejoice, and his whole heart was filled, because of the things which he had seen, yea, which the Lord had shown unto him." (1 Ne. 1:15.) Lest we hastily conclude that Lehi was but a typical wise man of his age, and no more, we have but to set up his story and his sermons beside the stories and sermons of his great contemporaries of the East and West. What a contrast! For all their moral fervor, nothing could be less like the inspired utterances of the man from Jerusalem than the teachings of the great Greeks, with their world-ly wisdom and their bleak pessimism.

Questions

1. Are the "representative men" of their time typi-cal or average men?

2. In what way are Joseph Smith and Brigham Young representative men?

3. What were Lehi's qualifications for his task? Which was more important, his training or his character? Explain.

4. What is significant in the resemblance between Lehi, Solon, and Thales a) as evidence of the authen-ticity of Nephi's account? b) as guaranteeing the quality of Nephite civilization?

5. What manner of man was Lehi? What were his weak points?

6. How did Lehi react to the world-crisis and moral degeneracy of his time?

7. What can the individual do in such a situation?

8. Is it an accident that the greatest religious found-ers known to antiquity were all contemporary with each other? With Lehi?

9. How does Lehi differ from the other representa-tive men of his age?

10. Compare Lehi's message to the world with the message which Solon has to give us.

Lesson 5

LEHI'S AFFAIRS

1. The Jews and the Caravan Trade

Prospectus of Lesson 5: Only within the last few years has it been realized that the ancient Hebrews were not the primitive agricultural people that scholars had always supposed they were, but among other things that they were always very active in trade and commerce. Their commercial contracts reached for many hundreds of miles in all directions, which meant an extensive caravan trade entailing constant dealings with the Arabs. In Lehi's day the Arabs had suddenly become very aggressive and were pushing Jewish merchants out of their favored positions in the deserts and towns of the north. To carry on large-scale mercantile activities with distant places it was necessary for merchants to have certain personal and official connections in the cities in which they did business; here we mention the nature of such connections. Jewish merchants were very active in Arabia in Lehi's day, diligently spreading their religion wherever they went, and settling down not only as tradesmen in the towns but as permanent cultivators and colonizers in the open country. Lehi's activity in this regard is more or less typical, and closely resembles that of his predecessor Jonadab ben Rekhab.

The New View of Israel's Economy: In the preceding lesson we showed that Lehi, the representative man, was in all probability a merchant. Now we shall consider the claim more closely.

Lehi's day was peculiar as a period of great private fortunes: "the artists no longer work only for the court and the temples," the archaeologists report of this age, "they had now to fill orders for a wealthy bourgeoisie. . . ."[1] But one did not acquire "exceeding great riches" by running a shop in Jerusalem or a farm in the suburbs. Almost a thousand years ago one of the greatest Arabic poets wrote:

To travel abroad replenishes one's wealth and generates a constant increase of prosperity; but keeping close to home injuries the faculties, and inevitably brings him who stays there into contempt . . .[2]

One of the surprising results of a recent scholarship is the impressive picture of a vast and uniform system of trade and commerce flourishing over the whole ancient world from the very earliest times.[3] The old conception of the oldest village communities as living under an economic system of "Hauswirtschaft" (independent local economy) in which trade and commerce were completely unknown[4] has given way to the realization that the astonishing transmission of raw materials and finished goods from the Indus to the North Sea in prehistoric times was largely the work of caravans. True to form the familiar evolutionary interpretation of everything led scholars for generations to conjure up pictures of the first Israelites as primitive village peasants unacquainted with trade and commerce:

> The impression has been generally conveyed (writes H. H. Gowen) that the Hebrews only passed from the agricultural to the commercial stage after the exile. I found, on the contrary, a very considerable number of trade terms which are so natively Semitic as even to have passed from the Hebrew into Greek and Latin and other European languages. Even some of the terms which may originally have been Egyptian or Indian have apparently passed to the west through a Semitic channel and in a Semitic form.[5]

This is not surprising when one considers, with Eduard Meyer, that the records from the very beginning "show a highly developed industry in the ancient East," with "the whole Syro-Arabian steppe and desert forming a single transmission area," feeding into the great cities of Syria and Phoenicia which grew fabulously wealthy as centers of trade and manufacturing.[6] "Already in the earliest period," writes Ebers, "we find the caravans of the Phoenicians and Syrians conveying the commerce of the Egyptian and Assyrian World Empires along all the military roads, and making use of the Babylonian weights and measures."[7] There are not a few records of expeditions sent into the desert by the kings of Babylonia and Assyria in order to secure the trade-routes used by their merchants.[8] At the beginning of Israel's history, the story of Joseph, as Ebers points out, shows the close

tie-up between Arabic caravans and Egyptian markets.[9]
At that time to the north of Sidon the wealthy and
sophisticated city of Ugarit "was a terminal of trade-
routes via the Euphrates for Mesopotamia and from the
metal-bearing regions of Anatolia (Turkey) and at the
same time a bridgehead of Egyptian and Mycenaean
Greece in Asia."[10]

With all their neighbors growing rich around them,
"is there any reason," Gowen asks, "to believe that the
Hebrews were so different from other branches of the
Semitic family that they were indifferent to commerce . . .
and content to leave the monoply to 'Ishmaelites' and
'Canaanites'?" There is every indication that they were
not. "From the earliest times the Hebrew carried within
himself two opposite tendencies . . . the story of Jacob
plainly reveals a man of immense commercial proclivity
fighting desperately to retain his instinctive appreciation
of the spiritual . . ."[11] Certainly Jacob's sons knew something about business when they made a deal with Arab
traders on their way to Egypt. "We must abandon once
for all," says Bertholet, "the idea that Israel from the
beginning kept strictly to itself," and he proceeds to point
out[12] that the Moabites exported wine by caravan in the
days of Isaiah; that Abraham had dealings with the
Qetura, who were Arab tribes engaged in the Ethiopian
incense trade; that Israelites were acquainted with the
markets of Tyre (Ez. 27:11, Gen. 43:11), and had their
own merchants' quarter in Damascus (I Kings 20:34,
16:6); that they were constantly being visited by foreign
caravans;[13] that foreign merchants and artisans enjoyed
concessions and had their own settlements in Israel,
where they formed regular commercial corporations.[14]
When the King of Damascus beat Israel's Omri, one of
the concessions he demanded in the peace treaty was the
right to set up a bazaar in Samaria. The story of the
Queen of Sheba shows Israel's interest in the old South
Arabia trade, while the ambitious expedition to Ophir
went even further afield — perhaps even to the distant
Zambesi country of Africa.[15]

Thus we see that the children of Israel, far from being an obscure and forgotten peasant community, as was so long believed of them, were doing business — and big business — in the desert long before Lehi's day and long after.

Overland Commerce: Jerusalem is an inland town, and hence all her trade, including that across the waters, had to move by caravan.

Almost every writer on the Holy Land has drawn attention to its character as a natural bridge connecting Egypt with the Empires of the Euphrates Valley. Two great highways of traffic passed through the land, the one along the coast . . . to Egypt, the other east of Jordan from South Arabia to Damascus. Along these roads trade flowed uninterruptedly from the earliest times to the days of Islam, and the inhabitants of Palestine were kept in touch with the products and markets of India and of Rome, of Libya and Arabia, of Egypt and Babylon, even of China and the Malay Peninsula.[16]

Of all types of commerce, Eduard Meyer concludes, "that across the desert played a particularly important role; to it men were beholden for the most precious and coveted of all nature's products, gold and incense. . . . On that trade rests the fact that in South Arabia among the Sabaeans about 1000 years before Christ a high civilization was developed, which was in direct commercial contact with the states on the Mediterranean."[17]

The story of this South Arabic trade is one of the most important and intriguing chapters in economic history, and it directly concerns the Book of Mormon. For many centuries the richest trade-route in the world was that which ran along the eastern shore of the Red Sea for almost the entire length of the Arabian peninsula.[18] This is the route that Lehi took when he escaped from Jerusalem — and even his skeptical family seemed to think that he knew what he was doing. Not only the wealth of the Indies, but even the more fabulous wealth of Africa passed through the *suqs* of Saba (Sheba) to Europe and the Near East, and from very early times the Israelites were in on the trade. "Commercial relations with Yemen (the southwest corner of Arabia) begun in Biblical times were later strengthened by Jewish merchants residing in Babylonia and trading with Sabaea and Abyssinia."[19] A succession of great Arab states controlled this trade and grew rich on it: "The Minaeans, Sabaeans, Katabanians, Hadhramautians, and Himyarites succeeded one another to monopolistic control of the lucrative trade-routes over which the riches of Asia and Africa flowed into the eastern Mediterranean seaboard."[20]

There is strong philological evidence that the trade of South Arabia with Palestine and the Mediterranean was very old indeed.[21] But in Lehi's day something happened that virtually put an end to the lucrative land-transport between the two regions. Exactly what it was that caused the Arabic center of gravity to shift from the south to the north we do not know, though it is not maintained that it may have been the discovery of the monsoon winds, enabling shippers to by-pass the South Arabian ports. At any rate, the great Arab merchant states in the south gave way to the greatly reduced activities of the *mukarribs,* independent merchants who closely resembled the Greek traders in the west, with whom in fact, they entered into extensive negotiations through Sidon and Tyre.[22] Along with this there took place in Lehi's day a general shift of business and population from South to North Arabia, where Jewish settlers and merchants lost the economic advantages which they had long enjoyed in those regions. As early as the 7th and 6th centuries B.C. Ammon and Moab received a large influx of desert Arabs, who at the same time were moving into Gaza and the Negev.[23] In the 5th century all the latter region became Nabataean country, the Nabataeans being an Arab merchant state which by the end of the century had become a great empire, even participating in the struggles among the Greek cities for economic control of islands in the Mediterranean.[24] At the same time this kingdom was founded, the son of Lehi's contemporary, Nebuchadnezzar, founded Teima on the north edge of the Hedjaz as a royal residence, since he "obviously realized its great importance on the con- verging north and south Arabian trade routes."[25]

In the Old Testament "with abrupt suddenness the word Arab suddenly appears in the literature in Jeremiah and Ezekiel, never to vanish again."[26] Jeremiah and Ezekiel, it will be recalled, were contemporaries of Lehi. Even the enterprise and aggressiveness of the Phoeni- cians and Syrians which gained them economic control of the whole Mediterranean failed, Eduard Meyer ob- serves, even to pose a serious threat to the Arabs' control of the caravan trade[27]—any great power that wanted to trade over the deserts had to buy their cooperation, and though the price was high, it was infinitely cheaper than the military conquest and occupation of an all but unin- habitable wilderness half the size of the United States.

World-wide Business Connections: The Jews had long learned the secrets of getting on with these people. Before the great "Arab push" of Lehi's day they had their merchants' quarters carrying on business by special agreement in the important caravan cities.[28] The same system seems to have operated here as in the rest of the ancient world. It takes two parties to carry on business, and the basic plan on which traders operated from the earliest times was what the Greeks called the *xenia*- contract, the Romans *hospitium,* and the Orientals *chuwa.* To do business in a foreign city you depended on the support of a friend in that city, and in return gave him your friendship and support when he visited your city. Such contracts of friendship could be entered into either by individuals or groups and were inherited from father to son through many generations. They go back to the heroic ages at the dawn of history.[29] Inscriptions show the presence of a Syrian merchant colony in far-off Puteoli in Italy not long after Lehi, and a colony of merchants from Tyre flourishing on the Greek Island of Delos, calling itself "The Society of Tyrian Merchants and Shippers."[30] Such contracts of friendship were most indispensable in dealing with the touchy and dangerous desert people, where in fact the *chuwa* still survives as a hold-over from prehistoric times. Al-Hariri gives us a glimpse of how it worked 900 years ago; when he writes of himself:

> "... So that I never entered a city
> or ventured into a strange place,
> without uniting (literally 'mixing') with its governor,
> as water mixes with wine,
> and strengthening myself by his patronage,
> as the body is strengthened by the soul."[31]

On entering a town, that is, one would go straight to the house of the most important man who could give one aid and protection. Just so in the immemorial usage of the desert one repaired directly to the tent of the sheikh of any tribe upon arriving in its area, to become his *dakhil* (protected guest) and ask for the protection and assistance which no noble chief could deny. It is still possible today, as it was centuries ago, for a town to enter into a fraternal covenant with a desert tribe, and for the payment of a yearly sum to enjoy safe passage through its terrain and protection from other tribes as well; for such an agreement of *chuwa* with a great sheikh guarantees not only his support but also that of the other desert chieftains with whom he has like contracts of brotherhood.[32]

Since such agreements of friendship were reciprocal and were always associated with trade, it is plain enough (as the cases of Isaac and Jacob make clear) that the great lords of the desert were in business from the first.

Hariri describes how he was "once returning from Damascus, on my way to Bagdad, accompanied by travellers on camels, of the tribe of Nomir (i.e., they were Arabs), men distinguished alike by excellence and affluence."[33] "I was one," says a typical sheikh of the desert, "distinguished alike by opulence and munificence, who had estates and villages and means of hospitality. ..."[34] It may seem a contradiction to have a desert chief the owner of landed estates, and indeed, the discovery in the 1930's that Abraham did not always dwell in tents

but may have owned a fine town-house came as a surprise to students: ". . . we had really learned something
about him," says Sir Leonard Woolley commenting on
this, "which, as a matter of fact, the literature did not tell
us and which we should never have guessed."[35] The
whole economy which we are describing has, in fact,
come to light only with the studies of recent years, yet
it is clearly if casually indicated in Nephi's account taken
from his father's journal.

Jewish Merchants among the Arabs: Now there is a
good deal of evidence that the Jewish merchants who
sallied forth into the desert places and cities of Arabia
exerted a very substantial pressure as missionaries on the
local populations. Solomon's reputation stood very high
in the land of Sheba in the extreme south of Arabia, and
if "the last Himyarite (South Arabic) king was an ardent
convert to Judaism" he must have been under some real
Jewish influence.[36] Everywhere the Jewish merchants
clung to their religion with great tenacity and often
tried to press it on others, earning in the Roman world
the epithet of proselytizing Jews." "The international
contacts developed by the language of trade," writes
Gower, "afforded the Jew a marvellous opportunity for
becoming the great missionary of monotheism."[37] Speaking specifically of the later Jewish merchants in Arabia
Wechter writes: "Though developing their own culture
and social patterns they kept in close touch with Babylonian and Palestinian Jewries, but especially with the
Tiberian center." And he quotes Herschberg: "The
documents and sources testify that Arabian Jewry did not
differ from that of all other lands . . . They lived in
accordance with accepted Jewish tradition."[38] The first
thing a Hebrew merchant would do upon settling down
in a place even for a limited stay was to set up an altar,
exactly as Lehi did at his first important camp. "It is to
be assumed without question that the settlement of Israelite merchants such as those at Damascus (I Kings 20:34)
had an altar that stood on Israelite earth (cf. II Kings

5:17). Without such it would have been impossible to
live after the manner of Israel."[39]

Jewish Colonies in the Desert: Even more significant
from the Book of Mormon point of view than the individual merchant contacts with the Arabs are those Israelite colonies which from time to time went forth to settle
in various parts of the wilderness. These were permanent colonies of farmers, as ardently Jewish as the merchants, "land cultivators who introduced into Arabia
vine and bee-culture, cultivated the palm and built dams
to store the rainfall. They also distinguished themselves
as craftsmen, especially as armorers and goldsmiths."[40]
When we remember that Lehi's people went into the
desert carrying "all manner of seeds of every kind, and
also the seeds of fruit of every kind" (1 Ne. 8:1), in the
confident expectation of settling down and planting those
seeds, and that they too showed great interest in vine
and bee-culture and betrayed an almost sentimental
love of fine workmanship in metals, especially weapons,
it appears that Lehi was certainly thinking more in terms
of the colonist than of the merchant when he left Jerusalem. However he may have acquired his great fortune,
he left the city under a cloud—an outcast "driven from
Jerusalem" with no hope or thought of returning. (1 Ne.
5:5, 7:14, 17:43-44.) His elder sons, who insisted on
discounting any divine guidance, assumed as a matter
of course that their father's favorite, Nephi, ". . . lies unto
us . . . that he may lead us away into some strange wilderness; and after he has led us away, he has thought to
make himself a king and ruler over us, that he may do with
us according to his will and pleasure." (1 Ne. 16:38.)
This to them seemed the natural explanation of what was
going on: Nephi and his father Lehi, to them, were running a colonizing project. When Xenophon was leading
the Ten Thousand out of Asia some accused him, so
he says, of planning to found a city, name it after himself, and lord it over the others.[41] This was a common
abuse of the colonizing technique. Equally common was
the naming of the colony after the leader — a regular

Book of Mormon practice, and perfectly familiar from Greek and Roman history and legend.

The Case of the Rekhabites: In the time of Jeremiah, or shortly before, a certain Jonadab ben Rechab had led a colony of permanent settlers from Jerusalem into the wilderness, where his descendants survived through all succeeding centuries as the strange and baffling nation of the Rekhabites.[42] What makes them baffling is their Messianic religion which is so much like primitive Christianity in many ways that it has led some scholars to argue that those people must have been of Christian origin, though the historical evidence for their great antiquity is unquestionable. When one considers that Jonadab's project was almost contemporary (perhaps slightly prior to) Lehi's, that his name, ending in *adab* is of a type peculiar to the period and to the Book of Mormon, and that the Book of Mormon specifically states that the Lord had led other people out of Jerusalem beside Lehi, and that the Rekhabite teachings are strangely like those in the Book of Mormon, one is forced to admit at very least the possibility that Lehi's exodus *could* have taken place in the manner described, and the certainty that other such migrations actually did take place.

When the great Nabataean kingdom arose after the fall of Jerusalem, it absorbed among other people of the desert the Idumaeans, Arabic-speaking nomads who "though Jews by religion since the time of Hyrcanus, to a large extent continued to live like Arabs according to their former customs, and they undoubtedly served as a medium whereby the tribes of Arabia were brought into contact with the Hellenistic world over which the Jews were spread."[43] Certainly they show how extensively the tribes of Arabia had been brought into contact with the Jewish world and religion in the preceding centuries.

Questions

1. How has our idea of the economic picture of 600 B.C. changed in recent years?

2. How do these changes influence the interpretation of Lehi's activities?

3. What business activities did the Jews of Lehi's day engage in?

4. Why would Lehi be obliged to have dealings with the Arabs?

5. What connections did Jewish merchants have with the Arabs? How would this economic background condition the nature of Lehi's exploit?

6. What kind of business ties would Lehi have in cities outside Jerusalem?

7. What was the religious attitude of the Hebrew merchants towards the people among whom they traveled and lived?

8. Why did they build altars?

9. In what respects could Lehi's party be called typical Jewish colonizers?

10. How does the case of the Rekhabites support the plausibility of Nephi's story?

Lesson 6

LEHI'S AFFAIRS

2. Lehi and the Arabs

Prospectus of Lesson 6: Here we discuss Lehi's personal contacts with the Arabs, as indicated by his family background and his association with Ishmael, whose descendants in the New World closely resemble the Ishmaelites (Bedouins) of the Old World. The names of Lehi and some of his sons are pure Arabic. The Book of Mormon depicts Lehi as a man of three worlds, and it has recently become generally recognized that the ancient Hebrews shared fully in the culture and traditions of the desert on the one hand and in the cultural heritage of Egypt on the other.

Lehi's ties with the Arabs are many and interesting. Since the only comprehensive study of this theme is a chapter of *Lehi in the Desert,* we can do no better in this lesson than to quote that chapter, with necessary alterations and additions.

Significance of Manasseh: Now of all the tribes of Israel Manasseh was the one which lived farthest out in the desert, came into the most frequent contact with the Arabs, intermarried with them most frequently, and at the same time had the closest traditional bonds with Egypt.[1] The prominence of the name of Ammon in the Book of Mormon may have something to do with the fact that Ammon was Manasseh's nearest neighbor and often fought him in the deserts east of Jordan; at the same time a prehistoric connection with the Ammon of Egypt is not at all out of the question. The seminomadic nature of Manasseh might explain why Lehi seems out of touch with things in Jerusalem. For the first time he "did discover" from records kept in Laban's house that he was a direct descendant of Joseph. Why hadn't he known that all along? Nephi always speaks of "the Jews at Jerusalem" with a curious detachment, and no one in First Nephi ever refers to them as "the people" or "our people" but always quite impersonally as "the Jews." It is interesting in this connection that the Elephantine letters speak only of Jews and Arameans, never of Israelites.[2]

"Call Me Ishmael": The proverbial ancestor of the Arabs is Ishmael. His is one of the few Old Testament names which is also at home in ancient Arabia.[3] His traditional homeland was the Tih, the desert between Palestine and Egypt, and his people were haunters of the "borders" between the desert and the town;[4] he was regarded as the legitimate offspring of Abraham by an Egyptian mother. His was not a name of good omen, for the angel promised his mother, ". . . he will be a wild man, his hand will be against everyone, and every man's hand against him. . . ."[5] So the chances are that one who bore his name had good family reasons for doing so, and in Lehi's friend Ishmael we surely have a man of the desert. Lehi, faced with the prospect of a long journey in the wilderness, sent back for Ishmael, who promptly followed into the desert with a large party. (1 Ne. 7:2-5.) Lehi's family charged him with irresponsibility and lack of candor in leading them out into the wastes, and in view of what they had to suffer and what they left behind they were, from the common sense point of view, quite right. The decision to depart into the wilderness came suddenly to Lehi, by a dream. (1 Ne. 2:2.) In the same way ". . . the Lord commanded him that I, Nephi, and my brethren, should again return unto the land of Jerusalem, and bring down Ishmael and his family into the wilderness." (1 Ne. 7:2)

Here there is no personal appeal of Lehi to Ishmael, no long arguments, discussions or explanations, no long preparation and planning: Ishmael immediately moves into the desert, ". . . and all the house of Ishmael" (1 Ne. 7:22), though his sons complained as bitterly as Laman and Lemuel. (1 Ne. 7:6) This means that he must have been hardly less adept at moving than Lehi himself. The interesting thing is that Nephi takes Ishmael (unlike Zoram) completely for granted, never explaining who he is or how he fits into the picture—the act of sending for him seems to be the most natural thing in the world, as does the marriage of his daughters with Lehi's sons. Since it has ever been the custom among the desert people for a man to marry the daughter of his paternal uncle (*bint al-ammi*)[6] it is hard to avoid the impression that Lehi and Ishmael were related. Yet, it is significant that Ishmael's descendants, Arab fashion, always retained a separate tribal identity (Jac. 1:13, Alma 47:35, 4 Ne. 1:38, Mor. 1:8-9), which strongly implies that their ancestral heritage was different—without a proud and independent tradition of their own they could hardly have preserved, as they apparently did, an independent tribal identity throughout the whole course of Book of Mormon history.[7]

Ishmaelites of Two Worlds: If it was common in the early days for antiquarians in America, being mostly ministers, to compare the Red Indians with the Hebrews, it has ever been the custom of a more critical class of observers down to the present time to compare them with the Bedouins of the East. Two hundred years ago Harmer wrote:

In the smallness of their clans, and in their terribleness to those of a more settled kind of life, there is some resemblance between the Arabs and the Indians of North America; shall we suppose that there is a conformity between the Emirs of the one and the Sashems of the other, as to the *slovenliness* in the way of life?

Then he presents a description of the good and bad points of the Bedouin that match those of the Indian in every detail.[8] Sir Richard Burton, one of the few men who have lived both among the Bedouins and the Indians, marvels that two people so much alike on all points could have had no common background: it just goes to prove, he concludes, that life under similar conditions will beget identical cultures,[9] a statement which has been exhaustively disproven since it was made. Whatever the connection, it is certain that life in a wild coun-

try confirmed the wild ways of the Lamanites. For example, *"it was the practice* of the Lamanites to stand by
the waters of Sebus to scatter the flocks of the people,
that thereby they might drive away many that were
scattered unto their own land, it being a practice of
plunder among them." (Alma 18:7.) If ever there was an
authentic piece of Bedouin mischief that is it. And of
course it led to fights and reprisals in the best desert
manner. (Al. 18:6) Among others these rascals scattered
the flocks of their own king and yet continued active
in the social and political life of the community—how
weak and poorly organized a government, and how
typical of the East! (Alma 17:26-27; 19:21)

But the Nephites as well as the Lamanites continued
their desert ways. Shortly after landing in America
Nephi himself took his tents and all who would follow
him and continued his wanderings in the new land as
in the old. (2 Ne. 5:5) The great man in his old age
still speaks the language of the desert: ". . . may I walk
in the path of the low valley, that I may be strict in the
plain road" (2 Ne. 4:32f), is the purest Bedouin talk
for "may I stick to the *wady* and not get off the clearly
marked mainline that everyone follows!" One hears the
echo of innumerable old desert inscriptions in his prayer:
". . . O Lord, wilt thou make a way for mine escape
before mine enemies! Wilt thou make my path straight
before me! Wilt thou not place a stumbling block in my
way—but that thou wouldst clear my way before me,
and hedge not up my way, but the ways of mine enemy."
(2 Ne. 4:33.) The immemorial desert custom which required a sheikh to place the edge of his robe (*kuffah*)
over the back of anyone seeking his protection is clearly
recalled in Nephi's cry: "O Lord, wilt thou encircle me
around in the robe of thy righteousness!" (*Ibid.*, 4:33.)

There is a remarkable association between the names
of Lehi and Ishmael which ties them both to the southern
desert, where the legendary birthplace and central shrine
of Ishmael was at a place called Beer Lehai-ro'i.[10] Well-
hausen rendered the name "spring of the wild-ox jaw-

bone," but Paul Haupt showed that Lehi (for so he reads the name) does not mean "jawbone" but "cheek,"[11] which leaves the meaning of the strange compound still unclear. One thing is certain however: that Lehi is a personal name. Until recently this name was entirely unknown save as a place name, but now it has turned up at Elath and elsewhere in the south in a form which has been identified by Nelson Glueck with the name Lahai which "occurs quite frequently either as a part of a compound, or as a separate name of deity or person, particularly in Minaean, Thamudic, and Arabic texts."[12] There is a Beit Lahi, "House of Lehi" among the ancient place names of the Arab country around Gaza, but the meaning of the name has here been lost.[13] If the least be said of it, the name *Lehi* is thoroughly at home among the people of the desert and, so far as we know, no-where else.

The name of Lemuel is not a conventional Hebrew one, for it occurs only in one chapter of the Old Testament (Proverbs 31:1, 4), where it is commonly supposed to be a rather mysterious poetic substitute for Solomon. It is, however, like Lehi, at home in the south desert, where an Edomite text from "a place occupied by tribes descended from Ishmael" bears the title, "The Words of Lemuel, King of Massa."[14] These people, though speaking a language that was almost Arabic, were yet well within the sphere of Jewish religion, for "we have nowhere any evidence that the Edomites used any other name for their God than Yahweh, the God of the Hebrews."[15]

Laman's name is discussed below.[16] It is a striking coincidence that Condon saw in the name *Leimun,* as he renders it (the vowels must be supplied by guesswork), a possible corruption of the name Lemuel, thus bringing these two names, so closely associated in the Book of Mormon, into the most intimate relationship.[17] Far more popular among the Arabs as among the Nephites was the name Alma, which can mean a young man, a coat of mail, a mountain, or a sign.[18] While Sam is a perfectly good Egyptian, it is also the normal Arabic form of Shem, the son of Noah.

Lehi's Three Worlds: Lehi, like Moses and his ancestor, Joseph, was a man of *three* cultures, being educated not only in "the learning of the Jews and the language of the Egyptians," but in the ways of the desert as well. "There is a peculiar color and atmosphere to the biblical life," says Professor Montgomery, "which gives it its special tone. . . . And that touch comes from the expansive and free-moving life of what we call Arabia. . . ."[19] The dual culture of Egypt and Israel would have been impossible without the all-important Arab to be the link between, just as trade between the two nations was unthinkable without the Bedouin to guide their caravans through his deserts. Without the sympathetic cooperation of the Arabs any passage through their deserts was a terrible risk if not out of the question, and the good businessman was ever the one who knew how to deal with the Arabs—which meant to be one of them.[20]

It should be noted in speaking of names that archaeology has fully demonstrated that the Israelites, then as now, had not the slightest aversion to giving their children non-Jewish names, even when those names smacked of a pagan background.[21] One might, in a speculative mood, even detect something of Lehi's personal history in the names he gave to his sons. The first two have Arabic names—do they recall his early days in the caravan trade? The second two have Egyptian names, and indeed they were born in the days of his prosperity. The last two, born amid tribulations in the desert, were called with fitting humility, Jacob and Joseph. Whether the names of the first four were meant, as those of the last two sons certainly were (2 Ne. 2:1, 3:1), to call to mind the circumstances under which they were born, the names are certainly a striking indication of their triple heritage, and it was certainly the custom of Lehi's people to name their children with a purpose. (Hel. 3:21, 5:6.)

Lehi at Home in the Desert: There is ample evidence in the Book of Mormon that Lehi was an expert on caravan travel, as one might expect. Consider a few general points. Upon receiving a warning dream, he is ready apparently at a moment's notice to take his whole "... family, and provisions, and tents" out into the wilderness. While he took absolutely nothing but the most necessary provisions with him (1 Ne. 2:4), he knew exactly what those provisions should be, and when he had to send back to the city to supply unanticipated wants, it was for records that he sent and not for any necessaries for the journey. This argues a high degree of preparation and knowledge in the man, as does the masterly way in which he established a base camp, that is, until the day when he receives the Liahona, he seems to know just where he is going and exactly what he is doing: there is here no talk of being "led by the Spirit, not knowing beforehand ..." as with Nephi in the dark streets of Jerusalem.

His family accuse Lehi of folly in leaving Jerusalem and do not spare his personal feelings in making fun of his dreams and visions, yet they never question his ability to lead them. They complain, like all Arabs, against the terrible and dangerous deserts through which they pass, but they do not include ignorance of the desert among their hazards, though that would be their first and last objection to his wild project were Lehi nothing but a city Jew unacquainted with the wild and dangerous world of the waste places.

Lehi himself never mentions inexperience among his handicaps. Members of the family laugh contemptuously when Nephi proposes to build a ship (1 Ne. 17: 17-20), and might well have quoted the ancient proverb, "Show an Arab the sea and a man of Sidon the desert."[22] But while they tell him he is "lacking in judgment" to build a ship, they never mock their brother's skill as a hunter or treat him as a dude in the desert. The fact that he brought a fine steel bow with him *from home* and that he knew well how to use that difficult weapon shows that Nephi had hunted much in his short life.

Lehi has strong ties with the desert both in his family and his tribal background. Twenty-six hundred years ago the Jews felt themselves much closer to the people of the desert than they have in subsequent times. "We come to realize," says Montgomery, "that Israel had its face turned towards those quarters we call the Desert, and that this was its nearest neighbor." The Jews themselves were desert people originally, and they never forgot it: "this constant seeping in of desert wanderers still continues. . . . There is no barrier of race or language or caste or religion," between them and their desert cousins.[23]

Lehi's Desert Background: Ever since the days of Sir Robert Wood, scholars have been pointing out the close parallels that exist between the way of life peculiar to the wandering Bedouins of the East and that of the ancient Patriarchs, especially Abraham.[24] "Rightly do the legends of Israel depict the father of the nation as living in tents," says a typical commentary, "for nomadizing is the proper business of the genuine old Hebrews, and indeed of the Semites in general."[25] Hugo Winckler pointed out that whereas the cities of Palestine were all in the north, the country of Judah was really Bedouin territory, being "the link between northern Arabia and the Sinai peninsula with their Bedouin life."[26] Since Thomas Harmer, 160 years ago attempted to test the authenticity of the Bible by making a close and detailed comparison between its description of desert ways and the actual practices of the Bedouins, hundreds of studies have appeared on that fruitful theme, and they are still being written.[27] In one of the latest, Holscher discovers that the word Arab as used in the Old Testament "designates originally no particular tribe, but simply the nomadic Bedouins. In this sense the ancestors of the Israelites were also Arabs before they settled down on cultivated ground."[28]

A Mixed Culture: But though their nomadic practices were by no means terminated by agricultural ones, we must not fall into the error of thinking of the ancient Patriarchs as desert nomads and nothing more. The discovery made in the 1930's that Abraham was a dweller in houses as well as a dweller in tents "came as a great surprise," though it could hardly have surprised readers of the Pearl of Great Price. The fact is that both the city and the wilderness figure prominently in the story of God's people from the beginning. Winckler showed years ago that the Bedouins have been in constant contact with the cities throughout history, while the city-dwellers of the East have always gone forth into the waste on business of various kinds.[29] There is indeed constant conflict between the two ways of life: but conflict also means contact, and in the Book of Mormon as in the Bible the city and the wilderness are always wonderfully close together.

In Bible times as today one could literally step from an ancient and crowded metropolis into a howling wilderness in the course of a short half-hour stroll![30] This state of things that seems so fantastic to us is actually typical of the East in every period. Lachish letter No. 6 in denouncing the prophet Jeremiah for spreading defeatism both in the country and in the city shows that Lehi, a supporter of the prophet, could have been active in either area of "the land of Jerusalem." The fact that Lehi "dwelt at Jerusalem in all his days" would be an aid rather than a hindrance to much travel, for "the wilderness of Judah is a long projection north from the Arabian deserts to the gates of Jerusalem."[31]

The Language of the Desert in the Book of Mormon: So the patriarchs of old were wandering Bedouins, though far from barbaric. Their language was that of the desert people, many of whose words are to this day closer to Hebrew than to modern Arabic.[32] As recently as 2000 B.C. Hebrew and Arabic had not yet emerged from "what was substantially a common language, un-

derstood from the Indian Ocean to the Taurus and from
the Zagros to the frontier of Egypt. This common language (excluding Accadian) was as homogeneous as
was Arabic a thousand years ago."[33] A curious persistent homogeneity of culture and language has character-
ized the people of the Near East in every age, so that
Margoliouth can affirm that "a Sabean (south Arabian)
would have found little to puzzle him in the first verse
of Genesis."[34] "The Hebrews remained Arabs," is the
verdict of a modern authority, "their literature . . . in
its recorded forms is of Arab scheme and type . . ."[35]
It is not surprising that Professor Margoliouth holds that
Arabic seems to hold "the key to every lock" in the study
of the Old Testament. It certainly is indispensable to
the study of Lehi's activities and background in his native country.

One interesting linguistic tie between Israel and
the Arabs should not be overlooked since it has direct
application to the Book of Mormon. We refer to those
Hebrew genealogies in which "the nomenclature is
largely un-Hebraic, with peculiar antique formations in
-an, -on, and in some cases of particular Arabian origin."[36] "The loss of the ending on is quite common in
Palestinian place-names," according to Albright, referring to places mentioned in Egyptian records.[37] One
can recall any number of Book of Mormon place names
—Emron, Heshlon, Jashon, Moron, etc., that have preserved this archaic -on, indicative of a quaint conservatism among Lehi's people, and especially of ties with the
desert people.

Place-names in the Desert: Lehi's intimacy with desert practices becomes apparent right at the outset of his
journey, not only in the skillful way he managed things
but also in the quaint and peculiar practices he observed,
such as those applying to the naming of places in the
desert.

The stream at which he made his first camp Lehi
named after his eldest son; the valley, after his second

son. (1 Ne. 2:8.) The oasis at which his party made
their next important camp ". . . we did call . . . Shazer."
(1 Ne. 16:13.) The fruitful land by the sea ". . . we
called Bountiful," while the sea itself ". . . we called
Irreantum. . . ." (1 Ne. 17:5.)

By what right do these people rename streams and
valleys to suit themselves? By the immemorial custom
of the desert, to be sure. Among the laws "which no
Bedouin would dream of transgressing" the first, according to Jennings-Bramley, is that "any water you may
discover, either in your own territory or in the territory
of another tribe, is named after you."[38] So it happens
that in Arabia a great *wady* (valley) will have different
names at different points along its course, a respectable
number of names being "all used for one and the same
valley. One and the same place may have several names,
and the *wadi* running close to the same, or the mountain
connected with it, will naturally be called differently by
different clans," according to Canaan,[39] who tells how
the Arabs "often coin a new name for a locality for
which they have never used a proper name, or whose
name they do not know," the name given being usually
that of some person.[40]

This confusing custom of renaming everything on
the spot seems to go back to the earliest times, and
"probably, as often as not, the Israelites named for themselves their own camps, or unconsciously co-founded a
native name in their carelessness."[41] Yet in spite of its
undoubted antiquity, only the most recent explorers have
commented on this strange practice, which seems to have
escaped the notice of travelers until explorers in our own
times started to make official maps.

Even more whimsical and senseless to a westerner
must appear the behavior of Lehi in naming a river after
one son and its valley after another. But the Arabs don't
think that way, for Thomas reports from the south
country that "as is commonly the case in these mountains, the water bears a different name from the wadi."[42]
Likewise the Book of Mormon follows the Arabic sys-

tem of designating Lehi's camp not by the name of the
river by which it stood (for rivers may easily dry up),
but rather by the name of the valley. (1 Ne. 10:16;
16:6.)

In closing we may note the increasing tendency of
recent years to equate Hebrew and Arab. Guillaume
concludes his study with the dictum that the two names
are actually derived from a common original, the name
of Eber, both alike signifying "sons of Eber."[43] According to Albright, "no sharp distinction is made between
Hebrews, Aramaeans, and Arabs in the days of the
Patriarchs,"—they were all one common culture and
race: the people of the desert.[44]

Questions:

1. How does the figure of Ishmael support the
authenticity of Nephi's record?

2. What is significant about Lehi's connection with
Manasseh?

3. What considerations make one hesitate to see
in the close resemblance of the American Indians to the
Bedouins a pure coincidence?

4. What indications are there that Lehi himself
was a man of the desert?

5. How can one explain the Arabic names of Lehi
and his sons? Why not Hebrew?

6. What is now claimed regarding the relationship
of Hebrews and Arabs?

7. What is significant in the triple cultural heritage
of Abraham, Joseph, Moses, Lehi? How many cultures
are represented in our Mormon heritage?

8. What indications are there in the Book of Mormon that Lehi was a man at home in the desert?

9. Is it possible for such a man to live in the city?
On a farm?

10. What indications are there in the Book of Mormon that Lehi spoke the language of the desert? How
would that language be related to his own native tongue?

Lesson 7

LEHI'S AFFAIRS

3. Dealings with Egypt

Prospectus of Lesson 7: The Book of Mormon insists emphatically and specifically that Lehi had acquired at least a veneer of Egyptian culture. Only within the last few decades have students come to appreciate the intimate cultural ties between Egypt and Palestine in Lehi's day. Here we note some of the discoveries that have brought about that surprising realization. Though Lehi's loyalty to Egypt seems mainly cultural, there is a good deal in the Book of Mormon to indicate business ties as well. Here we present two documents describing business dealings between Egypt and Palestine in ancient times: the one depicts the nature of overland traffic between two regions, the other gives a picture of trade by sea. That Lehi was interested also in the latter type of commerce is apparent from the prominence of the name of Sidon in the Book of Mormon.

Israel's Cultural Dependence on Egypt: Students have often speculated of recent years on the strange and suicidal devotion of the Jews to the cause of Egypt in the time of Zedekiah. We shall treat the political side of the question in the next lesson. Lehi was in the peculiar position of opposing the pro-Egyptian party (1 Ne. 7:14), while remaining an enthusiast for Egyptian culture. (1 Ne. 1:2, Mos. 1:4.) There is nothing paradoxical about that, Egypt had recently come under the sway of a corrupt and incompetent government, which in fact was about to fall to a popular revolution, but that did not mean that Egyptian cultural heritage had ceased to be the greatest in the world, and the Book of Mormon concern with Egypt is strictly cultural.

It has been learned within the last generation that cultural and economic ties between ancient Israel and Egypt were far stronger than anyone had hitherto supposed. J. W. Jack noted in 1938 that "excavations have shown a closer connection with the land of the Pharaohs than was suspected . . . the authorities at Lachish were probably using, or at least were accustomed to the

Egyptian calendar and the Egyptian system of numera-
tion in their local records." Though this goes for an
earlier time, "all indications point to this connection with
Egypt continuing unbroken right down to the end of the
Jewish monarchy."[1] One anthropologist went so far as
to claim that Lachish was actually an Egyptian colony,
but investigation shows that the same "Egyptian" physical type and the same predominance of Egyptian culture
prevails elsewhere in Palestine.[2] Recently found ivories,
seals, inscriptions, and the preliminary study of mounds
throughout the land all tell the same story — overwhelming and unexpected preponderance of Egyptian
influence, to the equally surprising exclusion of influences
from Babylonia and Assyria.[3] At Jerusalem itself, where
excavation is necessarily limited, sealings on jar handles
attest the same long reign of Egyptian culture.[4] At the
same time, the Elephantine papyri tell us another thing
that scholars never dreamed of and which they were at
first most reluctant to believe, namely, that colonies of
Jewish soldiers and merchants were entirely at home in
upper Egypt, where they enjoyed free practice of their
religion. The ties between Palestine and Egypt were,
moreover, of a very long standing, centuries of "a common Hebrew-Egyptian environment" being necessary
to produce the "permeation of Egyptian modes
of thought and expression into Hebrew," and to load the
Egyptian vocabulary with words out of Palestine and
Syria.[5] The newly identified *Aechtungstexte* show that
as early as 2000 B.C. "Palestine was tributary in large
part, at least, to Egypt," while the excavation of Byblos,
a veritable "little Egypt," proved the presence of
Egyptian empire in later centuries.[6]

To say that Egyptian culture is predominant in an
area is not necessarily to argue the presence of Egyptian
dominion. According to Hogarth, Egypt exercised the
following three degrees of empire. The first degree was
rule by direct force, the second by "fear of reconquest
which a few garrisons and agents and the prestige of
the conqueror could keep alive in the minds of indirect

administrators and native subjects," and the third degree
"meant little more than a sphere of exclusive influence,
from which tribute was expected but, not being secured
by garrisons or representatives, . . . tended to be inter-
mittent."[7] Thus we see that the position of Egypt as
"most favored nation" in Judah may represent any degree of decayed dominion — even to an "empire" of
fourth degree. It was the Egyptian cultural heritage
rather than her government that was all-powerful,
Egyptian influence being strongest in Palestine *after*
Egypt had passed her peak as a world power.

In the great days of Egypt the renowned Ipuwer
had said, "the foreigners have become Egyptians everywhere," and a near contemporary of Lehi can boast,
"Behold, are not the Ethiopian, the Syrian, and all
foreigners alike instructed in the language of Egypt?"[8]
For centuries it was the custom of the princes of Syria to
send their sons to Egypt to be educated.[9] No matter
how sorry the plight of Egypt, the boastful inscriptions
of her rulers — sometimes very feeble ones — proclaim
the absolute and unquestioned superiority of Egyptian
civilization to all others; with Egyptians that is an article
of faith. Like the English in our own days, the Egyptians
demonstrated time and again the ability to maintain a
power and influence in the world out of all proportion
to their physical resources; with no other means than a
perfect and tenacious confidence in the divine superiority
of Egypt and Ammon, Wenamon almost succeeded in
overawing the great prince of Byblos. Is it any wonder
then, that in a time when Egypt was enjoying the short
but almost miraculous revival of splendor that marked
the XXVI Dynasty, with its astonishing climax of world
trade, the credit of that country should stand high in the
land of Jerusalem?

Economic Ties: Lehi's main business was with
Egypt, carried on both by land and sea. The caravan
business with Egypt was of immense antiquity. The
names of merchants scratched on the hot rocks of the
passes leading into the Nile Valley can still be read,

and some of them go back to the Old Kingdom, or the very beginning of civilization.[10] By Lehi's day the endless centuries of coming and going had established a common system of weights and measures among the merchants of all the East, in which the Egyptian system predominated.[11] In brilliant tomb-paintings we still see the Amu from Syria and Palestine coming into Egypt with their wares, while from Arabia come inscriptions that confirm the story from the other side. "(This is) the sarcophagus of Zidbal, son of Zid . . . who imported myrrh and calamus perfumes for the temples of the Gods of Egypt . . ."[12] One particular document deserves to be cited at some length, since it is a firsthand account of intercourse across the desert between Egypt and Syro-Palestine in the days of the Pharaohs.

A Picture of Contacts between Egypt and Palestine: We refer to the journal of an Egyptian border official, written in 1222 B.C. and discovered on the back of the Papyrus Anastasi III in 1899.[13] This functionary kept a careful record each day of persons passing through an important outpost on the road between Egypt and Syria, giving their names, families, home towns, destination, and business. Thus on such and such a day, for example, Pa-mr-khetem the son of Any of the city of Mr-n-ptah in the Imr district is on his way to Egypt on official business as chief of the royal stables. He is carrying two important letters, one from a certain Pa-ra-m-hb. On another day, "To Syria, Nht-amon, son of T-r from the castle of M. in the regions of the borders of Jerrem, with two letters for Syria, one addressed to Pen-amon, a commander of occupation troops, and the other to the butler Ra-mes-sw-nekht, from the city." Again, there passes through the commander of the archers from the oasis-post of Mr-n-pth-htp-hr-ma in the mountains, on his way "to raise troops at the fortress which is called Sile." When one remembers that this is the sort of world with which Lehi's people were familiar, and that their whole culture is but an offshoot and reflection of this one, the strange resemblances of things and names in these letters to those in the Book of Mormon (e.g. the exchange of military letters, such expressions as the "borders of Jerrem" and the predominance of names compounded with the elements Pa-, mr-, and -amon) is not to be lightly brushed aside.

Sidon and the Sea Trades: But to carry on business with Egypt, ships were necessary as well as caravans, and for ships, Lehi would have to depend on the people of the coast. Even the Egyptians of 600 B.C., striving as they were to regain supremacy of sea-trade, had their huge seagoing ships manned exclusively by Syrian and Phoenician crews, though Egypt was a maritime nation.[14] But Israel had no ports at all; her one ambitious maritime undertaking had to be carried on with the aid and co-operation of Tyre, who took unscrupulous advantage of her land-lubber neighbor.[15]

But for centuries it had been Sidon that had taken the lead; it was Sidon that gave its name to all the Phoenicians — Homer's Sidonians, and Sidon still remained in business.[16] But now was Tyre's great day; by pushing and aggressive tactics she was running the show, and no doubt charging excessive rates.[17]

Now it is significant that whereas the name of Sidon enjoys great popularity in the Book of Mormon, in both its Egyptian (*Giddonah*) and Hebrew forms, the name of Tyre never appears in the book. That is actually as it should be, for in Lehi's day there was bitter rivalry between the two, and to support the one was to oppose the other. The upstart nobility that were running and ruining things at the court of Zedekiah were putting their money on Tyre, so to speak, and when Nebuchadnezzar came west on the fatal expedition that resulted in the destruction of Jerusalem one of his main objectives, if not the main one, was to knock out Tyre.[18] Up until quite recently it was believed that his thirteen-year siege of the city on the rock was unsuccessful, but now it is known for sure that Tyre was actually taken and destroyed, upon which Sidon enjoyed a brief revival of supremacy.[19] Now Lehi shared the position of Jeremiah

(1 Ne. 7:14), who was opposed to the policy of the court in supporting Egypt against Babylon; that meant that he was anti-Tyre and pro-Sidon.

A Harbor Sketch: To match the record of the Egyptian border official cited above, we have a recent discovery from Egypt which presents a most vivid picture of sea trade between that country and Syria-Palestine in the great days of the XVIII Dynasty. The walls of a newly opened tomb at Thebes (No. 162) are covered with pictures of Syrian merchants doing business in an Egyptian harbor in the time of Amenophis III (1405-1370 B.C.). "The event here recorded," write Davies and Faulkner, "was doubtless one of fairly frequent occurrence during the palmy days of the Empire. We probably shall not be far wrong if we see in this representation the beginnings of that maritime trade from Syrian ports which . . . culminated in the far-flung mercantile ventures of the Phoenicians,"[20] and which reached its peak, we might add, both for Egypt and Phoenicia, in the time of Lehi, when "Phoenician galleys filled the Nile mouths, and Semitic merchants . . . thronged the Delta."[21]

In the tomb in question, which was that of Qenamon, the mayor of the great city of Thebes, "in the lowermost shop a Syrian merchant is trying to sell a large jar of wine or oil . . . The small hand-scales being used by the two male shopkeepers suggests the possible use of gold-dust as a medium of exchange."[22] This would seem to support our statement in *Lehi in the Desert* p. 7, that "lists of goods imported into Egypt from Palestine show that the great men of the East took the gold of Egypt in return for their wine, oil, grain, and honey, the first three far outclassing all other commodities in importance." If the Jews had to trade for raw gold, they knew what to do with it when they got it, and some have maintained that the Hebrews were the greatest goldsmiths of antiquity. "Goods for sale," our authorities continue, "consist largely of great jars of wine or oil, but a notable item of cargo consists of two humped bulls of a foreign breed. Other articles offered consist of bowls containing costly materials of various kinds and specimens of the jewellers' craft in the form of vases of precious metal . . ."[22]

"Herzfeld estimates that some 133 different materials were brought to Palestine from these outside lands in addition to the 87 commodities produced at home;"[23] and Hoelscher described the Phoenician merchants as importing metals, slaves, and riding animals from overseas to exchange for the ivory, gold, jewels, spice, balsam, and woven stuffs brought in by the caravans.[24] The Egyptians always traded manufactured goods (weapons, jewelry, glassware, cloth, wine, cosmetics, etc.), for natural products: gold, myrrh, ebony, incense, aromatic wood, animals, antimony, ivory, tortoise-shell, slaves, etc.[25] In the Qenamon tomb, along with the big commerce "there seems to have been no regulation against small scale private trading. The waterside where the foreign ships moored was therefore lined with small booths in which Egyptian shopkeepers, women as well as men, plied a lively trade." In this petty trade the Egyptians try to sell the visiting sailors "textiles, sandals, foodstuffs and other items."[26]

Precious Things: Another Egyptian tomb depicting Syrian goods being brought to a local noble gives us a good idea of what passed as "precious things" in the world of Lehi; a vase rimmed with finely-wrought pomegranates and labelled in the picture "a vessel of gold", a blue cruse, a chariot, a bow and quiver, horses, a halberd, a blue double-handled jar labelled "vessel of lapis lazuli", a dagger, a jar of incense, an ointment horn, a jar labelled "silver vessel", a strip of cloth, a quiver, a decorated linen sash, a hardwood stick, another silver vessel so labelled, and bear on a leash.[27] It is interesting that the gold and silver items are so designated, while the rest go by the collective name of "precious things", since the same usage is evidenced four times in two chapters of 1 Nephi. (Chs. 2 & 3) Davies suggests that in the Theban tomb "No doubt some of the more precious and portable articles" were destined as a special gift for Qenamon himself in return for his services in smoothing the way as mayor and "as a commission on the deal."[28] One cannot help recalling at this point how Nephi and his brothers tried to bribe Laban by bringing to his court just such precious and portable articles, to smooth the way in their transaction with him.

Let us summarize by recalling what we first learned about Lehi from the Book of Mormon. He was exceedingly rich, and his wealth took the form of all manner of precious things, with an accent on gold and silver; his treasures were portable and he and his sons knew and appreciated fine metal work when they saw it. In a land that produced no precious metals, Lehi could have acquired these things only by inheritance or trade. What he got by inheritance, however, was an estate in the country, and the origin of his wealth may be confidently detected in his intimate knowledge of vine and olive culture. That he traded is clearly implied by his close — almost sentimental — ties with the great non-Jewish port of Sidon and with the great culture of Egypt. That he and his sons knew a good deal about caravan techniques is obvious, and yet we are explicitly told that they knew nothing at all about shipbuilding.[29] Why should they? Shipbuilding was the jealously-guarded monopoly of the coast people. As far as the business affairs of Lehi are set before us in the Book of Mormon, everything is exactly as it should be.

Questions

1. What has been the main trend of discovery regarding ancient contacts between Israel and Egypt?

2. How was trade carried on between the two countries?

3. What type of evidence indicates the cultural dependence of Palestine on Egypt? How extensive was that dependence?

4. What evidence bears out the report in the Book of

Mormon that an important man in Israel might learn Egyptian and have his children do the same?

5. What in the Egyptian frontier official's reports reminds one of the Book of Mormon?

6. What indication is there in the Book of Mormon that Lehi may have engaged in trade by sea?

7. What indication is there in the Book of Mormon that Lehi had any connections at all with Egypt?

8. What was the nature of Lehi's "precious things"? How and where could he have acquired them?

9. How can the prominence of the name Sidon (including its Egyptian form Giddonah) and the absence of that of Tyre, an even more important port, be explained? Why is Tyre snubbed?

10. How does the commission or bribe to Qenamon confirm the Book of Mormon account of business methods in dealing with high officials?

Lesson 8

POLITICS IN JERUSALEM

Prospectus of Lesson 8: Nephi tells us a great deal about conditions in Jerusalem in his day. Lessons 8, 9, and 10 take a
closer look at the city on the eve of its overthrow. From Nephi
we learn that the Elders of the Jews were running things, and
that these Elders hated Lehi. From other sources it is known
that Jerusalem at the time actually was under the control of the
Sarim, an upstart aristocracy that surrounded and dominated the
weak king and hated and opposed both the prophets and the old
aristocratic class to which Lehi belonged. This accounts for
Nephi's own coldness towards "the Jews at Jerusalem." Among
the considerable evidence in the Book of Mormon that identifies
Lehi with the old aristocracy, the peculiar conception and institution of "land of one's inheritance" deserved special mention.
Also the peculiar relationship between city and country has now
been explained, and with it the declaration of the Book of Mormon that Christ was born in the land of Jerusalem becomes a
strong argument in support of its authenticity. Another significant parallel between the Book of Mormon and the political
organization of Jerusalem in Lehi's day is the singular nature and
significance of the office of judges. The atmosphere of Jerusalem
as described in the first chapters of the Book of Mormon is completely authentic, and the insistence of Nephi on the greatness of
the danger and the completeness of the destruction of Judah has
recently been vindicated by archaeological finds.

The peculiar social organization of Jerusalem and
the social and political struggles that wracked the city
at the time of its fall have been the subject of a good
deal of recent investigation. Let us consider the newer
finds on each particular topic, after first seeing what the
Book of Mormon has to say about it.

The Rule of the Elders: Nephi tells us casually but
emphatically that things at Jerusalem were in control of
"the elders of the Jews," who were holding nocturnal
meetings with the powerful and influential Laban.
(1 Ne. 4:22-27.) Poor Zedekiah plays no part at all—
his name occurs half a dozen times in the Book of Mormon, but only to fix a date. These elders were no friends

of Lehi, for if they had been his life would never have
been in danger. As it was, he ". . . was driven out of
Jerusalem," (1 Ne. 7:14, Hel. 8:22) by the only people
who could have driven him out, the important people,
those responsible for the ". . . priestcrafts and iniquities"
that were to be the ruin of them at Jerusalem.
(2 Ne. 10:5.)

Bible students recognize today that affairs at Jerusalem were completely under the control of the "elders".
The word "elders" has been understood to mean "the
heads of the most influential families of a city."[1] In
1935 in the ruins of the city of Lachish, 30 miles southwest of Jerusalem, a remarkable body of documents was
found. They were military reports written at the very
time of the fall of Jerusalem and saved from the flames
of burning Lachish by being covered with rubble when
the watchtower in which they were stored collapsed.
Lachish was the last Jewish town to fall before Jerusalem
itself went down, so here, in the fragments of some
eighteen letters, we have a strictly first-hand, if limited,
account of what was going on.[2] Now in the Lachish
letters we learn that the men who are running—and
ruining—everything are the *sarim,* who actually are the
elders, the term *sarim* designating, according to J. W.
Jack, "members of the official class, i.e. officers acting
under the king as his counselors and rulers." In these
priceless letters "we find the *sarim* denouncing Jeremiah
to the king and demanding that he be executed because
of his bad influence on the morale of the people." In
accusing the prophet of defeatism, the leading men of
Jerusalem were supported by the majority of the people
and by a host of popular "prophets" suborned by the
court, by whose false oracles "Judahite chauvinism was
whipped to a frenzy."[3] To oppose this front, as Lehi
did was to incur the charges of subversion and defeatism.

The Old Aristocracy and the New: How did "the
elders of the Jews" get such power over the king? It
was not entirely Zedekiah's weakness that was to blame,

for the real showdown had come in the days of Hezekiah, whose every attempt at reform had been systematically frustrated by the *sarim*.[4] As in other ancient
states of the time, including those of Greece and Rome,
the king was traditionally a member of the old landhold-
ing aristocracy, to whom he was obliged to defer on
many points: he ruled by and with the consent and advice of a council whose nature and composition are still
recalled in our own word "senate," meaning "council of
elders." Isaiah, Jeremiah, and Lehi were themselves
members of this ruling class. There is evidence, according to Graetz, that the Talmud is right in reporting that
King Hezekiah actually married Isaiah's daughter after
the Assyrian danger was over,[5] and Winckler has shown
how the king at Jerusalem sought the advice and counsel
of Jeremiah as a wealthy and powerful man with important connections—though they were mostly Babylonian
connections, highly obnoxious to the ruling clique at
Zedekiah's court.[6] That clique had come into power in
the days of Hezekiah at which time "the aristocrats
possessed such extensive power in the state of Judah
that it almost surpassed that of the king."[7] These aristocrats were a new, upstart faction, however, and not that
to which Lehi and the prophets belonged: "The natural
nobility, that descended from the patriarchal conditions
of old, was, so to speak, pushed aside by an artificial
nobility of courtiers." Under Hezekiah, that is, the old
fashioned "Elders" of the first families were supplanted
by the new crowd, composed of the younger sons of the
kings and their families, an "appanage", along with the
families of the favorites of favorites of former kings.[8]

But how do we know that Lehi was a member of the
old aristocracy? His probable association with Jeremiah,
his education, his noble ancestry that could be traced
back to Joseph and related him to Laban himself,
the fact that a family record had been kept from very
ancient times on expensive bronze plates, his close and
long-standing cultural ties with Egypt and Sidon (rather
than Tyre, which was favored by the ruling group), the

quantity and nature of his possessions all tell the same story; but the key to the situation is to be found in the frequent mention by Nephi of "the land of his inheritance," which was both the source of his wealth and the place where he kept it. The pronounced distaste with which Nephi so often refers to "the Jews at Jerusalem" as a group to which his own people definitely do not belong makes it apparent that he is speaking of the Jewish faction that controlled Jerusalem, both the government and the populace, and also implies that Lehi's family did not think of themselves as living in the city. They are apparently the old landed aristocracy that do not go along with the crazy ways and policies of the new rulers.

"The Jews at Jerusalem": The worst thing Nephi can say about his brothers is that ". . . they were like unto the Jews who were at Jerusalem, . . ." (1 Ne. 2:13.) ". . . those who are at Jerusalem," he says, ". . . shall be scourged by all people," (1 Ne. 19:13), and he tells how when he thinks of what is to befall them ". . . all my joints are weak, for those who are at Jerusalem." (1 Ne. 19:20.) According to him, God takes the righteous away "from the knowledge of those who are at Jerusalem," (1 Ne. 22:4), while ". . . because of their priestcrafts and iniquities, they at Jerusalem will stiffen their necks against him. . . ." (2 Ne. 10:5.) Nephi refuses to preserve among his people ". . . the manner of the Jews" (2 Ne. 25:1-2); which he knows first-hand (2 Ne. 25: 5-6) but of which he strenuously disapproves. There is something distinctly patronizing in his announcement: "I have charity for the Jew—I say Jew, because I mean them from whence I came. I also have charity for the Gentiles. . . ." (2 Ne. 33:8-9.) That is, he has charity for the Jew because he is a Jew and has charity for everybody anyway! But when his brother Jacob says ". . . behold, the Jews were a stiffnecked people; . . ." and proceeds to expatiate upon their vices, he obviously

excludes himself and his own people from their number.
(Jac. 4:14f.)

Incidentally one should explain here the use of the
term "Jew" as applied to Lehi. The word was not used
to designate all Israelites before the exile, but it *was*
used to designate any citizen of the *state* of Judah, and
it is in *that* sense that the Book of Mormon specifically
employs it.[9]

"The Land of our Inheritance": The old aristocracy
had always—as in other ancient societies—been land-
holders and cultivators, and the reliable source of their
wealth remained the land.[10] Yet at the same time the
organization of these old families remained a nomadic
one, with families entering covenants of protection and
blood-relationship with each other. Galling has described how the old desert system was adjusted to a
settled and localized patriarchal order in which the
"Elders" ruled because of their wealth, which wealth
had to be derived in turn from "the lands of a man's
inheritance."[11] We have shown elsewhere at considerable length how the constitutions of the earliest civilized
societies all rested on a feudal order. Whenever the
promised land is occupied by an invading host, the king's
heroes and supporters are rewarded with lands, and
these become the lands of their families' inheritance and
the title of their nobility. So far as is known to date,
there is no ancient civilization whose records do not open
with the description of a feudal order of society, and
every feudal aristocracy is both a migratory and a landed
nobility. Though their wealth is in "the lands of their
inheritance," they never cease to travel, hunt, and trade.[12]

Such was the old aristocracy of Israel. Eduard
Meyer says that all their power and authority went back
originally to the first land-allotments made among the
leaders of the migratory host when they settled down
in their land of promise. Regardless of wealth of influence or ability, no one could belong to the old aristocracy who did not still possess "the land of his in-

heritance."[13] This institution—or attitude—plays a remarkably conspicuous role in the Book of Mormon. Not
only does Lehi leave "the land of his inheritance," but
whenever his people wish to establish a new society they
first of all make sure to allot and define the lands of their
inheritance, which first allotment is regarded as inalien-
able. No matter where a group or family move to in
later times, the *first* land allotted to them is always regarded as "the land of their inheritance," thus Alma
22:28, 54:12-13, Ether 7:16—in these cases the expression "land of *first* inheritance" is used. (Cf. Mor. 2:27-
28, 1 Ne. 13:15, Alma 35:9, and 14, 43:12, Jac. 3:4,
Alma 27:12, 62:42, Mor. 3:16, etc.) This is a powerful
argument for the authenticity of the Book of Mormon
both because the existence of such a system is largely
the discovery of modern research and because it is set
forth in the Book of Mormon very distinctly and yet quite
casually.

The City and the Country: But along with this no-
madic-agrarian background, there is yet a third element
in the picture, for from their very first settlement in
Judea the Israelites entered into close and constant contact with the *city* economy of the Canaanites, which they
imitated and adopted. The imposition of a feudal pattern
on city organization produced, we are told, the peculiar
arrangement expressed in the formula: "the city of N . . .
and her daughter-cities."[14] In each city the Elders were
the ruling body and represented the voice of the free
and traditionally independent citizenry as against the
king's representative or the *Rabu;* in the capital city they
were a check on the king himself, and in Jerusalem no
king could be crowned without their approval or pass
important laws without their consent.[15]

One important aspect of the early land organization and control remains to be mentioned, and that is the
control of an area, already noted, by a "mother city," to
whom the other cities were "daughters." Rome was
originally the name of a city and nothing else, yet at all

times all land under control of that city was called
Roman and its inhabitants if they were free at all had
to be citizens of Rome and had to go to Rome every
year to vote, just as if they lived there. Finally all the
civilized world became Rome and its inhabitants Romans.
It is only in scale and not in nature that this differs from
other cities. Socrates, Sophocles and Euripides were all
Athenian citizens and described themselves as men of
Athens—yet they were born and reared and lived in
villages many miles apart—none of them actually in the
city. In the same way, while the Book of Mormon refers
to the city of Jerusalem plainly and unmistakably over
sixty times, it refers over forty times to another and
entirely different geographical entity which is always
designated as "the land of Jerusalem." In the New
World also every major Book of Mormon city is surrounded by a *land of the same name.*

The land of Jerusalem is *not* the city of Jerusalem.
Lehi ". . . dwelt at Jerusalem in all his days . . ." (1 Ne.
1:4), yet his sons had to ". . . go down to the land of
our father's inheritance, . . ." to pick up their property.
(1 Ne. 3:16, 21.) The apparent anomaly is readily explained by the Amarna Letters, in which we read that
"a city of the land of Jerusalem, Bet-Ninib, has been
captured."[16] It was the rule in Palestine and Syria from
ancient times, as the same letters show, for a large area
around a city and all the inhabitants of that area to bear
the name of the city.[17] It is taken for granted that if
Nephi lived at Jerusalem he would know about the surrounding country: ". . . I, of myself, have dwelt *at*
Jerusalem, wherefore I know concerning the regions
round about. . . ." (2 Ne. 25:6.) But this was quite
unknown at the time the Book of Mormon was written
—the Amarna Letters were discovered in 1887. One
of the favorite points of attack on the Book of Mormon
has been the statement in Alma 7:10 that the Saviour
would be born "at Jerusalem which is the *land* of our
forefathers." Here Jerusalem is not the city "*in* the
land of our forefathers," it *is* the land. Christ was

born in a village some six miles from the city of Jerusalem; it was not in the city, but it was in what we now know the ancients themselves designated as "the land of Jerusalem." Such a neat test of authenticity is not often found in ancient documents.[18]

The Rule of the Judges: In Zedekiah's time the ancient and venerable council of elders had been thrust aside by the proud and haughty *judges*, the spoiled children of frustrated and ambitious princes, who made the sheet anchor of their policy a strong alliance with Egypt and preferred Tyre to Sidon, the old established emporium of the Egyptian trade, to which Lehi remained devoted. The institution of the judges deserves some attention.

Since the king no longer sat in judgment, the ambitious climbers had taken over the powerful and dignified—and for them very profitable—"*judgment seats*", and by systematic abuse of their power as judges made themselves obnoxious and oppressive to the nation as a whole while suppressing all criticism of themselves—especially from recalcitrant and subversive prophets.[19] It was an old game. In 1085 B.C. one Korihor, the chief priest of Ammon, had actually seized the throne of Egypt, where for a long time the priests of Ammon ran the country to suit themselves in their capacity as judges of the priestly courts. These courts had at first competed with the king's courts and then by murder and intrigue, quite forced them out of business.[20] This story reads like a chapter out of the Book of Mormon.

But it is in the New World that we see the old institutions revived in full force. When King Mosiah suggested an improvement on the monarchical system (by which a king, no matter how unrighteous, had to remain in office until his death) the one alternative that presented itself was rule by judges. ". . . let us appoint judges," he says, (Mos. 29:11) and everyone seems to know exactly what he means, for in his speech, which is given in full, he does not have to explain the system to his hearers at all, and they adopt his suggestions quite readily and without any of the confusion and jamming that always goes with a shift from one type of government to a wholly different one. If Mosiah and his officers "newly arrange the affairs of this people," it is certainly along familiar lines. This is definitely indicated in the case of Korihor, who was able to gain a great following in the land by charging that ". . . the high priest, and also the chief judge over the land, . . ." under the new system were simply reviving ". . . ordinances and performances which are laid down by *ancient priests,* to usurp power and authority. . . ." (Alma 30:21-24.)

That there was a real danger of reviving an ancient priest-rule is apparent from the fact that the new system had no sooner been established than a certain Nehor, in the first case to be tried by the new chief judge, is charged with being "first to introduce priestcraft among this people." The chief judge on this occasion observes that such a business if allowed by the people ". . . would prove their entire destruction." (Alma 1:12.) So the abuses of the system and its ties with priestcraft were still vividly remembered from the Old World. The Nephites in fact regarded themselves as fugitives from the ". . . priestcrafts and iniquities . . ." of Jerusalem (2 Ne. 10:5), and while the Nephites ". . . did not reckon after the manner of the Jews who were at Jerusalem; neither did they measure after the manner of the Jews, . . ." (Alma 11:4), they *did* continue to build their sanctuaries, and also their synagogues after the manner of the Jews. That is, they retained certain sacral aspects of the older civilization. The manner of Nehor's execution in itself is ample illustration of the unbroken ties between the cultic legal practices of the Old and New World. (Alma 1:15.)

Mosiah's system of judges worked well for many years, but with the increase of unrighteousness crime and lawlessness became so general that several chief judges were murdered; the high office became an object of intrigue and manipulation by political cliques and

finally by criminal gangs, with the ". . . Gadianton robbers filling the judgment seats—. . ." in the end. (Hel.
7:4.) The extreme prominence of judges and judgment
seats in the Book of Mormon, apparent from a glance
at the concordance, is a direct and authentic heritage of
the Old World in Lehi's day.

Foreign Policy: As to foreign policies, the Amarna
Letters show at great length how the corrupt and ambitious lords of Palestine and Syria lost everything many
centuries before Lehi by counting too much on Egyptian
aid that never came. In the time of Hezekiah Judah had
preserved a delicate and precarious neutrality.[21] She
would have preferred continuing free of entanglements
with either side in Zedekiah's time as well, but the
pressure was too great. The geographic and strategic
location of Jerusalem constantly forced its people to
make decisions which they would gladly have avoided.
For two and a half centuries, since the conquests of
Assurbanipal, every state in the East had been constantly involved in endless underground activities, plots
and intrigues, espionage, revolts, punitory expeditions
and secret alliances. The division of Jerusalem in two
parties was thoroughly typical, the same division existing in Tyre and Damascus at the time.[22] Judah had to
choose between Babylon and Egypt; both were at the
peak of their splendor and prosperity which was actually
a fool's paradise built on a war-time boom economy.
Who would have guessed that within forty years both
of them would be under the rule of a nation of simple
nomads that hardly anyone had ever heard of! This was
Babylon's last fling, as it was Egypt's.[23]

Chaos and Destruction: When the bubble burst
everything went at once. Wiedemann sees no reason
for doubting that the prophecy of Jeremiah about Apries
of Egypt was literally fulfilled and that the king lost
his life in a revolution.[24] When the blow fell on Judah
it was far more catastrophic than scholars have hitherto
been willing to believe, with "all or virtually all, of the

fortified towns in Judah razed to the ground."[25] It was not until 1925 that we learned that "Tyre actually fell" at that time.[26] It is now believed, in fact, that in 586 southern Judah was "so frightfully depopulated" that the Arabs simply moved into the vacuum and occupied the southern country without opposition forever after.[27]

The unsurpassed destruction of Judah was preceded by an unparalleled atmosphere of terror and gloom that still speaks to us in the Lachish Letters. The country was divided into two factions, "the two parties, pro-Egyptian and pro-Babylonian, existed side by side in the land," each accusing the others of bad faith and bad judgment.[28] It was "a time of dissension and heart burning, when divided counsels rent the unhappy city of Jerusalem," and, as things became ever worse in an atmosphere "charged with unmixed gloom Zedekiah stubbornly followed the path to ruin by conspiring with Pharaoh."[29] Other cities were divided by the same faction and strife, "but it was especially at Jerusalem that passions ran high."[30] The vivid and imaginative description of a French scholar tells how towards the end, "In Jerusalem things were desperate. All the cities of Judah, except Lachish and Azekah, had fallen to the enemy; the country of Benjamin was a mass of ruins among rivers of blood. At the six gates of the city the guards had been doubled, but desertions became more numerous every day. Passions were at their height. The crowd disputed at the street-corners day and night, and their discussions were always accompanied by the steady hammering of the battering rams."[31] The false prophets continued their foolish and mercenary activities to the end, while the Elders charged the true prophets with treason and "the sarim were in permanent session in the Palace" sitting day and night to try cases of defection— a hysterical attempt to run down "subversives" when it was all too late.[32]

For years scholars insisted that the "destruction" of Jerusalem in 586 was not a real destruction at all but just the taking away of a number of noble hostages.

Today they know better. The Book of Mormon was quite right after all in insisting on describing that event as a complete destruction: ". . . for I know that the day must surely come that they must be destroyed, save a few only, who shall be led away into captivity." (1 Ne. 17:43.) What the Book of Mormon describes with particular clarity and power is the atmosphere of tension and gloom in the city leading up to the final catastrophe. Nowhere is the "dissension and heart-burning that rent the unhappy city of Jerusalem" more clearly shown forth than in those impassioned scenes within Lehi's own household. Two of his sons supported him, but the two eldest, taking the part of the Jews at Jerusalem, resisted and protested in the bitterest terms; they beat their younger brother, they exerted influence on their mother, and finally went so far as to try to put their father out of the way: ". . . the Jews also sought to take away his life; yea, and ye also have sought to take away his life; wherefore, ye are murderers in your hearts and ye are like unto them." (1 Ne. 17:44.) These are terrible words to be spoken in a family, and they plainly show what the conflict was about. While Lehi ". . . truly testified of their wickedness and their abominations; . . ." the Jews simply laughed at him (1 Ne. 1:19), and his older sons went along with them, protesting to their father that ". . . the people who were in the land of Jerusalem were a righteous people; for they kept the statutes . . . according to the law of Moses; wherefore, we know that they are a righteous people. . . ." (1 Ne. 17:22.) So Lehi's family was incorrigibly split right down the center, even as Jerusalem itself and all the cities surrounding it.

Questions:

    1. Who were "the Elders of the Jews"?
    2. To what did they owe their power?
    3. How does the role of Zedekiah in the Book of Mormon agree with what is now known of the man's character and history?

4. What was the composition of the "new aristocracy"? Of the old?

5. What indications are there that Lehi was a member of the old aristocracy?

6. What is Nephi's attitude towards "the Jews at Jerusalem"? How can that attitude be explained?

7. Is it correct to call Lehi a "Jew"?

8. What is designated by the expression "the land of one's inheritance" in the Book of Mormon? What is the significance of the concept as evidence for the authenticity of the book?

9. How does the statement in Alma 7:10 that the Lord would be born in Jerusalem actually support the authenticity of the Book of Mormon?

10. How is the institution of judges in the Book of Mormon related to conditions in Israel in Lehi's day?

11. How does the situation within Lehi's family as described in the Book of Mormon compare with conditions in Jerusalem at the time, as scholars now describe them?

12. How does the "atmosphere" at Jerusalem as described by Nephi agree with that depicted in such recent finds as the Lachish Letters?

ESCAPADE IN JERUSALEM

Prospectus of Lesson 9: There is no more authentic bit of Oriental "culture-history" than that presented in Nephi's account of
the brothers' visits to the city. Because it is so authentic it has
appeared strange and overdrawn to western critics unacquainted
with the ways of the East, and has been singled out for attack
as the most vulnerable part of the Book of Mormon. It contains
the most widely discussed and generally condemned episode in
the whole book, namely, the slaying of Laban, which many have
declared to be unallowable on moral grounds and inadmissible
on practical grounds. It is maintained that the thing simply could
not have taken place as Nephi describes it. In this lesson these
objections are answered.

Two Missions in Jerusalem: The final business of
Lehi's people in Jerusalem was conducted during a
couple of quick and dangerous visits to the city by his
sons. After the family was well out of Jewish territory
and camping Bedouin fashion "deep in the wilderness,"
it was necessary to send the young men back to town
on two important missions. The second was only to
"the land of Jerusalem" to pick up Ishmael. The fact
that this was a simple and uncomplicated assignment
at a time when things would have been very hot for the
brothers in the city itself (where they had been chased
by Laban's servants on their former expedition, and
would be instantly recognized), implies that Ishmael,
like Lehi, may have lived well out in the country.
(1 Ne. 7:2-5)

But the first mission was an exciting and dangerous
bit of work in the city itself. It was not undertaken
originally as a raid, for we are explicitly told that the
young men took their tents with them, (1 Ne. 3:9),
which was never done on a raid and which showed their
intentions to be peaceful and honorable. They went in
boldly and openly to Laban and frankly stated their
business to him. Yet they were expecting trouble and,
in the immemorial and inevitable manner of the desert,

drew lots to see who would go in to Laban—they knew
their man, and none of them wanted the job! (1 Ne.
3:11) After they failed to gain their point with Laban
the trouble began. The record tells of hiding without the
walls (as Arabs do when they reconnoiter a town),
daring exploits in the dark streets, mad pursuits, dangerous masquerading, desperate deeds, and bitter quarrels
—a typical Oriental romance, one might say, but typical
because such things actually do, and always did, happen
in eastern cities.

It has ever been an established and conventional bit
of gallantry for some Bedouin bravo with a price on his
head to risk his life by walking right through a city
under the noses of the police in broad daylight—a very
theatrical gesture but one which my Arab friends assure
me has been done a thousand times. It was while reading
the *Beni Hilal* epic that the writer was first impressed by
the close resemblance of the behavior of Lehi's sons on
that quick trip to Jerusalem to that of the young braves
of the *Beni Hilal* when they would visit a city under like
circumstances. The tales of the wanderings of the 'Amer
tribe tell the same story—camping without the walls,
drawing lots to see who would take a chance, sneaking
into the city and making a getaway through the midnight streets[1]—it is all in 1 Nephi, chapters 3 and 4 and
all quite authentic.

The All-Important Records: The purpose of the first
return trip to Jerusalem was the procuring of certain
records which were written on bronze plates (the Book
of Mormon like the Bible always uses "brass" for what
we call bronze—a word that has become current only
since its translation). Lehi had a dream in which he was
commanded to get these records which, as he already
knew, were kept at the house of one Laban. Nephi does
not know exactly the reason for this and assumes, in-
correctly as it turned out, that the object was to "preserve unto our children the language of our fathers."
(1 Ne. 3:19.) It is interesting that the *Beni Hilal* in

setting out for their great trek felt it necessary to keep a record of their *fathers* and to add to it as they went, "so that the memory of it might remain for future generations." The keeping of such a *daftar,* as it was called, was also known to other wandering tribes.[2]

It was in fact the keeping of such records that distinguished civilized nomads from the floating riffraff of the desert, to judge by Jawad Ali's remarks in the opening of his big new work on the Arabs before Islam. The *Jahiliyah,* or "time of ignorance," gets its name, he says, not as has commonly been supposed from the ignorance of the true religion in which the primitive Arabs lived, but from the fact that it describes a period in which the people were ignorant of reading and writing: "They were nomadic tribesmen, living in ignorance and sloth, having no contacts with the outer world, and keeping no records."[3] Actually their ancestors had reached a very high peak of civilization, but after the fall of the great kingdoms they had kept no records, and so had degenerated into the state of desert tramps—a condition which has always been regarded as utterly deplorable by the highest type of nomad, to whom *adab,* the preservation and cultivation of a literary tradition and especially the pure language of the fathers, is the highest human virtue. At the beginning of their long wandering, the Sheikh of the *Beni Hilal* ordered them to keep a record of each important event, "that its memory might remain for the members of the tribe, and that the people might read it and retain their civilized status" (*ifadah*). Accordingly verses recited on notable occasions were written down on the spot, just as Nephi wrote down his father's utterances by the river of Laban.[4]

Nephi's Wild Night: The records were in possession of a certain Laban—kept in his house. The figure of Laban will receive special attention hereafter; here it is the picture of Jerusalem that concerns us. Having failed in two attempts to get the records from Laban, and having in the process completely ruined their chances of any kind of a bargain, what were the brothers to do? The elder men worked off their frustration by beating their brother, but he proposed to risk it alone the third time. Leaving the others hidden without the walls, "I, Nephi, crept into the city and went forth towards the house of Laban." (1 Ne. 4:5) It was very late at night and this was not the strictly legitimate way of going about things; but Nephi had been encouraged by an angel and he was resolved to get the plates by fair means or foul. "I was led by the Spirit, not knowing beforehand the things which I should do." (1 Ne. 4:6.) He had reached the end of his resources and his situation was completely desperate. Not far from Laban's house, where he had been so roughly and meanly treated before, Nephi stumbled upon the prostrate form of Laban, lying dead drunk in the deserted street. (1 Ne. 4:7) The commander had been (so his servant later told Nephi) in conference with "the elders of the Jews out by night among them" (1 Ne. 4:22), and was wearing his full dress armor. What a world of inference in this! We sense the gravity of the situation in Jerusalem which "the elders" are still trying to conceal; we hear the suppressed excitement of Zoram's urgent talk as he and Nephi hasten through the streets to the city gates (1 Ne. 4:27), and from Zoram's willingness to change sides and leave the city we can be sure that he, as Laban's secretary,[5] knew how badly things were going. From the Lachish letters it is clear that informed parties in Jerusalem were quite aware of the critical state of things at Jerusalem, even while the *sarim*, "the elders," were working with all their might to suppress every sign of criticism and disaffection. How could they take counsel to provide for the defense of the city and their own interests without exciting alarm or giving rise to general rumors and misgivings? By holding their meetings in secret, of course, such midnight sessions of civil and military leaders as Laban had just been attending.

The Death of Laban: With great reluctance, but urged persistently by "the voice of the Spirit," Nephi took Laban's own sword and cut off his head with it. This episode is viewed with horror and incredulity by people who recently approved and applauded the far less merciful slaughter of far more innocent men on the islands of the Pacific. Samuel ibn Adiyt, the most famous Jewish poet of Arabia in ancient times, won undying fame in the East by allowing his son to be cruelly put to death before his eyes rather than give up some costly armor which had been entrusted to his care by a friend.[6] The story, true or not, is a reminder that eastern and western standards are not the same, and that the callousness of Americans in many matters of personal relationships would shock Arabs far more than anything they do shocks us.

A famous test-case for liberal scholars in Islam was whether God would permit children to die in the Deluge or not: to answer that in the affirmative was to mark oneself a blind reactionary.[7] Yet children still die in floods every year. Does the self-styled liberal with his glib and fastidious horror of killing ever stop to consider his own behavior pattern? What is meant, for example, by "backing the attack"? Anyone who has backed attacks both from the front line and the rear can affirm that "backing the attack" simply means sharing the full guilt of the slaughter without sharing the redeeming risk of combat. The front line soldier is exposed to a danger at least equal to that to which he exposes his opponent— each has a sporting chance of getting as much as he is giving. There might conceivably be some merit or honor in that. But what excuse is there for one who has supplied the means and enjoyed the profits of war in perfect safety to affect a sanctimonious and enlightened superiority to the base business of slaughter? Those who would strike the story of Laban's death from the Book of Mormon as immoral or unbelievable are passing hasty judgment on one of the most convincing episodes in the whole book.

The Book of Mormon is no more confined to mild and pleasant tales than is the Bible; it is for the most part a sad and grievous tale of human folly. No one seems more disturbed by the demise of Laban, however, than Nephi himself, who takes great pains to explain his position. (1 Ne. 4:10-18) First he was "constrained by the Spirit" to kill Laban, but he said in his heart that he had never shed human blood and became sick at the thought: "I shrunk and would that I might not slay him." The Spirit spoke again, and to its promptings Nephi adds his own rationalizings:

> I also knew that he had sought to take away mine own life; yea, and he would not hearken unto the commandments of the Lord; and he also had taken away our property.

But this was still not enough; the Spirit spoke again, explaining the Lord's reasons and assuring Nephi that he would be in the right; to which Nephi appends yet more arguments of his own, remembering the promise that his people would prosper only by keeping the commandments of the Lord:

> . . . and I also *thought* that they could not keep the commandments . . . save they should have the law.

which the dangerous and criminal Laban alone kept them from having.

> And again, I knew that the Lord had delivered Laban into my hands for this cause. . . . Therefore I did obey the voice of the Spirit.

At long last, and with great reluctance, Nephi did the deed. If the Book of Mormon were a work of fiction, nothing would have been easier than to have Laban already dead when Nephi found him (killed perhaps in a drunken brawl) or simply to omit altogether an episode which obviously distressed the writer quite as much as it does the reader, though the slaying of Laban is no more reprehensible than was the beheading of the unconscious Goliath.

Is the Laban Episode Believable?: From time to time the claim is put forth, that the story of Laban's death is absurd, if not impossible. It is said that Nephi could not have killed Laban and made his escape. Those who are familiar with night patrolling in wartime, however, will see in Nephi's tale a convincing and realistic account. In the first place, the higher critics are apparently not aware that the lighting of city streets, except for festivals, is a blessing unknown to ages other than our own. Many passages might be cited from ancient writers, classical and Oriental, to show that in times gone by the streets of even the biggest towns were perfectly dark at night, and very dangerous. In the famous trial of Alcibiades for the mutilation of the Hermes, we have the testimony of one witness who, all alone, beheld by moonlight the midnight doings of a drunken band in the heart of downtown Athens, from which it is clear that at that time the streets of the greatest city in the western world were unlighted, deserted, and dangerous at night.[8] To move about late at night without lamp bearers and armed guards was to risk certain assault, as we are reminded by Juvenal's immortal satire:

> Consider now the various dangers that confront you by night. You are just plain crazy if you go out to dinner without having made out your will—as if nothing could happen to you! For when you go about at night danger lurks in every open window: you can consider yourself lucky if they confine themselves to dumping garbage on your head. Then there is the drunk and disorderly character, who hasn't killed anybody yet that night and can't sleep until he has. However much on fire with youth and wine he will give a wide birth to the rich escort with torches and bronze lanterns. But I who go by moonlight or with the stub of a candle am fair game. He blocks the way and orders me to halt: I comply—what else can you do if the guy is crazy and twice as strong as you are? "Where do you think you're going?" he shouts, "what strange synagogue do you hide out in?" . . . Well, it's the poor man's privilege to request his assailant, as he is being beaten up, to allow him to retain a few teeth. But that is not all you have to worry about: for you can always count on being robbed if you stay at home—even after everything has been tightly locked and barred—when some armed bandit is on the loose in the neighborhood.[9]

These are the perils of night in the streets of the greatest city in the world, at the very height of its grandeur and sophistication. The extreme narrowness of ancient streets made their blackout doubly effective. From the Greek and Roman comedy and from the poets we learn how heavily barred and closely guarded the doors of private houses had to be at night, and archaeology has shown us cities farther east (e.g., Mohenjo-Daro) in which apparently not a single house window opened onto the public street, as few do even today at ground level. East and West, the inmates simply shut themselves in at night as if in a besieged fortress. Even in Shakespeare's day we see the comical terror of the nightwatch passing through the streets at hours when all honest people are behind doors. In a word, the streets of any ancient city after sundown were a perfect setting for the committing of deeds of violence without fear of detection.

It was very late when Nephi came upon Laban (1 Ne. 4:5, 22); the streets were deserted and dark. Let the reader imagine what he would do if he were on patrol near enemy headquarters during a blackout and stumbled upon the unconscious form of some notoriously bloodthirsty enemy commander, renowned for his brutal and treacherous treatment of friend and foe alike. By the rough code of war the foe has no claim to a formal trial, and it is now or never. Laban was wearing armor, so that the only chance of dispatching him quickly, painlessly, and safely was to cut off his head—the conventional treatment of even petty criminals in the East, where beheading has always been by the sword, and where an executioner would be fined for failing to decapitate his victim at one clean stroke. Nephi drew the sharp, heavy weapon and stood over Laban for a long time, debating his course. (I Ne. 4: 9-18.) He was an expert hunter, a skilled swordsman, and a powerful man:[10] with due care such a one could do a quick and efficient job and avoid getting much blood on himself. But why should he worry about that? There was not one chance in a thousand of meeting any honest citizen, and in the dark no one would notice the blood anyway. What they *would* notice would be the armor that Nephi put on, and which, like the sword, could easily be wiped clean. The donning of the armor was the natural and the shrewd thing for Nephi to do. A number of instances from the last war could be cited to show that a spy in the enemy camp is never so safe as when he is wearing the insignia of a *high* military official —provided he does not hang around too long, and Nephi had no intention of doing that. No one dares challenge "big brass" too closely (least of all a grim and hot-tempered Laban); their business is at all times "top secret", and their uniform gives them complete freedom to come and to go unquestioned.

Nephi tells us that he was "led by the spirit." He was not taking impossible chances, but being in a tight place he followed the surest formula of those who have successfully carried off ticklish assignments. His audacity and speed were rewarded, and he was clear of the town before anything was discovered. In his whole exploit there is nothing in the least improbable.

How Nephi disguised himself in the clothes of Laban and tricked Laban's servant into admitting him to the treasury is an authentic bit of Oriental romance, (e. g. Haroun al-Rashid) and of history as well. One need but think of Sir Richard Burton's amazingly audacious masquerades in the East, carried on in broad daylight and for months on end with perfect success, to realize that such a thing is entirely possible.[11]

Questions

1. Why was it so important for Nephi to get the brass plates?

2. Did Nephi and his brethren go back to Jerusalem as brigands or outcasts?

3. Does the account of the behavior of the brethren when they got to Jerusalem ring true? Can it be checked against real experience?

4. What conditions enabled Nephi to carry out his dangerous mission undetected?

5. What are the implications of the night meetings of the Elders in Jerusalem?

6. How does the unpleasantness of the episode of the killing of Laban speak for its authenticity? What is Nephi's attitude toward that exploit?

7. Was the killing of Laban a physical impossibility? Is Nephi's escape incredible?

8. Is the story of Nephi's exploits in Jerusalem too dramatic and exciting to be believed?

9. In times of war and revolution people do things they would not normally do, and do them differently. Is a student who has spent every day of his life safe within the four walls of an institution in a position to judge whether Nephi and his brethren could or would have done this or that?

10. Explain the saying: "Wo to the generation that understands the Book of Mormon!"

PORTRAIT OF LABAN

Prospectus of Lesson 10: Laban is described very fully, though casually, by Nephi, and is seen to be the very type and model of a well-known class of public official in the Ancient East. Everything about him is authentic. Zoram is another authentic type. Both men provide food for thought to men of today: both were highly successful yet greatly to be pitied. They are representatives and symbols of a decadent world. Zoram became a refugee from a society in which he had everything, as Lehi did, because it was no longer a fit place for honest men. What became of "the Jews at Jerusalem" is not half so tragic as what they became. This is a lesson for Americans.

Laban as a Representative Man: Laban of Jerusalem epitomizes the seamy side of the world of 600 B.C. as well as Lehi or Jeremiah or Solon do the other side. With a few deft and telling touches Nephi resurrects the pompous Laban with photographic perfection—as only one who actually knew the man could have done. We learn in passing that Laban commanded a garrison of fifty, that he met in full ceremonial armor with "the elders of the Jews" for secret consultations by night, that he had control of the treasury, that he was of the old aristocracy, being a distant relative of Lehi himself, that his house was a depository of very old family records, that he was a large man, short-tempered, crafty, and dangerous, and to the bargain cruel, greedy, unscrupulous, weak, vainglorious, and given to drink. All of which makes him a *Rabu* to the life, the very model of an Oriental *Pasha*. He is cut from the same cloth as Jaush, his contemporary and probably his successor as "military governor of the whole region, in control of the defenses along the western frontier of Judah, and an intermediary with the authorities of Jerusalem," or as Hoshiah, "apparently the leader of the military company situated at some outpost near the main road from Jerusalem to the coast," who shows his character in the Lachish Letters to be one of "fawning servility."[1]

Ever since the time of Hezekiah the greatest check on the power and authority of the king at Jerusalem had come from the leader of the new aristocracy of which we have spoken, that scheming and arrogant nobility which ran things with a high hand. Their chief bore only the harmless title of "Head of the Palace" (*'al-ha-Bait*), yet like other Mayors of the Palace in later ages he knew how to make all things bow to his tyrannical will, and the prophets called him the "wrecker" or "despoiler," he being stronger than the king himself.[2]

For ages the cities of Palestine and Syria had been more or less under the rule of military governors of native blood, but in theory at least, answerable to Egypt. "These commandants (called *Rabis* in the Amarna Letters) were subordinate to the city-princes (*chazan*), who commonly addressed them as 'Brother' or 'Father.' "[3] They were by and large a sordid lot of careerists whose authority depended on constant deception and intrigue, though they regarded their offices as hereditary and sometimes styled themselves kings. In the Amarna Letters we find these men raiding each other's caravans, accusing each other of unpaid debts and broken promises, mutually denouncing each other as traitors to Egypt, and generally displaying the usual time-honored traits of the high officials in the East seeking before all things to increase his private fortune. The Lachish Letters show that such men were still the lords of creation in Lehi's day—the commanders of the towns around Jerusalem were still acting in closest cooperation with Egypt in military matters, depending on the prestige of Egypt to bolster their corrupt power, and still behaving as groveling and unscrupulous timeservers.

Laban's office of headman is a typical Oriental institution: originally it was held by the local representative or delegate of a king, who sent out his trusted friends and relatives to act for him in distant parts of the realm. The responsibilities of such agents were as vague as their powers, and both were as unlimited as

the individual chose to make them. The system of ancient Empires was continued under the Caliphate, who
copied the Persian system in which "the governor, or
Sahib, as he was then called, had not only charge of the
fiscal administration but also had jurisdiction in civil and
penal matters . . . the sovereign power never gave up in
full its supreme rights over every part of the body poli-
tic, and this right devolved upon his representative;"
so that in theory the *rabi* could do anything he wanted
to. In the appointment of such a trusted official character counts for everything—in the end his own honor and
integrity are the only checks upon him; but in spite of
all precautions in their selection, and as might be expected, "the uprightness of the Cadis depended only
too often upon the state of society in which they lived."[4]
And the moral fibre of Laban's society was none too
good.

The Typical Pasha: Al-Maqrizi (1364-1442 A.D.)
has left a classic description of the typical pasha in his
glory, which we reproduce here from Gottheil:

> The rank of such a one was the highest of the dignitaries of
> the turband and the pen. Sometimes the same was also a preach-
> er . . . All religious matters were in his care. He took his seat
> every Saturday and Tuesday . . . upon a divan ('matress') and
> a silken cushion . . . Near him were five attendants; two in front,
> two at the door of his private room, and one to introduce those
> that came to him as litigants. Four guards stand near to him;
> two facing two. He has an ink stand and ornamented with sil-
> ver, which is brought to him from the state treasury; a bearer is
> appointed for it, who is paid by the government. From the
> stables there is brought for him a gray mule; one of such a color
> being reserved for him alone. From the saddle-magazine a
> saddle is brought for him, richly adorned, on the outside of
> which is a plaque of silver. In the place of hide, silk is used.
> Upon state occasions he wears chains and robes of honor faced
> with gold . . . When he is appointed preacher as well as judge
> . . . the accompaniment of the dignity of the preacher is the
> drum, the clarion, and special flags; for this one is the keeper
> of the flags with which the Wazir 'Chief of the Sword' is hon-
> ored . . . He is borne (in state) by the lieutenants of the gate
> and the attendants. No one approaches his presence . . . nor

does messenger or mission approach, except they receive permission . . . The head of the Treasury must report to him. He
has, also, to watch over the Diwan of the Mint, in order to
render an account of the money that is minted.[4]

One need only compare this officer with some digni-
taries in the court of Pharaoh (including Joseph himself) thousands of years before, to realize how little
some things change in the East. The pampering, the
magnificence, the armed guards and servants, the broad
and general powers, especially those connected with
the treasury, the forbidding presence and frightening
display of power and temper in one who is supposedly
a public servant—one can see Laban in every sentence!

Laban as a Man of the World: On the other hand,
it must be admitted in all fairness that Laban was a
successful man by the standards of his decadent society.
He was not an unqualified villain by any means—and
that as much as anything makes Nephi's account of him
supremely plausible. Laban had risen to the top in a
highly competitive system in which the scion of many an
old aristocratic family like his own must have aimed at
the office which he held and many an intriguing upstart
strained every effort to push him from the ladder that
all were trying to climb. He was active and patriotic,
attending committee meetings at all hours of the night;
he was shrewd and quick, promptly recognizing his
right and seizing his opportunity to confiscate the property with which Nephi and his brethren attempted to
bribe him—a public official. The young men wanted
some family records from him; they wanted them very
badly but would not tell what they wanted them for.
They were willing to pay almost anything to get them.
There was obviously something shady about the deal
from Laban's point of view. Very well, he could keep
his mouth shut, but would it be sound business practice
to let the plates go for nothing? With his other qualifications Laban was a big impressive figure of a man—
not a man to be intimidated, outsmarted, worn down, or

trifled with—he was every inch an executive. Yet he
plainly knew how to unbend and get drunk with the
boys at night.

Laban at Work: One of the main functions of any
governor in the East has always been to hear petitions,
and the established practice has ever been to rob the pe-
titioners (or anyone else) wherever possible.   The Eloquent Peasant story of fifteen centuries before Lehi and
the numerable Tales of the Qadis of fifteen centuries
after him are all part of the same picture, and Laban fits
into that picture as if it were drawn to set off his portrait:

> . . . and Laman went in unto the house of Laban, and he
> talked with him as he sat in his house.
> And he desired of Laban the records which were engraven
> upon the plates of brass, which contained the genealogy of my
> father.
> And . . . Laban was angry, and thrust him out from his
> presence; and he would not that he should have the records.
> Wherefore, he said unto him: Behold thou art a robber, and I
> will slay thee.
> But Laman fled out of his presence, and told the things
> which Laban had done, unto us. (1 Ne. 3:11-14.)

Later the brothers returned to Laban laden with
their family treasure, hoping to buy the plates from him.
This was a perfectly natural procedure.   In Lesson 8
on ancient merchants we saw that the Syrians who
came to trade in Egypt reserved their most precious
things, portable treasures of gold and silver, as a "present" for Qen-amon the mayor of Thebes, that is, the
King's personal representative in that great city, and
that the editor of the text regarded that present as "perhaps . . . a commission on the deal."   The behavior of
Lehi's sons in this instance shows that they had been
brought up in a family of importance, and knew how
things were done in the world; they were afraid of Laban, knowing the kind of man he was, but they were
not embarrassed to go right in and "talk with him as he
sat in his house," dealing with the big man on an equal
footing.   They might have known what would happen:

And it came to pass that when Laban saw our property, and that it was exceeding great, he did lust after it, insomuch that he thrust us out, and sent his servants to slay us, that he might obtain our property.

And it came to pass that we did flee before the servants of Laban, and we were obliged to leave behind our property, and it fell into the hands of Laban. (1 Ne. 3:25-26.)

Compare this with the now classic story of Wenamon's interview with the rapacious Zakar Baal, governor of Byblos, almost exactly five hundred years before. The Egyptian entered the great man's house and "found him sitting in his upper chamber, leaning his back against a window," even as Laman accosted Laban "as he sat in his house." When his visitor desired of the merchant prince and prince of merchants that he part with some cedar logs, the latter flew into a temper and accused him of being a thief ("Behold thou art a robber!" says Laban), demanding that he produce his credentials. Zakar Baal then "had the journal of his fathers brought in, and had them read it before him," from which it is plain that the important records of the city were actually stored at his house and kept on tablets. From this ancient "journal of his fathers" the prince proved to Wenamon that his ancestors had never taken orders from Egypt, and though the envoy softened his host somewhat by reminding him that Amon, the lord of the universe, rules over all kings, the hard-dealing official "thrust him out" and later even sent his servants after him—not, however, to slay him, but to check up on him and bring him something in the way of refreshment as he sat sorrowing. With cynical politeness the prince offered to show Wenamon the graves of some other Egyptian envoys whose missions had not been too successful, and when the business deal was finally completed, Zakar Baal, on a legal technicality, turned his guest over to the mercies of a pirate fleet lurking outside the harbor.[5] And all the time he smiled and bowed, for after all Wenamon was an Egyptian official, whereas Lehi's sons lost their bargaining power when they lost their fortune. The Laban story is an eloquent commentary on the ripeness of Jerusalem for destruction.

The Garrison of Fifty: As to Laban's garrison of fifty, it seems pitifully small for a great city. It would have been just as easy for the author of 1 Nephi to have said fifty-thousand, and made it really impressive. Yet even the older brothers, though they wish to emphasize Laban's great power, mention only fifty (1 Ne. 3:31), and it is Nephi in answering them who says that the Lord is "mightier than Laban and his fifty," and adds, "or even than his tens of thousands." (1 Ne. 4:1.) As a high military commander Laban would have his tens of thousands in the field, but such an array is of no concern to Laman and Lemuel: it is the "fifty" they must look out for—the regular, permanent garrison of Jerusalem. The number fifty suits perfectly with the Amarna picture where the military forces are always so surprisingly small and a garrison of thirty to eighty men is thought adequate even for big cities. It is strikingly vindicated in a letter of Nebuchadnezzar, Lehi's contemporary, wherein the great king orders: "As to the fifties who were under your command, those gone to the rear, or fugitives return to their ranks." Commenting on this, Offord says, "In these days it is interesting to note the indication here, that in the Babylonian army a platoon contained fifty men";[6] also, we might add, that it was called a "fifty"—hence, "Laban with his fifty." Of course, companies of fifty are mentioned in the Bible, along with tens and hundreds, etc., but not as garrisons of great cities and not as *the* standard military unit of this time. Laban, like Hoshaiah of Lachish, had a single company of soldiers under him as the permanent garrison, and like Jaush (his possible successor) worked in close cooperation with "the authorities in Jerusalem."

The Case of Zoram: An equally suggestive figure is Zoram, Laban's trusted servant whom Nephi met carrying the keys to the treasury as he approached the

building. Zoram naturally thought the man in armor
with the gruff voice was his master who he knew had
been out by night among the elders of the Jews. (1 Ne.
4:22.) Nephi, who could easily have been standing in
the dark, ordered the man to go in and bring him the
plates and follow after him, and Zoram naturally thought
that a need for consulting the documents had arisen in
the meeting, "supposing that I spake of the brethren of
the church," in which case he would act with great dis-
patch in order not to keep the officials waiting. He hurried in, got the plates, and hastened after the waiting
and impatient commander, but not, it must be admitted,
"without another word,"—for he talked and talked as
he hurried after Nephi through the dark streets towards
the gates. What did he talk about? "The elders of the
Jews," about whose doings he evidently knew a good
deal. For Zoram, as Laban's private secretary and
keeper of the keys, was himself an important official, and
no mere slave. Professor Albright has shown that the
title "servant" by which Nephi designates him, meant in
Jerusalem at that time something like "official representative," and was an honorable rather than a menial
title.[7]

That the *sarim*, who, as we saw in another lesson
"were in permanent session in the Palace," were full of
restless devices is implied not only in their strange hours
of meeting but in the fact that Zoram seemed to think
nothing strange of the direction or place where Nephi
was taking him. But when he saw the brethren and
heard Nephi's real voice he got the shock of his life
and in a panic made a break for the city. In such a situation there was only one thing Nephi could possibly
have done, both to spare Zoram and to avoid giving
alarm—and no westerner could have guessed what it
was. Nephi, a powerful fellow, held the terrified Zoram
in a vice-like grip long enough to swear a solemn oath
in his ear, "as the Lord liveth, and as I live" (1 Ne.
4:32), that he would not harm him if he would listen.
Zoram immediately relaxed, and Nephi swore another

oath to him that he would be a free man if he would join
the party: "Therefore, if thou wilt go down into the
wilderness to my father thou shalt have place with us."
(1 Ne. 4:34.)

The Oath of Power: What astonishes the western reader is the miraculous effect of Nephi's oath on
Zoram, who upon hearing a few conventional words
promptly becomes tractable, while as for the brothers, as
soon as Zoram "made an oath unto us that he would
tarry with us from that time forth . . . our fears did cease
concerning him." (1 Ne. 4:35, 37.)

The reaction of both parties makes sense when one
realizes that the oath is the one thing that is most sacred
and inviolable among the desert people and their descendants: "Hardly will an Arab break his oath, even if
his life be in jeopardy,"[8] for "there is nothing stronger,
and nothing more sacred than the oath among the nomads,"[9] and even the city Arabs, if it be exacted under
special conditions. "The taking of an oath is a holy
thing with the Bedouins," says one authority, "Wo to
him who swears falsely; his social standing will be dam-
aged and his reputation ruined. No one will receive
his testimony, and he must also pay a money fine."[10]

But not every oath will do. To be most binding
and solemn an oath should be by the *life* of something,
even if it be but a blade of grass. The only oath more
awful than that "by my life" or (less commonly) "by
the life of my head," is the *wa hayat Allah* "by the life
of God," or "as the Lord Liveth," the exact Arabic
equivalent of the ancient Hebrew *hai Elohim*.[11] Today
it is glibly employed by the city riff raff, but anciently it
was an awful thing, as it still is among the desert people.
"I confirmed my answer in the Bedouin wise," says
Doughty, "By his life . . . he said, 'Well, swear by the
life of Ullah' (God)! . . . I answered and thus even the
nomads use, in a greater occasion, but they say *by the
life of thee* in a little matter."[12] Among both Arabs and
Jews, says Rosenblatt, "an oath without God's name is

no oath," while "both in Jewish and Mohammedan societies oaths by 'the life of God' are frequent."[13]

So we see that the only way that Nephi could possibly have pacified the struggling Zoram in an instant was
to utter the one oath that no man would dream of break-
ing, the most solemn of all oaths to the Semite: "As the
Lord liveth, and as I live!" (1 Ne. 4:32.)

Transferred Loyalty: Now Zoram was the most
trusted of secretaries, as his intimacy with the most secret
affairs of state, his liberty to come and go at all hours,
and his possession of the keys to the treasury and archives attest.   Yet in a single hour he shifted all his allegiance from the man who trusted and leaned on him to
a stranger.   The oath was enough to confirm such a
move, but how could a man be so readily forced to take
that oath?   He was not forced into it at all, but talked
into it, softened and persuaded by Nephi's words, in
particular the promise "that he should be a free man like
unto us if he would go down in the wilderness with us."
(1 Ne. 4:33.)   Plainly with all his influence and privileges Zoram did not think of himself as a free man, and
his relationship with Laban was not one of trust and
affection.   Zoram's behavior is an even more eloquent
commentary than that of his master on the true state of
things in a society that had lost its balance and its faith
and sought only after power and success, "the vain
things of the world."

Questions

1. There is no passage in the Book of Mormon describing Laban, yet he is very fully described by hints
dropped here and there throughout the narrative. How
does this support the claim that the Book of Mormon
is not a work of fiction?

2. In what ways was Laban a typical Oriental
potentate?   What could Joseph Smith have known about
typical Oriental potentates?

3. What actual functionaries in ancient Israel exactly match Laban in his official capacity?

4. What reflection does Laban suggest on the nature of worldly success?

5. Is Laban a type characteristic of decadent societies? Do we have his like among us today?

6. In what way is the Laban story "an eloquent commentary on the ripeness of Jerusalem for destruction"?

7. What is the significance of "Laban and his fifty" as historical evidence?

8. What was the position of Zoram? How do his role and character enhance the plausibility of the story?

9. What did Zoram probably think when he recognized that he was among strange men? How did Nephi handle him? (Hint: at this time there were plots and conspiracies in every city and much espionage.)

10. Was Zoram a weak character? Why did he not consider himself a free man? Are you a free man?

Lesson 11

THE FLIGHT INTO THE WILDERNESS

Prospectus of Lesson 11: To appreciate the setting of much of Book of Mormon history it is necessary to get a correct idea of what is meant by "wilderness". That word has in the Book of Mormon the same connotation as in the Bible, and usually refers to desert country. Throughout their entire history the Book of Mormon people remain either wanderers in the wilderness or dwellers in close proximity to it. The motif of the Flight into the Wilderness is found throughout the book, and has great religious significance as the type and reality of the segregation of the righteous from the wicked and the position of the righteous man as a pilgrim and an outcast on the earth. Both Nephites and Lamanites always retained their nomadic ways.

What is a "Wilderness"?: Without the wilderness to provide a frequent diversion and perpetual background for its story, Book of Mormon history would be quite unthinkable. The word "wilderness" occurs at least 336 times in the Book of Mormon. There has always been a prejudice in favor of interpreting the word "wilderness" as signifying forest or jungle, both out of courtesy to the jungles of Central America, the classic Book of Mormon country, and to the language of our fathers, which grew up in a world happily unfamiliar with deserts. To our ancestors deserted land was land grown wild—overrun and choked with vegetation. Yet according to the *Oxford Dictionary* that is the fourth and least common meaning of the word, which properly refers to desert country. Certainly there is no doubt at all that the Book of Mormon is speaking of desert most of the time when it talks about wildernesses.

Wilderness in the Bible: We have the Bible to guide us here, for the Book of Mormon opens in Bible country, and in the Bible "wilderness" almost always means desert. Thus when Lehi assures his wife that the Lord will bring their sons "down again unto us in the wilderness", even while the young men "journeyed in the

wilderness up to the land of Jerusalem" (1 Ne. 5:5-6),
we know beyond a doubt that the wilderness in question was the country between Jerusalem and the Red
Sea, all of which is very dry and desolate. When in
Arabia, Lehi's people had to be "keeping in the most fertile parts of the wilderness", in order to survive (1 Ne.
16:14), it is clear what sort of country they were in.

The Wilderness in Book of Mormon Tradition: The
eight years of wandering in the deserts of Arabia which
the next few lessons of this series describe, are
simply an introduction to the wilderness — the Book
of Mormon people never entirely leave it. Wandering
in the wilderness is at one and the same time for them
both a type and a reality. One of their first patriarchs
begins a great discourse by comparing his own times to
"the provocation in the days of temptation while the
children of Israel were in the wilderness" (Jac. 1:7),
and recalls that Abraham in the *wilderness* offering up
his son was the type of Christ being offered in the
world. (Jac. 4:5.)

When Nephi spoke of his own wandering in terms
of the Exodus: "I will also be your light in the wilderness; and I will prepare the way before you, if it so be
that ye shall keep my commandments . . . ye shall be led
towards the promised land . . ." (1 Ne. 17:13), he was
perfectly aware of the parallel, for he tells us that he
"did liken all scriptures unto us, that it might be for our
profit and learning." (1 Ne. 19:23.) Hundreds of years
later Mosiah referred to Nephi's wanderings as a type
and pattern in full effect in his own day: " . . . as they
were unfaithful they did not prosper nor progress in their
journey, but were driven back, and . . . were smitten
with famine and sore afflictions, . . ." (Mos. 1:7.) A
later prophet explaining this says, " . . . they tarried in
the wilderness, or did not travel a direct course, and
were afflicted with hunger and thirst, because of their
transgressions. . . . And now I say, is there not a type
in this thing? For just as surely as this director did

bring our fathers, by following its course, to the promised land, shall the words of Christ, if *we* follow their course, carry us beyond this vale of sorrow into a far better land of promise." (Alma 37:42-45.)

Just as Lehi's descendants were constantly reminded, as Israelites are everywhere, of the sufferings and deliverance of their fathers in the wilderness of the Exodus, so they were reminded of later wanderings and deliverances in the wilderness of the New World:

> . . . Go and remember the captivity of thy fathers in the land of Helam, and in the land of Nephi; and remember how great things he has done for them . . . (Mos. 27:16.)
> . . . having been brought out of bondage time after time, and having been kept and preserved until now; and they have been prospered until they are rich in all manner of things . . . (Alma 9:22.)

It was the wandering in the wilderness that could teach the people better than anything else what they needed most to learn: the feeling of absolute and complete dependence on God at all times for all they had and were. (Mos. 4:21 ff.)

Quarantining the Wicked: The resemblance of one migration of God's people to another is not an accident, according to the Book of Mormon. In every age when the wicked reach a point of no return they are stopped from frustrating God's plan (which allows men to be *righteous* as well as wicked if they so choose), by bringing about a forceful separation between the two. One might call it a form of quarantine:

> . . . the Father hath commanded me, and I tell it unto you, that ye were separated from among them because of their iniquity; therefore it is because of their iniquity that they know not of you. And verily, I say unto you again that the other tribes hath the Father separated from them; and it is because of their iniquity that they know not of them. (3 Ne. 15:19-20.)

Thus the Lord himself explains the principle on which these things are done. The flight from the wicked world and wandering in the wilderness is by no means a unique event, but takes place in every dispensation:

> . . . he has also brought our fathers out of the land of Jer-
> usalem; and he has also . . . delivered them out of bondage and
> captivity, *from time to time* even down to the present day; and
> I have always retained in remembrance their captivity; yea, and
> ye also ought to retain in remembrance, as I have done, their
> captivity. (Alma 36:29.)

Though the righteous go into the desert, it is the
wicked who are cut off and lost; it is they who are put
under quarantine:

> And not at any time hath the Father given me command-
> ment that I should tell it unto your brethren at Jerusalem. Neither
> at any time hath the Father given me commandment that I should
> tell unto them concerning the other tribes of the house of Israel,
> whom the Father hath led away out of the land. (3 Ne. 15:14.)

It is the Jews at Jerusalem who are left behind and
abandoned:

> . . . I go my way, and ye shall seek me, and shall die in
> your sins: whither I go, ye cannot come. (John 8:21.)
> . . . he leadeth away the righteous into precious lands, and
> the wicked he destroyeth, and curseth the land unto them. . . .
> (1 Ne. 17:38.)

Such was always the Lord's way. When he brought
Lehi out of Jerusalem, "no one knew about it save it were
himself and those whom he brought out of the land."
Exactly so did the Lord bring Moses and the people
in secret out of the wicked land of Egypt, and Abraham
fled by night and secretly from Ur of the Chaldees as
Lot did from Sodom and Gomorrah, and so was the city
of Enoch removed suddenly to an inaccessible place.
And in every case, the wicked world thus left behind is
soon to be destroyed, so that those who leave the fleshpots and the "precious things" behind and lose all for
a life of hardship are actually losing their lives to save
them. It would be hard to say whether this pattern is
more clearly set forth in the Old Testament or the New,
but certainly it is most fully exemplified in the Book of
Mormon.

The Flight from Babylon, a Type and a Reality: Lehi's
flight from Jerusalem was more than an escape, it was

a conscious and deliberate renunciation of a whole way of life: "I have charity for the Jew," Nephi announces, "I say Jew, because I mean them from whence I came." (2 Ne. 33:8); yet he will not teach his people the ways of the Jews as he knows them,

> For I, Nephi, have not taught them many things concerning the manner of the Jews; for their works were works of darkness, and their doings were doings of abominations. (2 Ne. 25:1-2.)
>   . . . I have not taught my children after the manner of the Jews. (2 Ne. 25:6.)

Even in temporal matters the Nephites "did not reckon after the manner of the Jews who were at Jerusalem; neither did they measure after the manner of the Jews." (Alma 11:4.) Why this deliberate break with a tradition which had been so carefully preserved through the ages and was yet to be preserved through many generations? Nephi's successor gives the Lord's explanation:

> . . . I have lead this people forth out of Jerusalem, . . . that I might raise up unto me a righteous branch from the fruit of the loins of Joseph. Wherefore, I . . . will not suffer that this people shall do like unto them of old. (Jac. 2:25.)

There comes a time when the general defilement of a society becomes so great that the rising generation is put under undue pressure and cannot be said to have a fair choice between the Way of Light and the Way of Darkness. When such a point is reached the cup of iniquity is full, and the established order that has passed the point of no return and neither can nor will change its ways must be removed physically and forcibly if necessary from the earth, whether by war, plague, famine or upheavals of nature. (Mor. 2:13-15.) When the Chosen People do wickedly, according to a doctrine often stated in the Talmud, all nature suffers, and to save the world and restore the balance of good and evil God destroys the old generation and raises up a new people in righteousness. Lehi's people were neither the

first nor the last to be led into the wilderness to escape
the wrath to come:

> And as one generation hath been destroyed among the Jews
> because of iniquity, even so have they been destroyed from gen-
> eration to generation according to their iniquities; and never hath
> any of them been destroyed save it were foretold them by the
> prophets of the Lord. (2 Ne. 25:9.)

Other parties before and after the Nephites have
been led even to the New World: the Jaredites at the
time of the great destruction in the days of the Tower,
the people of Zarahemla who "came out from Jerusalem
at the time that Zedekiah, king of Judah, was carried
away captive into Babylon" (Omni 15), and various
communities on the islands of the sea:

> . . . as it says isles (in the plural), there must needs be more
> than this, and they are inhabited also by our brethren. For be-
> hold, the Lord God has led away from time to time from the
> house of Israel, according to his will and pleasure. And . . . the
> Lord remembereth all of them who have been broken off, where-
> fore he remembereth us also. (2 Ne. 10:21-22.)

The Wandering Continued in the New World: Nephi's
wanderings in the wilderness, undertaken in the fullest
awareness that they continued the traditions of the
fathers, were resumed almost immediately upon arrival
in the New World. This is an extremely important aspect of Book of Mormon history which is too often overlooked. These people did not regard their journey from
Jerusalem to America simply as a transportation project
to carry them from one settlement to another. They
were travelers before they left Jerusalem, and they remained so forever after. Lehi calls the deserts of Arabia
"the wilderness of mine afflictions," (2 Ne. 3:3) showing that to him the wilderness was both figurative and
real. Hardly had his party landed in the New World
when, Nephi reports, "The Lord did warn me, that I,
Nephi, should depart from them and flee into the wilderness, and all those who would go with me. . . . And we
did take our tents . . . and did journey in the wilderness
for the space of many days." (2 Ne. 5:5-7.) What

Nephi describes here is an immediate continuation of
their Old World wanderings; neither their ways nor
their customs had had time to change before they were
"fleeing into the wilderness" again, tents and all! And
when Nephi's party finally settled down and founded
communities and their descendants built cities, people
went right on fleeing from *them* into the wilderness, just
as their fathers had from Jerusalem. (This theme is
treated more fully below in Lesson XXIX.)

Next after Nephi, Jacob describes his people in
terms of "the days of temptation while the children of
Israel were in the wilderness" (Jac. 1:7); and that this
is more than mere imagery. That he is thinking in very
concrete as well as figurative terms, is brought out in
one of the most moving passages not only in the Book
of Mormon but of all the literature we have ever read:

> And it came to pass that I, Jacob, began to be old; and . . .
> I conclude this record, declaring that I have written according
> to the best of my knowledge, by saying that the time passed
> away with us, and also our lives passed away like as it were
> unto us a dream, we being a lonesome and a solemn people,
> wanderers, cast out of Jerusalem, born in tribulation, in a wilder-
> ness, and hated of our brethren, which caused wars and conten-
> tions; wherefore, we did mourn out our days. (Jac. 7:26.)

The Nephites never ceased to think of themselves
in those melancholy terms. Five hundred years after
Jacob, Alma could write that his people were both blessed
and sorrowful in their wandering state. Because of their
isolation, he says, God gives them special revelation,
and glad tidings "are made known to us in plain terms,
that we may understand, that we cannot err; and this
because of our being wanderers in a strange land; therefore, we are thus highly favored, . . ." (Alma 13:23.)
God, he says,

> has been mindful of this people, who are a branch of the
> tree of Israel, and has been lost from its body in a strange land;
> yea, I say, blessed be the name of my God who has been mind-
> ful of us, wanderers in a strange land. (Alma 26:36.)

Nephites and Lamanites both Wander: If the Nephites continued their nomadic ways, so no less did the Lamanites. From the first we find them "dwelling in tents, and wandering about in the wilderness." (Enos 20.) At least four hundred years after those words were written, Alma tells us that "the more idle part of the Lamanites (most of the nation) lived in the wilderness, and dwelt in tents; . . ." (Alma 22:28.) At the same time on the Nephite side we read how Mosiah was "warned of the Lord that he should flee out of the land of Nephi, and as many as would hearken unto the voice of the Lord should also depart out of the land with him, into the wilderness . . . and they were led by many preachings and prophesyings. . . ." (Omni 12.) It is the Jerusalem pattern all over again. On more than one occasion an afflicted people ". . . could find no way to deliver themselves out of bondage, except it were to take their women and children, and their flocks, and their herds, and their tents, and depart into the wilderness. . . ." (Mos. 22:2.) Sometimes a holy man like Samuel the Lamanite or Nephi the son of Helaman "departed out of the land, and whither he went, no man knoweth."

All these movements were religious in nature. Mosiah's people "were led by many preachings and prophesyings" in the wilderness. Such societies are met with often in the Book of Mormon. Alma founded such a group by the waters of Mormon, (Mos. 18), and moved about with them in the wilderness. (Mos. 23.) At that particular time such movements into the desert seem to have been popular, many people being "desirous to become even as Alma and his brethren, who had fled into the wilderness" (Mos. 21:31, 34), while Alma's people actually collided with another religious group settled in the waste — a community of refugee priests. (Mos. 23:31.) Nephi, like Alma, built up communities in the wilderness (Hel. 16:4), and other groups practiced rebaptism in the wilderness. (3 Ne. 7:24 f.)

All this reminds us powerfully of the Qumran Community of the recently discovered Dead Sea Scrolls and the peculiar type of Judaism that is represented. This we shall discuss presently, but what we wish to emphasize here is that the Book of Mormon deals with national, tribal, cultural and military history, only as incidental to its main theme, which is the doings of a small segment of the inhabitants of the New World, namely that minority of the faithful who continued to attempt to live the Law in its purity by escaping into the wilderness.

Questions

1. Why is a correct interpretation of the word "wilderness" essential to an examination or understanding of the Book of Mormon?

2. What is usually meant by "wilderness" in the Book of Mormon? The Bible? English?

3. What is the place of the wilderness in the religious traditions of the Nephites?

4. Was it a real wilderness or a "spiritual" one?

5. How does God "quarantine the wicked"? Why?

6. What comfort did the Nephites take in their wanderings?

7. Why did the Nephites continue their wanderings in the New World?

8. Why did the Lamanites? Were they more numerous than the city-dwellers?

9. What is the answer to the charge that the Book of Mormon is but an unimaginative repetition of the Bible? How does one explain recurrent situations and events in various dispensations?

10. In what things did Lehi's people make a break with the past? Why?

11. In what things did they retain and preserve their ties with the past? Why?

12. Why does the Lord not want us to be "at ease in Zion"? What is the meaning of the expression? See 2 Ne. 28:21.

Lesson 12

THE PIONEER TRADITION AND THE TRUE CHURCH

Prospectus of Lesson 12: The Israelites always looked back upon the days of the wandering in the wilderness as the true schooling of the Chosen People and the time when they were most nearly fulfilling the measure of their existence. The concept of man as a wanderer and an outcast in a dark and dreary world is as old as the records of the human race. The desert has always had two aspects, that of refuge and asylum on the one hand, and of trial and tribulation on the other: in both respects it is a place where God segregates and tests his people. Throughout the history of Israel zealous minorities among the people have gone out into the wilderness from time to time in an attempt to get back to the ways of the Patriarchs and to live the old Law in its purity, fleeing from Idumea or the wicked world. This tradition remained very much alive among the early Christians, and is still a part of the common Christian heritage, as can be seen from numerous attempts of Christian groups to return to the ways of Israel in the desert. Only the restored Church of Jesus Christ, however, has found itself in the actual position of the ancient saints, being literally driven out into the desert.

The Pioneer Background, a Book of Mormon Tradition: Time and again the Book of Mormon people were admonished by their leaders always to remember the trials and deliverances of Abraham in the wilderness, of the Children of Israel in the Exodus, of Lehi in his wanderings, and of the tribulation and release of various wandering saints and ancestors in the New World.[1] This is another example of the significant timing of the Book of Mormon, for none knew at the time of its appearance that the saints of the new dispensation would soon be continuing that great tradition of tribulation and triumph in the wilderness. The Book of Mormon was the best preparation and training-manual for what was to come.

Recently scholars have become aware as never before of the importance and significance of the wilderness and the wandering in the religious teachings both of ancient Israel and the primitive Christian Church. A number of important studies have appeared on the subject, and these supply a welcome commentary and confirmation for the rich fund of information that the Book of Mormon gives us about the ways of the wilderness.

The Hebrews and the Wandering: It has often been pointed out that the Hebrews always idealized the desert life as the good life. For the prophets of Lehi's time the years of Israel in the wilderness were in spite of all hardships "Israel's ideal time," when the people were nearer to God than ever before or after.[2] It was to recapture the spirit of that time that Jonadab ben Rekhab and his followers, fleeing from "paganizing influences in law and religion," settled in the desert some hundred years before Lehi.[2] The idea was much older than that, however. "The narrative of the exodus," writes Daube, "is dominated by the concept of God as *go'el,* 'redeemer', of the nation, as the mighty relative or legitimate owner who enforces his right to recover a member of the family or property subjected to foreign domination."[3] That is, the Exodus was not only a real event, but also "a type and a shadow of things," representing both escape from the wicked world and redemption from the bondage of sin.

Man the Outcast: Now the idea that this life is a pilgrimage through the desert did not originate with the Christians or even the Jews: it has been the religious memory of the human race from the earliest dispensations of the Gospel. The apocryphal writings are full of it, and the great antiquity of the tradition they report may be judged from Haldar's study of the oldest known temple texts—those of the Sumerians. The religious activity of the Sumerians centered about a ritual drama that took place at the temples (built for that purpose) at the New Year, celebrating and dramatizing the creation of the world, the fall of man, the redemption and resurrection. The ritual drama began by depicting the original home of man as a Garden of Eden, "a beautiful place adorned with greenery," in which the hero, the father of the race, resided; next "the enemies enter the

edin (for such the Sumerians called the place), destroy-
ing and carrying off the god to another place, also called
edin . . ."[4] *Edin* is thus the world before and also after
its transformation, when it becomes a dark and dreary
place: "we meet with a kind of 'exodus' into the desert
as an equivalent to the *descensus ad inferos,"* in which
man becomes a homeless wanderer in a land of desolation,[5] a place *not* to be confused, however, with the underworld or place of the dead.[6]

As Halder summarizes it,

> In the beginning we meet with the 'steppe' flourishing with
> verdure being the pasture of the herds. Then, the enemies from
> the desert enter the god's field, destroy it, and make it a desert;
> at this moment the god descends to the Nether World. Then
> the change occurs, and finally, the god's triumph over his ene-
> mies and his return to life are celebrated, the field again becom-
> ing the flourishing dwelling place of the cattle.[7]

What we should notice here is not the important resurrection theme, or the Garden of Eden motif, or the
appearance in the earliest known human records not only
of an "eschatology of woe," but also of a millennial hope
and "eschatology of bliss," but the specific reference to
this world as a desert. Man has lost his paradise and
though he shall regain it eventually through the sacrifice of the hero who overcomes death, he must live mean-
while as an outcast in a dark and dreary place. In the
greatest Sumerian epic, man is represented by the wandering and homeless hero Gilgamesh (often identified
by scholars with Adam), who travels through a dark
desert in search of the water of life and the plant or tree
of immortality (of which a serpent deprives him). Hundreds of parallels to this have been found in folklore
and ritual literature everywhere; it is the great heritage of
the whole human race.[8]

The Desert's Two Faces: The desert has two faces;
it is a place both of death and of refuge, of defeat and
victory, a grim coming-down from Eden and yet a sure
escape from the wicked world, the asylum alike of the

righteous and the rascal. The pilgrims' way leads
through sand and desolation, but it is the way back to
paradise; in the desert we lose ourselves to find ourselves. These familiar paradoxes are literal as well as
figurative: "It may be said, without any exaggeration,"
wrote the celebrated Burckhardt from much personal experience, "that the poorest Bedouin of an independent
tribe smiles at the pomp of a Turkish Pasha."[9] In the
midst of poverty that we can hardly imagine, the man of
the desert deems himself rich. "Among themselves,"
says Burckhardt, "the Bedouins constitute a nation of
brothers," but only as they keep to the desert: ". . . in
proportion as they reside near to a town, an avaricious
spirit becomes more general among them."[9] Our Mormon
missionaries have often noted that the same thing holds
true of the Indians among whom they have worked:
the farther from the highway they live, the higher are
their moral standards and the purer their traditions. "The
Bedouins are sober," a recent observer reports, "because
they cannot be otherwise. Since they must carry everything with them, they must ration everything, always
counting on the possibilities of being held up at every
departure and every arrival. They accept their lot because they know no other."[10] There is no escape from
the discipline of desert life, and no compromise with city
ways: there is always trouble when the two come into
contact.

The Desert as an Escape: Bitter experience has
taught the desert people that the world envies and re-
sents their hard-bought freedom. The mass and inertia
of a city civilization is a terrible thing: since none can
stand against it, the only hope of opposing it lies in
escaping from its reach. The skill of the Arabs in "silently stealing away," dissolving like a wraith into the
trackless sands, is proverbial. So is their quick and deadly reaction to the presence of strangers in their midst.
Robbed at every turn by the smooth manipulators of the
city, the Arabs can hardly be blamed for thinking that

robbery is the normal form of human economy and making themselves masters of the craft.   Upon turning his
talents to business many a simple desert sheik has dis-
played a capacity that seemed nothing short of genius.
Since their land is unproductive, these people must deal
in goods that they neither produce nor consume; they
become carriers and conveyors, skillful middlemen art-
fully turning every situation to their own advantage. The
Arabs feel perfectly justified in raiding the caravans
which do not buy their protection.   There is nothing
cynical about their ancient and established blackmail,
which is simply the application in their own country of
business methods learned in the city—they sell what
they have to sell for all they can get.   If the outside
world forces itself upon them, the outside world must
pay the price, for they know that the only hope of preserving their integrity is to avoid contact with the outside world altogether, even at the risk of appearing
morbidly anti-social.

Volumes have been written on the pure and noble
character of the Bedouin in his native state. "I was inclined in the prime of my past," writes an ancient poet,
"to make my residence among the people of the desert,
in order to acquire their high-minded temperament, and
their pure Arab language."[12] Both are very hard to find,
and totally beyond the reach of the short-time visitor:
"In order to form a really good estimation of Arab
character, it would be necessary to live in these remote
districts for many years, following the migrations of one
of their great tribes. . . ."[13] One can no more get to know
these people by casual contacts in and around the towns
than one can get to know our Indians by talking to them
in trading-posts. Theirs is a secret and hidden life to
which access is only possible for one who is willing to
share that life all the way.

Thus it is no exaggeration to say that the dwellers
in the wilderness are utterly removed from the ordinary
affairs of men. When "the world" becomes too much
for the Arabs, "they withdraw into the *depths* of the

wilderness, where none can follow them with hopes of success."[14] This suggested to Harmer that the Biblical term *"dwelling deep,* which Jeremiah recommends to some Arab tribes (Jer. 49:8, 30) means this plunging far into the deserts; rather than going into deep caves, and dens, as commentators suppose."[15] To this day the proximity of the desert to the town "at the best of times . . . hampers the government by offering a refuge and recruiting ground to all the enemies of order."[16] But fleeing into the wastes, which from the point of view of the city people is the act either of insane or criminal persons, all such refugees being lumped together as outlaws,[17] has been the resort of the righteous as well as the wicked from the beginning: "Come out of her, O my people! Partake not of her sins lest ye partake of her plagues!"

Come out of Her, O My People!: Careful studies of the apocryphal writings have revealed that in olden times the Jews believed that even the Ten Tribes "in order to be able to live the Law without molestation, resolved . . . to depart from the society of mankind and migrate *in terram aliam,* that is, to the Other World 'in a land beyond, where no member of the human race had ever before lived.' "[18] Such was certainly the case of the Jaredites who at the beginning of history were ordered to leave the wicked and fallen world of the Tower and betake themselves "into that quarter where there never had man been." (Ether 2:5) The Rekhabites who went out into the desert before Lehi's day are typical of the back-to-the-wilderness movements among the Jews in every age, the *paritsim,* or "those who separated themselves from the nation," and were viewed accordingly as traitors and outlaws by "the Jews at Jerusalem."[19] Lehi could never have gone back to Jerusalem even if he had wanted to. In 1 Maccabees 2:29 (written about 175 B.C.), we are told that "at that time many who were seeking after righteousness and judgment went down into the desert (or wilderness) to settle, with their children and their wives and their property, being sore op-

pressed by the evils of the time."[20] In the Dead Sea
Scrolls we have the contemporary records of just such a
community. Another such were the Ebionites who from
their teachings have the peculiar appearance, even as the
Dead Sea people and Lehi's own community do, of being both Christians and Jews at once.[21] From the Talmud
we learn that any Jew was free to take the *Nasir* oath
that bound him to observe the severe and simple ways
of Israel in the wilderness—a way of life that never
ceased to appeal to individuals and groups.[22]

    "Idumea, or the World . . .":   In Jewish tradition the
pious man who flees to the desert is represented by Elias,
according to Käsemann, "as the counterpart of Adam,
the sum and type of all righteous souls," as well as the
pattern of the High Priest. This Elias-Adam, the great
High-priest, is a stranger on the earth, or "wicked Idumea," where only his holy office and mission enable him
to survive at all, and where when that mission is completed he is put to death by the wicked.[23] Idumea is the
desert to the south of Judaea, where Lehi began his wanderings as an outcast, having been "driven out of Jerusalem,"—a classic place both of suffering and of temptation. In using the expression "Idumea, or the world,"
the Lord opens his book of revelations for this last dispensation by reminding us that we too are travelers and
outcasts in the wilderness.[24]

    Käsemann begins his remarkable study of the
Christian community of ancient times as God's people
wandering in the wilderness by observing that a state of
homeless migration is the "normal manner of existence
of those who are the bearers of revelation."[25] The early
Christians, he says, "regarded themselves as wholly led
by revelation: for them everything is directed from the
Other Side; their whole life is oriented towards the
epangelia, the promise, which is the goal of their journeyings." Their life and mission on earth was for them
"a confident journeying" from a heavenly past to a
heavenly future,[26] or in the words of the Apostolic

Fathers and the Dead Sea Scrolls, "the way of light is out of one eternity and into another."[27] Käsemann further notes that this way through life was one set out in God's plan from the beginning of the world, and though its continuity has often been broken by the wickedness of man, "God constantly restores it to earth by his Word, as at the beginning." By this way the saints must walk while they are in the earth, their life here being an *apodemia,* both figuratively (as in the Jewish philosopher Philo) and literally, i.e., a temporary sojourn in a strange land.[28] Such being the case, the journey in the wilderness is, in the primitive Christian view, God's special way of training and educating his people. As they travel through the wilderness they are led and sustained by revelations from on high, exactly as Alma describes it (Alma 13:23); yet they are also given an earthly leader, who is properly designated as the High Priest.[29] Like the early Hebrews and the later Jews, the first Christians thought of themselves as walking in the ways of their spiritual ancestors, "a band of homeless saints passing over the earth in search of their heavenly home."[30]

It is not surprising, then, to find the Dead Sea sectaries organized in camps in deliberate imitation of Israel in the desert,[31] or to learn that many scholars see in John the Baptist, the voice in the wilderness, the surest link between those sectaries and the first Christians.[32] Some have detected wandering Israel in the organization of the Apostolic Church, in which all the general authorities "received nomadic apostolate."[33] John's description of the Church as a woman who flees to the wilderness always captivated the imagination of later churchmen, who never knew quite what to make of it.[34]

Attempts to return to the Old Ways: Just as pious Christians have always looked for "Letters from Heaven" and willingly accepted forgeries when the real article has failed to appear, so Christian communities in every century have made determined attempts to get back to the ways of the wilderness and the wandering, and not hesitated to produce by artificial means the conditions and surroundings necessary to put themselves in a situation resembling that of Israel in the Desert of the Exodus. Like the Jewish sectaries before them, enthusiasts of the Christian monastic movement diligently sought out the wildest deserts they could find as the only proper setting for a way of life pleasing to God.[35] In the same spirit the pilgrims of the Middle Ages inflicted upon themselves all the hardships of wandering in strange lands and thirsty deserts in the endless search for a heavenly Jerusalem,[36] while in modern times Protestant sects have attempted to relive at their camp-meetings the very life of ancient Israel on the march. These and many like practices bear eloquent testimony to the deep and abiding influence of the wandering and the desert in the Christian and Jewish traditions. Throughout the whole course of the history of the Christian churches, one detects the powerful working of the conviction that God's people must always be travelers in the wilderness, both literally and figuratively.

The Real Church in the Real Wilderness: While some groups such as the Quakers and Pilgrim Fathers have been driven into the wilderness against their will— though always with a measure of calculation on their part—one church alone has had the honor of resembling Israel on the march in all details without having to resort to any of the usual artificial devices and theatrical props.

The parallels between the history of the restored Church and the doings of the ancients are so numerous and striking that even enemies of the Church have pointed them out again and again—what writer has not compared Brigham Young to Moses, for example? But I think in the case of the Latter-day Saints these resemblances have an extraordinary force, and that for two main reasons: (1) that they are not intentional, and (2) that they actually are the fulfillment of modern-day prophecy.[37]

The prophecy in question is found in the Doctrine and Covenants 49:24-25:

But before the great day of the Lord shall come, Jacob shall flourish in the wilderness, and the Lamanites shall blossom as the rose. Zion shall flourish upon the hills and rejoice upon the mountains, and shall be assembled together unto the place which I have appointed.

It is significant that all three of these "chosen people" were to suffer and dwell in the wilderness before the days of their rejoicing. The trials and tribulations of Zion in a very real wilderness in the remotest regions of the earth were matched by those of the Lamanites, driven from their lands and reduced to the last extremes of poverty and hardship in miserable and out-of-the-way tracts of wood and desert, and even more closely resemble the untold labors and dangers of the heroic settlers in the barren wastes of modern Palestine. All this is a sequel and vindication of the Book of Mormon, binding the Old World and the New together in a single divine economy, as the prophets foretold.[38] The principal actors of the mighty drama are still the descendants of Lehi on the one side and the children of "the Jews at Jerusalem" on the other, and the scene of their trials and victories is still as ever the desert.

A Constant Theme: One often hears it suggested that perhaps the Latter-day Saints overdo the "pioneer business." Yet as far as can be discovered the true church in every age has been one of pioneers—wanderers and settlers in the wilderness in the most literal sense. And in every age the Church has been careful to preserve and recall in the midst of its own trials the pioneer stories of its own early days and of still earlier dispensations, thousands of years ago. If the stories are all strangely alike that is no accident: we can do no better than to "liken all scriptures unto us," as did Nephi of old, "that it might be for our profit and learning."

Questions

1. Is the recollection and admiration of the deeds of pioneer ancestors peculiar to the Church of this dispensation alone?

2. What was anciently the purpose in rehearsing those deeds and recalling those tribulations?

3. Why did the Hebrews always look back upon the years of the wandering as "Israel's ideal time"?

4. How old is the religious concept of man's life as a wanderer in the wilderness? What theories might account for its origin?

5. What does the desert have to offer to the righteous? To the wicked?

6. How was the tradition of the desert kept alive among the more pious members of the Jewish society?

7. How do desert conditions enforce an austere and abstemious way of life?

8. What is there in the New Testament to illustrate the early Christian concept of life as a pilgrimage?

9. Name some instances of attempts by Christian groups to revive the old life of Israel in the wilderness.

10. What is singular about the relationship of the Latter-day Saints to the wilderness? What aspects of their flight to the West are peculiarly like those of ancient times?

11. Is the pioneer theme overemphasized in the Church today?

12. What is the significance of the flight-into-the-wilderness theme for modern Americans? Where do we go now?

Lesson 13

CHURCHES IN THE WILDERNESS

Prospectus of Lesson 13: As outcasts and wanderers the Nephites took particular pains to preserve unbroken the records and traditions that bound them to their ancestors in the Old World. Special emphasis is laid in the Book of Mormon on one particular phase of the record; namely, the care to preserve intact that chain of religious writing that had been transmitted from generation to generation by these people and their ancestors "since the world began". The Book of Mormon is a religious history. It is specifically the history of one religious community, rather than of a race or nation, beginning with the "people of Nephi" who became established as a special minority group at the very beginning of Book of Mormon times. The Nephite prophets always preached that the nation could only maintain its integrity and its very existence by remaining a pious religious society. Alma founded a church based on religious traditions brought from the Old World: it was a Church in the Wilderness, a small group of pious dissenters who went forth into the desert for the purpose of living the Law in its fullness. This church was not unique among the Nephites; other "churches of anticipation" flourished in the centuries before Christ, and after Christ came many churches carrying on in the apocalyptic tradition.

The Unbroken Chain: If Lehi's people, as we have seen, continued to view themselves as Israel on the march in a literal as well as a figurative sense, their ties with the past were far more than a mere matter of sentiment. They were the key to their identity as a people, the sheet anchor of their civilization; as a branch "broken off from its parent" they had no other roots than the records and traditions they carried with them. They were acutely conscious of that fact. At the very outset Nephi explained to his brothers why they should be willing to run any risk to get the brass plates:

. . . behold, it is wisdom in God that we should obtain these records, that we may preserve unto our children the language of our fathers; And also that we may preserve unto them the words which have been spoken by the mouth of all the holy prophets . . . *since the world began,* even down unto this present time. (1 Ne. 3:19-20.)

The purpose of the plates, as he saw it, was to preserve the cultural heritage of the past for generations to
come, and especially to retain intact the unbroken religious tradition of God's people back to the very beginning.

This is the announcement that launches the vast
and restless record-keeping project of Lehi's descendants, determined to keep intact the chain of writings that
bound them to the righteous of every age in a single unbroken faith and tradition. For the ancients all history
was sacred history; but it was Eduard Meyer who first
pointed out that "scientific" history first began with the
Jews, who in their passion for keeping full and accurate
records amassed a great deal of material which we
would call "secular history." "There are many records
kept of the proceeding of this people," says one Nephite
historian, "by many of this people, which are particular
and very large, concerning them. But behold, a hun-
dredth part of the proceedings of this people . . . cannot be contained in this work." (Hel. 3:13-14.) Mere
mass made it necessary to edit. From the first Nephi
had stated the guiding principle in the preserving of
plates and records: "Wherefore, the things which were
pleasing unto the world I do not write, but the things
which are pleasing unto God and unto those who are
not of the world." (1 Ne. 6:5.) The primary and
original aim of keeping those records which make up the
Book of Mormon was to preserve the *religious* tradition of the righteous few who down through the centuries have heeded God's word and been guided by
his prophets.

The history of God's dealings with men is a timeless one, a story of things "not of this world." It is interesting that the latest studies of Primitive Christianity,
especially since the coming out of the Dead Sea Scrolls,
see in John the Baptist and the Apostle John the chief
links between Christianity and Judaism; for Nephi proceeds to give a circumstantial account of the mission of

John the Baptist (1 Ne. 10:8 f.), while designating the other John by name as a fellow worker who shall write records that will substantiate his own, "sealed up to come forth in their purity." (1 Ne. 14:12-27.) He thinks of himself and his father as engaged in a single vast and timeless project along with all the other righteous prophets who ever lived. ". . . Ye need not suppose," he reminds us speaking for his own day, "that I and my father are the only ones that have testified . . . (1 Ne. 22:31.) ". . . the mysteries of God," says Nephi, "shall be unfolded . . . as well in these times as in times of old, and as well in times of old as in times to come; wherefore, the course of the Lord is one eternal round." (1 Ne. 10:19.)

Nephi Preserves the Religious Tradition: Lehi in fleeing from Jerusalem represents the righteous minority whose history is the main concern of the Book of Mormon. Hardly had the party landed in America when it was necessary for Nephi in turn to "depart . . . and flee into the wilderness." (2 Ne. 5:5.) With him he took a select group: ". . . And all those who would go with me were those who believed in the warnings and the revelations of God; wherefore they did hearken unto my words." (2 Ne. 5:6.) It was, that is, strictly a *religious body* that went forth, taking their tents and journeying "in the wilderness for the space of many days." (2 Ne. 5:7.) They settled down as a religious community, calling themselves the "people of Nephi." (2 Ne. 5:9.) Though they were only a minority group, viewed forever after as traitors and dissenters from the main body, it was they who preserved unbroken and intact all the religious ties with the Old World: it was they who had the records that were brought from Jerusalem (stolen, said the Lamanites!), and the ball and sword that were to become the traditional national treasures (2 Ne. 5:12-14); and as soon as they settled in the wilderness they built a temple "after the manner of the temple of Solomon" (2 Ne. 5:16), which many of them had seen with

their own eyes.   Most important is the all-embracing
rule of life they followed:

> And we did observe to keep the judgments, and the statutes,
> and the commandments of the Lord in all things according to
> the law of Moses. (2 Ne. 5:10.)

In all things they were simply following in the established line without any break from the past.   In teaching his people, Nephi tells us, he "did liken all scriptures
unto us, that it might be for our profit and learning."
(1 Ne. 19:23.)

Nephi's successor and brother, Jacob, explains very
clearly why his people kept the law of Moses while actually believing in Christ, the Anointed One to come:
". . . we knew of Christ . . . many hundred years before
his coming; and . . . also all the holy prophets which were
before us . . . and for this intent we keep the law of
Moses, it pointing out souls to him; . . ." (Jac. 4:4-5.)
A later prophet explains the law of Moses as "a law of
performances and of ordinances, a law which they were
to observe strictly from day to day, to keep them in remembrance of God and their duty towards him.   But
. . . all these things were types of things to come." (Mos.
13:30-31.)   Until the Lord himself should come, the
people were to be guided by Moses . . . and even all the
prophets who have prophesied ever since the world began . . ." (Mos. 13:33.)

Two Nations, Two Churches: The nation founded by
Nephi was strictly a religious society, the prophet himself remaining "their ruler and their teacher," though refusing to become their king, as they wanted him to. (2
Ne. 5:18-19.)   And a religious society it remained. Jacob and Joseph, having "been consecrated priests and
teachers of this people, by the hand of Nephi," (Jac. 1:
18) labored mightily to keep them on the path in the
face of growing disaffection and worldliness.   His
teaching was that if the nation was to survive it could
never forget its peculiar *religious* nature and calling:

Wherefore, thus saith the Lord, I have led this people forth out of the land of Jerusalem, by the power of mine arm, that I might raise up unto me a righteous branch from the fruit of the loins of Joseph. Wherefore, I the Lord God will not suffer that this people shall do like unto them of old. (Jac. 2:25-26.)

For him as for Nephi there are just two sides to the question. He groups all factions and complexions of people into two arbitrary categories. After naming seven different groups, he adds, "but I shall call them Lamanites that seek to destroy the people of Nephi, and those who are friendly to Nephi I shall call Nephites . . ." (Jac. 1:14.) In the same way, Nephi had explained: ". . . he that fighteth against Zion, *both Jew and Gentile* . . . are they who are the whore of all the earth." (2 Ne. 10:16.) By this reasoning there are *never* more than "save two churches only" in the world, and indeed Nephi's much-commented remark to that effect (1 Ne. 14:10) reads more like a statement of general principle than the denunciation of one particular church among many.

When Lehi bade farewell to his people, he spoke to them as a group who could only escape "captivity" by being united in the closest bonds of social unity: ". . . arise from the dust, my sons, and be men, and be determined in one mind and in one heart, united in all things, that ye may not come down into captivity." (2 Ne. 1:21.) Such intimate bonds of affection could only be implemented by a religious allegiance, and when Jacob tries to stem the tide of secularization he appeals passionately for the preservation of the old rules of equality on a religious basis:

Think of your brethren like unto yourselves, and be familiar with all and free with your substance, that they may be rich like unto you. But before ye seek for riches, seek ye for the kingdom of God . . . the one being is as precious in his sight as the other. And all flesh is of the dust; and for the selfsame end hath he created them, that they should keep his commandments and glorify him forever . . . (Jac. 2:17-21.)

But the world went its wicked way, and down through Book of Mormon history the righteous remain, as always, in the position of dissenting minorities. The fullest and most interesting description of such churches comes from the time and activities of the great Alma almost 500 years after Nephi.

Abinadi Preaches the Tradition: The story begins with the activities of the prophet Abinadi in the days of the wicked King Noah. (Mosiah 11:20.) When his preaching of repentance put his life in danger, Abinadi "came among them in disguise, that they knew him not, and began to prophesy among them, . . ." (Mos. 12:1.) The people protested: ". . . We teach the law of Moses. And again he said unto them: If ye teach the law of Moses why do ye not keep it? . . ." (Mos. 12:29.) It is still the same old issue of the Law of Moses as a type and a preparation for the Messiah and greater things to come *versus* the law of Moses as an end in itself and a full justification of the status quo. That was the argument with which the Book of Mormon began (1 Ne. 17:22), and it has never ceased to be the main issue between the two great traditions of Israel. *Reading* to them the voice of God in the first person, Abinadi explains exactly wherein the force and virtue of the Law of Moses— to which these people claim such loyal devotion—really reside, (Mos. 13:30), showing them that not only Moses looked forward to the coming of the Messiah, but "all the prophets who have prophesied ever since the world began—have they not spoken more or less concerning these things?" (Mos. 13:33.) It is significant that the bulk of Abinadi's teachings and prophecies was *read* by him to the people out of the books: "And now I read unto you the remainder of the commandments of God, for I perceive that they are not written in your hearts; I perceive that ye have studied and taught iniquity the most part of your lives." (Mos. 13:11.) This is a beautiful touch of prophetic irony, incidentally, in the best tradition of the great prophets, with its clever play on the words "read", "write", and "study".

Alma Founds a Church: When one of the priests

who attended on the king, a young man by the name of Alma, tried to persuade the king to spare the prophet's life he only succeeded in putting his own life in jeopardy and had to run away. (Mos. 17:2-3.) ". . . And he being concealed for many days did write all the words which Abinadi had spoken." (Mos. 17:4.) Thus Alma equipped himself with a full written account of the traditions as Abinadi had read it to his hearers at great length; it took him "many days" to do the job, and we can be sure that when he emerged from hiding he was steeped in the traditions not only of the priests (for he was one of them) but of the prophets as well. He was ready to organize his church: First he ". . . went about privately among the people, and began to teach the words of Abinadi." (Mos. 18:1.) Then . . .

. . . as many as did believe him did go forth to a place which was called Mormon . . . having been infested, by times or at seasons, by wild beasts. Now, there was in Mormon a fountain of pure water, and Alma resorted thither, there being near the water a thicket of small trees, where he did hide himself in the daytime from the searches of the king. (Mos. 18:4-5.)

The nature of the place is clear: it is in wild, open, desert country—not a jungle—an oasis where some small trees grew around a spring.

Alma baptized the people who came to him there (Mos.18:10), and when some 204 of them had congregated in the desert he organized them into a church, "and they were called the Church of God, or the Church of Christ, from that time forward.

And whosoever was baptized by the power and authority of God was added to his church. (Mos. 18:17.)

And . . . Alma having authority from God, ordained priests; even one priest to every fifty of their number did he ordain to preach unto them, and to teach them concerning the things pertaining to the kingdom of God. (Mos. 18:18.)

And he commanded them that they should teach nothing save it were spoken by the mouth of the holy prophets. (Mos. 18: 19.)

And he commanded them that there should be no contention one with another, but that they should look forward with one eye . . . having their hearts knit together in unity and in love one towards another. . . . And thus they became the children of God. (Mos. 18:21-22.)

A Picture of Alma's Church in the Wilderness: C o nsistent with the ancient practices which he was consciously following, Alma insisted on absolute equality, teaching "his people, that every man should love his neighbor as himself, that there should be no contention among them." (Mos. 23:15)   The priests worked for their living, ". . . the preacher was no better than the hearer, neither was the teacher any better than the learner; and thus they were all equal." (Alma 1:26.) "And they did impart of their substance, every man according to that which he had, . . . they were liberal to all, . . . whether out of the church or in the church." (Alma 1: 27, 30.)   For all their liberality and humanity, Alma's people thought of themselves as completely severed from the rest of the nation: ". . . come ye out from the wicked," he said to them, "and be ye separate, and touch not their unclean things; . . . the names of the wicked shall not be numbered among the names of the righteous. . . ." (Alma 5:57.) Just as his followers were not allowed to touch unclean things, so none from the outside and none unwilling to accept their own strict standards could mingle with them; ". . . that the word of God may be fulfilled, which saith: The names of the wicked shall not be mingled with the names of my people." (Alma 5:57.)

This was more than a spiritual segregation—it was a real organization: ". . . they did assemble themselves together in different bodies, being called churches; every church having their priests and their teachers, and every priest preaching the word according as it was delivered to him by the mouth of Alma." (Mos. 25:21.) There were seven such churches, "And they were called the people of God." (Mos. 25:24.)   Everything remained strictly under Alma's control, for he ". . . was

their high priest, he being the founder of their church"
(Mos. 23:16) who personally consecrated the priests
and teachers who ". . . did watch over their people, and
did nourish them with things pertaining to righteousness." (Mos. 23:17-18.) Moreover the people had
their own territory, which "they called the land of
Helam" (Mos. 23:19), and they built their own city,
"which they called the city of Helam." (Mos., 23:20)

Other "Churches of Anticipation": This revival of
the old ways continued down to the time of Christ. A
generation after Alma the Nephite nation broke up into
all sorts of independent groups—unholy as well as holy,
in which ". . . their leaders did establish their laws, every
one according to his tribe." (3 Ne. 7:11.) At such a
time, Nephi, another mighty religious leader, came forward and began calling the people back to the right way,
". . . that there were none who were brought unto repentance who were not baptized with water." (3 Ne.
7:24) For the people ". . . went forth and sought for
Nephi; . . . desiring that they might be baptized" (Hel.
16:1), while his work went forward, ". . . baptizing, and
prophesying, and preaching, crying repentance unto the
people, showing signs and wonders, working miracles
among the people, that they might know that the Christ
must shortly come. . . ." (Hel. 16:4.) But again it was
only the more righteous minority who were interested—
those who believed the words of the prophet Samuel—
the rest remaining as they were in town and country.
(Hel. 16:5-7.)

False Churches: Now when Christ finally came
and established his Church, it was very much like those
"churches of anticipation" we have been describing, (4
Ne. 1:1 ff), and indeed the multitude to which Jesus
appeared was a small one. (3 Ne. 19:2-3, 17:25.) And
after the Lord had departed in time came the usual cor-
rupters: "False Christs, . . . false prophets, and false
preachers and teachers among the people, . . . and many
dissensions away unto the Lamanites." (Words of

Mormon, 15-16.) King Benjamin and King Mosiah both tried to make the nation identical with the Church — God's people, and preached the same doctrine and practices as Alma and Nephi had, thus confirming the original and unchanging concept of the nation and church as God's elect, looking forward to the coming of the Messiah. The whole scheme of things as to doctrine, organization, and tradition is fully and carefully set forth in the Book of Mormon, always with the clear understanding that what is done is but a continuation of what was done of old — it is almost impossible to find any innovation in the Book of Mormon, or any religious institution or practice that did not rest its case on the ways of the ancients and the timeless and unchanging nature of God's dealings with his children.

Questions

1. In what specific ways do the Nephites display attachment and devotion to their past in the Old World?

2. Why is it important to realize that the Book of Mormon is primarily the history of a religious community?

3. What evidence is there that the Book of Mormon is primarily a religious history?

4. Into what two categories do Nephi and Jacob divide all society? What is significant in this division with regard to the identity of the "great and abominable church"?

5. Describe the rise and organization of Alma's Church.

6. Who authorized Alma to found a church?

7. How can there have been a plurality of churches among the righteous part of the Nephites if there is only one true church?

8. What is a "Church of Anticipation"?

Lesson 14

UNWELCOME VOICES FROM THE DUST

Prospectus of Lesson 14: The mystery of the nature and organization of the Primitive Church has recently been considerably illuminated by the discovery of the so-called Dead Sea Scrolls. There is increasing evidence that these documents were deliberately sealed up to come forth at a later time, thus providing a significant parallel to the Book of Mormon record. The Scrolls have caused considerable dismay and confusion among scholars, since they are full of things generally believed to be uniquely Christian, though they were undoubtedly written by pious Jews *before* the time of Christ. Some Jewish and Christian investigators have condemned the Scrolls as forgeries and suggest leaving them alone on the grounds that they don't make sense. Actually they make very good sense, but it is a sense quite contrary to conventional ideas of Judaism and Christianity. The Scrolls echo teachings in many apocryphal writings, both of the Jews and the Christians, while at the same time showing undeniable affinities with the Old and the New Testament teachings. The very things which made the Scrolls at first so baffling and hard to accept to many scholars are the very things which in the past have been used to discredit the Book of Mormon. Now the Book of Mormon may be read in a wholly new light, which is considered here in lessons 14, 15, 16, and 17.

The Mystery of the Primitive Church: One of the great mysteries of history has been the nature and organization of the Primitive or original Christian Church, that is, the tangible Church founded by Christ. Was there a church organization at all? If so what became of it? Did they really expect the end of the world? Were they for the law of Moses or against it? It is hard for us to realize how completely in the dark the scholars have always been on these vitally important matters, how varied and contradictory their theories, how weak and speculative all their evidence.[1] Only with the discovery of vitally important documents, beginning with the Didache in 1875, did the dense impenetrable fog that already baffled the great Eusebius in his researches into the Primitive Church, begin to lift.[2] We cannot discuss here the many sensational discoveries that have forced the learned, with the great-

est reluctance, to acknowledge that the strange and unfamiliar form that is becoming clearer every day through
the rising mists is the solid reality of a forgotten Church
that once truly existed. But we cannot avoid touching
upon the most sensational find of modern times—that of
the Dead Sea Scrolls. For the Scrolls put us constantly
in mind of the Book of Mormon and, we believe, confirm
it on many points.

Certitude and the Dead Sea Scrolls: At   present   the
Scrolls are floating in a sea of controversy, but there are
certain things about them which have either never been
disputed or have now become the object of universal
consensus. It is to such non-controversial things that we
shall confine our study for obvious reasons. It is universally agreed today, for instance, that Dead Sea Scrolls
were produced by a community of Jews living in the
desert of Judaea a long time ago, a community of whose
existence no one was aware before the present decade.[3]
Even the terrible Professor Zeitlin, though he claims that
the sect was not nearly as ancient as the other experts
believe it was, and insists that the writer or writers of the
Scrolls were disgustingly ignorant and wrote only non-
sense, would agree to that much. And that is all the
information we need to make a very significant comparison between what we find written in the Scrolls and what
we find written in the Book of Mormon. Furthermore,
the finding of writings in not one or two but in more than
thirty caves, (and that by men whose competence ranges
from that of illiterate Bedouin boys to that of the very top
men in Hebrew and Christian studies), does away with
the argument once vehemently put forward that the
Scrolls were a plant or were never found in the caves at
all. The excavation of extensive ruins lying in the immediate vicinity of the most important caves has brought
forth a wealth of artifacts (notably certain jars of peculiar shape) resembling those found in the caves and
nowhere else, along with more than 400 coins which
make it possible to determine the date of activities in the
desert with great accuracy. "Excavation of the settle-

ment at Kh. Qumran has established beyond a doubt that all the material was deposited in these caves late in the first century A.D."[4] That, of course, is only the terminal date; the life of the Qumran community belongs to the preceding centuries.[5]

"Sealed up to come forth in their purity"?: Even before one knows what is in the Dead Sea Scrolls, the story of their coming forth, "a marvelous account," as Dupont-Sommer rightly calls it, immediately puts the Latter-day Saint in mind of the Book of Mormon.[6] In 1953 the author of these lessons wrote of the Scrolls:

The texts that have turned up with such dramatic suddenness in the last few years, as if a signal had been given, are the first ancient documents which have survived not by accident but by design.

We then quoted a passage from the apocryphal Assumption of Moses, "in which Moses before being taken up to heaven is instructed by the Lord to 'seal up' the covenant:

Receive this writing that thou mayest know how to preserve the books which I shall deliver unto thee: and thou shalt set in order and anoint them with oil of cedar and put them away in earthen vessels in the place which he made from the beginning of the creation of the world.[7]

The purpose of this hiding, we are told, is to preserve the books through a ". . . period of darkness when men shall have fallen away from the true covenant and would pervert the truth." We then pointed out that the Dead Sea Scrolls had been preserved in just such a manner as that prescribed to Moses:

In specially-made earthen jars, wrapped in linen which was 'coated with wax or pitch or asphalt which proves that the scrolls were hidden in the cave for safe preservation, to be recovered and used later again.' By whom? The peculiar method of storage also indicates very plainly that the documents were meant for a *long* seclusion, for to lay a roll away with the scrupulous care and after the very manner of entombing an Egyptian mummy certainly indicates a long and solemn farewell and no mere temporary storage of convenience.[8]

Since these words were written, it has been pointed out in high places that "... those who hid their precious scrolls did not return to claim them",[9] ... and that while "... in the case of our scrolls and wrappers, they may, as suggested, have been concealed in the cave in a time of national panic it is important to remember that burial in caves was the custom of the country, and so this conceal-ment may only be the equivalent of the correct cemetery burial of the contents of a *Genizah.*"[10] That is, it is now suggested that the scrolls were not hidden away tempo-rarily during a time of crisis and danger, as has been generally held, but were actually given a formal burial in the manner of books laid away in a Genizah. A Geni-zah was a walled-off bin in an ancient synagogue in which old worn-out copies of scripture were placed to be gotten out of the way and forgotten forever. They could not be destroyed since they contained the sacred Tetra-grammon, the mysterious name of God, yet the old tat-tered texts were no longer usable—and so they were pushed behind the wall and forgotten. But the Dead Sea Scrolls were not thus thrust aside. The whole emphasis in the manner of their bestowal was for preservation— preservation over a very long time, and since the Ascen-sion of Moses is actually one of the fragments found in the caves, it is certain that these people knew all about the tradition according to which the righteous men of one dispensation would hide up their records, "... sealed up to come forth in their purity, according to the truth which is in the Lamb, in the own due time of the Lord, unto the house of Israel." (1 Ne. 14:26) From this and many other considerations it is apparent that the people who left us the Dead Sea Scrolls had something of the Book of Mormon idea concerning books and rec-ords.

Israel and the Church: Were they one?: Another im-portant disclosure of the Dead Sea Scrolls to the world, and one of which all scholars are now aware, was the dis-covery of large areas of Jewish and Christian doctrine and practice of which the scholars had been totally ignorant, and these areas, far from being mere bits of obscure detail, lie at the very heart of Judaism and Christianity in their older and purer forms. The discovery of the scrolls has proven very upsetting to the experts. The Jewish scholars who twitted the Christians for being alarmed by the discovery that the religion of Christ was not a novel and original thing suddenly introduced into the world for the first time with the birth of Jesus, were in turn thrown into an even greater turmoil by the discovery that doctrines which they had always attributed to Christian cranks and innovators were really very old and very Jewish. Israel and Christianity, heretofore kept in separate and distinct compartments by the professors of both religions (except for purely symbolic and allegorical parallels) are seen in the Scrolls to have been anciently confounded and identified. Suddenly a window is opened on the past and we behold Israel full of what is Christian and the early Church full of Israel! With this discovery, as we have pointed out elsewhere, "the one effective argument against the Book of Mormon, (i. e. that it introduces New Testament ideas and terminology into a pre-Christian setting) collapses.[11]

On the one hand, the Jewish nature of the scrolls could not be denied. It is only fair and right that the Hebrew University should in the end have been willing to pay the high price for the possession of these old texts that no one else was willing to pay, and that the study of the scrolls, originally left largely to the Christians, is now rapidly becoming a Jewish monopoly.[12] On the other hand, none could fail to see that the scrolls talk a language very like that of the *New* Testament. The manner in which the scrolls treat the scriptures, for example, "has no parallel either in Hellenistic or Pharisaic Judaism, in allegory, philosophizing exegesis or in legalistic interpretation. But it precisely follows the pattern of the New Testament exegesis of the Law and the Prophets."[13] Professor Harding notes that "many authorities consider that Christ himself studied with them (the "Scrolls" people)" and he is personally quite convinced that John the Baptist did.[14]

Alarm of the Christian World: Since the first publication of the Dead Sea Scrolls, devout scholars have been busy reassuring their co-religionists that "no Christian need stand in dread of these texts,"[15] while admitting, for example, that ". . . the Isaiah scroll was received with consternation in some circles,"[16] . . . and that ". . . the results were shocking," . . . when they started to study the new-found text of Samuel.[17]   Nevertheless, the defensive tone of such reassurances, with their frequent references to alarm and misgiving, shows plainly enough that the "startling disclosure: that the sect possessed, years before Christ, a terminology and practice that have always been considered uniquely Christian,"[18] has administered a severe shock to the complacency of conventional Christianity.   "It is as though God had added to his 'once for all' revelation," writes a devout Presbyterian scholar,[19] while the readers of the *Catholic World* are assured that "It is only to be expected that there will be certain likenesses between the community at Qumran and the Church of the New Law, both of them 'seeking' the true God and striving to be perfect, each in his own way. The revelation of the New Testament was not, so to speak, built up on a vacuum."[20]

If that is "only to be expected" why has the Book of Mormon been so savagely attacked by ministers on the very grounds of likeness between the Book of Mormon pre-Christian churches and the Christians?[21]   If it was "only to be expected" why did it prove so startling and upsetting?   Because of the scrolls, writes F. M. Cross, ". . . the strange world of the New Testament becomes less baffling, less exotic."[22]   The charge of being "baffling", "strange", and "exotic" is that most constantly hurled at the Book of Mormon description of the religious world of the ancient Americans.   Have the scholars any reason to believe it was any less so than the relatively familiar "world of the New Testament"?

Neither Christian nor Jewish—yet Both! The Jewish scholar Teicher avoids the embarrassment of having to accept an early Judaism shot through with Christian ideas by denying that the scrolls are Jewish at all. He points out that the teachings of the scrolls exactly correspond to those of the Primitive Christian Church, especially with regard to the Messiah:

> The judge of mankind in the Last Day is thus, according to the Habbakuk Scroll, the Elect, the Christian Messiah, that is, Jesus. Is then Jesus referred to explicitly in the Scroll? He is; under the appelation of *Moreh ha-sedeq*, which should be correctly translated the 'True Teacher'—the title applied to Jesus both in Mark and among the Jewish-Christian sect of the Ebionites.[23]

His conclusion from this is that the Scrolls *must* be a Christian production, yet his Jewish colleagues do not agree with him. The scrolls are typically Christian and yet they are Jewish, typically Jewish and yet Christian! Moreover they are typically Biblical in style and composition, and yet not Biblical. "The hymns in the collection are reminiscent of the latest Biblical psalms, and more especially the psalms in the prologue of Luke. They draw heavily on the Psalter and Prophetic poetry for inspiration, and borrow direct phrases, cliches, and style. However, neither in language, spirit nor theology are they Biblical."[24] How can such a thing be possible? The Book of Mormon holds the answer, or, the other way around, however you may hate to accept the thesis of the Book of Mormon, the "marvelous finds" of Qumran certainly confirm its position. The Book of Mormon is Christian yet Jewish, it is Biblical yet not Biblical.

Can the Scrolls Be Read?: In studying the Dead Sea Scrolls there is first of all the little problem of translation. Recently Dr. Zeitlin has stated flatly that the scrolls cannot be translated:

> Even the best scholar of the Hebrew medieval period could not do justice in translating these scrolls because most of them are untranslatable. It is indeed folly to attempt to translate these scrolls into any modern language. It would be a waste of time.

Then he quite undermines his own position with the following dictum: "In rendering an ancient text into a modern language the translator must not add words to or subtract words from the text."[25] That is a meaningless statement if there ever was one, for "so completely does any one-to-one relationship vanish between the vocabularies of languages that reflect widely different cultures that it may be necessary to translate one line of a text by a whole page or a page by a single line!"[26] If one insists, with Dr. Zeitlin, on a literal word-for-word translation, one might as well insist on a letter-for-letter translation. The only alternative is Willamowitz' definition of a translation as "A statement in the translator's own words of what he thinks the author had in mind." There is no such thing as a text that can be read but not translated; whoever can read a foreign language so that it means something to him, can certainly express that meaning in his own words—and such an expression is no more nor less than a translation. If one cannot express it in one's own words, one has not understood it. Zeitlin is wrong on both points. Any text that can be read can be translated, but no text can ever be translated literally.

But how can we know if we are understanding a text correctly? Zeitlin admits loudly and often that the scrolls make no sense to him, they are not in his language; yet he heaps scorn on "all the scholars who deal with the scrolls with the aid of a dictionary."[27] Since nobody alive speaks the language of the scrolls it is hard to see how anyone can get very far without a dictionary. The same is true of any ancient language—yet ancient languages are read! The first rule of exegesis is, that if a text means something it means something! That is to say, if a writing conveys a consistent message to a reader there is a good chance that that text is being at least partly understood correctly. The longer the text is that continues thus to give forth consistent and connected meaning, the greater the probability that it is being read rightly; and the greater the number of people who derive the same meaning from a text independently, the greater the prob-

ability that that meaning is the right one. It should never
be forgotten, however, that the interpretation of an ancient text never rises above the level of a high plausability
—there is no final certainty.   The history of scholarship
is the story of one man who dares to rebuke and correct
all the other scholars in the world on a point in which they
have been in perfect agreement for hundreds of years—
and proves them wrong! That is one reason why an inspired translation of the Book of Mormon is infinitely to
be preferred to the original text, for if we had the original
all the scholars could very easily be wrong in their reading
of any passages.   None the less, in the long run the statistical argument is the one we must appeal to in cases of
doubt.

From first to last the scrolls have told a single consistent story; their message has been picked up independently by scores of scholars, and the fact that they have
recognized a single message, even though they have found
it strange and disconcerting, is ample proof that a real
message has been conveyed.   This is the message we
convey here.   Every one of our "dictionary translations"
that follow can be substantiated by the independent verdict of far better scholars than we are, and in cases where
our interpretation may seem extreme or forced we have
called upon such men for confirmation.   If the scrolls
were only a few scattered fragments of half a dozen lines
or so one would always be in doubt, but we have to do
here with a good-sized book whose contents are ample
and varied enough to make the test of internal evidence
alone quite decisive.

Connections Everywhere: From the first, scholars recognized that the scrolls talked the familiar language of
certain canonical and apocryphal writings.   It was not
difficult to detect in the first fragments discovered close
affinities to the Gospels (especially John), and Epistles.[28]
and also to such important apocryphal writings as the
Testament of the Twelve Patriarchs, the Book of Enoch,
Sibylline writings (Jewish and Christian), the Apocalypse of Baruch, the Assumption of Moses, the Psalms

of Solomon, the Lives of Adam and Eve, the Apocalypse of Abraham, and others.[29] Moreover the scrolls used the peculiar language and expressed the peculiar ideas found in the earliest Christian writings after the Apostles, especially in the Pseudo-Clementine writings to which we have so often referred in other places as the key to the thinking of the Early Christian Church.[30] As if that were not enough, the scrolls "may be said, with some exaggeration, to have been written in code", and to employ the devices of cryptography of secret Jewish sects.[31] "The intertestamental works soon reveal their identity by key words and characteristic phraseology," writes Cross, noting that the scrolls teach us for the first time "the theological vocabulary of contemporary Judaism in both its Hebrew and Aramaic branches".[32]

The Emerging Pattern: That we have in the scrolls and the New Testament a single tradition is admitted, however reluctantly, by all scholars today. That they are also in direct line of descent from the Old Testament prophets as the traditional teachings of certain Jewish sectaries has also been pointed out. Furthermore, aside from being found in the same sacred library with a great many works of the Jewish Apocrypha, they contain many surprising ties with the later Christian apocryphal writings. Moreover these connections are by no means haphazard. There is a definite tendency behind them. What indicates a revision of conventional ideas about early Christianity, for example, is not the discovery of new doctrines and ideas (Zeitlin makes great to-do about the complete *un*originality of the scrolls), but the emergence of a pattern of emphasis and orientation which had not been heretofore attributed to Christians; it is the emphasis and orientation found in the Book of Mormon and discussed in our last lesson. In the Dead Sea Scrolls we have a fairly large body of *datable* documents that seem to be a common meeting ground for Jewish and Christian ideas expressed both in the canons of the Old and New Testament and in the Jewish and Christian Apocrypha.

At last enough of the hitherto hidden background of the Old and New Testament is beginning to emerge to enable students before long to examine the Book of Mormon against that larger background of which it speaks so often and by which alone it can be fairly tested.

Questions

1. What are the Dead Sea Scrolls?

2. What is peculiar about the nature of their preservation?

3. What is significant for Book of Mormon study in the discovery of pre-Christian texts that speak the language of the New Testament?

4. Why has the message of the scrolls been an unwelcome one to certain Christians?

5. Why to the Jews?

6. How can scholars prove their claim to be able to read ancient records?

7. With what other ancient documents do the scrolls display affinity?

8. What possible connection can exist between the Qumran people and those who produced other writings resembling the scrolls?

9. How do objections to the authenticity of the scrolls resemble those brought forward against the Book of Mormon?

10. Are the Dead Sea Scrolls scripture?

Lesson 15

QUMRAN AND THE WATERS OF MORMON

Prospectus of Lesson 15: Alma's church in the wilderness was a typical "church of anticipation". In many things it presents striking parallels to the "church of anticipation" described in the Dead Sea Scrolls. Both had gone forth into the wilderness in order to live the Law in its fullness, being dissatisfied with the official religion of the time, which both regarded as being little better than apostasy. Both were persecuted by the authorities of the state and the official religion. Both were strictly organized along the same lines and engaged in the same type of religious activities. In both the Old World and the New these churches in the wilderness were but isolated expressions of a common tradition of great antiquity. In the Book of Mormon Alma's church is clearly traced back to this ancient tradition and practice, yet until the recent discovery of the Dead Sea Scrolls no one was aware of its existence. We can now read the Book of Mormon in a totally new context, and in that new context much that has hitherto been strange and perplexing becomes perfectly clear.

The Church of Anticipation in the Book of Mormon: Let us go back to Alma's community at the oasis of Mormon. We have seen that it was organized after an accepted pattern as a "church of anticipation". Lehi himself had belonged to that great tradition of faithful Israelites who ran afoul of the official party at Jerusalem ("teachers and rulers," Justin Martyr called them) and because of their "priestcrafts and iniquities" (2 Ne. 10:5) had to flee to the desert. "Our father Lehi was driven out of Jerusalem because he testified of these things. Nephi also testified of these things, and also almost all of our fathers, even down to this time; yea, they have testified of the coming of Christ, and have looked forward, and have rejoiced in his day which is to come." (Hel. 8:22.)

All the Book of Mormon churches before Christ were "churches of anticipation". ". . . they shall not be ashamed that wait for me," was their slogan from the beginning (2 Ne. 6:7), ". . . For the people of the Lord are they who wait for him; for they still wait for the coming of the Messiah." (2 Ne. 6:13.) ". . . Notwithstand-

ing we believe in Christ," Nephi explains, "we keep the
law of Moses, and look forward with steadfastness unto
Christ, until the law shall be fulfilled." (2 Ne. 25:24.)
In this hope the people were fully justified: ". . . we also
had many revelations, and the spirit of much prophecy;
wherefore, we knew of Christ and his kingdom, which
should come. . ." (Jac. 1:6 cf. 4:6.) "For for this intent
have we written these things," says Jacob, "that they may
know that we knew of Christ, and we had a hope of his
glory many hundred years before his coming; and not
only we ourselves had a hope of his glory, but also all
the holy prophets which were before us. . . And for this
intent we keep the law of Moses, it pointing our souls to
him; . . ." (Jac. 4:4-5.)

Centuries later the great prophet, Abinadi, who converted Alma, gave a wonderful sermon on this doctrine,
which the people had well-nigh forgotten. It comprises
the whole fifteenth chapter of Mosiah, in which he says
". . . that whosoever has heard the words of the prophets,
. . . and believed that the Lord would redeem his people,
and have looked forward to that day for a remission of
their sins, I say unto you, that these are his seed, or they
are the heirs of the kingdom of God." (Mos. 15:11.)
". . . notwithstanding the law of Moses," Alma reports
of the Nephites of his own day, "they did look forward
to the coming of Christ, considering that the law of Moses
was a type of his coming, and believing that they must
keep those outward performances until the time he should
be revealed unto them. Now they did not suppose that
salvation came by the law of Moses; but the law of Moses
did serve to strengthen their faith in Christ." (Alma 25:
15-16.) ". . . begin to believe in the Son of God, that he
will come," this Alma implores his people, ". . . that he
shall suffer and die . . . that he shall rise again from the
dead, which shall bring to pass the resurrection, that all
men shall stand before him, . . ." (Alma 33:22.) Many
followed his advice and ". . . took upon them, gladly, the
name of Christ, or Christians as they were called, because
of their belief in Christ who should come . . ." (Alma

46:15—remember that this is a translation! What the
old Nephite word for "Christians" was we cannot even
guess.)[1]

Alma's Community in the Desert: We have seen that
Alma went forth and founded a community in the desert
and in time established and presided over seven churches.
What concerns us here is the early desert community
which set the pattern of strictness followed by the others.
One aspect of life by the waters of Mormon was the
strict observance of the old Jewish Sabbath (Mos. 18:
23), combined with observances on another day of the
week as well: ". . . there was one day in every week that
was set apart that they should gather themselves together to teach the people, and to worship the Lord their God,
and also, as often as it was in their power, to assemble
themselves together." (Mos. 18:25.)[2]

On one of these days of assembly the king's agents,
who had been on the lookout for this sort of thing, ". . . the
king, having discovered a movement among the people,"
reported to Noah, who "sent his army to destroy them."
(Mos. 18:32-33.)

> And it came to pass that Alma and the people of the Lord
> were apprised of the coming of the king's army; therefore they
> took their tents and their families and departed into the wilder-
> ness. And they were in number about four hundred and fifty souls.
> (Mos. 18:34-35.)

Many sympathizers were left behind among the
people, and when things got worse at home ". . . they
would have gladly joined with them," (Mos. 21:31) but
it was too late, and for the present there was nothing to
do but wait:

> Therefore they did not at that time form themselves into
> a church, waiting upon the Spirit of the Lord. Now they were
> desirous to become even as Alma and his brethren, who had fled
> into the wilderness. (Mos. 21:34.)

Alma's people in their flight took grain with them
(Mos. 23:1), and after ". . . eight days journey into the
wilderness . . . they pitched their tents, and began to till

the ground, and began to build buildings; . . ." (Mos. 23:3-5), establishing a new community, the order of which is described in the 23rd chapter of Mosiah. This community ran into trouble with a rival settlement led by Amulon and some priests of king Noah, and so they decamped again and after traveling twelve days in the wilderness arrived at the city of Zarahemla. (Mos. 25.) There the king, Mosiah, called a great public assembly at which the king ". . . read, and caused to be read, . . . the account of Alma and his brethren, and all their afflictions, . . ." (Mos. 25:4-6.)[3]

From first to last these people are conscientious record-keepers, passionately devoted to reading and writing. Armed with voluminous writings of the traditions of the prophets penned by himself, Alma had gone forth and founded his community by the waters of Mormon, and from their long wanderings the society returns with full and careful records of all that has happened.

The Qumran Community: Now let us turn to the Qumran community—the people who wrote and hid up the Dead Sea Scrolls. The one thing that emerges most clearly from all the Dead Sea documents is the picture of a pious community of Israelites who had gone out into the desert in order to live the law of Moses in its perfection. This society can best be described by quotations from their "Manual of Discipline" or *Serek* Scroll, which we here indicate by column (Roman numerals) and line (Arabic numerals). As to the purpose of the group:

V, 7-8: Everyone who comes to the united order shall enter into the covenant of God before the eyes of all those who have dedicated themselves, and he shall place himself under solemn obligation by a strong oath to turn (or return) to the Law of Moses even to all he commanded, with all his heart and all his soul insofar as it has been revealed to the Sons of Zadok, the priests who keep the covenant.[4]

VIII, 15: Teaching the Law (and all that) he commanded (or established) by the hand of Moses, to carry out all that has been revealed from time to time even as the holy prophets have explained (or revealed) it by the Holy Ghost (or Spirit of his Holiness).

These people deliberately separated themselves from "the Jews at Jerusalem" because they were convinced that the nation as a whole under the guidance of ambitious priests and kings had fallen into a state of apostasy.[5] All new candidates had to attend a meeting at which

I, 22 f: the Levites must read of the iniquities of the Children of Israel, and all their transgressions and sins in the rule of Belial. Those entering the Covenant will confess after them saying: We have gone astray . . . we have done evil even we. . . . His judgment is come upon us and our fathers.

V, 5 f: They have come to "lay foundation of truth for Israel," the people having become "uncircumcised of heart and stiff-necked."

They knew the meaning of persecution, considered themselves as living "under the rule of Belial, and required an oath of their members

I, 17-18: not to return from following (God) out of any fear whether of intimidation or testing by fire in the kingdom of Belial.

The society was very well organized:

I, 11 f: "And all who embrace the truth must bring with them all their mind, might, and possessions to the church of God. To purify their *minds* in truth of the statutes of God, and their *physical strength* (or might) as a test of fine gold of his ways, and all their *property* as following a righteous counsel.[6]

II, 24 f: "No one shall stumble from his appointed position nor be thrown from his appointed place, for everyone shall be active (valid, good) in the church (or unity).

VIII, 1 f: "In the council of the church twelve men, and three priests, perfect in all that has been revealed touching all the Law, to execute truth and righteousness and judgment in love, mercy and humility, for every man with his neighbor. To keep faith in the earth, to build up the established order, and a broken spirit, and to atone for the evil by doing judgment and putting to the test, with (due) observance of time."[7]

They covenant to love one another (I, 7-8) and,

I, 19: when they enter the covenant the priests and Levites will declare blessed the God of Salvation and all who observe (do) his truth, and all those entering the covenant shall say after them: 'Amen! Amen!'

VI, 8: This is the arrangement (*serek*) for the seating of the (general) assembly, each man according to his position: the priests shall sit first in order, the elders second, and the rest of all the people (and all the remaining people) shall sit each man in his place.

XI, 19: (At the initiation,) "the priests come first in order one by one, and then the Levites, and after them all the people . . .

21: "And they shall pass by three according to order (rank), one after the other, for thousands, and hundreds and fifties and tens, according to knowledge (or so that every man of Israel may know), every man of Israel as man of the house of his standing in the church of God. . .

Rules of initiation and examination were strict. Most remarkable is the mention of baptism:

III, 4 f: (Of one who enters the covenant with any reservations) : "he shall not be purified among the redeemed nor cleansed in the water of purification (or grace), and he shall not sanctify himself in the waters and the rivers, and he shall not be purified in all the waters of washing. . .

III, 6 f: "His sin is forgiven him and in the humility of his soul he is for all the Laws of God; his flesh is cleansed shining bright in the waters of purification, even in the waters of baptism (*dukh*); and he shall be given a new name in due time to walk perfect in all the ways of God.[8]

The Qumran "Church of Anticipation": All this and much else is so very Christian that the Qumran community has been called a "Church of Anticipation".[9] Everything looks to the future:

VIII, 4 f: When these things shall come to pass in Israel, and the designated organization truly established, planting the seed for eternity—a holy Temple for Aaron, true witnesses to testify and those of proven hearts; to make atonement for the earth (or land) and assure the wicked their just desserts. This is the tested wall, the precious cornerstone whose foundations will not tremble nor be removed from their place . . . a true and perfect temple in Israel, to establish a covenant for eternal ordinances (or statutes).

VIII, 12: ". . . and when these things shall come to pass in Israel by these dispositions, they shall be removed from the midst of the seats of the wicked to go into the desert and prepare there the way of the Lord, as it is written: 'In the desert prepare a highway for the Lord make straight in the wilderness a road

for our God. . . .' This preparation is the study of the Law, as
he established it by the hand of Moses. . ."

IX, 3: "And when these things come to pass in Israel,
according to all these patterns for establishing the Holy Spirit,
for the eternal truth, for the atonement of sins and transgressions
. . . at that time the men of the community will be set apart as a holy
house (temple) for Aaron, being united as a holy of holies and
a common temple for Israel, the pure in heart."

V, 5-6: "To circumcise in the Church the uncircumcised
of heart, even the stiffnecked, so as to lay a foundation of truth
for Israel, for a church and an eternal covenant, for the salvation
(atonement) of all who are willing to accept it, for the sanctifi-
cation of Aaron and a True Temple in Israel."

This "church of anticipation" considered itself only
a temporary organization, living the old Law as fully as
possible and marking time until the coming of a new dispensation:

IX, 11: All these regulations are for Aaron and Israel
"until there shall come a prophet and anointed ones (messiahs)
of Aaron and Israel."

These people believed that God took the fullness of
the Gospel from among men because of sin (V, 10).
Those to whom this knowledge was imparted were not
to divulge it to the general public:

IX, 16 f: There must be no discussion or argument about
these things with "the men of the pit, so that the counsel of the
Law may be kept secret in the midst of men of iniquity . . ."

V, 2 f: They must keep themselves far from all evil and
designing men, but cling to unity in the Law and property . . ."

Other Churches in the Desert: These few passages
will serve to give some insight into the general nature of
the Qumran organization. Just as resemblances of expression and doctrine can be found in the writings of
many other societies, Jewish and Christian, so the scholars
have easily perceived resemblances in the nature and
function of the society itself with those of other ancient
communities. There has been a good deal of argument
as to which group the Qumran people most closely resemble, and for a while it was widely believed that they
were actually the Essenes or a branch of them. Not

enough is known about the Essenes (or what is known is so contradictory as to cancel out a good deal of it) to justify the position, but after all the problem of nomen-culture is not the important thing. The nature of the so-ciety itself is what counts.

Molin's Summary: The fullest study of the commun-ity of Qumran yet to appear is that of the Austrian Georg Molin. The main points of his study represent the com-mon reaction of scholars to the scrolls and few would dispute them. For economy of space we give them here.[10]

1. The Qumran people formed a *church* in the plain and orig-inal sense of the word, "a society of people specially chosen and set apart . . . an ekklesia, a host of elect spirits called for a special mission upon this earth." (p. 138.)

2. "As a chosen group it is however at the same time the ideal or perfect Israel." This goes back to the time of such proph-ets as Hosea, Jeremiah, and Ezekiel, to whom, in spite of all its hardships, Israel's best time—its ideal time—was the years spent in the desert, when they were nearer to God than in later periods. "The paganizing of law and religion led already about 800 B.C. to the founding of the Rekhabite society, whose members . . . wanted to continue the simple way of life of the desert." (p. 140.)

3. "Their minds made up, this holy army separated them-selves from the people of God who had betrayed God, from their priests and kings, who had been foremost in iniquity . . . They saw themselves surrounded by signs of impending calamity on all sides. They had read their prophets well (especially Isaiah, Ezekiel, Haggai, Zechariah, and Malachi)." (p. 146.)

4. They fulfilled the conditions of the Old Covenant as perfectly as they could be carried out, and though that was a great deal, it left them unsatisfied, cramped by limitations beyond which they could not go (p. 186). Doctrine interested them far more than cult and ordinance and they were looking and waiting for light, filled with the feeling that "the time was growing near and every day could be the last." (p. 186.) "Apocalyptic thoughts are constantly and everywhere in evidence (in the scrolls), and taken completely for granted. One has the impression that their readers or hearers already possessed a very respectable knowledge of apocalyptic teachings." (p. 15.)

5. These people were no starry-eyed fanatics: "They viewed their present condition with a complete lack of any illu-sions, even with some pessimism, but with no lack of courage. A new age is coming . . . in which the plan which was laid down for

the world from the beginning will go into fulfillment. It even
seems that the world is to be completely changed, so that its physical structure as well as its basic plan is to be altered." (p. 124.)

6. "Thus the whole way of life of the sect appears constantly
in the light of the Last Days. 'LATTER-DAY SAINTS' a
certain 'Christian' sect of a later time called themselves. One
can correctly attribute the title to the sect we are dealing with
here. They knew no other way than the Jewish way, but they
pursued that way with a holy devotion that puts us to shame."
(p. 146.)

The last remark quoted from Molin is indeed a significant concession—the more so since it is a very grudg-
ing one. The Mormons have been guilty of stealing this
ancient sectarian thunder—a hundred years before anybody knew about it! But as a matter of fact all this *was*
clearly set forth before the restored church was organized—in the Book of Mormon.

The Resemblance Is Not Accidental: The astonishing
parallels between the churches of the Book of Mormon
and that of the Qumran community—the reader may
search out any number of them—are more than mere coincidence. Molin has observed that people were behaving in the manner of the Qumran Jews as early as 800
B.C., and there is evidence that such a group was living
at Qumran itself as early as the 7th century B.C., that is,
before and during the time of Lehi.[11] There is no question of any of these groups being the *true* church—what
we are interested in here is simply to point out that there
were just such churches before the time of Christ. We
were at pains to show that the Book of Mormon churches
of anticipation got their whole tradition and practice from
the Old World in unbroken succession, Lehi himself being one of those who were driven out into the wilderness
because he insisted on preaching about the coming of the
Messiah and denouncing the Jews for false ideas regarding the law of Moses. And so the Scrolls from the Dead
Sea are teaching us, as they are teaching the Christian
world, how little we really know about the Bible—and
especially about the Book of Mormon!

Questions

1. Why was Lehi driven out of Jerusalem?

2. What evidence for "churches of anticipation" is there among the Nephites?

3. Was Alma aware of the Old World tradition of churches in the wilderness when he went forth to found his church? What evidence for that?

4. How does Alma's community resemble the Qumran sect in purpose and spirit?

5. How does it resemble the Qumran community in organization and function? In the keeping of records?

6. What is the significance for the Book of Mormon of the fact that evidence for sects of the Qumran variety in the desert goes back to the time of Lehi and earlier?

7. What evidence is there that Alma's church was not the only community of its kind in the Book of Mormon? What is the significance of that? Was it the first of its kind?

8. Is it possible that the Qumran church was really led by revelation? Was Alma's church?

9. What are the implications of Molin's suggestion that the best name for the Qumran church would be Latter-day Saints? Did they really live in the last days?

10. List the arguments for and against the proposition that the remarkable resemblance between Alma's church and the Qumran community is purely accidental.

Lesson 16

THE APOCRYPHA AND THE BOOK OF MORMON

Prospectus of Lesson 16: In the light of the Dead Sea Scrolls, all
the Apocryphal writings must be read again with a new respect.
Today the correctness of the 91st Section of the Doctrine and
Covenants as an evaluation of the Apocrypha is vindicated with
the acceptance of an identical view by scholars of every persuasion, though a hundred years ago the proposition set forth
in the Doctrine and Covenants seemed preposterous. What all the
apocryphal writings have in common with each other and with the
scriptures is the Apocalyptic or eschatological theme. This theme
is nowhere more fully and clearly set forth than in the Book of
Mormon. Fundamental to this theme is the belief in a single
prophetic tradition handed down from the beginning of the world
in a series of dispensations, but hidden from the world in general
and often confined to certain holy writings. Central to the doctrine is the Divine Plan behind the creation of the world which
is expressed in all history and revealed to holy prophets from
time to time. History unfolds in repeating cycles in order to
provide all men with a fair and equal test in the time of their
probation. Every dispensation, or "Visitation", it was taught, is
followed by an apostasy and a widespread destruction of the
wicked, and ultimately by a refreshing or a new visitation.

What are the Apocrypha?: The discovery of the Dead
Sea Scrolls has directed the attention of the learned as
never before to the study of that vast and neglected field
of literature known as the Apocrypha. The significance
of these writings for Book of Mormon study will become
apparent as soon as we consider what they are and what
they say.

First, as to what the Apocrypha are. An apocryphal writing is one that had been accepted as inspired
scripture by *any* Christian or Jewish group at *any* time.
When such texts are brought together and examined,
they are found almost without exception to reveal all the
characteristics of real scripture.[1] The manuscripts that
contain them are just as old as and sometimes older than
many of those of the canonical books i.e., the books of
the Bible; they are found in the same places and condi-

tions; they were anciently put to the same uses; they talk about the same things in the same terms and make the same claim to divine origin. It is clear, for example, that Qumran community considered the Book of Jubilees, the Testament of the XII Patriarchs, the Apocalypse of Baruch, the Assumption of Moses, the Psalms of Solomon, and many other writings just as sacred as anything in the Bible. So closely in fact do these documents resemble the scriptures and each other that to this day there is no agreement among their pious readers or among the specialists who study them as to what is really "apocryphal" in the Bible and what is really Biblical in the Apocrypha. It is no wonder that scholars have been driven to distraction trying to decide how to classify the Apocryphal writings. The key to the problem of the Apocrypha was given 133 years ago in the 91st Section of the Doctrine and Covenants:

> Verily, thus saith the Lord unto you concerning the Apocrypha, there are many things contained therein that are true, and it is mostly translated correctly; There are many things contained therein that are not true, which are interpolations by the hands of men ... Therefore, whoso readeth it, let him understand, for the Spirit manifesteth truth; and whoso is enlightened by the Spirit, shall obtain benefit therefrom; and whoso receiveth not by the Spirit, cannot be benefited ...

The Changing Attitude Towards Scripture: This was a shocking declaration at the time it was written and long afterward. The apocryphal writings contained in the Septuagint and Vulgate, for example, were regarded as wholly inspired by a large section of the Christian world, but by most Protestants they were looked upon as purely human creations. Other Apocrypha were dismissed as the productions of diseased and undisciplined Oriental minds.[2] The thought that the Apocrypha might be both divinely inspired *and* corrupted by men seemed utterly contradictory for, as St. Augustine protested to Jerome, how could a book of which God was the author have any corruption in it at all or be anything but absolutely perfect? Unless it believes in revelation a church must, as

Irenaeus insisted long ago, believe that its scriptures are absolutely perfect, otherwise no certitude is possible, all things being resolved in a conflict of opinion and speculation of men.[3] Yet today both Catholics and Protestants not only accept new and revised translations of the Bible, but engage in the diligent compilation of new and changing editions of the "original" text! In Joseph Smith's day all Christians believed that the Bible was the only divinely dictated book in the world; the existence of a large and ancient literature that closely resembled the Bible both in form and content was largely ignored and its materials consigned to a wholly different category from that of the Bible. Yet the Jews never made such a distinction:

> One cannot emphasize strongly enough the fact that, literally speaking, there are no Apocrypha in the Jewish literature . . . The idea of the Canon and, in consequence, the idea of books not forming part of that Canon, belongs exclusively to the church and not to the synagogue . . . Not all the books in the Hebrew Bible share among the Jews the same authority . . . Even the Prophets are not considered as having a binding legal force . . .[4]

The Christian Canon is a product of the post-Apostolic Church that had ceased to claim revelation. It is a late and artificial thing and the true church is not bound by it.[5]

What do the Apocrypha Say?: Now as to what the Apocrypha say, it is true that they are full of bizarre and peculiar things. Such things by their very oddity can sometimes be traced back to their uninspired sources and "the interpolations of men". But along with dubious information it is even more apparent that "there are many things therein that are true". In the Old Testament, New Testament, Jewish Apocrypha, Christian Apocrypha, and Dead Sea Scrolls we have five bodies of documents every one of which has numerous points of resemblance to all the other four. By the process of boiling them all down to those teachings which are shared by *all of them in common*, scholars hope, and often claim, to discover the original pattern of thought common to all of them, and in the end to reveal the true nature and origin of the gospel.

What results from this process is always the same thing.
The common denominator of *all* the apocryphal writings
and all the scriptures is the "apocalyptic" or "eschatological" theme. There is no clearer or fuller exposition of
this theme than the Book of Mormon.

The Apocalyptic Themes and the Book of Mormon:
The best explanation of what "apocalyptic" is about may
be had by considering the apocalyptic elements in that
book. As we go we shall "control" each point by some
reliable matter from the apocryphal writings.

1. *The Great Tradition.* In the lesson on *Churches
in the Wilderness* we saw that the Book of Mormon people always thought of the righteous as a single timeless
community, preaching and believing the same gospel
along with Moses and all the prophets, and Abraham,
and those who were before Abraham, "since the very
beginning of the world," and right down to the end of
the world.

What all apocalyptic writers have in common, a recent study concludes, is the claim to be telling a story
that was given to man by revelation and was had among
the most ancient prophets from the beginning; this history
has been transmitted to the righteous down through all
periods of time.[6]

2. *The Secret Teaching.* According to the Book of
Mormon the knowledge possessed by the righteous
prophets down through the ages has not been shared by
the rest of the world. From time to time God has "sent
angels, and conversed with men, and made known unto
them the plan . . . prepared from the foundation of the
world." (Alma 12:29, Moroni 7:22.) Those who have
believed in the plan have been few, and God has always
hidden them away from the wicked.

In the scrolls we read that God causes the righteous
"to discern and to know the Most High and the wisdom
of the Sons of Heaven, and to understand the perfection
of the way . . ." But this knowledge is not to be divulged
to or discussed with the outside world, "the children of
the pit".[7]

3. *The Holy Book.* In every age the inspired prophets have put down their knowledge in books. "I have
spoken to you concerning all things which are written
from the creation of the world . . ." says Jacob to his
people. (2 Ne. 6:3.) The Book of Mormon opens
with Lehi "carried away in a vision" which is from its
content a model of all apocalyptic visions; in the vision he
reads from a book. (1 Ne. 1:11-12.) His son speaks of
a sealed book in which "the revelation which was
sealed shall be kept in the book until the own due time
of the Lord . . . for behold they reveal all things from
the foundation of the world unto the end thereof." (2 Ne.
27:10.) The Lamanites were converted to the true
religion specifically by being "taught the records and
the prophecies which were handed down even to the present time." (Alma 23:5.) Nephi tells us that his writing is
directed to people of another age, living in the last days,
"for their good I have written them". (2 Ne. 25:8.)
Lehi himself learns as much from the books as from direct
revelation (2 Nephi 2:17), and these books contained
the words "Spoken by the mouth of all the holy prophets
. . . since the world began". (1 Ne. 3:20.)

"The apocalyptic writer," writes R. H. Charles,
". . . professedly addressed his book to future generations. Generally directions as to the hiding and sealing
of the book were given in the text. . . ." The belief was
that this practice had obtained from the days of the
earliest patriarchs.[8]

4. *The Plan.* As the books themselves are brought
forth from time to time throughout the whole span of history, so the subject they deal with is always the Big Picture, God's Plan for the world from beginning to end.
"God knowing all things . . . sent angels to minister unto
the children of men . . . (Moroni 7:22 ff), and himself
"conversed with men, and made known unto them the
plan . . . which had been prepared from the foundation
of the world." (Alma 12:29) God sees all things "from
eternity to all eternity, according to his foreknowledge
. . ." (Alma 13:7) and the purpose of all revelation is "to

bring about his eternal purposes in the end of man." (2 Ne. 2:15, 2:11.)

According to R. H. Charles, all apocalyptic writing conceives of the whole of human history as being "determined from the beginning in the counsels of God. . . ."[9] In the Serek Scroll we are told, "From God is the knowledge of all that exists or will exist. And before their existence he established (or prepared) all their design, and when they exist the manner of their operation as to the Plan of His Glory. They fulfill their functions and no changes are made therein."[10]

6. *Revelation.* For all their devotion to the ancient books and the constant tradition, the people who cultivate apocalyptic literature always claim revelation in their own time. "We search the prophets," says Jacob at the beginning, "and we have many revelations and the spirit of prophecy; and having all these witnesses we obtain a hope. . . ." (Jac. 4:6, cf. 1:6.) "Is it not as easy," Alma asks, "at this time for the Lord to send his angel to declare these glad tidings unto us as unto our children, or as after the time of his coming?" (Alma 39:19.) "Have miracles ceased because Christ hath sat down on the right hand of God?" another prophet asks, ". . . nay, neither have angels ceased to minister unto the children of men. . . ." (Moroni 7:27-29.)

Charles notes that every apocalyptic writing claims divine revelation, and that "the reality of the visions is to some extent guaranteed by the writer's intense earnestness and by his manifest belief in the divine origin of his message." Charles himself hesitates "to assume that the visions are a literary invention and nothing more," though he concludes that "there will always be a difficulty in determining what belongs to his actual vision and what to the literary skill or free invention of the author. . . ."[11]

Strictly speaking, in apocalyptic thinking prophecy is not the divination of the future but the awareness of a pattern. If you know the plot of a typical western drama, you can always tell how it's going to turn out, not because you are clairvoyant, but because the course of events is clearly prescribed by the characters and setting of the play. There are those among our teachers of religion today who say that God cannot know the future. To say that God can only know what is happening right now is as simple as to argue that he can only know what is happening right here. Many of the children of men journeying in this wilderness know neither where they have been or where they are going, yet to one viewing their movements from above it would all be perfectly clear. Even the poet knows we are marooned "on this bank and shoal of time," not because that represents the whole universe, but because that bleak and narrow view represents all we know about it.

7. *Time and Timelessness.* The plan and the true story of man's life on earth, being "eschatological," i.e. beyond the limits of local time and space, is timeless. Mosiah can speak quite naturally of "things to come as though they had already come" (Mos. 16:6), and Mormon can address unborn generations "as if ye were present, and yet ye are not. . . ." (Mor. 8:35.) Yet as far as this earth is concerned everything is in terms of times and periods. The history of God's people is a *repeating cycle of events*—a dispensation of the visiting of angels and of God's conversing with men followed by an apostasy and in turn by a general destruction from which the righteous remnant are rescued by being led away. This you will find in 2 Ne. 9:2; 25:8-9 ("destroyed from generation to generation"), 2 Ne. 29:8ff. God speaks to every nation in its dispensation, Moroni 7:22, 24, 31. It was the nature of a "church of anticipation" to consider future events as present.

Today new emphasis is being placed on the concept of "prefiguration" in the early Jewish and Christian teachings, i.e., the idea that the history of one age or dispensation prefigures events in another. "This approach," writes Flusser, "which sees world history as an organic whole, is typical of the workings of the apocalyptic mind. To such a mind it is quite plausible, not only that the sons of Jacob predicted the future history of the nation, but also that their deeds had some direct bearing on the events of the author's lifetime, however many years later."[12] "Everything liveth and abideth forever," says Sirach, but then he describes the earthly economy as a series of temporal visitations, each under a great patriarch, each having its heralds, its glorious manifestations, and its end in a fall and apostasy.[13] It is all one story, however, which Enoch is declared to have read in "the book of all the deeds of mankind." The peculiar type of thinking that sees all the past and future as embodied in the present is nowhere more strikingly illustrated than in the Dead Sea document known as the Habbakuk commentary,[14] and nowhere is the principle of scriptural interpretation embodied in that commentary more perfectly described than in the words of Nephi in which he explains his own method of teaching in the wilderness: "I did liken *all* scriptures unto *us*, that it might be for our profit and learning." (1 Ne. 19:23.)

8. *The Messiah.* The center and pivot of the whole plan of history is of course the Messiah in the Book of Mormon: ". . . none of the prophets have written, nor prophesied, save they have spoken concerning this Christ. . . ." (Jac. 7:11.) "All the prophets . . . ever since the world began . . . have they not spoken more or less concerning these things?" (Mos. 13:33.)

Compare this with the teaching of the Talmud: "All the prophets have prophesied of nothing save the days of the Messiah, that is, of the eternal order to come."[15] Gunkel, before the discovery of the Dead Sea Scrolls, found in the *prechristian* apocryphal writings frequent reference to a divine redeemer, a new heaven and a new earth, the millennial rule of the Lord in person on earth, a Messiah who is to come as a human being and yet be more than human, a carefully cultivated "Wisdom" literature, the doctrine of the resurrection of the flesh, the practice of baptism in water, the belief that the eighth day rather than the seventh is the holiest of days, the reports of a Lord who is meek and humble, despised and put to death, resurrected, ascended to heaven, and who

visits the spirits in prison. Also he found in the apocalyptic writings the use of such baffling code-words as
"water of life," "second death," "first Adam," etc., and
a conception of cosmology and world history totally at
variance with that of the official schools of the Jews and
Christians.[16] All this sort of thing has been brought to
light by the studies of the last two generations.

9. *The Doctrine of Probation.* According to the
Plan of Life and Salvation, fixed and determined before
the foundation of the world, the earth was made to be a
place of testing, men being free while here to choose the
way of light or the way of darkness. The Book of Mormon has a great deal to say about this. Our earth life is
the "days of probation," (1 Ne. 15:31-32, 10, 21),
". . . and the days of the children of men were prolonged,
according to the will of God . . . wherefore their state
became a state of probation, and their time was length-
ened, . . ." (2 Ne. 2:21.) "Walk in the straight path
which leads to life, and continue in the path until the end
of the day of probation." (2 Ne. 33:9.) ". . . this life
became a probationary state; a time to prepare to meet
God; a time to prepare for that endless state . . . which
is after the resurrection of the dead." (Alma 12:24.)
"This life is the time for men to prepare to meet God . . .
improve your time while in this life . . . if ye have pro-
crastinated the day of your repentance, behold, ye have
become subjected to the Spirit of the devil." (Alma
34:32-33, 35.) What we do during this brief time of
probation will determine our state forever hereafter; the
effect of the plan being "everlasting, whether on the one
hand or on the other—either unto peace and life eternal,
or unto the deliverance . . . into captivity. . . ." (1 Ne.
14:7.)

This theme is treated at length in the *Serek* Scroll,
sometimes in the very words used in the Book of Mormon.
According to this source the operation of the plan on this
earth takes place in set dispensations. Every man is tested and rewarded by the test of the particular period in
which he lives, some coming sooner, some later, but all

in their properly appointed time. Every man will be
tested in the situation of his particular dispensation, but
whatever he earns, whether great or small, is for keeps.[17]
This is exactly the doctrine of Alma 13:3 ff and 1 Ne.
14.7. What we do in this life will determine our status
forever and ever. In the scrolls the newly baptized member is admonished "in his times to walk perfect in all the
ways of God as he has commanded for the set seasons of
his appointed times."[18] The teaching of the community,
moreover, is for all types of men "for all the kinds of their
spirits in their characteristics, for all their deeds in their
time-cycles and for visitations of their smitings, while the
limited time of their prosperity shall last."[19] For the
next passage we shall follow Brownlee's translation, lest
we appear to be overdoing things:

> In these (two spirits) are the families of all mankind . . . ac-
> cording to the inheritance of each, whether much or little, for
> all the *period* or the *ages*. For God has set them in equal parts
> until the *last period* . . . Now God through the mysteries of his
> understanding and through his glorious wisdom has appointed
> a *period* for the existence of wrong-doing; but at the *season* of
> *visitation* he will destroy it forever.[20]

There is no more emphasized doctrine in the Apocrypha, especially the Christian Apocrypha, than the teaching of the *Two Ways*, the Way of Light and the Way of
Darkness. We have seen Nephi counselling his people
to "walk in the straight path which leads to life until the
end of the day of probation." (2 Ne. 33:9.) Constantly
the Book of Mormon people are told to choose between
life and death, with emphasis on the fact that man is
placed on this earth in the peculiar position of being able
to choose either good or bad as long as he is here: ". . . remember that you are free to act for yourselves—to choose
the way to everlasting death or the way of eternal life."
(2 Ne. 10:23, cf. Hel. 14:30 f, Alma 12:29, 31. Alma
13:3 ff., 42:27 f., 1 Ne. 14:7 f.) The closest parallels to
these passages are extremely abundant in the apocryphal
literature.[21] Thoroughly characteristic is also the Book of
Mormon emphasis on the "light." (2 Ne. 3:5, 17:13; Jac.

6:5, Alma 19:6 mentions "light" six times in one verse.) This is also very "Johannine."[22]

10. *The Doctrine of Apostasy.* From the first, according to the apocalyptic concept of history, men have chosen the darkness rather than the light. This teaching receives great emphasis in the Book of Mormon, where a constantly recurring event is the apostasy of God's church from the way of righteousness. Such general apostasies are described in Alma 62:44-46; Hel. 4: 11-12, 21-23; 3 Ne. 7:7; 4 Ne. 27-31, 38-46. Behind this is the general weakness of the human race and "the nothingness of the children of men" (Hel. 12:4-7), which makes this world inevitably the kingdom of darkness and the dominion of Satan, "which comes by the cunning plans which he hath devised to ensnare the hearts of men." (Alma 28:13) For the devil has *his* plan which opposes God's plan for the human race—"that cunning plan of the evil one!" (2 Ne. 9:28.) Just so, in the Dead Sea Scrolls the wicked, who are perfectly free to do as they choose, reject God's plan, preferring one of their own, for as might be expected, the devil counters God's plan with a parallel plan:

> The self-willed go the way of their own heart, wandering after his heart and his own eyes and according to the plan (or counsel) of his own devising and his own gods . . .[23]
> By the king of darkness go astray all the sons of righteousness (ZDK), and all their sins and trespasses and iniquities and the perversity (transgressions) of their deeds are under his government, according to the secret plan of God, until the end that he has decreed. And all their smitings (buffetings) and the set period of their afflictions (are) in the government of his judgments. But all the spirits of his election (or testing) are for teaching the sons of Light.[24]
> The ways of the wicked shall be crooked in the kingdom of perversion until the set time of judgment that has been fixed.[25]

The church is to work with the wicked, protesting, provoking, and where possible correcting, so it may be a "witness against all who transgress the Law."[26] Nevertheless, the plan remains hidden to those who are in dark-

ness and is to be known only "by those who fear the
spirit of self-will."[27]

> All who go the way of evil . . . who seek not the Lord nor try
> to find his truth, in the secret things have fallen away . . . they shall
> bring upon themselves great judgments for eternal destruction
> without remnant.[28]

Man is always falling away; from Eden to the present moment the human race is in revolt. The chosen people themselves regularly fall from grace and must be
called to repentance. "Because of the shedding of blood,"
says the Talmud, "the holy house (the temple—the same
expression is used in the scrolls) is destroyed, and God
withdraws (literally, 'takes back up') his presence from
Israel." Then it quotes Numbers 35:33: "But if you
defile it (the land), you shall not dwell in it either. Because of whoredom and idolatry and the neglect of due
offerings the world is visited by desolation (lit. 'banish-
ment'); the people are swept away from it and others
come and settle down in their place."[29] Some of the
Tanaim say that the end of the blessed age when God
gave revelations to men came in the days of Hosea, others
in the days of Hazael, others that "since the days of
Elijah" men have been without the ancient blessing, and
still others from the days of Hezekiah.[30] But all are
agreed that the Lord does withdraw and *has* withdrawn
his spirit, and that in keeping with a clearly-stated general
principle. God lets his spirit descend upon the people
when they are righteous and "takes it back up again"
when they are not.[31]

11. *The Apocalypse of Woe.* Since the world is the
domain of Belial it is doomed in the end to destruction—
but only in the final end. The image most commonly in-
voked by the word, apocalyptic, is that of the great destruction of the world, but that comes only at the
consummation of times. Meantime there are many
ends.[32] We see that from the Book of Mormon. The
saints can only expect persecution "in the domain of
Belial," but must not weaken for that reason. "Thus shall
they do," says the rule, "year by year for all the days of

the rule of Belial." (Serek II, 19.) There shall surely come a "time of refreshing," we are told in the scrolls even as in the New Testament, but meantime the world "shall roll itself in the ways of evil, in the sway (or government) of iniquity, until the established judgment of the set time." This is precisely the teaching of the *Didache* and the *Pastor of Hermas*, the two most important Christian Apocrypha.[33]

All apocryphal traditions, according to Gunkel, in view of the wickedness of the world tell of "a series of plagues, occurring in strictly ordered periods, by which, however, the human race remains unconverted, and goes right on sinning until the final and most terrible of all bring corruption and destruction." Pending this final consummation, in each of these "ordered periods" God sends light into the world by revealing the Great Plan in its fullness to chosen prophets, who call the world to repentance and bear testimony to it, that its blood may not be on their heads. Each of these visitations, as they are called, sees the general rejection of the Gospel Plan by the human race, followed by a general apostasy of those who did accept it, save for a faithful remnant who are removed from the scene. Finally when the number of spirits has been fulfilled, a culmination of wickedness is followed by a culminating destruction, after which in the last and greatest visitation of all the Messiah comes personally to rule upon the earth.[34]

These and other teachings, set forth with great power and clarity in the Book of Mormon, make up the substance of the apocryphal as well as the scriptural teaching, but their great importance for the understanding of the true nature both of Christianity and of Judaism has only begun to be appreciated. With the new discoveries the Apocrypha must be read in a wholly new context that gives them a new meaning and importance. Even the Bible must now be viewed in the light of new knowledge; but especially the Book of Mormon must undergo a change of status. Apocalyptic ideas, as is well known, have flourished among groups of religious enthusiasts,

Christian and non-Christian, in every age, but in only one source do we find the full and consistent picture of the old eschatology that scholars today are reconstructing from many pieces of evidence, and that source is the Book of Mormon.

Questions

1. What are the Apocrypha?

2. How has the discovery of the Dead Sea Scrolls enhanced their importance?

3. What has been the attitude of the Christian world towards the Apocrypha? Of the Latter-day Saints? (Sect. 91).

4. What fundamental teachings do the Apocrypha and the Scriptures have in common?

5. Wherein do they differ?

6. What is "apocalyptic"?

7. What teachings common to all apocalyptic writings are also found in the Book of Mormon, regarding the Great Tradition? The secret teaching of the gospel? The sealing and transmission of sacred records? The divine Plan? Continued revelation? Time and history? The Messiah? This life as a probation? The Two Ways? Apostasy and restitution?

8. Do the Latter-day Saints believe that God has infinite foreknowledge? Did the Nephites?

9. Does the predominance of apocalyptic themes in the Book of Mormon support or weaken its claims to authenticity? What was the status of the Apocrypha in Joseph Smith's day?

10. What apocalyptic themes are particularly popular with revivalists? What apocalyptic themes do they ignore? Which of these are most emphasized in the Book of Mormon?

Lesson 17

A STRANGE ORDER OF BATTLE

Prospectus of Lesson 17: This lesson is on an unusual theme. The Book of Mormon story of Moroni's "Title of Liberty" gives valuable insight into certain practices and traditions of the Nephites which they took as a matter of course but which are totally unfamiliar not only to the modern world but to the world of Biblical scholarship as well. Since it is being better recognized every day that the Bible is only a sampling (and a carefully edited one) of but one side of ancient Jewish life, the Book of Mormon must almost unavoidably break away from the familiar things from time to time, and show us facets of Old World life untouched by the Bible. The "Title of Liberty" story is a good example of such a welcome departure from beaten paths, being concerned with certain old Hebrew traditions which were perfectly familiar to the Nephites but are nowhere to be found either in the Bible or in the apocryphal writings. These traditions, strange as they are, can now be checked by new and unfamiliar sources turned up in the Old World, and shown to be perfectly authentic.

A New Discovery: It has always been known, if only from the pages of Varro and Livy, that the ancients had a ritual concept of war. The closely related functions of hunting and warfare were never undertaken without certain observations of a ritual or cultic nature, which are everywhere hinted at in ancient literature but nowhere fully expounded. It was the discovery among the Dead Sea Scrolls of a long and beautifully preserved text, now designated as the *Milhamah* ("Battle") Scroll, that for the first time cast a flood of light on the nature of sacred warfare among the Jews. The same text serves to illustrate and explain most remarkably a strange and wonderful episode in the Book of Mormon, which should serve as a reminder that the ways of the ancients are not our ways, and that to produce the Book of Mormon would have required far more than luck and learning of any man.

Moroni rouses the People: The episode to which we refer is the story of the Title of Liberty. One of those

strong and ambitious men around whom the usual resist-
ance to the Church crystalized in the first century B.C.
was Amalickiah, ". . . a man of cunning device and a man
of many flattering words . . ." (Alma 46:10), whose am-
bition was to be king, and whose chief support came from
". . . the lower judges of the land, and they were seeking
for power. . . ." (Alma 46:4-5.) He made a deal with the
judges and began openly to rally his forces, whereupon
". . . Moroni, who was the chief commander of the armies
of the Nephites, . . ." and who had shortly before won a
magnificent victory over the traditional enemy, ". . . was
angry with Amalickiah." (Alma 46:11.)

And it came to pass that he rent his coat; and he took a piece
thereof, and wrote upon it—IN MEMORY OF OUR GOD,
OUR RELIGION, AND FREEDOM, AND OUR PEACE,
OUR WIVES, AND OUR CHILDREN—and he fastened it
upon the end of a pole. (Alma 46:12.)

Then he dressed himself in his full armor,

and he took the pole, which had on the end thereof his rent coat,
(and he called it the title of liberty) and he bowed himself to the
earth, and he prayed mightily unto his God for the blessings of
liberty to rest upon his brethren . . . (Alma 46:13.)

And it came to pass that when he had poured out his soul to
God, he named all the land which was south of the land Desolation, yea . . . all the land . . . A chosen land, and the land of
liberty. (Alma 46:17.)

And he said: Surely God shall not suffer that we, who are
despised because we take upon us the name of Christ, shall be
trodden down and destroyed, until we bring it upon us by our
own transgression. (Alma 46:18.)

Then Moroni ". . . went forth among the people,
waving the rent part of his garment, that all might see
the writing which he had written upon the rent part,
. . ." and calling upon ". . . whosoever will maintain this
title upon the land, . . ." to ". . . come forth in the strength
of the Lord, and enter into a covenant, that they will
maintain their rights, and their religion, that the Lord
God may bless them." (Alma 46:19-20.) All who were
willing to join came together dressed for war, ". . . rend-
ing their garments in token, or as a covenant, that they

would not forsake the Lord their God; or, in other words, if they should transgress . . . and be ashamed to take upon them the name of Christ, the Lord should rend them even as they had rent their garments." (Alma 46:21.) Then at the mustering place apparently ". . . they cast their garments at the feet of Moroni; . . ." witnessing to the chief that they asked God to ". . . cast us at the feet of our enemies, even as we have cast our garments at thy feet to be trodden under foot, if we shall fall into transgression." (Alma 46:22.)

The Garment of Joseph: Moroni then reminded the multitude that they were actually a remnant of the seed of Jacob, and also ". . . a remnant of the seed of Joseph, whose coat was rent by his brethren into many pieces; . . ." and if they should do wickedly ". . . our garments shall be rent by our brethren, and we be cast into prison, be sold, or be slain." (Alma 46:23.)   Then Moroni told an apocryphal story of how Jacob

before his death . . . saw that a part of the remnant of the coat of Joseph was preserved and had not decayed. And he said —Even as this remnant of garment of my son hath been preserved, so shall a remnant of the seed of my son be preserved . . . while the remainder of the seed of Joseph shall perish, even as the remnant of his garment. (Alma 46:24.)

Moroni suggested that the lost remnant of the garment may actually represent the Nephites who had fallen away from the church. (Alma 46:27.)

To the modern and the western mind all this overobvious dwelling on types and shadows seems a bit overdone, but not to the ancient or Oriental mind. The whole Arabic language is one long commentary on the deepseated feeling, so foreign to us but so characteristic of people who speak synthetic languages, that if things are *alike* they are the *same*. In the Israelite way of thinking, writes Pedersen, "the clothes follow and partake of the total character of the soul. . . . There may be garments, so penetrated by a definite physical substance, that they are indissolubly connected with its forms of manifestation. This holds good where special importance is attached to the functions. Thus . . . the honour and glory of the priest is bound up with his garment (Sirach 50, 11). . . . The anxiety lest the holy garments should be defiled, appears from the careful ritual for the Day of Atonement, preserved in the Mishna."[1]   It is interesting that the principal evidence here given comes from non-Biblical, that is, apocryphal sources, since the entire episode from the Book of Mormon has no parallel in the Bible and yet may be substantiated as genuine old Israelite lore from apocryphal texts.

When Moroni and his agents went around everywhere gathering recruits, all who would not join ". . . to stand against Amalickiah, and those who had dissented, . . ." they classed as Amalickiahites, (Alma 46:28.) Amalickiah tried to play the Lamanites against Moroni as his trump card, but Moroni beat him to it by making ". . . a covenant to keep the peace, . . ." while intercepting Amalickiah's forces before they could make contact with the Lamanites. (Alma 46:31.)   Since Moroni had just won a miraculous victory over the Lamanites, who for a time had threatened the whole Nephite nation with extinction, it was nothing but the basest treason for Amalickiah, a Nephite, to go over to the Lamanites and try to revive the war.   Moroni took strong but legitimate measures to put down the sedition:

> And it came to pass that whomsoever of the Amalickiahites that would not enter into a covenant to support the cause of freedom, that they might maintain a free government, he caused to be put to death; and there were but few who denied the covenant of freedom. (Alma 46:35.)

One of the most remarkable aspects of the story is the manner in which Moroni sought to stir up patriotic fervor by appealing to ancient and traditional devices. He connected the whole business of the rent garment with the story of the tribal ancestors Jacob and Joseph, and suggested that ". . . those who have dissented from us . . ." were the very ". . . remnant of the seed of Joseph . . ." to which the dying Jacob prophetically referred. (Alma 46:27.) It was not merely a resemblance or a type, but the very event foreseen by the patriarch of old. Plainly the whole background and explanation of Moroni's strange behavior is to be sought in the Old World and among traditions not preserved in the Bible.

The Battle Scroll: The *Milhama* ("Battle") is the title now given to the scroll that opens with that word, and which has heretofore been designated either as "The War of the Sons of Light with the Sons of Darkness," or "The Rule of Battle for the Sons of Light."[2]   There has been a good deal of argument over whether the wonderful order of battle prescribed in the text actually represents an attempt at military organization, or whether it is purely a ritual or spiritual army that is described.[3]   For our purposes it makes little difference, since we are concerned only with the fact that there was such a concept of holy war, whether ritual or actual. The arrangement of God's army and the conduct of warfare as described in this text is a highly idealized and impractical one, but is obviously of great antiquity, as is clear especially in the imagery of the hymn that comes near the end of the scroll.

An important part of this text is taken up with certain slogans and war cries which the army writes boldly upon its trumpets and banners, calling itself both the army of God and "the assembly of the congregation."

> When they are gathered together to the house of meeting they shall write 'The Testimonies of God for the Holy Council' . . . On the trumpets of the ranks of battle they shall write 'The Ranks of the Banners of God for the Vengeance of His Anger against all the Sons of Darkness,' 'The Powers of God for Scattering the Enemy and Putting to Flight Those Who Hate Righteousness' . . .[4]

This is the sort of slogan they march under. On the "trumpets of return" they describe themselves as "The Gathering of God," and on another devise designate the enemy as "The Faithless Slain."[5] They are the Church of God united for the extermination of all the Sons of Darkness, who are faithless betrayers. This is even clearer from the writings placed upon the banners of the various military units. Thus for the hundreds, "The

Hundred of God, a Hand of War against all Erring Flesh," for the fifties (see above, Lesson X) and tens, "The Camps of God," "The Congregation of God," "The Banners of God," "The Victory of God," "The Help of God," "The Deliverance of God," etc. etc., emphasizing as did Moroni's standard the program of deliverance from bondage and preservation of liberty. We are reminded of the great care the ancients took to establish the moral guilt of their enemies and thereby clear themselves of their blood by an inscription on a ritual dart: "Flashing of a Sword Consuming the Iniquitous Slain in the Judgment of God."[6] This dart was to be hurled ritually at the enemy before battle—three darts cast seven times. The Romans also before making war on a nation would throw three darts in its direction, dedicating it to destruction in the archaic rite of the *feciales,* the great antiquity of which establishes both the age and the genuineness of the Jewish practice.[7]

As to the army itself, the *Milhama* scroll specifies that they "shall all be volunteers for war (as were Moroni's host), blameless in spirit and flesh, and ready for the day of vengeance . . . for holy angels are together with their armies . . . And no indecent, evil thing shall be seen in the vicinity of any of your camps."[8]

Such ideal armies, consciously dramatizing themselves as the righteous host, are also met with in the Book of Mormon, notably in the case of Helaman and his two thousand sons. (Alma 53:17 ff.) The chief banners of the army described in the scroll are "the great ensign placed at the head of all the army," which bore the inscription: " 'Army of God' together with the name of 'Israel and Aaron' and the names of the twelve tribes of Israel," and the ensigns of the thousands which bore the title: "Wrath of God, full of anger, against Belial and all the people of his party, without any survivors." Throughout the many ensigns the same motifs predominate as in Moroni's program, namely the freedom of the host from all transgression and the dedication of all the opposition to extermination. Israel is the first and foremost name occurring on the sacred banners, and in Moroni's exploit he is careful to trace the real origin of his banner and the custom he is following to Jacob himself, who is Israel, explaining the symbolism of all he is doing in terms of the actual teaching of Jacob.

The *Milhama* document is just as spiritual or "mystical" as the other scrolls, Dupont-Sommer has observed, but ". . . it is at the same time specifically military and ardently warlike, . . ."[9] which is exactly how Moroni wished to make his people. The priests and Levites ". . . have a role to play in the battle right in the midst of the combatants, . . ." actually directing each phase of the combat by means of blasts on sacred trumpets.[10] It is they also who like the Roman *feciales* (and like Moroni) formally dedicate the enemy to destruction. Before the battle the chief priest gives an address to the troops telling them not to fear since ". . . God goes with you to fight for you against your enemies to save you." Then he turns to the enemy and pronounces them the ". . . congregation of wickedness, the host of darkness, the troops of Belial, the seven nations of vanity, . . ." who are about to be overcome not by a savage army but by ". . . the poor whom thou hast redeemed." "Then the priest intones a warlike song, woven entirely of Biblical texts— truly a song of triumph of this mystical army, . . ." but a very savage and "Asiatic" one that bears all the marks of great antiquity.[11]

Moroni's Banner and Kawe's Banner: One interesting aspect of the Dead Sea Scrolls that many writers have commented on is the strong and undeniable affinity between certain important traditions and doctrines contained in them and the teachings of the ancient Iranians.[12] This connection hardly came as a surprise, since such a tie-up has often been noted in the apocryphal writings and many studies have pointed out the strongly "Iranian" nature of Jewish eschatology.[13] The Jews ranked Cyrus, the founder of the Persian nation, next to Solomon and David alone in glory and authority, and how well the Jews and Persians got to know each other is clear to everyone from the Book of Esther. For the New Testament times we have the Lord hailed at his birth by the Magi. Though the apocalyptic side of the Book of Mormon naturally shares with the rest of Hebrew eschatology many of those things for which the scholars insist on detecting a possible Iranian background, we have in the Title of Liberty episode a clear and independent parallel, for Moroni's banner is just like the "Flag of Kawe" (*dirafsh-i-kawiyani*), the legendary founder of the Magi. In the beginning, runs the story, Iran was under the rule of the serpent, the oppressor, "the man of the Lie and king of madmen," Dahhak, who reigned a thousand years and forced all men to subscribe their names in the Book of the Dragon. To liberate the people there rose up in Isfahan a mighty man, a blacksmith named Kawe, who took the leather apron he wore at his work and placed it on the end of a pole; this became the symbol of liberation and remained for many centuries the national banner of the Persians as well as the sacred emblem of the Magi. Going about with his banner, Kawe called upon the people to rise in revolt and shake off the oppressor; to lead the people the hero Threataona was raised up in the mountains by a shepherd (like Cyrus), and he put Kawe in charge of raising and leading an army.[14] This Threatoana is a doublet of King Cyrus, the founder of the Persian nation and in Jewish lore the holiest of kings next to Solomon and David.

The parallel with the story of Moroni's banner is very striking, and it is certainly more than a mere coincidence. The Dead Sea Scrolls provide the link between the two, for along with the many clear Iranian affinities that have so impressed students of the doctrines and expressions found in the Scrolls, we have in the *Milhama* scroll revealed for the first time the actual practice and concern of the ancient Hebrews with regard to holy banners and the mustering of the holy army (cf. the Magi) of liberation.[15] Thus we find in the Old World a peculiar combination of things: 1) the garment as a banner, 2) the program of liberation from the wicked oppressor (compare the treasonous Amalickiah with the usurper Dahhak, the "Man of the Lie"), 3) the peculiar custom of putting long sermonizing inscriptions on banners to rouse up and excite the people to a holy cause, 4) the proclamation of allegiance to God, religion, freedom, wives, children, etc. (Kawe, we are told, was only driven to revolt by the evil king's threat to his family), 5) the formal and legal condemnation to death of all opponents as transgressors and children of darkness, and 6) the attributing of the invention of the banner to the founder and ancestor of the nation—in the Scrolls and the Book of Mormon it is Jacob or Israel.

The Torn Garment, an Apocryphal Tale: When Moroni (Alma 46:24) begins his story by saying ". . . let us remember the words of Jacob . . ." he is plainly reminding his hearers of a tale that is familiar to them all. Yet who in the West has ever known anything about the story that follows, in which the words of Jacob are: "Even as this remnant of garment of my son hath been preserved, so shall a remnant of the seed of my son be preserved . . . while the remainder of the seed of Joseph shall perish, even as the remnant of his garment?" Here the survival of Joseph's garment guarantees and typifies the survival of Joseph.

In the tenth century of our era the greatest antiquarian of the Moslem world, Muhammad ibn-Ibrahim ath-Tha'labi, collected in Persia a great many old tales and legends about the prophets of Israel. After the fall of Jerusalem and the scattering of the Jews, many of the sectaries, such as those that once lived around the Dead Sea, moved East to be under the protection of the Persians. Thus groups of Jews representing various sects and shades of belief were scattered all over central Asia in the Middle Ages, and it is from such, no doubt, that Tha'labi gets his amazing fund of information, which is worthy to be set up beside the most enlightening volumes of Apocrypha. Among other things, Tha'labi tells a number of stories, which we have not found anywhere else, about Jacob and the garment of Joseph. In one, Joseph's

brethren bring his torn garment to their father as proof
that he is dead, but Jacob after examining the garment,
("and there were in the garment of Joseph three marks
or tokens when they brought it to his father") declares
that the way the cloth is torn shows him that their story
is not true; "Behold, if the bear had eaten him he surely
would have rent his garment, and since he would (naturally) have fled towards the gate, verily the garment
should have been torn behind. . . ." But since this is not
the case it may be that Joseph still lives. Another account
is the case of "the vizier" Potiphar, who by examining the
tears in Joseph's garment knew that he was innocent and
spared his life, "for he knew that if he (Joseph) had attacked his wife the tear would have been in front. . . ."
So again his torn garment declared that Joseph should
live.[16]

Most significant is Tha'labi's discussion of the two
remnants of Joseph's garment, from which we quote:

And when Joseph had made himself known unto them (his
brethren) he asked them about his father, saying, 'What did my
father after (I left)?' They answered, 'He lost his eyesight (from
weeping).' Then he gave them his garment (qamis, long outer
shirt). According to ad-Dahak that garment was of the weave
(pattern, design) of Paradise, and the breath (spirit, odor) of
Paradise was in it, so that it never decayed or in any way
deteriorated (and that was) a sign (omen). And Joseph gave
them that garment, and it was the very one that had belonged to
Abraham, having already had a long history. And he said to
them, 'Go, take this garment of mine and place it upon the face
of my father so he may have sight again, and return (to me) with
all your families. And when they had put Egypt behind them and
come to Canaan their father Jacob said, 'Behold, I perceive the
spirit (breath, odor) of Joseph, if you will not think me wandering
in my mind and weakheaded from age. . . . (for) he knew that
upon all the earth there was no spirit (breath, odor) of Paradise
save in that garment alone . . . And as-Sadi says that Judah said
to Joseph, 'It was I who took the garment bedaubed with blood to
Jacob, and reported to him that the bear had eaten Joseph; so
give me this day thy garment that I might tell him that thou art
living, that I might cause him to rejoice now as greatly as I caused
him to sorrow then. And Ibn-Abbas says that Judah took the
garment and went forth in great haste, panting with exertion and

anxiety . . . and when he brought the garment he laid it upon his face, so that his sight returned to him. And ad-Dahak says that his sight returned after blindness, and his strength after weakness, and youth after age, and joy after sorrow." (then follows a dialogue between Jacob and the King of Death).[17]

Note here that there were *two* remnants of Joseph's garment, one sent by *Joseph* to his father as a sign that he was still alive (since the garment *had not decayed*), and the other, torn and smeared with blood, brought by *Judah* to his father as a sign that Joseph was dead. Moroni actually quotes Jacob ("Now behold, this was the language of Jacob") as saying: "Now behold, this giveth my soul sorrow; nevertheless, my soul hath joy in my son . . ." (Alma 46:25 f.) Compare this with Judah's statement in the Old World account, that the undecayed garment caused Jacob as much joy as the bloody garment caused him sorrow. In both accounts Jacob is described as being near to death—hence Judah's haste to reach him with the garment and make amends for the evil he has done.

Surely there is "a type and a shadow" in this story, for the particular concern of Israel is with Joseph and Judah and how, after working at cross purposes they were reconciled after many years by the magnanimity of the one and the remorseful repentance of the other. It is another form of the symbolic story of the Two Sticks told in the 37th chapter of Ezekiel. But aside from the great symbolic force of the tale, there can be no doubt that the story told by Moroni as one familiar to all the people actually was one that circulated among the Jews in ancient times and was taken to the East by them, being like much early Jewish lore completely lost in the West. It was totally unknown to the world in which Joseph Smith lived.

These interesting little details are typical apocryphal variations on a single theme, and the theme is the one Moroni mentions; the rent garment of Joseph is the symbol both of his suffering and his deliverance, misfortune and preservation. Such things in the Book of Mormon illustrate the widespread ramifications of Book of Mormon culture, and the recent declaration of Albright and other scholars that the ancient Hebrews had cultural roots in every civilization of the Near East. This is an acid test that no forgery could pass; it not only opens a window on a world we dreamed not of, but it brings to our unsuspecting and uninitiated minds a first glimmering suspicion of the true scope and vastness of a book nobody knows.

Questions

1. Why has the denunciation of war and the awareness of its evils in no way diminished the frequency of ferocity of wars?

2. Was Moroni justified in putting to death those who would not "support the cause of freedom"? Was that real freedom?

3. Is there any justification for war? Can we break the commandments of God every day and then profess indignation because he allows us to suffer the effects of our folly?

4. What things are strange and unfamiliar in the Title of Liberty story?

5. What Old World parallels are there to these things?

6. What common origin is indicated to explain the resemblance?

7. How does the concept of war in the *Milhama* Scroll and Alma differ from the modern view?

8. What considerations justify seeking illuminating parallels between the Book of Mormon customs and beliefs and practices as far away as Iran? Could there be any real connection between the two?

9. What indication is there in the story of Moroni's banner that the Nephites were familiar with apocryphal teachings since lost to the world?

10. Discuss the attitude of the Book of Mormon towards types and symbols.

To what extent can such things be realities?

Lesson 18

LIFE IN THE DESERT

1. Man versus Nature

Prospectus of Lesson 18: In Nephi's description of his father's eight years of wandering in the desert we have an all but foolproof test for the authenticity of the Book of Mormon. It can be shown from documents strewn down the centuries that the ways of the desert have not changed, and many first-hand documents have actually survived from Lehi's age and from the very regions in which he wandered. These inscriptions depict the same hardships and dangers as those described by Nephi, and the same reaction to them. A strong point for the Book of Mormon is the claim that Lehi's people survived only by "keeping to the more fertile parts of the wilderness," since that is actually the custom followed in those regions, though the fact has only been known to westerners for a short time. Nephi gives us a correct picture of hunting practices both as to weapons and methods used. Even the roughest aspects of desert life at its worst are faithfully and correctly depicted.

The Unchanging Ways of the Desert: The problem of survival in the deserts has two aspects—the challenge of nature and the challenge of man. It would be hard to say which was the more formidable danger of the two in the Arabian desert of Lehi's day or, so far as one can tell, of any day before or since. "The way of life of these desert tribes has changed but little through the millennia," writes Ebers. "The ancients already describe them as being robbers who also engage in trade."[1] The immense corpus of Arabic poetry which has survived and increased through the last thousand years depicts the same dangers and problems of life in the desert that confront the traveler today; a thousand years before the poets we find a vast number of inscriptions scratched in the rocks by travelers and now gathered into massive collections from all parts of the peninsula; many of these inscriptions go back to Lehi's day. Older than the inscriptions and the poets are the Babylonian and Egyptian accounts that tell us of the same forbidding and dangerous wastes and of their equally forbidding and dangerous inhabitants. Egyptian texts four thousand years old speak with pity and contempt of the "poor Amu" who can never stop wandering in his terrible wild country.[2]

But before going into the Old World record, we shall, according to our plan, first present what the Book of Mormon has to say about the perils and hardships which nature put in the way of Lehi's party in the desert. (In the next lesson we shall consider the human obstacles.)

Hardship in the Desert: "We have wandered much in the wilderness," the daughters of Ishmael complained on their father's death, ". . . and we have suffered much affliction, hunger, thirst, and fatigue; and after all these sufferings we must perish in the wilderness with hunger." (1 Ne. 16:35.) Lehi's sons confidently expected to perish in the wilderness and in despair their mother cried out to Lehi ". . . . we perish in the wilderness!" (1 Ne. 5:2.) On the last long stretch they ". . . did travel and wade through much affliction in the wilderness; . . . and did live upon raw meat in the wilderness. . . ." (1 Ne. 17:1-2) From the first they ". . . suffered many afflictions and much difficulty, yea even so much that we cannot write them all. . . ." (1 Ne. 17:6) At times their sufferings and afflictions in the wilderness became so great that even Lehi began to murmur! (1 Ne. 16:20.) While in the best Arab fashion they kept to " . . . the more fertile parts of the wilderness. . . ." (1 Ne. 16:16), and thus kept their animals in motion, for themselves a good deal of the time there was only meat, for they got their food by ". . . slaying food by the way, with our bows and our arrows and our stones and our slings." (1 Ne. 16:15.) So dependent were they on hunting for food that when Nephi broke his fine steel bow, the wooden bows having " . . . lost their springs . . ." (1 Ne. 16:21), there was no food at all to be had and the party was in great danger of

starvation: " . . . being much fatigued, because of their
journeying, they did suffer much for the want of food."
(1 Ne. 16:19.) When Nephi finally returned from a
mountain top with game, and " . . . they beheld that I
had obtained food, how great was their joy! . . . "
(1 Ne. 16:30-32.)

Along with hunger and thirst sheer exhaustion plays
its part. The effort of travel entailed much fatigue, sufferings and afflictions, much difficulty and wading
through much affliction. The difficulty of the terrain often made hard going, as we shall see in the account of Lehi's dreams, but behind everything one feels
the desolation and exhaustion of a sun-cursed land.
Where else would it be necessary for well-equipped
and experienced travelers to suffer *thirst?* (1 Ne. 16:35.)

The Arabs Testify: Turning now to the corpus of
inscriptions, we find an eloquent commentary to Nephi's
text. An inscription of Lehi's own contemporary, Nebuchadnezzar, tells us, referring to the deserts between
"the upper sea" and the "lower sea", i.e., North Arabia,
of "steep paths, closed roads, where the step is confined. There was no place for food, difficult roads,
thirsty roads have I passed through . . . "[3] "O Radu,"
says one old writing scratched by some Bedouin in the
rocks of Lehi's desert, "help Shai' in a country exposed
to the sun!"[4] Here Radu is a tribal deity, and Shai is the
wanderer. Another writes: that "he journeyed with the
camels in the years in which the heat of the sun was intense (?), and he longed for Saiyad his brother. So O
Allat (a female deity) (grant) peace and coolness!"[5]
"O Radu," another prays, "deliver us from adversity,
and may we be saved!"[6] The word for "saved" *nakhi*, reminds us of what was said above of the feeling of dependence on God which the desert forces upon men. The
constant feeling of being lost, and the realization that
without help one can never be saved is a real as well as a
"spiritual" one in the desert. "O Radu, deliver us from
misfortune, that we may live!"[7] This inscription from

the Thamud country just east of Lehi's route, sounds like
scripture—but there is nothing figurative about it. "O
Allat," another traveler prays, "deliver 'Abit from burning thirst!"[8] "On a journey," Burckhardt tells us, "the
Arabs talk but little; for . . . much talking excites thirst,
and parches up the palat . . ."[9] No wonder they give the
impression of being "a lonesome and solemn people!"
"It is no exaggeration," writes a present-day authority,
"to say that the Bedouin is in an almost permanent state
of starvation."[10] "Many times between their waterings,"
Doughty reports, "there is not a single pint of water
left in the greatest *sheikh's* tent."[11]

Rate of March: Lehi's party is described as moving
through the desert for a few days (three or four, one
would estimate) and then camping "for the space of a
time." This is exactly the way the Arabs move. Caravan speeds run between two and one-quarter and
three and nine-tenths miles an hour, thirty miles being,
according to Cheesman, "a good average" for the day,
and sixty miles being the absolute maximum."[12] "The
usual estimate for a good day's march is reckoned by
Arab writers at between twenty-eight and thirty miles;
however, in special or favorable circumstances it may
be nearly forty."[13] On the other hand, a day's slow
journey "for an ass-nomad, moving much slower than
camel-riders, is twenty miles."[14]

The number of days spent camping at any one place
varies (as in the Book of Mormon) with circumstances.
"From ten to twelve days is the average time a Bedouin
encampment of ordinary size will remain on the same
ground," according to Jennings Bramley, who, however,
observes, "I have known them to stay in one spot for
as long as five or six months."[15] The usual thing is to
camp as long as possible in one place until "it is soiled
by the beasts, and the multiplication of fleas becomes
intolerable, and the surroundings afford no more pas-
tureage, (then) the tents are pulled down and the men
decamp."[16] "On the Syrian and Arabic plain," accord-

ing to Burckhardt "the Bedouins encamp in summer . . .
near wells, where they remain often for a whole month."[17]
Lehi's time schedule thus seems to be a fairly normal
one, and the eight years he took to cross Arabia argue
neither very fast nor very slow progress—the Beni Hilal
took twenty-seven years to go a not much greater distance. After reaching the seashore Lehi's people simply
camped there "for the space of many days," until a revelation again put them in motion.

The More Fertile Parts of the Wilderness: "The goal of
the migration is always the watering place," we are told.[18]
"Ranging from one spring to another," writes Conder,
" . . . the nomads seem to resemble the Jews at the
period when, for forty years, they lived in the wilderness."[19] The resemblance was not lost on Lehi's people.
Speaking of the wells which Abraham dug, "and which
had to be reopened by Isaac," Conder notes that they
"were perhaps similar to the hufeiyir, or 'pits' which
the Arabs now dig in the beds of the great valleys. . . ."[20]
These were "the more fertile parts of the wilderness"
of which Nephi speaks. "The wadis," writes Norman
Lewis, " . . . actually simplify long distance travel. In
the dry season they become natural roads of great
length and in places are often several hundred yards
wide. Their beds are firm and flat, and in them is to
be found whatever moisture or vegetation exists in an
arid country. For these reasons they are a boon to caravans, which often follow their courses for hundreds of
miles."[21] Not long ago Professor Frankfort wrote of
the south desert, "The secret of moving through this
desolation has at all times been kept by the Bedouin.
. . ."[22] Intrepid explorers of our own day have learned
the secret, however, and Lehi knew of it too. Like a
sudden flash of illumination comes the statement that
Lehi by divine instruction " . . . led us in the more fertile
parts of the wilderness." (1 Ne. 16:16.) Woolley and
Lawrence describe such "more fertile parts" as "stretching over the flat floor of the plain in long lines like

hedges . . ."[23] They are the depressions of dried-up watercourses, sometimes hundreds of miles long. They furnish, according to Bertram Thomas, "the arteries of life in the steppe, the path of Bedouin movement, the habitat of animals by reason of the vegetation—scant though it is—which flourishes in their beds alone . . ."[24] In Arabia it is this practice of following "the more fertile parts of the wilderness" that alone makes it possible for both men and animals to survive. Cheesman designates as "touring" the practice followed by men and beasts of moving from place to place in the desert as spots of fertility shift with the seasons.[25]

Hunting on the Way: Mainzer has maintained that no ancient people were less given to hunting than the Jews.[26] If that is so, it is one more thing that sets Nephi off from "the Jews at Jerusalem," for he and his brothers, like the Arabs and the early Hebrews were great hunters. "My food is the chase, the earth my only bed . . ." is the boast of the true desert man.[27] As recently as Burckhardt's time ostriches were hunted quite near to Damascus and gazelles were "seen in considerable numbers all over the Syrian desert."[28] And there are still a few tribes, "the real men of the desert, who live by hunting gazelles, whose meat they dry and whose skin they wear. They have no flocks or camels, but travel as smiths, with asses as their beasts of burden. Even the Bedouins call them "the people of the desert, *'oma l-khala,* "dogs of the desert" or "people of the asses . . ." because they keep asses instead of camels. The early Egyptian tomb paintings show the people of the eastern deserts coming to Egypt always with asses instead of camels, yet on the other hand the Assyrian pictures show the desert people of Lehi's time as camel riders.[29] From the point of view of Nephi's story it makes little difference; in either case they would have hunted, sought the watering places, kept to the more fertile parts, and waded through much affliction!

Hunting Weapons: "Every Bedouin is a sportsman both from taste and necessity," writes one observer, who explains how in large families some of the young men are detailed to spend all their time hunting.[30] Nephi and his brothers took over the business of full-time hunters and in that office betray the desert tradition of the family, for Nephi had brought a fine steel bow from home with him, and he knew how to use it. He explicitly tells us that the hunting weapons he used were "bows, arrows, stones, and slings," (1 Ne. 16:15.) That is another evidence for the Book of Mormon, for Mainzer found that those were indeed the hunting weapons of the early Hebrews, who never used the classic hunting weapons of their neighbors, the sword, lance, javelin and club.[31] "The bow," he tells us, "was . . . usually made of hard, elastic wood, but quite often of *metal*. We do not know whether it resembled the Arabic or the strong Persian bow."[32] Evidence for metal bow he finds in 2 Sam. 22:35; Ps. 18:35; and Job 20:24. No need to argue, as we once did, in favor of a *partly* metal bow.[33]

Things looked dark when Nephi broke his fine steel bow, for the wooden bows of his brothers had ". . . lost their springs . . ." (1 Ne. 16:21, note the peculiarly Semitic use of the plural for a noun of quality), and though skilled in the art of hunting, they knew little enough about bow-making, which is a skill reserved to specialists even among primitives. Incidentally, archery experts say that a good bow will keep its spring for about one hundred thousand shots; from which one might calculate that the party at the time of the crisis had been traveling anything from one to three years. It was of course out of the question to make the familiar composite bow, and was something of a marvel when Nephi "did make out of wood a bow," (1 Ne. 16:23); for the hunter, the most conservative of men, would never dream of changing from a composite to a simple bow. Though it sounds simple enough when we read about it, it was almost as great a feat for Nephi to make a bow as it was for him to build a ship, and he is justly proud of his achievement.

According to the ancient Arab writers, the only bow-wood obtainable in all Arabia was the *nab'* wood that grew only "amid the inaccessible and overhanging crags" of Mount Jasum and Mount Azd, which are situated in the very region where, if we follow the Book of Mormon, the broken bow incident occurred.[34] How many factors must be correctly conceived and correlated to make the apparently simple story of Nephi's bow ring true! The high mountain near the Red Sea at a considerable journey down the coast, the game on the peaks, hunting with bow and sling, the finding of bow-wood viewed as something of a miracle by the party— what are the chances of reproducing such a situation by mere guesswork?

Beasts of Prey: Nephi mentions in passing the carnivora of the desert, which were one of the standard terrors and dangers of the way to the lone traveler. His brothers, he says, " . . . sought to take away my life, that they might leave me in the wilderness to be devoured by wild beasts." (1 Ne. 7:16.) Whether he was to be left living or dead (and both practices were followed),[35] the danger would be the same, for in any case he would be left alone. Thus we read in the ancient inscriptions of the desert of one who "encamped at this water-place; then the lion wounded him . . ."[36] Another reports that he "came from perilous places in the year in which Ahlan was ripped!"[37] Others tell of having their animals attacked by lions.[38] Another tells how "there pursued him a wolf that continued a year to assault him from a hiding-place."[39] All these were lone victims, and it is being alone that Nephi says would expose him to the beasts.

There was once carried on in certain learned journals a lively discussion on whether the Hebrews raised bees or not.[40] Certain it is that they knew and treasured wild honey, even as Lehi did (1 Ne. 17:5), who "prepared . . . honey in abundance" to take with him on his voyage across the ocean. (1 Ne. 18:5) It was wild honey, and there is no mention of his taking bees to the New World. Indeed bees and honey are never mentioned in the Book of Mormon as being in the New World at all.

Hunting in the mountains of Arabia to this day is carried out on foot and without hawks or dogs.[41] Nephi's discovery that the best hunting was only at " . . . the top of mountains . . ." (1 Ne. 16:30) agrees with later experience, for the oryx is "a shy animal that travels far and fast over steppe and desert in search of food but retires ever to the almost inaccessible sand-mountains for safety . . ."[42] In western Arabia the mountains are not sand but rock, and Burckhardt reports that "in these mountains between Medina and the sea, all the way northward (this is bound to include Lehi's area), mountain goats are met, and the leopards are not uncommon."[43] Julius Euting has left us vivid descriptions of the danger, excitement, and exhaustion that go with the hunting of the big game that abounds in these mountains, which are, by the way, very steep and rugged.[44]

Raw Meat: Nephi vividly remembers the eating of raw meat by his people in the desert and its salutary effect on the women, who "did give plenty of suck for their children, and were strong, yea, even like unto the men; . . ." (1 Ne. 17:2.) "Throughout the desert." writes Burckhardt "when a sheep or goat is killed, the persons present often eat the liver and kidney raw, adding to it a little salt. Some Arabs of Yemen are said to eat raw not only those parts, but likewise whole slices of flesh; thus resembling the Abyssinians and the Druses of Lebanon, who frequently indulge in raw meat, the latter to my own certain knowledge."[45] Nilus, writing fourteen centuries earlier, tells how the Bedouin of the Tih live on the flesh of wild animals, failing which "they slaughter a camel, one of their beasts of burden, and nourish themselves like animals from the raw meat," or

else scorch the flesh quickly in a small fire to soften it
sufficiently not to have to gnaw it "like dogs."[46] Only
too well does this state of things match the grim economy
of Lehi: " . . . they did suffer much for want of food,
. . ." (1 Ne. 16:19) ". . . we did live upon raw meat in
the wilderness. . . ." (1 Ne. 17:2.)

The Desert Route: It is obvious that the party went
down the eastern and not the western shore of the Red
Sea (as some have suggested) from the fact that they
changed their course and turned east at the nineteenth
parallel of latitude, and " . . . did travel nearly eastward
from that time forth . . . ," passing through the worst
desert of all, where they ". . . did travel and wade
through much affliction . . . ," and " . . . did live upon
raw meat in the wilderness. . . ." (1 Ne. 17:1-2) Had
the party journeyed on the west coast of the Red Sea,
they would have had only water to the east of them at
the 19th parallel and for hundreds of miles to come. But
why the 19th parallel? Because Joseph Smith is reliably
reported to have made an inspired statement to that
effect.[47] He did not know, of course, and nobody knew
until the 1930's, that only by taking a "nearly eastward"
direction from that point could Lehi have reached the
one place where he could find the rest and the materials
necessary to prepare for his long sea voyage.

Of the Qara Mountains which lie in that limited
sector of the coast of South Arabia which Lehi must
have reached if he turned east at the 19th parallel,
Bertram Thomas, one of the few Europeans who has
ever seen them, writes:

What a glorious place! Mountains three thousand feet high
basking above a tropical ocean, their seaward slopes velvety with
waving jungle, their roofs fragrant with rolling yellow meadows,
beyond which the mountains slope northwards to a red sand-
stone steppe . . . Great was my delight when in 1928 I suddenly
came upon it all from out of the arid wastes of the southern
borderlands.[48]

As to the terrible southeastern desert, "The Empty

Quarter," which seems from Nephi's account to have been the most utter desolation of all, Burton could write as late as 1852:

Of Rub'a al-Khali I have heard enough, from credible relators, to conclude that its horrid depths swarm with a large and half-starving population; that it abounds in Wadys, valleys, gullies and ravines, that the land is open to the adventurous traveler.[49]

The best western authority on Arabia was thus completely wrong about the whole nature of the great southeast quarter a generation after the Book of Mormon appeared, and it was not until 1930 that the world knew that the country in which Lehi's people were said to have suffered the most is actually the worst and most repelling desert on earth.

In Nephi's picture of the desert everything checks perfectly. There is not one single slip amid a wealth of detail, the more significant because it is so casually conveyed.

Questions

1. What evidence is there for the claim that conditions of life in the deserts of the Near East have remained virtually unchanged for thousands of years?

2. Why is this important in examining Nephi's narrative?

3. What are the natural obstacles to travel in the wilderness according to the Book of Mormon?

4. According to the ancient inscriptions? What is the nature of these inscriptions?

5. What is meant by "the more fertile parts of the wilderness"? Does the Book of Mormon refer to them in the correct context?

6. What were the hunting methods of Nephi and his brethren? What weapons did they use?

7. What is the significance of these weapons as evidence for the authenticity of the story?

8. What are the implications of eating raw meat? Can such things be?

9. What route did Lehi's people take through the desert?

10. What is the significance of the 19th parallel as evidence for the authenticity of Nephi's account? How does the story of the broken bow confirm the record?

Lesson 19

LIFE IN THE DESERT

2. Man versus Man

Prospectus of Lesson 19: A valuable passage about fire-making in 1 Nephi furnishes the perfect clue to the nature of Lehi's contacts in the desert. He avoided all contact whenever possible. This behavior is perfectly consistent with the behavior of modern Arabs and with known conditions in the desert in Lehi's day. The whole story of Lehi's wandering centers about his tent, which in Nephi's account receives just the proper emphasis and plays just the proper role. Another authentic touch is Lehi's altar-building and sacrificing. The troubles and tensions within Lehi's own family on the march, and the way they were handled and the group led and controlled by Lehi's authority are entirely in keeping with what is known of conditions both today and in ancient times. The description of the role and the behavior of women in 1 Nephi are also perfectly consistent with what is known of actual conditions from many sources.

Nephi's account is very enlightening on the subject of human relationships in the desert. These are to be considered under two heads: (1) contacts with other parties in the desert, and (2) relationships within the group.

"Not Much Fire": The key to the first of these is an enlightening comment on cooking and firemaking:

For the Lord had not hitherto suffered that we should make much fire, as we journeyed in the wilderness; for he said: I will make thy food become sweet, that ye cook it not; and I will also be your light in the wilderness . . .(1 Ne. 17:12-13.)

It was only "as we journeyed" that the Lord restricted fire-making; there was no restraint once they reached the seashore, nor was fire ever forbidden absolutely, but only "much fire". Since there was nothing wrong with fire as such, why the limitation? "I well remember," writes Bertram Thomas, "taking part in a discussion upon the unhealthfulness of campfires by night; we discontinued them forthwith in spite of the bitter cold."[1] Major Cheeseman's guide would not even let him light a tiny lamp to jot down star readings, and they never dared build a fire on the open plain where it "would attract the attention of a prowling raiding party over long distances and invite a night attack."[2] Once in a while in a favorably sheltered depression "we dared to build a fire that could not be seen from a high spot," writes Raswan.[3] That is, fires are not absolutely out of the question, but rare and risky—not *much* fire, was Lehi's rule. And fires in the daytime are almost as risky as at night. Palgrave tells how his party were forced "lest the smoke of our fire should give notice to some distant rover, to content ourselves with dry dates," instead of cooked food.[4]

Shunning Human Contacts the Safe Rule: We have seen that Lehi left Jerusalem secretly and that the Lord is careful to conceal from the wicked the movements of those whom he "leadeth away into precious lands." Nephi persuaded Zoram to join Lehi's party "that the Jews might not know concerning our flight into the wilderness." (1 Ne. 4:36.) It was policy on Lehi's part to avoid human contact in the desert as much as he possibly could, but even had his party been ordinary Arabs they would have done the same. The only contacts travelers through the desert should make are those necessary to obtain escorts, but often it is impossible to get any escort at all. "We still feared to proceed without the company of an escort," writes Hariri of a journey across the Syrian desert to Damascus, "And we therefore sought one from all the tribes of the Bedu and tried everything to get it; but still it was impossible to find any escort." So they went without, in fear and trembling.

And after that we proceeded on our intended journey with prayers instead of drivers to encourage our camels, and words instead of warriors to protect our goods . . .[5]

Everyone is suspicious of everyone else in the desert, because no one is exactly sure of his status. "The camps are scarcely ever placed in the immediate

neighborhood of water, but the Arab women go perhaps a mile away from the tents and bring the needful
supply in black skins," Conder reports. "I have often
asked the Arabs why they did not pitch close to the
water, but never got a satisfactory answer. They have
probably learned from experience that the great requisite
for a camp seems to be shelter and concealment."[6] While
in the desert the Arab dreads the approach of anyone—
even a friend. Hariri tells how when he saw a figure
approaching his camp, "I discovered his turning aside
to the place that I occupied, and commended myself
to God for protection against intruders."[7]

Many have noted that "the Bedouins are not
ashamed of acting like cowards,"[8] and that they will
always beat a retreat unless "they are really in a safe
majority, and if they are outnumbered, they hide in
the undulations of the ground, in a manner which would
excite the admiration of any military man."[9] The inscriptions are full of scouting, spying, dodging, evading:

> N. was on the lookout for his imprisoned fellows. So, O
> Baal-Samin, rest to those who are distressed.[10]
> N. went away in the evening in order to go eastward into
> the desert. So, O Allat, grant return and protection from the
> enemy![11]
> N. was heavy-hearted on account of his brother and on
> account of his father and on account of his uncle. And he was
> afraid of the enemy. So, O Allat and Gad-'Awihh, grant pro-
> tection. And he found traces of his fellows and longed for
> them. . . .[12]

That is a grim little testimony to the sort of thing
that might easily have happened to Lehi's family!

> N. was on the lookout. So, O Allat, (give) deliverance from
> the plotter.[13]

One group of inscriptions, that can be dated 123-4
A.D., contains the names of many who describe themselves as "on the lookout" and the Thamud inscriptions
contain a whole class of texts dealing with "spying
and being on the lookout."[14] One is "by W. son of
Malik son of I., and he escaped with the cattle into
this valley. So O Allat (give) peace."[15]

All these dramatic little inscriptions, which are counted by the hundreds, have been discovered within the last sixty years. How eloquently they recall Lehi and his predicament! Thomas lays down a rule which is to be observed by all travelers in the desert, even to this day—"An approaching party may be friend, but is always assumed to be foe."[16] In the words of the ancient poet Zuhair, "He who travels should consider his friend to be his enemy."[17]   St. Nilus describes Bedouins on the march in the fifth century as possessed by the same jittery nervousness and unbearable tension that make the accounts of Cheeseman, Philby, Thomas, Palgrave, Burckhardt, and the others such exciting reading.   At the merest sign of an armed man, he says, his Bedu fled in alarm "as if seized by panic fear," and kept on fleeing, "for fear makes them exaggerate danger and causes them to imagine things far beyond reality, magnifying their dread in every instance."[18] Just so their modern descendants "live always under the impression that an invasion is on the way, and every suspicious shadow or movement on the horizon calls for attention," according to the astute Baldensperger.[19] This almost hysterical state of apprehension is actually a prime condition of survival in the desert: "A bedawy never tells his name," says the writer just quoted, "nor his tribe, nor his business, nor the whereabouts of his people, even if he is in a friendly district. They are and must be very cautious . . . a word out of season may bring death and destruction."[20] When the Beni Hilal migrate, it is "under the darkness of the night, under the obscuring veil of the rain," by-passing settled places in darkness and in silence. What can better describe such a state of things than the Book of Morman expression, "a lonesome and a solemn people"? Doughty said he had never met a "merry" man among the Arabs— and there is no humor in the Book of Mormon. This mood is hardly accidental. If the Hebrew gets his brooding qualities from his desert ancestors, why not the Lamanite?

A Hostile Land: But what was there to be afraid of? First of all, resentment of intrusion. "A Chinese wall seems to surround this land," a recent visitor reports, "jealously guarded from foreign intrusion." Everyone, he says, not excluding Moslems, is suspect, and "it is extremely difficult to invent a plausible reason for one's presence there."[21] What kind of a reason could Lehi invent? The whole of Arabia proper is "to this very day almost absolutely closed to the investigations of science."[22] "The Arab tribes are in a state of almost perpetual war against each other. . . ." Burckhardt says,[23] but even friends do not trust each other: "They often treat their *confederates,* of a more peaceful turn of mind than themselves, in a very oppressive way," Harmer reports, citing I Sam. 25:7.[24]

Now we have seen that in Lehi's day the whole Arabian Peninsula was in a state of great upheaval and unrest; it was a time of major migrations when nobody knew who was trespassing where. When Lehi's party was the smaller one it would skillfully avoid contact, when it was the larger one the other side would just as skillfully avoid contact! The wilderness of Judaea, writes Dupont-Sommer, "throughout the history of Palestine, has served as a place of refuge for bandits and outlaws and all wanted men."[25] But this was far more conspicuously the case in the Nejd, the southern desert of Idumea into which Lehi escaped.[26] Lehi's position was pretty much that of the sheikh of the Amer, one of whose young men killed the vicious and oppressive Sherif or Governor of Mecca. So the family had to flee, and exactly reversing Lehi's route went north through the Arabah to Gaza and thence to Moab, where they became the ruling tribe in the Middle Ages.[27] In their wanderings, spying and scouting is their main activity, their whole march is one protracted reconnaissance in enemy territory; they are uprooted and homeless, outcasts from their native city, and to survive must play a skillful game of dodging and evading.[28]

The Raiders: But the main danger to travel in the desert, even in the best of times, has always been the raiders. *Tul-ma henna hayyun inghaziy:* "as long as we breathe we must make raids!" is the saying of the Bedouins.[28] The raid is a highly honorable and traditional undertaking, and includes attacks on neighboring tribes as well as on traveling caravans. It is undertaken whenever possible. "The Arabs may be styled a nation of robbers," Burckhardt writes, "whose principal occupation is plunder, the constant subject of their thoughts. . . . The Arab robber considers his profession honorable; and the term *haramy* (robber) is one of the most flattering terms that could be conferred on a youthful hero. The Arab robs his enemies, his friends, and his neighbors. . . . The Bedouins have reduced robbery, in all its branches, to a complete and regular system. . . ."[29] A hundred years before Burckhardt, Harmer tells us that "the Arabs wait for caravans with the most violent avidity, looking about them on all sides, raising themselves up on their horses, running here and there to see if they cannot perceive any smoke, or dust, or tracks on the ground, or any other marks of people passing along." Once they have spotted a caravan they follow it all day, keeping just out of sight, "and in the night they silently fall upon the camp, and carry off one part of it before the rest are got under arms."[31] And so it was in Lehi's day, when his friend and contemporary Jeremiah wrote: "Thou hast laid in ambush for them, as the Arabians in the wilderness." (Jer. 3:2.)

The Tent: It is most significant how Nephi speaks of his father's tent; it is the official center of all administration and authority. First the dogged insistence of Nephi on telling us again and again that "my father dwelt in a tent." (1 Ne. 2:15, 9:1, 10:16, 16:6.) So what? we ask, but to an Oriental that statement says everything. Since time immemorial the whole population of the Near East have been either tent-dwellers or house-dwellers, the people of the *bait ash-sha'r* or the *bait at-tin,* "houses of hair or houses of clay."[32] It was Harmer who first pointed out that one and the same person may well alternate between the one way of life and the other, and he cites the case of Laban in Genesis 31, where "one is surprised to find both parties so suddenly equipped with tents for their accommodation in traveling," though they had all along been living in houses.[33] Not only has it been the custom for herdsmen and traders to spend part of the year in tents and part in houses, but "persons of distinction" in the East have always enjoyed spending part of the year in tents for the pure pleasure of a complete change.[34]

It is clear from 1 Ne. 3:1, 4:38, 5:7, 7:5, 21-22, 15:1, 16:10, that Lehi's tent is the headquarters for all activities, all discussion and decisions.

". . . Have Place with Us": Nephi's invitation to Zoram was: ". . . if thou wilt go down into the wilderness to my father, thou shalt have *place* with us. . . . (1 Ne. 4:34.) Accordingly after an exchange of oaths, ". . . We departed into the wilderness, and journeyed unto the tent of our father," (1 Ne. 4:38)—with their own tents, of course. (1 Ne. 3:9.) The first thing a suppliant does seeking "place" with a tribe is to "put up his tent near that of his protector, take a woolen string from his head and lay it around the neck of his new patron saying, 'I seek protection with thee, O So-and-so.'" To this the answer is: "Be welcome to my authority! We receive all of you but what is bad. Our *place* is now your *place*."[35] From that moment the newcomer is under the full protection of the sheikh and "has place" with the tribe. The immemorial greeting of welcome to those accepted as guests in any tent is *Ahlan wa-Sahlan wa-Marhaban*: in which *ahlan* means either a family or (as in Hebrew) a tent, *sahlan* a smooth place to sit down and *marhaban* the courteous moving aside of the people in the tent so as to make room for one more. The emphasis is all on "having place with us".[36]

Councils in the Tent: The main activity in the sheikh's

tent is always the same. It is talk. In every Arab tribe
the sheikh's tent is before all the place where the councils
of the tribe are held; says Musil, "the tent of tryst."[36]
When they are not raiding and hunting, the men of
the tribe sit in the chief's tent and talk.[37]   To make up
for the long silence on the march—necessary to avoid
undue thirstiness, "When they assemble under their tents,
a very animated conversation is kept up among them without interruption."[38]   So it is the most natural thing in
the world for Nephi after being out alone to return to
the tent of his father and find his brothers there," . . .
and they were disputing one with another concerning
the things which my father had spoken unto them."
(1 Ne. 15:1-2.) And it was perfectly natural for him
to join the discussion and win the day with a long and
eloquent speech.

"The tent is the family hearth, the common bond
and something of the incarnation of the family," writes
De Boucheman. "*Beyt* means 'house' in Arabic in the
sense that we speak of a royal or princely 'house'; it is
likewise the term designating the family group, and em-
braces more than just one family *ahl* but is less comprehensive than the tribe."[39]   That is a perfect description
of the society that traveled with Lehi—more than one
family, less than a clan—properly designated by the
peculiar word tent, exactly as Nephi uses it.   Zoram
came not to his father's family or tribe, but to his tent.
In modern times a great tribe would number about 1000
people or 300 tents, the average tribe about 100 tents.
But "the scantiness of pasture and water supplies obliges
the Arabs to divide themselves into numerous small
camps . . . The Sheikh of the tribe, with his family, generally collects the largest encampment round his tent,
and this forms the rendezvous of the rest."[40]   To seek
pasture "the whole tribe . . . spreads itself over the
plain in parties of 3 or 4 tents each . . ."[41]

Lehi's Altar: As his first act, once his tent had been
pitched for his first important camp, Lehi ". . . built
an altar of stones, and made an offering unto the Lord,

and gave thanks to the Lord" (1 Ne. 2:7)   It is for all the world as if he had been reading Robertson Smith. "The ordinary mark of a Semitic sanctuary [Hebrew as well as Arabic, that is] is the sacrificial pillar, cairn, or rude altar . . . upon which sacrifices are presented to the god. . . . In Arabia we find no proper altar but in its place a rude pillar or heap of stones beside which the victim is slain."[42]   It was at this same altar of stones that Lehi and his family ". . . did offer sacrifice and burnt offerings . . . and they gave thanks unto the God of Israel" (1 Ne. 5:9) upon the safe return of his sons from their dangerous expedition to Jerusalem. When Raswan reports, "A baby camel was brought up to Mishal'il's tent as a sacrificial offering in honor of the safe return of Fuaz," we cannot help thinking of some such scene before the tent of Lehi on the safe return of his sons.[43] This is what the Arabs call a *dhabiyeh-l-kasb,* a sacrifice to celebrate the successful return of warriors, hunters, and raiders to the camp. "This sacrifice," writes Jaussen, "is always in honor of an ancestor,"[44] and Nephi twice mentions the tribal ancestor Israel in his brief account. In the best desert manner Lehi immediately after the thanksgiving fell to examining the "spoils". (1 Ne. 5:10.)

To this day the Bedouin makes sacrifice on every important occasion, not for magical and superstitious reasons, but because he "lives under the constant impression of a higher force that surrounds him . . ." St. Nilus in the oldest known eyewitness account of life among the Arabs of the Tih says, "They sacrifice on altars of crude stones piled together."[45]   That Lehi's was such an altar would follow not only the ancient law demanding uncut stones, but also from the Book of Mormon expression "an altar of stones," which is not the same thing as "a stone altar." Such little heaps of stones, surviving from all ages, are still to be seen throughout the south desert.

We have seen that the first thing the Jewish merchant in Arabia would do on settling in a place, whether

a camp or town, was to set up an altar.[46] Bertholet has
argued that since the family and the house were identical
in the common cult of hospitality, to be received as a
guest was to be received into the family cult of which
the center was always the altar.[47]

Family Affairs: But how do the members of such
closed corporations get along together? It is the domestic history that presents the real challenge to whoever would write a history of Bedouin life. To handle
it convincingly would tax the knowledge of the best
psychologist, and woe to him if he does not know the
peculiar ways of the eastern desert, which surprise and
trap the unwary westerner at every turn.

The ancient Hebrew family was a peculiar organization, self-sufficient and impatient of any authority beyond its own. "These are obviously the very conditions,"
writes Nowack, "which we can still observe today among
the Bedouins."[48] Thus, whether we turn to Hebrew or
to Arabic sources for our information, the Book of Mormon must conform. Lehi feels no pangs of conscience
at deserting Jerusalem, and when his sons think of home,
it is specifically the land of their inheritance, their own
family estate, for which they yearn. Not even Nephi
evinces any loyalty to the "Jews at Jerusalem," split
up as they were into squabbling interest-groups.

While Lehi lived, he was the sheikh, of course,
and the relationship between him and his family as
described by Nephi is accurate in the smallest detail.
With the usual deft sureness and precision, the book
shows Lehi leading—not ruling—his people by his per-
suasive eloquence and spiritual ascendancy while
his murmuring sons follow along exactly in the manner
of Philby's Bedouins—"an undercurrent of tension in
our ranks all day . . ." great difficulty to "appease their
evil, envious souls. . . ."[49] "We left Suwaykan," says
Burton, "all of us in the crossest of humors. . . . So
'out of temper' were my companions, that at sunset, of
the whole party, Omar Effendi was the only one who
would eat supper. The rest sat upon the ground, pouting

and grumbling . . . Such a game as naughty children, I have seldom seen played even by Oriental men . . ."[50]

"Hate and Envy Here Annoy": The character and behavior of Laman and Lemuel conform to the normal pattern. How true to the Bedouin way are their long bitter brooding and dangerous outbreaks! How perfectly they resemble the Arabs of Doughty, Burton, Burckhardt and the rest in their sudden and complete changes of heart after their father has lectured them, fiery anger yielding for the moment to a great impulse to humility and an overwhelming repentance, only to be followed by renewed resentment and more unhappy wrangling! They cannot keep their discontent to themselves, but are everlastingly "murmuring." "The fact that all that happens in an encampment is known, that all may be said to be related to each other, renders intrigue almost impossible."[51] "We were all one family and friendly eyes," Doughty recollects, but then describes the other side of the picture—"Arab children are ruled by entreaties. . . . I have known an ill-natured child lay a stick to the back of his good cherished mother, and the Arabs say, 'many is the ill-natured lad among us that, and he be strong enough, will beat his own father'."[52]

The fact that Laman and Lemuel were grown-up children did not help things. "The daily quarrels between parents and children in the desert constitute the worst feature of the Bedouin character," says Burckhardt, and thus describes the usual source of the trouble: "The son . . . arrived at manhood is too proud to ask his father for any cattle . . . the father is hurt at finding that his son behaves with haughtiness towards him, and thus a breach is often made."[53] The son, especially the eldest one, does not feel that he is getting what is coming to him and behaves like the spoiled child he is. The father's attitude is described by Doughty, telling how a great sheikh dealt with his son—"The boy, oftentimes disobedient, he upbraided, calling him his life's torment, Sheytan, only never menacing him, for that were far from a Bedouin father's mind."[54]   It is common, says Burckhardt (*Ibid.,* I, 114) for mothers and sons to stick together in their frequent squabbles with the father, in which the son "is often expelled from the paternal tent for vindicating his mother's cause."[55] Just so Sariah takes the part of her sons in chiding her own husband, making the same complaints against him that they did (1 Ne. 5:2), and she rates him roundly when she thinks he has been the cause of their undoing.

Authority in the Family: Is it any wonder that Laman and Lemuel worked off their pent-up frustration by beating their youngest brother with a stick when they were once hiding in a cave? Every free man in the East carries a stick, the immemorial badge of independence and of authority and every man asserts his authority over his inferiors by his stick, "which shows that the holder is a man of position, superior to the workman or day-labourers. The government officials, superior officers, tax-gatherers, and schoolmasters use this short rod to threaten—or if necessary to beat—their inferiors, who-ever they may be."[56] The usage is very ancient. "A blow for a slave" is the ancient maxim in Ahikar, and the proper designation of an underling is *abida-l'asa,* "stick-servant." This is exactly the sense in which Laman and Lemuel intended their little lesson to Nephi, for when the angel turned the tables he said to them, ". . . Why do ye smite your younger brother with a rod? Know ye not that the Lord hath chosen *him* to be a ruler over *you* . . .?" (1 Ne. 3:29.)

Through it all, Laman, as the eldest son, is the most disagreeable actor. "When only one boy in the family, he is the tyrant, and his will dominates over all."[57] So we see Laman still thinking to dominate over all and driven mad that a younger brother should show superior talents. The rivalry between the sons of a sheikh "often leads to bloody tragedies in the sheikh's household,"[58] and Nephi had some narrow escapes.

In the sheikh's tent the councils of the tribe are held and all decisions concerning the journey are made (1 Ne. 15:1 ff), but "no sheikh or council of Arabs can

condemn a man to death, or even inflict a punishment . . .
it can only, when appealed to, impose a fine; it cannot
even enforce the payment of this fine.''[59]   Why, then,
if there was no power to compel them, did not Laman
and Lemuel simply desert the camp and go off on their
own, as discontented Arabs sometimes do?[60]   As a matter
of fact, they tried to do just that (1 Ne. 7:7), and in the
end were prevented by the two things which, according
to Philby, keep any wandering Bedouin party together—
fear and greed. For they were greedy. They hoped for
a promised land and when they reached the sea without finding it, their bitter complaint was, ''Behold, these
many years we have suffered in the wilderness, which
time we might have enjoyed our possessions . . .'' (1
Ne. 17:21.) And their position was precarious. Nephi
pointed out to them the danger of returning to Jerusalem
(1 Ne. 7:15), and where would they go if they deserted
their father? As we have seen, with these people, family
was everything, and the Arab or Jew will stick to ''his
own people'' because they are all he has in the world.
The family is the basic social organization, civil and
religious, with the father at its head. To be without
tribe or family is to forfeit one's identity in the earth;
nothing is more terrible than to be ''cut off from among
the people,'' and that is exactly the fate that is promised
Laman and Lemuel if they rebel. (1 Ne. 2:21.) ''Within
his own country,'' says an Arab proverb, ''the Bedouin
is a lion; outside of it he is a dog.''[61]

The Women: The women particularly had a hard
time in the wilderness (1 Ne. 17:20), as they always
do, since they do all the work, while the men hunt and
talk. ''The Arab talks in his tent, cares for the animals,
or goes hunting, while the women do all the work.''[62]
The women have their own quarters, which no man may
invade; and an older woman may talk up boldly to the
sheikh when no one else dares to, just as Sariah took
Lehi to task when she thought her sons were lost in
the desert. (1 Ne. 5:2-3.) All that saved Nephi's life
on one occasion was the intervention of ''one of the

daughters of Ishmael, yea, and also her mother, and one of the sons of Ishmael," (1 Ne. 7:19), for while "the Arab can only be persuaded by his own relations," he can only yield to the entreaties of women without losing face, and indeed is expected to yield to them, even robbers sparing a victim who appeals to them in the name of his wife, the daughter of his uncle.[63] "If a courageous woman demands that a raiding sheikh give back something so that her people will not starve, he is in honor bound to give her a camel. . . ."[64] Nephi marvelled at the strength that the women acquired in the midst of their trials and toils. ". . . Our women did give plenty of suck for their children, and were strong, yea, even like unto the men; . . ." (1 Ne. 17:2.) This phenomenon has aroused the wonder and comments of travelers in our own day.[65]

Mourning Customs: It was the daughters of Ishmael who mourned for him and chided Lehi for his death. (1 Ne. 16:34-35.) Budde has shown that the Old Hebrew mourning customs were those of the desert, in which "The young women of the nomad tribes mourn at the grave, around which they dance singing lightly." The Arabs who farm also put the body in a tent around which the women move as they mourn. "At the moment of a man's death, his wives, daughters, and female relations unite in cries of lamentation, (*welouloua*), which are repeated several times. . . ."[66] It is common in all the eastern deserts for the women to sit in a circle in a crouching position while the woman nearest related to the dead sits silently in the middle—in Syria the corpse itself is in the middle; while singing, the women move in a circle and whenever the song stops there is a general wailing. The singing is in unison, Indian fashion. In some parts the men also participate in the rites, but where this is so the women may never mix with the men. They have a monopoly and a mourning tradition all of their own.[67] Mourning begins immediately upon death and continues among the Syrian Bedouins for seven days, a few hours a day. "All mourning is by mourning women and female relatives. No men are present . . .''[68] As is well known, no traditions are more unchanging through the centuries than funerary customs.[69]

Questions

1. What are the implications of the restrictions on campfires in the Book of Mormon?

2. What would Lehi's attitude be towards human contacts in the desert? Why?

3. What is the normal attitude of travelers in the desert to meetings with other parties?

4. Politically, what was the general state of things in the desert in Lehi's day?

5. What has always been the principal peril to travelers in the deserts of the Near East?

6. Was it so in Lehi's day? What is the evidence?

7. Why does Nephi so often repeat that his father dwelt in a tent?

8. What is the significance as evidence of Nephi's invitation to Zoram: "Thou shalt have place with us"?

9. Was Lehi guilty of a pagan practice in setting up an altar?

10. Is the behavior of Laman and Lemuel exaggerated or overdrawn in the Book of Mormon?

11. Is the part of the women in Nephi's account convincingly described?

12. What is the authentic touch in Nephi's account of the mourning for Ishmael?

LIFE IN THE DESERT

3. Lehi's Dreams

Prospectus of Lesson 20: Long ago Sigmund Freud showed that
dreams are symbolic, that they take their familiar materials from
everyday life and use them to express the dreamer's real thoughts
and desires. Lehi's dreams have a very authentic undertone of
anxiety of which the writer of 1 Nephi himself seems not fully
aware; they are the dreams of a man heavily burdened with
worries and responsibilities. The subjects of his unrest are two:
the dangerous project he is undertaking, and the constant opposition and misbehavior of some of his people, especially his two
eldest sons. It may be instructive for the student to look for
these two themes in the dreams discussed here. This lesson is
devoted to pointing out the peculiar materials of which Lehi's
dreams are made, the images, situations, and dream-scenery which
though typical can only come from the desert world in which
Lehi was wandering. These 13 snapshots of desert life are submitted as evidence for that claim.

A Desert Album, 13 Typical View Shots: In reporting
his father's dreams, Nephi has handed us, as it were, a
dozen vivid little snapshots or colored slides of the desert
country, that should prove to the most skeptical that
somebody who had a hand in the writing of the Book of
Mormon actually lived there.

1. The first is a picture of a lone traveler, Lehi
himself, in "a dark and dreary waste," (1 Ne. 8:4-7);
he has "traveled for the space of many hours in darkness," and in desperation "Began to pray unto the
Lord that he would have mercy on me."

Now if we turn to the vast photo-album of Arabic
lyric poetry or to the actual photographs of inscriptions
scratched on a thousand red rocks we will find almost
countless duplications of this particular snapshot—the
lone wanderer lost in the darkness. Of all the images
that haunt the early Arab poets this is by all odds the
commonest. It is the standard nightmare of the Arab;
and it is the supreme boast of every poet that he has

traveled long distances through dark and dreary wastes all alone.[1] That the poetry is born of grim reality may be seen from the inscriptions. One fellow, many centuries ago, reminds us of an event that took place "in the year in which he walked the whole night in the mire."[2] In the inscriptions a thousand lone wanderers send up in desperation prayers for help: "O Radu, help Shai!" "O Allat and Gad-'Awidh, grant protection!"[3] The great Abu Zaid said there was one prayer that he had learned in a dream which alone was his guarantee of safety in the desert: "Preserve me, O God . . . guard me in my person and my property . . . cover me with the curtain of thy grace. . . ."[4] Just as Nephi prays: "O Lord wilt thou encircle me around in the robe of thy righteousness!" as he wanders "in the path of the low valley." (2 Ne. 4:32-33.)

2. In the next picture we see "a large and spacious field" (1 Ne. 8:9), "a large and spacious field, as if it had been a world." (1 Ne. 8:20.) This in Arabic is the symbol of release from fear and oppression, the state of being "mabsut" or spread out. The Arab poet describes the world as a *maidan*, or large and spacious field,[5] an image borrowed by the earliest Christian writers, notably The Pastor of Hermes and the Pseudo-Clementines, for the religious symbolism of the *maidan* is as old as it is obvious.[6] Heroic literature is full of it.

3. The next picture is a close-up of a tree "the beauty thereof was far beyond, yea exceeding of all beauty; and the whiteness thereof did exceed the whiteness of the driven snow." (1 Ne. 11:8) ". . . whose fruit was desirable to make one happy . . . most sweet, above all that I ever before tasted . . . the fruit thereof was white, to exceed all the whiteness that I had ever seen . . . desirable above all other fruit." (1 Ne. 8:10-12.)

Where would one find such a tree in the poets? Only in the gardens of kings. The Persian King, and in imitation of him, the Byzantine Emperor and the Great Khan had such trees constructed artificially out of pure silver to stand beside their thrones and represent the

Tree of Life,[7] and if the reader has a genuine Persian or Turkish rug in his home he may discover that the central pattern, though stylized almost beyond recognition, represents either a flowing vase (the water of life) or a tree. The naturalistic curves and tendrils that surround the tree and run to the ornamental border are nothing less than the garden of Eden and the tree in the center is the Tree of Life." The rug pattern turns up on Cappadocian seals four thousand years old. Many hundreds of books and articles have been written on the Tree of Life as a symbol and a cult-object, but in no land on earth is the sight of a real tree, and especially a fruit-bearing one, greeted with more joy and reverence than in treeless Arabia, where certain trees are regarded as holy because of their life-giving propensities.[8]

4. In the next picture the man who has found the tree all by himself is looking for his family, that they too might be revived by the fruit. ". . . I began to be desirous that my family should partake of it also . . . and as I cast my eyes round about, that perhaps I might discover my family . . ." (1 Ne. 8:12-13.)

Perhaps the commonest and most touching theme in the vast corpus of Arabic desert inscriptions is the theme of longing and looking for one's family. When the writer comes to water and rests, he wishes for his family, and is usually smitten with terrible longing to see them. The desire is often intensified by the sudden recognition of some long forgotten landmark, as in the poets, or by noting an inscription put there, maybe years ago, by the lost loved ones, or some other little reminder of an earlier and happier visit to the place. Thus: "N. encamped in this place yearning . . . and he yearned for Shal-bal." ". . . and he found the inscriptions of A. and of his father, so he yearned for them."[9] ". . . and he found the inscription of his uncle, so he yearned for him." ". . . and he found the inscription of his uncle, and he longed . . ."[10] "N. camped here . . . and he was looking out for his imprisoned fellows. So O Baal-Samin, rest to those who are distressed."[11] "H. . . . found the inscriptions of his fellows and was sad. . . ."[12] "N. N. laid a stone on the tomb of his brother who was killed. . . . And he was looking out for his two brothers. . . ."[13]

5. In the next picture we see the missing family resting at a spring and trying to decide which way to go. From the spring comes "a river of water and it ran along, and it was near the tree . . . and I saw the head thereof a little way off. . . ." (1 Ne. 8:13-14.) This is the authentic "scenery of a desert oasis, with its rivers springing miraculously from nowhere and emptying themselves again perhaps in the desert sands."[14] The expression "river of water" is used only for small, local streams,[15] and here Lehi is so near the source of the clear little stream that he can recognize people standing there.

6. The next picture is largely a blur, for it represents ". . . a mist of darkness, insomuch that they who had commenced in the path did lose their way, that they wandered off and were lost." (1 Ne. 8:23.) We see other dim figures, guiding themselves to the tree by holding on to a rod or railing of iron as they ". . . did press forward through the mist of darkness. . . ." (1 Ne. 8:24)

In the many passages of Arabic poetry in which the hero boasts that he has traveled long distances through dark and dreary wastes all alone, the main source of terror (the heat and glare of the day, though nearly always mentioned, are given second place), and the culminating horror is almost always a "mist of darkness," a depressing mixture of dust, and clammy fog, which, added to the night, completes the confusion of any who wander in the waste.[16] Quite contrary to what one would expect, these dank mists are described by travelers in all parts of Arabia, and el-Ajajja, one of the greatest of early desert poets, tells how a mist of darkness makes it impossible for him to continue a journey to Damascus.[17] In its nature and effect Lehi's mist of darkness conforms to this strange phenomenon most exactly, always bearing in mind that this dream-mist was a super-mist, "exceeding great." A very ancient

Arabic tale recounts how when the Pharaoh of Joseph's time was on an expedition in the desert he found himself "in a dark valley, in which he heard a great outcry, yet he could see no people because of the thick darkness. . . ." There he did a strange thing—he built a great and wonderful castle of light, which was destroyed when Nebuchadnezzar conquered the Egyptian lands.[18]

7. This strongly suggests the picture of ". . . a great and spacious building; and it stood as it were in the air, high above the earth, on the other side of the river in the dark valley." (1 Ne. 8:26-27.) By now most of us have seen photographs of those wonderful ancient Arab houses (first "discovered" in the 1930's) built after the Babylonian design of Lehi's day, "ten and twelve-story skyscrapers that . . . represent genuine survivals of ancient Babylonian architecture,"[19] with their windows beginning, for the sake of defense, twenty to fifty feet from the ground. At night these lighted windows would certainly give the effect of being suspended above the earth. The eighth book of Hamdani's al-Iklil is devoted to describing the early castles of Arabia, "great and spacious buildings" which "stood as it were in the air, high above the earth." "And the castle of Ghumdan," writes Hamdani of one of the most famous, "had twenty stories of upper chambers, one above another. There is disagreement as to its heighth and breadth, for some say each of its walls measured a thousand by a thousand (i.e., cubits: a "great and spacious building" indeed!), while others say it was greater, and that each of its stories was ten cubits (15 feet) high."[20] In Arabic parlance the prime index of elegance and ease in any house or dwelling (including tents) is always "spaciousness."

8. The next picture shows a party going on in the big house: "And it was filled with people, both old and young, both male and female; and their manner of dress was exceeding fine; and they were in the attitude of mocking and pointing their fingers towards those who had come at and were partaking of the fruit." (1 Ne.

8:27.) As others came and joined the party they also joined in the mockery. (1 Ne. 8:33.) For "... the large and spacious building, which my father saw, is vain imaginations and the pride of the children of men. ..." (1 Ne. 12:18.) "And the multitude of the earth was gathered together; and I beheld that they were in a large and spacious building, like unto the building which my father saw ... the great and spacious building was the pride of the world; and it fell, and the fall thereof was exceeding great. ..." (1 Ne. 11:35-36.)

Now speaking of the great castle of Ghumdan, the poet Al-A'asha tells us:

And never was there a more splendid assemblage of people than the people of Ghumdan when they gathered. But dire calamity befell them, even as a wailing woman who has been utterly bereft.[21]

Hamdani gives other accounts of this and other castles, whose legends and whose silent ruins all point to the same moral lesson—the magnificent gathering in the great and spacious building high above the earth is doomed to the destruction reserved for the haughty and the wicked, just as Pharaoh's shining "castle of light" in the desert was said to have been destroyed by the same conqueror who leveled the pride of Jerusalem and Tyre in Lehi's day.

9. The mockery, mimicry and finger-pointing that passed for sport among the smartly-dressed people in the spacious house were directed at a poor little bedraggled band of wanderers, hungrily eating the fruit of the tree that stood nearby and terribly humiliated at having their poverty made an object of public merriment. "And after they had partaken of the fruit of the tree they did cast their eyes about as if they were ashamed" (1 Ne. 8:25), for all the fine people upstairs were "mocking and pointing their fingers towards those who had come and were partaking of the fruit. And after they had tasted of the fruit they were ashamed, because of those that were scoffing at them; ..." (1 Ne. 8:27-28.)

"The Bedouin in a town appears to be a very dif-

ferent man from the same person in the Desert," writes
Burckhardt, "He knows that the townspeople, whom
he despises, entertain absurd notions respecting his nation. . . . The wandering Arabs have certainly more wit
and sagacity than the people who live in the towns; their
heads are more clear, their spirits unimpaired by de-
bauchery . . ."[22] What is more natural than that the
"city Arabs" should "mock their desert cousins (whom
they secretly envy) with every show of open contempt"?
"The 'million' are educated in the towns," a recent
observer reports, "and they have always despised the
Bedouins, like a certain inhabitant of Jericho whom I
met in 1947, who, though quite uneducated himself, made
fun of certain poor desert Arabs who were passing by
with all their baggage: women, children, camels, chick-
ens, and the rest,"[23] a funny sight indeed. While every
visitor is impressed by the pride and nobility of the desert
Arab at home and notes his contempt for sedentary life;
this contempt is met by equal contempt, and "both sides
would consider themselves degraded" by a marriage
between the desert people and the dwellers in houses of
clay.[24] In town the Arab is, so to speak, on enemy
ground, and keenly sensitive to his position. Nobody
likes mockery — least of all the proud and touchy Arab.

10. As a result of being scoffed at, the victims beat
a retreat in confusion and humiliation: "and they fell
away into forbidden paths and were lost." (1 Ne. 8:28.)
If this seems an extreme reaction to a little loss of face,
we need only contemplate a touching inscription cut in
the rocks by one who "encamped at this place . . . and
he rushed forth in the year in which he was grieved by
the scoffing of the people: he drove together and lost
the camels . . . Rest to him who leaves (this inscription)
untouched!"[25]

11. Our snapshots include a number of moving
little pictures of parties lost in the desert. Because of the
mist of darkness one group "who had commenced in the
path did lose their way, that they wandered off and were
lost." (1 Ne. 8:23.) Many on their way to the great

and spacious building "were lost from his (Lehi's) view, wandering in strange roads." (1 Ne. 8:32.) It is the devil, we are told, who "leadeth them away into broad roads, that they perish and are lost." (1 Ne. 12:17.)

Need we say that to get lost in the desert is the chief waking dread and commonest nightmare of the Arab? The first westerner to explore Lehi's desert in modern times was Edward Robinson, who writes: "On the course northwest we launched forth into the 'great and terrible wilderness' . . . the desert, however, could not be said to be pathless; for the many camel-tracks showed that we were on a great road . . ."[26] To stray from that broad way, to become separated from one's party, is fatal. The religious imagery of "going astray" needs no long commentary. "No one will succeed in having his pilgrimage accepted," says Hariri, "who goes astray from the broad road of rectitude."[27] It is pure insanity to strike off for oneself in a moment of vain glory and self-sufficiency. "He went astray and made a hasty journey," one inscription recounts, "and O Dusares, protect him . . . !"[28] Another man tells us how "he found traces of his fellows and longed for them," while being "heavy hearted on account of his brother and on account of his father and on account of his uncle, and he was afraid of the enemy."[29] That is a sad little reminder of how families could get separated forever in the desert. Many of the personal inscriptions in the huge collection of Littmann are messages left behind in the desperate attempt to get in touch with relatives. Typical is No. 156: "By S. . . . and he found the inscription of his uncle, and he longed for him. So, O Allah, peace to him who leaves (this inscription untouched), and relief! . . ."[30]

12. To symbolize what is utterly inaccessible, Lehi is shown "a great and terrible gulf" (1 Ne. 12:18) "an awful gulf" (1 Ne. 15:28), a tremendous chasm with one's objective (the tree of life) maddeningly visible on the other side; all who have traveled in the desert know the feeling of utter helplessness and frustration at finding

one's way suddenly cut off by one of those appalling
canyons with perpendicular sides — nothing could be
more abrupt, more absolute, more baffling to one's plans,
and so will it be with the wicked in a day of reckoning.
Hariri describes death as "a chasm dread" which sooner
or later confronts all mortals.[31] Many recent photographs
show us that Burton was not exaggerating when he
described the "titanic walls, lofty donjons, huge pro-
jecting bastions, and moats full of deep shade," that are
a characteristic of Lehi's desert.[32] It is very much like the
"red rock" country of our own Southwest.

13.   One of the most remarkable of our snapshots is
that of a "fountain of filthy water" (1 Ne. 12:16) ". . .
the water which my father saw was filthiness." (1 Ne.
15:27.)

"And . . . many were drowned in the depths of the
fountain . . ." (1 Ne. 8:32.) This was a typical desert
sayl, a raging torrent of liquid filth that sweeps whole
camps to destruction. In the year 960 A.D., according
to Bar Hebraeus, a large band of pilgrims returning from
Mekkah "encamped in the bed of a brook in which water
had not flowed for a long time. And during the night,
whilst they were sleeping, a flood of water poured down
upon them all, and it swept them and all their possessions
out into the Great Sea, and they all perished."[33] Even
a mounted rider if he is careless may be caught off guard
and carried away by such a sudden spate of "filthy
water," according to Doughty.[34] One of the worst places
for these gully-washing torrents of liquid mud is in "the
scarred and bare mountains which run parallel to the
west coast of Arabia . . . the rainstorms break against
this long ridge and produce almost in a moment raging
torrents — the Arabic *sail*, spate — which sweep away
all obstacles without warning and with loss of life of
man and cattle."[35] This was the very region through
which Lehi traveled on his great trek.

"The situations (for camps) are not always, however, wisely chosen," one observer reports, "for, in more
than one instance, a sudden thunderstorm in the hills

has brought a flood down the great valleys, in the bottom of which smaller groups of tents are often found and the water has carried away and drowned the whole settlement, together with its flocks."[36]   Quite recently a visitor to Arabia has pointed to another interesting scriptural parallel:

A temptation exists to build villages to cater for the needs of the caravan traffic in the wadis (the more fertile parts of the wilderness) which are thought to have permanently dried up. Thus it happens that the parable of the house built upon the sand still finds periodical illustration in actual fact. Recently, after many years of drought and consequent security, one such village near the Yemen road was suddenly obliterated when the wadi filled once again with a raging torrent of water from the mountain.[37]

The most minute and careful description of such an event is one recorded by a German engineer working in Palestine early in the present century. On May 18, 1913, there occurred a typical flash-flood in which "people from the Bedouin camps, camels, sheep, and also wild animals were swept away and killed by the terribly rapid rising of the floodwaters."[38] The engineer, visiting two valleys two days later was impressed more than anything else by the filthiness and mess of the thing.   "Thick yellow mud, mixed with desert sand, clung to the bushes on the bank . . . In the freshly-dried desert mud I found dead snakes, lizards, grasshoppers, beetles, shreds of blue cloth that belonged to the Bedouins, a piece of woolen rope and elsewhere small, half-petrified animals. . . ."[39] Such storms as this, he says, occur about every ten or twelve years in the desert. Lehi had good reason to worry — and dream — about them! In the inscriptions we read of one who was "driven away from the watering-place of the camels by a torrent, in the year in which the tribe of Qadam drove away the tribe of Harim."[40] Another inscription is "By A., and the *sail* drove him away at the water-place of the camels."[41] "By An., and the *sail* drove him away at Rass."[42] Another "abode in the springtime in this valley, in the year in which the torrent passed along with his camels." To which Littmann appends a note: "It seems that a torrent took away the camels of Sawad. A sudden torrent sometimes tears down tents and seizes upon men and animals."[43]

Lehi's dreams are summed up in the words of a single brief poem by Rubah who in a few lines describes the terror of loneliness of the long journey, in the mist of darkness (sultry and thick) the "awful gulf," the broad ways, and the paths that stray.[44]

Joseph Smith, Sr., according to his wife, once had the classic dream (as who has not?) of being lost and alone in a vast empty waste, only in his case he "could see nothing save dead, fallen timber."[45] That is natural enough, for men dream by night only of the things they see by day—that is what makes Lehi's dreams so convincing as authentic testimony. Only one who had actually seen those things could have dreamed them; only one who had been haunted by those fears and frightened by those situations would ever have been visited by them in a dream of the night.

Questions

1. Why are casual and incidental details such as those that abound in Lehi's dreams particularly valuable as evidence?

2. Are the 13 pictures which we have taken from Lehi's dreams peculiar to the Near East?

3. Could they be duplicated in Joseph Smith's own environment? How much of the world had Joseph Smith seen before 1830?

4. Of what part of the world are these dream-pictures characteristic?

5. Is the undertone of anxiety in Lehi's dreams psychologically authentic?

6. What specifically do Lehi's dreams show him to be worrying about?

7. What features of Lehi's dreams remain to be explained? Can you suggest an everyday experience that might furnish material for the iron rod image?

8. Which of the dream images do you find most interesting? Why?

9. What things in Lehi's dreams are characteristic of dreams in general?

10. Why have dreams lost their importance and authority in our society?

Lesson 21

LIFE IN THE DESERT

Lehi the Poet—A Desert Idyll.

Prospectus of Lesson 21: One of the most revealing things about Lehi is the nature of his great eloquence. It must not be judged by modern or western standards, as people are prone to judge the Book of Mormon as literature. In this lesson we take the case of a bit of poetry recited extempore by Lehi to his two sons to illustrate certain peculiarities of the Oriental idiom and especially to serve as a test-case in which a number of very strange and exacting conditions are most rigorously observed in the Book of Mormon account. Those are the conditions under which ancient desert poetry was composed. Some things that appear at first glance to be most damning to the Book of Mormon, such as the famous passage in 2 Ne. 1:14 about no traveler returning from the grave, turn out on closer inspection to provide striking confirmation of its correctness.

An Eloquent Race: On one occasion Nephi returned to the tent of his father to find his brothers hotly disputing there ". . . concerning the things which my father had spoken unto them. . . ." (1 Ne. 15:1 ff.) Nephi, who had just before been conversing with the Lord, entered into the discussion, and ". . . did exhort them with all the energies of my soul, and with all the faculty which I possessed, . . ." (1 Ne. 15:25), until finally ". . . they did humble themselves . . ." (1 Ne. 16:5), even against their nature. Wonderful is the power of speech among the desert people. Against the proud and touchy Bedouins, eloquence is the only weapon the sheikh possesses, and Lehi had it in great abundance. A good part of Nephi's account is taken up with his powerful words, of which, we are told, only a tiny part are given. The true leader, says an ancient Arab poetess, "was not one to keep silent when the contest of words began." When the men assemble in the chief's tent to take counsel together, the leader "addresses the whole assembly in a succession of wise

counsels intermingled with opportune proverbs," exactly in the manner of Lehi with his endless parables.[1]
"People of any other country hearing them speak,"
says our informant, "would simply suppose them filled
with a supernatural gift." "Poetical exclamations . . .
rose all round me," Burton recalls, "showing how deeply
tinged with imagination becomes the language of the
Arab under the influence of strong passion or religious
enthusiasm . . . "[2]

Inspired Speech: The most notable thing about
this type of eloquence is the nearness of poetry to inspiration. "With the destruction of the Temple," says
one authority, "the magic power (of uttering oracles)
was transferred to individuals—the so-called 'whispers,'
pious men of faith."[3] "Magic" is a modern verdict, but
the ancient "whisperers," may well have been those by
whom the words of God ". . . hiss forth . . . ," (2 Ne.
29:2-3; Moro. 10:28).   Since they no longer had the
temple, which was soon to be destroyed, Lehi's people
were obliged, as Alma later explains, to carry their own
inspiration with them. In the migrations great and small,
it was always the patriarch or leader of the group who
was the peculiar recipient of revelation. Even the pagan
legends of colonizers speak of divine signs and omens
vouchsafed the leaders. Such men had wonderful powers of concentration. Conder recalls how during a wild
and savage war dance in an Arab camp "the Sheikh of
the tribe could be seen, a few yards off, engaged in
prayer during the greater part of the time that this
strange dance was going on. His attention appeared to
be in no way distracted by the noise . . . "[4] So might
Lehi have prayed as his sons caroused in the ship. (1 Ne.
18:9 f.) There were two ways of delivering oracles
among the ancient Semites, Haldar concludes in his
study of the subject, 1) by technical oracle methods, and
2) by a priest in a state of ecstacy, but "no clear distinction can be made between the 'sacerdotal' and the 'prophetic' oracles."[5] Confusion of types of revelation is also

the rule in the Book of Mormon, as when Lehi says, ". . . I have dreamed a dream or in other words, I have seen a vision. . . ." (1 Ne. 8:2) Which was it? It makes no difference, as long as the experience came from without by the Spirit of the Lord. As to the form the oracles took, all inspired utterance seems to have been given in stately formal language, while all true poetry was regarded as real inspiration. On such matters, Margoliouth reminds us, "We must suspend judgment because of the bewildering character of the evidence before us . . ."[6] Everything seems to run into everything else. If there is nothing that might be called distinctively poetic in pre-Islamic literature it is because as Abu Taman observes, the entire literature *is* poetry.[7]

Literary Standards: In a way, the Arab is incapable of speaking prose, but we must not get the idea that his poetry is anything like our poetry. No Semitic verse can be made into anything remotely resembling good literature in English and still preserve a trace of its original form or content. Nicholson notes that the very best Oriental poetry contains "much that to modern taste is absolutely incongruous with poetic style. Their finest pictures . . . often appear uncouth or grotesque, because without an intimate knowledge of the land and the people it is impossible for us to see what the poet intended to convey, or to appreciate the truth and beauty of its expression."[8] "As long as our ignorance is so great," writes T. E. Peet, "our attitude towards criticism of these ancient literatures must be one of extreme humility. . . . Put an Egyptian or Babylonian story before a layman, even in a good translation, he is at once in a strange land. The similes are pointless and even grotesque for him, the characters are strangers, the background, the allusions, instead of delighting, only mystify and annoy. He lays it aside in disgust."[9] How well this applies to certain "literary" critics of the Book of Mormon!

Lehi's Qasidah: In Lehi's day an inspired leader

had to be a poet, and there is in our opinion no more remarkable episode in the Book of Mormon than that recounting how he once addressed his wayward sons in verse.

It was just after the first camp had been pitched, with due care for the performance of the proper thanksgiving rites at the "altar of stones," that Lehi, being then free to survey the scene more at his leisure (for among the desert people it is the women who make and break camp, though the *sheikh* must officiate in the sacrifice), proceeded, as was his right, to name the river after his first-born and the valley after his second son. (1 Ne. 2:6-8, 14). The men examined the terrain in a place where they expected to spend some time, and discovered that the river "emptied into the fountain of the Red Sea," at a point "near the mouth thereof" not far above the Straits of Tiran. When Lehi beheld the view, perhaps from the side of Mt. Musafa or Mt. Mendisha, he turned to his two elder sons and recited his remarkable verses. Nephi seems to have been standing by, for he takes most careful note of the circumstance: "And when my father saw that the waters of the river emptied into the fountain of the Red Sea, he spake unto Laman, saying: O that thou mightest be like unto this river, continually running into the fountain of all righteousness! And he also spake unto Lemuel: O that thou mightest be like unto this valley, firm and steadfast, and immovable in keeping the commandments of the Lord!" (1 Ne. 2:9-10.)

The common practice was for the inspired words of the leader to be taken down in writing immediately. When Abu Zaid returned by night from a wonderful experience, Hariri reports, "We called for ink and pens and wrote it at his dictation."[10] Another time when a wise man feels inspiration upon him he calls, "Prepare thy inkhorn, and take thy implements to write . . . "[11] So Lehi might have spoken to his sons.

The Oldest Oriental Poetry: On all the once controversial matters, certain aspects of the earliest desert poetry are now well agreed on, though of course there is no agreement or proof as to just how old they might be.

First, there is the occasion. It was the sight of the river flowing into the gulf which inspired Lehi to address his sons. In a famous study, Goldziher pointed out that the earliest desert poems ever mentioned are "those *Quellenlieder* (songs composed to fresh water) which, according to the record of St. Nilus, the ancient Arabs used to intone after having refreshed and washed themselves in some fountain of running water discovered in the course of a long journeying."[12] Nilus' own account is a vivid picture of what Lehi's party went through:

> The next day . . . after making their way as is usual in the desert by devious routes, wandering over the difficult terrain, forced to turn aside now this way, now that, circumventing mountains, stumbling over rough, broken ground through all but impenetrable passes, they beheld in the far distance a spot of green in the desert; and striving to reach the vegetation by which the oasis might provide a camp or even sustain a settlement for some of them as they conjectured, they turned their eyes towards it as a storm-tossed pilot views the harbor. Upon reaching it, they found that the spot did not disappoint their expectations, and that their wishful fantasies had not led them to false hopes. For the water was abundant, clean to the sight, and sweet to the taste, so that it was a question whether the eye or the mouth more rejoiced. Moreover, there was adequate forage for the animals; so they unloaded the camels and let them out to graze freely. For themselves, they could not let the water alone, drinking, splashing and bathing as if they could not revel in it enough. So they recited songs in its praise (the river's), and composed hymns to the spring. . . .[13]

The antiquity of this passage, or rather the author's first-hand knowledge of the desert people, has recently been seriously questioned, yet the language, though Greek, is strangely like that of the Arabs themselves, and certainly the main fact, the holiness of springs and the practice of conjuring by them, as Lehi does, is substantiated by the very ancient Babylonian formula: "I would have thee swear, by springs, valleys, mountains, rivers, must thou swear."[14]

Ibn Qutaiba, in a famous work on Arabic poetry,

quoted a great desert poet, Abu Sakhr, as saying that
nothing on earth brings verses so readily to mind as the
sight of running water and wild places.[15] This applies
not only to springs, of course, but to all running water.
Thomas recounts how his Arabs upon reaching the Umm
al-Hait hailed it with a song in praise of the "continu-
ous and flowing rain," whose bounty filled the bed of
the wady, "flowing along between sand and stream
course. . . ."[16] Just so Lehi holds up as the most admir-
able of examples "this river, continually flowing . . .";
for to the people of the desert there is no more miraculous and lovely thing on earth than continually running
water. When the Beni Hilal stopped at their first oasis,
the beauty of it and the green vegetation reminded them
again of the homeland they had left, "and they wept
greatly remembering it." It was precisely because Laman
and Lemuel were loud in lamenting the loss of their
pleasant ". . . land of Jerusalem . . . and their precious
things . . ." (1 Ne. 2:11), that their father was moved
to address them on this particular occasion.

Two interesting and significant expressions are
used in Nephi's account of his father's *qasidah* to Laman
and Lemuel. The one is "the fountain of the Red Sea,"
and the other "this valley," firm and steadfast. Is the
Red Sea a fountain? For the Arabs any water that does
not dry up is a fountain. Where all streams and pools
are seasonal, only springs are abiding—water that never
runs away or rises and falls and can therefore only be a
"fountain." This was certainly the concept of the Egyptians, from whom Lehi may have got it.[17] Hariri describes a man whose income is secured and unfailing as
being "like a well that has reached a fountain."[18] Nicholson quotes one of the oldest Arab poets, who tells how
the hero Dhu 'l-Qarnayn (who may be Alexander the
Great) "Followed the Sun to view its setting when it
sank into the sombre ocean *spring*."[19]

As to this valley, firm and steadfast, who, west
of Suez, would ever think of such an image? We, of
course, know all about everlasting hills and immovable

mountains, the moving of which is the best-known illustration of the infinite power of faith, but who ever heard
of a steadfast valley? The Arabs to be sure. For them
the valley, and not the mountain, is the symbol of per-
manence. It is not the mountain of refuge to which they
flee, but the valley of refuge. The great depressions that
run for hundreds of miles across the Arabian peninsula
pass for the most part through plains devoid of mountains. It is in these ancient riverbeds alone that water,
vegetation, and animal life are to be found when all
else is desolation. They alone offer men and animals escape from their enemies and deliverance from death by
hunger and thirst. The qualities of firmness and steadfastness, of reliable protection, refreshment, and sure
refuge when all else fails, which other nations attribute
naturally to mountains, the Arabs attribute to valleys.[20]
So the ancient Zohair describes a party like Lehi's:

> And when they went down to the water, blue and still in its
> depression, they laid down their walking-sticks like one who has
> reached a permanent resting place.[21]

In the most recent study on the qasida, Alfred
Bloch distinguishes four types of verse in the earliest
desert poetry: (1) the *ragaz*, or verses to accompany
any rythmical repeated form of work or play, (2) verses
for instruction or information, (3) elegies, specializing
in sage reflections on the meaning of life, and (4) *Reise-
lieder* or songs of travel, recited on a journey to make the
experience more pleasant and edifying.[22] Lehi's *qasida*
meets all but the first of these specifications—and to be
genuine it only needs to meet one of them. It also meets
the requirements of the *saj'*, or original desert poetry, as
Nicholson describes it: " . . . rhymed prose . . . which
originally had a deeper, almost religious significance as
the special form adopted by poets, soothsayers, and the
like in their supernatural revelations and for conveying
to the vulgar every kind of mysterious and esoteric
lore."[23]

Lehi's Qasidah: If the earliest desert poems were songs inspired by the fair sight of running water, no one today knows the *form* they took. But it can be conjectured from the earliest known form of Semitic verse that that form was the *saj'*, a short exhortation or injunction spoken with such solemnity and fervor as to fall into a sort of chant. Examples of this would be magical incantations, curses, and the formal pronouncements of teachers, priests, and judges.[24] From the earliest times the *saj'* was the form in which inspiration and revelation announced themselves.[24] Though the speaker of the *saj'* did not aim consciously at metrical form, his words were necessarily more than mere prose, and were received by their hearers as poetry. The *saj'* had the effect, we are told, of overawing the hearer completely, and was considered absolutely binding on the person to whom it was addressed, its aim being to compel action.[25]

Lehi's words to his sons take just this form of short, solemn, rhythmical appeal. The fact that the speech to Laman exactly matches that to his brother shows that we have here such a formal utterance as the *saj'*. The proudest boast of the desert poet is, "I utter a verse and after it its brother," for the consummation of the poetic art was to have two verses perfectly parallel in form and content. Few ever achieved this, and Ibn Qutaiba observes that the usual verse is followed not by a "brother" but at best by a "cousin."[26] Yet Lehi seems to have carried it off. Of the moral fervor and didactic intent of his recitation there can be no doubt; the fact that Nephi recounts the episode in a record in which there is, as he says, only room for great essentials, shows what a deep impression it made upon him.

In addressing his sons in what looks like a little song, Lehi is doing just what Isaiah does (Isaiah 5:1-7) when he speaks to Israel in a *shirat dodi*, "a friendly chant," a popular song about a vine which, once the hearer's attention has been won, turns into a very serious moral tirade.[27] On another occasion, as we have noted, he employs the popular figure of the olive tree. The stock

opening line of the old desert poems is, "O my two beloved ones! (or friends)," an introduction which, says
Ibn Qutaiba, should be avoided, "since only the ancients
knew how to use it properly, uniting a gentle and natural
manner with the grandiose and magnificent."[28]   Lehi's
poem is an example of what is meant: he addresses his
two sons separately but each with the peculiar and typical Arabic vocative "O that thou. . .!" (*Ya laitaka*), and
describes the river and valley in terms of unsurpassed
brevity and simplicity and in the vague and sweeping
manner of the real desert poets, of whom Burton says,
"there is a dreaminess of idea and a haze thrown over the
object, infinitely attractive, but indescribable."[29]   Lehi's
language is of this simple, noble, but hazy kind.

According to Richter, the best possible example of
the primitive Arabic *qasid* (the name given to the oldest
actual poetry of the desert) is furnished by those old
poems in which one's beloved is compared to a land "in
which abundant streams flow down . . . with rushing and
swirling, so that the water overflows every evening and
continually."[30] Here the "continually flowing" water is
compared to the person addressed, as in Lehi's "song" to
Laman. The original *qasid*, the same authority avers, was
built around the beseeching (*werbenden*, hence the name
qasid) motif, not necessarily erotic in origin, as was once
thought, but dealing rather with praise of virtue in general (*Tugendlob*).[31] Ibn Qutaiba (Sect. 12) even claims
that the introductory love theme was merely a device to
gain attention of male listeners and was not at all the real
stuff of the poem.   The standard pattern is a simple one:
(a) the poet's attention is arrested some impressive natural phenomenon, usually running water; (b) this leads
him to recite a few words in its praise, drawing it to the
attention of a beloved companion of the way, and (c)
making it an object lesson for the latter, who is urged to
be like it.   Burton gives a good example: at the sight of
the Wady al-Akik the nomad poet is moved to exclaim,

O my friend, this is Akik, then stand by it,
Endeavoring to be distracted by love, if not really a lover.

This seems to be some sort of love song, albeit a peculiar one, and some have claimed that all the old *qasidas* were such.[32]   But Burton and his Arabs know the real meaning, "the esoteric meaning of this couplet," as he calls it, which quite escapes the western reader and is to be interpreted:

> Man! This is a lovely portion of God's creation:
> Then stand by it, and here learn to love the perfections of thy Supreme Friend.[33]

Compare this with Lehi's appeal to Lemuel:

> O that thou mightest be like unto this valley, firm and steadfast,
> And immovable in keeping the commandments of the Lord!

Note the remarkable parallel.   In each case the poet, wandering in the desert with his friends, is moved by the sight of a pleasant valley, a large *wady* with water in it; he calls the attention of his beloved companion to the view, and appeals to him to learn a lesson from the valley and "stand by it," firm and unshakable in the love of the ways of the Lord.   Let us briefly list the exacting conditions fulfilled by Nephi's account of his father's *qasidas* and demanded of the true and authentic desert poet of the earliest period:

(1) They are *Brunnen-* or *Quellenlieder,* as the Germans call them, that is, songs inspired by the sight of water gushing from a spring or running down a valley.

(2) They are addressed to one or (usually) two traveling companions.

(3) They praise the beauty and the excellence of the scene, calling it to the attention of the hearer as an object lesson.

(4) The hearer is urged to be like the thing he beholds.[34]

(5) The poems are recited extempore on the spot and with great feeling.

(6) They are very short, each couplet being a complete poem in itself.[35]

(7) One verse must be followed by its "brother," making a perfectly matched pair.

Here we have beyond any doubt all the elements of a situation of which no westerner in 1830 had the remotest conception. Lehi stands before us as something of a poet, as well as a great prophet and leader, and that is as it should be. "The poetic art of David," says Professor Montgomery, "has its complement in the early Arabic poets . . . some of whom themselves were kings. . . ."[36]

Lehi and Shakespeare: No passage in the Book of Mormon has been more often singled out for attack than Lehi's description of himself as one " . . . whose limbs ye must soon lay down in the cold and silent grave, from whence no traveler can return; . . ." (2 Ne. 1:14.) This passage has inspired scathing descriptions of the Book of Mormon as a mass of stolen quotations "from Shakespeare and other English poets."[37] Lehi does not quote Hamlet directly, to be sure, for he does not talk of "that undiscovered country, from whose bourne no traveler returns," but simply speaks of "the cold and silent *grave,* from whence no traveler can return." In mentioning the grave, the eloquent old man cannot resist the inevitable "cold and silent" nor the equally inevitable tag about the traveler—a device that, with all respect to Shakespeare, Lehi's own contemporaries made constant use of. Long ago Friedrich Delitzsch wrote a classic work on ancient Oriental ideas about death and after life, and a fitting title of his book was *Das Land ohne Heimkehr*—"The Land of No Return."[38] In the story of Ishtar's descent to the underworld the lady goes to the *irsit la tari,* "the land of no return." She visits "the dark house from which no one ever comes out again," and travels along "the road on which there is no turning back."[39] A recent study of Sumerian and Akkadian names for the world of the dead lists prominently "the hole, the earth, the land of no return, the path of no turning back, the road whose course never

turns back, the distant land, etc."[40]   A recently discovered fragment speaks of the grave as "the house of
Irkallu, where those who have come to it are without
return. . . . A place whose dead are cast in the dust, in
the direction of darkness . . . (going) to the place where
they who came to it are without return."[41]   This is a good
deal closer to Lehi's language than Shakespeare is.   The
same sentiments are found in Egyptian literature, as in a
popular song which tells how "the gods that were afore-
time rest in their pyramids . . . None cometh again from
thence that he may tell of their state . . . Lo none may take
his goods with him, and none that hath gone may come
again."[42]   A literary text reports: "The mockers say,
'The house of the inhabitants of the Land of the West
is deep and dark; it has no door and no window . . . there
the sun never rises but they lie forever in the dark.' "[43]

Shakespeare should sue; but Lehi, a lover of poetic
imagery and high-flown speech, can hardly be denied
the luxury of speaking as he was supposed to speak.
The ideas to which he here gives such familiar and conventional expression are actually *not* his own ideas about
life after death—nor Nephi's nor Joseph Smith's, for
that matter, but they are the ideas which any eloquent
man of Lehi's day, with a sound literary education such
as Lehi had, would be expected and required to use. And
so the most popular and obvious charge of fraud against
the Book of Mormon has backfired.

Questions

1. Why was eloquence a necessity for Lehi?
2. How does eastern eloquence differ from our
own?
3. Discuss the relationship between inspiration,
revelation, visions, dreams, prophecies, ecstasy, eloquence, poetry and scripture. Does the Book of Mormon make the same distinction between them that we do?
4. What are some of the peculiar characteristics of
ancient desert poetry?
5. Can these be detected in Lehi's speeches?

6. Are we justified in calling his address to his two sons poetry?

7. Why is the average student or professor of literature unqualified to pass judgment on the Book of Mormon as literature?

8. How is the literary strangeness of the Book of Mormon an indication of authenticity?

9. What are the normal objections to calling the Red Sea a fountain? To calling a valley firm and steadfast?

10. What indications are there in the Book of Mormon that Lehi might have read and studied poetry?

Lesson 22

PROPER NAMES IN THE BOOK OF MORMON

Prospectus of Lesson 22: In this lesson we test certain proper names in the Book of Mormon in the light of actual names from Lehi's world, unknown in the time of Joseph Smith. Not only do the names agree, but the variations follow the correct rules and the names are found in correct statistical proportions, the Egyptian and Hebrew types being of almost equal frequency, along with a sprinkling of Hittite, Arabic, and Greek names. To reduce speculation to a minimum, the lesson is concerned only with highly distinctive and characteristic names, and to clearly stated and universally admitted rules. Even so, the reader must judge for himself. In case of doubt he is encouraged to correspond with recognized experts in the languages concerned. The combination of the names Laman and Lemuel, the absence of Baal names, the predominance of names ending in -iah—such facts as those need no trained philologist to point them out; they can be demonstrated most objectively, and they are powerful evidence in behalf of the Book of Mormon.

Forty years ago a psychologist by analyzing the proper names in the Book of Mormon believed he was able to prove beyond any doubt that the Book originated in the world of Joseph Smith. His verdict is still accepted.[1] This is another illustration of the futility of testing any ancient document by the criteria of any other age than that which it claims for its origin. For, by the method employed, our psychologist could have proven with equal ease that the Book of Mormon was written in any century to which he chose to attribute it.

There is no happier hunting-ground for the half-trained scholar than the world of words. For unbridled license of speculation and airy weakness of evidence only the authority on ancient geography (including Book of Mormon geography) can surpass the homemade philologist. There are no rules and no limits in a game in which the ear decides for itself whether or not a resemblance in sound is to be taken as accidental or significant, yet there are quite enough peculiar proper names in the Book of Mormon to provide a rigorous and exacting test for the authenticity of the Book, provided of course that a properly trained ear does the testing.[2] Since we cannot lay claim to such an ear, we shall in this lesson lean over backward to confine ourselves to a few minimum claims which it would be very hard for anyone to dispute. Let us limit ourselves to ten points.

The Test Cases:—1. There is in the Book of Mormon within one important family a group of names beginning with Pa-. They are peculiar names and can be matched exactly in Egyptian. Names beginning with Pa- are by far the most common type in late Egyptian history, but what ties Pahoran's family most closely to Egypt is not the names but the activities in which the bearers of those names are engaged; for they sponsor the same institutions and engineer the same intrigues as their Egyptian namesakes did centuries before — and in so doing they give us to understand they are quite aware of the resemblance!

2. There is a marked tendency for Egyptian and Hebrew names in the Book of Mormon to turn up in the Elephantine region of Upper Egypt. It is now believed that when Jerusalem fell in Lehi's day a large part of the refugees fled to that region.

3. The most frequent "theophoric" element by far in the Book of Mormon names is Ammon. The same is true of late Egyptian names. The commonest formative element in the Book of Mormon names is the combination Mor-, Mr-; in Egyptian the same holds true.

4. Egyptian names are usually compound and formed according to certain rules. Book of Mormon names are mostly compound and follow the *same* rules of formation.

5. Mimation (ending with -m) predominated in Jaredite names, nunation (ending with -n) in Nephite and Lamanite names. This is strictly in keeping with the development of languages in the Old World, where mimation was everywhere succeeded by nunation around

2000 B.C., that is, well after the Jaredites had departed, but long before the Nephites.

6. A large proportion of Book of Mormon names end in -iah and ihah. The same ending is peculiar to Palestinian names of Lehi's time but not of other times.

7. The names in the Book of Mormon that are neither Egyptian nor Hebrew are Arabic, Hittite (Hurrian) or Greek. This is strictly in keeping with the purported origin of the book.

8. Lehi is a real personal name, unknown in the time of Joseph Smith. It is always met with in the desert country, where a number of exemplars have been discovered in recent years.

9. Laman and Lemuel are not only "Arabic" names, but they also form a genuine "pair of pendant names," such as ancient Semites of the desert were wont to give their two eldest sons, according to recent discoveries.

10. The absence of "Baal-" names (that is names compounded with the theophoric Baal element), is entirely in keeping with recent discoveries regarding common names in the Palestine of Lehi's day.

Familiar Names in Familiar Situations: Let us now briefly consider the evidence for each of these ten points in order.

1. Paanchi, the son of Pahoran Sr., and pretender to the chief-judgeship has the same name as one of the best-known kings in Egyptian history, a contemporary of Isaiah and chief actor in the drama of Egyptian history at a time in which that history was intimately involved in the affairs of Palestine.[3] Yet his name, not mentioned in the Bible, remained unknown to scholars until the end of the 19th century. This Egyptian Paanchi, whose name means "He (namely Ammon) is my life," was the son of one Kherihor (the vowels are guesses!), the High Priest of Ammon, who in a priestly plot set himself up as a rival of Pharaoh himself, while his son Paanchi actually claimed the throne. This was four hundred years before Lehi left Jerusalem and

it had historic repercussions of great importance; not only did it establish a new dynasty, but it inaugurated the rule of priestcraft in Egypt; from that time on "the high priest of Amon . . . could and constantly did reduce the king to a position of subservience."[4]

Now in the Book of Mormon both Paanchi and Korihor are involved in such plots and intrigues of priestcraft. The former to gain the chief judgeship for himself tried to achieve the assassination of his two elder brothers, who bore the good Egyptian names of Pahoran (meaning "man of Syria or Palestine," —a Horite) and Pacumeni (Cf. Egyptian Pakamen), while the latter charged the judges with trying to introduce into the New World the abuses of priestcraft which the people knew had been practiced in the Old, ". . . ordinances and performances which are laid down by ancient priests, to usurp power and authority. . . ." (Alma 30:23.) It is apparent that with their Old World names and culture, Lehi's people brought over many Old World memories and ideas with them, as was only to be expected.

Geographical Bull's-eye:—2. In *The Improvement Era* for April, 1948, the author published a map showing the clustering of Book of Mormon names in the up-river country of Egypt, south of Thebes. The map bore the caption:

> The tendency of Book of Mormon names to turn up in definite limited areas and in close association with each other is strong indication that the resemblances between the Old and the New World titles are not accidental.[5]

As a reader of the article will perceive, we were at that time at a loss to explain a phenomenon which we felt was "not accidental." But soon after we came across the answer in Professor Albright's observation that when Jerusalem fell the very Jews who had persecuted Lehi ". . . hid in the wilds during the siege . . . ," and when all was lost fled to Egypt. In particular they went to upper Egypt, where the Jews had a very special settlement at Elephantine, far up the Nile.[6] Albright even suggests that the main colonization of Elephantine took place as a result of the flight from Jerusalem at that time.[6] Since Egypt was then the lone survivor against Nebuchadnezzar, it was only to Egypt that his enemies could fly. But since Egypt was also an objective of Nebuchadnezzar's victorious campaign, the safest place for any refugee to that land would be as far up the river as he could get. That is therefore where one would logically expect to find the Book of Mormon names, that is, the Jewish names of Lehi's days; but before he even knew the explanation, this writer was puzzled by the fact, which to him seemed paradoxical, that our Book of Mormon names should congregate so very far from home.

Mixed Nationalities: Recently there have been discovered lists of the names of prisoners that Nebuchadnezzar brought back to Babylon with him from his great expedition into Syria and Palestine.[7] These represent a good cross section of proper names prevailing in those lands in the days of Lehi, and among them is a respectable proportion of Egyptian names, which is what the Book of Mormon would lead us to expect.[8] Also in the list are Philistine (cf. Book of Mormon *Minon* and *Pathros!*) Phoenician, Elamite, Median, Persian, Greek, and Lydian names—all the sweepings of a campaign into Lehi's country. According to D. H. Thomas, this list shows that it was popular at the time to name children after Egyptian hero kings of the past.[8] A surprisingly large number of the non-Hebraic Nephite names are of this class. Thus the name Aha, which a Nephite general bestowed on his son, means "warrior" and was borne by the legendary first hero king of Egypt. Himni, Korihor, Paanchi, Pakumeni, Sam, Zeezrom, Ham, Manti, Nephi and Zenoch are all Egyptian hero names.[9] Zeniff certainly suggests the name Zainab and its variants, popular among the desert people, of which the feminine form of Zenobia was borne by the most glamorous woman of ancient times next to Cleopatra and that other desert queen, the Queen of Sheba. Recently Beeston has identified Zoram in both its Hebrew and Arabic forms.[10] In another old name list, the Tell Taannek list, the elements *bin, zik, ra,* and *-andi* are prominent, as in the Book of Mormon.[11]

Rules of Name-building:—3. The commonest name heard in the Egypt of Lehi's day was the commonest name heard among the Nephites, that of Amon or Ammon (the two spellings are equally common, and Gardiner favors Amun), the god of the empire, who unlike other Egyptian deities never took animal form, was regarded as the universal god, and seems to have been an importation into Egypt from the time of Abraham.[12] His name is very often used in the building of other names, and when so employed it changes its sound according to definite rules. Gardiner in his *Egyptian Grammar* (page 431) states:

> A very important class of personal names is that containing names known as theophorous; i.e., compound names in which one element is the name of a deity. Now in Graeco-Roman transcriptions it is the rule that when such a divine name is stated at the *beginning* of a compound (the italics are Gardiner's) it is less heavily vocalized than when it stands independently or at the end of a compound.

The author then goes on to show that in such cases *Amon* or *Amun* regularly becomes Amen, while in some cases the vowel may disappear entirely. One need only consider the Book of Mormon *Aminidab, Aminadi, Amminihu, Amnor,* etc., to see how nearly the rule applies in the West. In the name Helaman, on the other hand, the strong vocalization remains, since the "divine name" is not "stated at the *beginning*" of the compound. Since the Semitic "l" must always be rendered as "r" in Egyptian (which has no "l") Helaman would in "*unreformed*" Egyptian necessarily appear as the typically Egyptian *Heramon.*

By checking the long Egyptian name lists in Lieblein and Ranke's works, the reader may satisfy himself that the element *Mr* is, next to *Nfr* alone, by far the commonest.[13]　It is very common in the Book of Mormon also. In Egyptian it means a great many things though its commonest designation in proper names is "beloved." Thus the Egyptian king Meryamon or Moriamon is "beloved of Amon."

4. Another illustration of name-formation in Nephite and Egyptian may be seen in the names *Zemna-rihah* (Nephite) and *Zmn-ha-re* (Egyptian), where the same elements are combined in different order. The elaborate Nephite names of Gidgiddoni and Gidgiddonah may be parallels to the Egyptian *Djed-dihwti-iw-f* and *Died-djhwti-iw-s;* in each case the stem is the same, sounding something like "Jidjiddo-." To this the suffix -*iw-f,* and *iw-s* are added in Egyptian with the word *ankh,* signifying "he shall live" and "she shall live," respectively,[14] the two names meaning "Thoth hath said he shall live" and "Thoth hath said she will live." The suffixes in the two Nephite names are different, -*iw-ni* and *iw-nah,* but they are perfectly good Egyptian and indicate "I shall live" and "we shall live" respectively. The agreements are much too neat and accurate to be accidental.　Any student with 6 months heiroglyphic will recognize the Nephite Gidianhi as the typical Egyptian name "Thoth is my life," -*Djhwty-ankh-i.*

Mimation and Nunation:—5. Jirku had shown that mimation was still current in the Semitic dialects of Palestine and Syria between 2100 and 1800 B.C., when the nominative case still ended in -m. From Egyptian and Hittite records it is now clear that the dialects of Palestine and Syria dropped this mimation in the first half of the second millennium B.C., and it is preserved in the Bible only in a few pre-Hebraic words used in very ancient incantations and spells, and in the mysterious and archaic words *Urim* and *Thummim,* which it now appears are not Hebrew plurals at all.[15]　This is significant since the Book of Mormon favors -m endings for

Jaredite names. The Jaredites must have taken mimation
with them some time before 2000 B.C., when the change
to nunation occurred. Nunation itself, however, which
is extremely common in the Book of Mormon proper
names, is an old-fashioned thing which in Lehi's day was
a sign of conservatism and most frequently found among
the desert people. It turns up in old Hebrew genealogies
in which "the nomenclature is largely un-Hebraic, with
peculiar antique formations in -an, -on, and in some
cases of particular Arabian origin."[16] This nunation or
ending in -n has left traces in all Semitic languages, but
mostly among the desert people, being retained completely in classical Arabic.

6. In *Lehi in the Desert*, page 33, we wrote: "Since
the Old Testament was available to Joseph Smith, there
is no point in listing Hebrew names, but their Book of
Mormon *forms* are significant. The strong tendency to
end in -*iah* is very striking, since the vast majority of
Hebrew names found at Lachish (i.e., from records contemporary with Lehi) end the same way, indicating that
-*iah* names were very frequent in Lehi's time." Since
that was written our view has been confirmed by a study
made by D. W. Thomas, who noted that a "striking"
peculiarity of Hebrew names in the age of Jeremiah is
". . . the many personal names which end in -*iah*."[17]
Thus Reifenberg lists from the ancient Hebrew seals of
the time such names as Yekamiahu (Jekamiah), Shepa-
tiahu son of Assiahu, Iaazaniahu, Gadiahu (cf. Book of
Mormon Gadiandi, Giddianhi), Hilkiahu, Gealiahu,
Aliahu, etc.[18] This -*iahu* ending (German -jahu) is our
Biblical -*iah*, -*ijah*, and by a common metathesis also become the extremely common Book of Mormon name ending -*ihah*.

Non-Semitic Names:—7. The Hittite names in the
Book of Mormon all come to us in an Egyptianized form,
which is what one would expect in Lehi's Palestine where
Hittite names still survived even though Hittite language
was probably not used.[19] Thus the Nephite Manti while

suggesting the Egyptian Manti, Monti, Menedi, etc., also recalls the Egyptian name of a Hittite city, Manda. A highly characteristic element of Hittite and Hurrian names is *Manti, -andi,* likewise common in the Book of Mormon. The Nephite Kumen, Kumen-onhi, Kishkumen certainly remind one of the Egyptian-Hittite name of an important city, Kumani; Nephite Seantum is cognate with Egyptian-Hittite Sandon, Sandas; the Jaredite Akish and Kish are both found in the Old World, where they are of very great antiquity; Akish being the Egyptian-Hittite name for Cyprus.[20] Most interesting is the Nephite city of Gadiandi, whose name exactly parallels the Egyptian rendering of the name of a Hittite city, Cadyanda.[21] It should be borne in mind that one of the great discoveries and upsets of the twentieth century has been the totally unsuspected importance and extent of the Hittite penetration of Hebrew civilization. Every year the Hittites receive new importance in the Hebrew story. The Book of Mormon has not overdone its *-andis* and *-antis!*

The occurrence of the names Timothy and Lachoneus in the Book of Mormon is strictly in order, however odd it may seem at first glance. Since the fourteenth century B.C. at latest, Syria and Palestine had been in constant contact with the Aegean world, and since the middle of the seventh century Greek mercenaries and merchants closely bound to Egyptian interest (the best Egyptian mercenaries were Greeks), swarmed throughout the Near East.[22] Lehi's people, even apart from their mercantile activities, could not have avoided considerable contact with these people in Egypt and especially in Sidon, which Greek poets even in that day were celebrating as the great world center of trade. It is interesting to note in passing that Timothy is an Ionian name, since the Greeks in Palestine were Ionians (hence the Hebrew name for Greeks: "Sons of Javanim"), and—since "Lachoneus" means "a Laconian"—that the oldest Greek traders were Laconians, who had colonies in

Cyprus (Book of Mormon Akish) and of course traded with Palestine.[23]

Important Names in the Book of Mormon: —8. The name of Lehi occurs only as part of a place-name in the Bible.[24] And only within the last twenty years a potsherd was found at Elath (where Lehi's road from Jerusalem meets "the fountain of the Red Sea") bearing the name of a man, *LHI*, very clearly written on it. Since then Nelson Glueck has detected the name in many compound names found inscribed on the stones of Arabia.[25] On a Lihyanite monument we find the name of one *LHI-TN*, son of Pagag, whose name means "Lehi hath given." The *LHI* name is quite common in inscriptions.[26] Nfy[27] and Alma[28] are equally common, and Mormon may be of Hebrew, Egyptian, or Arabic origin.[29] While Glueck supplies the vowels to make the name Lahai, Paul Haupt in a special study renders it Lehi, and gives it the mysterious meaning of "cheek" which has never been explained.[30] There is a Bait Lahi, "House of Lehi" among the ancient place names of the Gaza country occupied by the Arabs in the time of Lehi, but the meaning of the name is lost.[31]

9. The name of *LMN* is also found among the inscriptions. Thus in an inscription from Sinai: "Greetings Lamin, son of Abdal." (SHLM LMINU BN ABDL).[32] Recently the name Laman (written definitely with a second "a") has turned up in south Arabia and been hailed by the discoverers as "a new name."[33] In an inscription reading "Lamai son of Nafiah erected this monument, . . ." Jaussen noted that the final *Yod* is defective and suggests that the word is really Laman.[34] In Palestine the name of Laman is attributed to an ancient Mukam or sacred place. Most of these Mukams are of unknown date, many of them prehistoric. In Israel only the tribe of Manasseh (Lehi's tribe) built them.[35] The name of Lemuel, as we have seen, also comes from the deserts of the south.[36]

Pendant Names: But the most striking thing about the

names of Laman and Lemuel is the way they go together; as we saw above it has been suggested that the
former is but a corruption of the latter.[36] Whether that
is so or not, the musical pair certainly belong together
and are a beautiful illustration of the old desert custom
of naming the first two sons in a family with rhyming
twin names, "a pair of pendant names," as Spiegel puts
it, ". . . like Eldad and Medad, Hilleq and Billeq or
Jannes and Jambres. The Arabs particularly seem to
enjoy putting together such assonant names Yagyg and
Magyg (Gog and Magog), Harun and Quarun (Aaron
and Korah), Qabil and Habil (Cain and Abel), Khillit
and Millit (the first dwellers in hell). . . ."[37] Spiegel is
here discussing the names Heyya and Abeyya, and might
well have included in his parallels the recently discovered
romance of Sul and Shummul. Harut and Marut were
the first two angels to fall from grace, like Laman and
Lemuel, according to Arab tradition of great antiquity.
These names never go in threes or fours but only in pairs,
designating just the first two sons of a family with no
reference to the rest. This "Dioscuric" practice has a
ritual significance which has been discussed by Rendel
Harris,[38] but of the actual practice itself, especially
among the desert people, there can be no doubt, for we
read in an ancient inscription: "N. built this tomb for
his sons Hatibat and Hamilat."[39] One could not ask for a
better illustration of this little-known and, until recently,
unsuspected practice than we find in the Book of Mormon where Lehi names his first two sons Laman and
Lemuel.

Baal Names:—10. The compiler of these studies was
once greatly puzzled over the complete absence of *Baal*
names from the Book of Mormon. By what unfortunate
oversight had the authors of that work failed to include
a single name containing the element *Baal,* which thrives
among the personal names of the Old Testament? Having discovered as we thought, that the book was in error,
we spared no criticism at the time, and indeed had its neg-

lect of *Baal* names not been strikingly vindicated in recent years it would be a black mark against it. Now we learn, however, that the stubborn prejudice of our text against *Baal* names is really the only correct attitude it could have taken, and this discovery, flying in the face of all our calculation and preconceptions, should in all fairness, weigh at least as heavily in the book's favor as the supposed error did against it.

It happens that for some reason or other the Jews at the beginning of the sixth century B.C. would have nothing to do with *Baal* names. An examination of Elephantine name lists shows that ". . . the change of Baal names, by substitution, is in agreement with Hosea's foretelling that they should be no more used by the Israelites, and consequently it is most interesting to find how the latest archaeological discoveries confirm the Prophet, for out of some four hundred personal names among the Elephantine papyri, not one is compounded of Baal . . ."[41]

Since Elephantine was settled largely by Israelites who fled from Jerusalem after its destruction, their personal names should show the same tendencies as those in the Book of Mormon. Though the translator of that book might by the exercise of superhuman cunning have been warned by Hosea 2:17 to eschew Baal names, yet the meaning of that passage is so far from obvious that Albright as late as 1942 finds it ". . . very significant that seals and inscriptions from Judah, which . . . are very numerous in the seventh and early sixth centuries, seem never to contain any *Baal* names."[41] It is significant indeed, but hardly more so that the uncanny acumen which the Book of Mormon displays on the point.

To these ten points many others might be added, but we must be careful at this stage of the game not to be too subjective in our interpretations nor to distinguish too sharply between languages. There is an increasing tendency to fuse ancient languages together as ancient cultures were fused. Thus Jirku finds in Egyptian name lists many place-names that occur both in the Old Testament and in the cuneiform sources, "and many of these are still preserved in the modern Arabic names of the tells" or ruins that mark their sites. Thus the same names turn up in Egyptian, Hebrew, Babylonian, and Arabic.[42] In Lehi's day the Aramaic and the Arabic spoken in the cities were almost identical, "every distinction between them in the pronunciation of certain sounds must have vanished."[43] Before that time Hebrew personal names had a strong national color and served as a reliable source for the study of the religious history of the people; but in the cosmopolitan age foreign names became as popular as native ones, both with the Jews and with other people.[44]

Out of a hundred possible points we have confined ourselves to a mere sampling, choosing ten clear-cut and telling philological demonstrations by way of illustration. The force of such evidence inevitably increases with its bulk, but we believe enough has been given to indicate that Eduard Meyer did not consider all the factors when he accused Joseph Smith of "letting his fancy run free" in inventing the Book of Mormon names.[45] The fact is that nearly all the evidence for the above points has come forth since the death of Meyer. Let us be fair to him, but let us in all fairness be fair to the Book of Mormon as well.

Questions

1. Why must one use caution in dealing with names as evidence?

2. If the Book of Mormon had been first published in 1900 instead of 1830, how would the close resemblance of the proper names in it to those actually occurring in the Old World be hailed as absolute proof of fraud? As it is, why is that resemblance not hailed as equally convincing proof of authenticity?

3. How can one account for the clustering of Book of Mormon names in the Elephantine region of the Upper Nile? Why so far from Jerusalem?

4. How does the large variety of name-types in the Book of Mormon support its authenticity? How long have the name-lists from Lehi's time been known to scholars?

5. Why are the Book of Mormon names never exactly like their Old World counterparts?

6. How do you account for the frequency of the name of Ammon in the Book of Mormon?

7. How can one be sure that the resemblance between two names is significant?

8. Is it conceivable that pious Israelites would give non-Hebraic names to their children? Even pagan names?

9. What are the principal derivations of name-types of the Book of Mormon?

10. How can one explain the presence among the Nephites of Egyptian names? Greek? Arabic? Hittite?

11. How does one explain the absence of Baal names?

Lesson 23

OLD WORLD RITUAL IN THE NEW WORLD

Prospectus of Lesson 23: In the writer's opinion, this lesson presents the most convincing evidence yet brought forth for the authenticity of the Book of Mormon. Very likely the reader will be far from sharing this view, since the force of the evidence is cumulative and based on extensive comparative studies which cannot be fully presented here. Still the evidence is so good, and can be so thoroughly tested, that we present it here for the benefit of the reader who wishes to pursue the subject further. Since Gressmann, Jeremias, Mowinckel, and many others began their studies at the start of the century a vast literature on the subject of the Great Assembly at the New Year and the peculiar and complex rites performed on that occasion has been brought forth. Yet nowhere can one find a fuller description of that institution and its rites than in the Book of Mormon. Since "patternism" (as the awareness of a single universal pattern for all ancient year rites is now being called) is a discovery of the last thirty years, the fact that the now familiar pattern of ritual turns up in a book first published almost 130 years ago is an extremely stimulating one. For it is plain that Mosiah's account of the Great Year Rite among the Nephites is accurate in every detail, as can be checked by other year-rites throughout the world.

Ancient Society was "Sacral": Within recent years scholars have become aware as never before of the completely "sacral" nature of ancient society in the Near East. "The order of the state," as Kees says of Egypt, "as well as of the universe itself, goes back to the time of the gods."[1] State and cult are inseparable in the ancient East, and all things center in a single supreme rite, performed in its completeness only at a particular place, the shrine that stands at the center of the earth, and a particular time, the New Year's day when all things are born and the earth is created anew.[2] Since everyone was required by law to be present at this great event, to do homage to the king and receive his blessing for the new age, the result was a tremendous assembly.

At hundreds of holy shrines, each believed to mark the exact center of the universe and represented as the point at which the four quarters of the earth converged—"the navel of the earth" —one might have seen assembled at the New Year—the moment of creation, the beginning and ending of time—vast concourses of people, each thought to represent the entire human race in the presence of all its ancestors and gods. A visitor to any of these festivals . . . would note that all came to the celebration as pilgrims, often traversing immense distances over prehistoric sacred roads, and dwelt during the festival in booths of green boughs.

What would most command a visitor's attention to the great assembly would be the main event, the now famous ritual year-drama for the glorification of the king. In most versions of the year-drama, the king wages combat with his dark adversary of the underworld, emerging victorious after a temporary defeat from his duel with death, to be acclaimed in a single mighty chorus as the worthy and recognized ruler of the new age.

The New Year was the birthday of the human race and its rites dramatized the creation of the world; all who would be found in "the Book of Life opened at the creation of the World" must necessarily attend. There were coronation and royal marriage rites, accompanied by a ritual representing the sowing or begetting of the human race; and the whole celebration wound up in a mighty feast in which the king as lord of abundance gave earnest of his capacity to supply his children with all the good things of the earth. The stuff for this feast was supplied by the feasters themselves, for no one came "to worship the King" without bringing his tithes and first fruits.

Thus we wrote some years ago, citing a dozen well-documented cases in widely separated parts of the ancient world to show that this identical Year-Rite took place everywhere.[3] But in more than two hundred separate descriptions of this festival gathered over a number of years we never thought to include one of the most impressive of all—for who would think to turn to the Book of Mormon for such information?

Yet it is there, and very conspicuously so. We have already found abundant evidence in the Book of Mormon for the religious orientation of the believing *minority;* but if the people as a whole took their culture directly from the Old World, as we have so emphatically maintained, then we should also expect the worldly majority to have *their* traditional piety and express it on formal occasions in ritual patterns based on the immemorial usages brought from the old country. And that is exactly what we do find. In the Book of Mormon we have an excellent description of a typical Great Assembly or Year Rite as we have briefly described it above. Though everything takes place on a far higher spiritual plane than that implied in most of the Old World ritual texts, still not a single element of the primordial rites is missing, and nothing is added, in the Book of Mormon version. In the Old World itself the rites were celebrated at every level of spirituality, from the gross licentiousness of Rome and Babylon to the grandiose imagery and austere morality of Pindar and some of the old apocalyptic writings. It is the latter tradition that meets us in the national rites of the Nephites.

King Benjamin and the Ways of the Fathers: There was a righteous king among the Nephites named Benjamin, and he was a stickler for tradition. He insisted that his three sons "should be taught in all the languages of his father," (Mos. 1:2) just as Nephi had been of old; "and he also taught them concerning the records which were engraven on the plates of brass," being convinced that without such a link to the past they "must have suffered in ignorance." (Mos. 1:3.) He cited the case of Lehi who learned Egyptian and had his children learn it, so that they could read the old engravings "that thereby they could teach them to *their* children," and so on, "even down to this present time." (Mos. 1:4.) Without these written records, Benjamin observed, his people would be no better off than the Lamanites, who had nothing but the corrupt and incorrect traditions of their fathers to guide them. (Mos. 1:5.) It would appear that the grand passion of King Benjamin's life was the preservation intact of the mysteries and practices of his people as they went back to the beginning, as set forth, for example, in the brass plates. (1 Ne. 5:11-16.)

When King Benjamin "waxed old, and said that

he must very soon go the way of all the earth, he made preparation to confer the kingdom upon one of his sons." Now the transfer of kingship is the central act of the great rite to which we referred above, no matter where we find it. And it is this rite which is fortunately described by Mosiah in considerable detail.

The "Year Rite" in America: Let us mark the various details descriptive of the rite in the Book of Mormon, numbering them as we go. The first thing King Benjamin did in preparation was to summon his successor, Mosiah, and authorize him (for it is always the new king and never the old king that makes the proclamation) to (1) "make a proclamation throughout all this land among all this people . . . that thereby they may be gathered together;[4] for on the morrow I shall proclaim unto this my people out of mine own mouth that thou art a king and a ruler over this people, whom the Lord our God hath given us. And moreover, (2) I shall give this people a name, that thereby they may be distinguished above all the people which the Lord God hath brought out of the land of Jerusalem." (Mos. 1:10-11.) Then (3) "he gave him charge concerning all the affairs of the kingdom," (Mos. 1:15), and consigned the national treasures to his keeping: the plates, the sword of Laban, and the Liahona, with due explanation of their symbolism. (Mos. 1:16-17.)[5]

The Order of the Meeting: Obedient to Mosiah's proclamation, (4) "all the people who were in the land of Zarahemla . . . gathered themselves together throughout all the land, that they might go up to the temple to hear the words which king Benjamin should speak unto them." (Mos. 1:18, 2:1, in which the formula is repeated.) There was so great a number, Mosiah explains, (5) "that they did not number them," this neglect of the census being apparently an unusual thing. (Mos. 2:2.)[6] Since these people were observing the law of Moses and their going up to the temple was in the old Jewish manner, (6) "they also took of the firstlings of their flocks, that they might offer sacrifice and burnt offerings according to the law of Moses." (Mos. 2:3.) The "firstlings" mark this as (7) a New Year's offering, and just as the great *Hag* was celebrated after the Exodus in thanksgiving for the deliverance from the Egyptians, so the Nephite festival was (8) "to give thanks to the Lord their God, who had brought them out of the land of Jerusalem, and who had delivered them out of the hands of their enemies" in the New World. (Mos. 2:4.)

The multitude (9) pitched their tents round about the temple, "every man according to his family . . . every family being separated one from another." (Mos. 2:5.) (This is the Passover practice according to the Talmud.) (10) Every tent was erected "with the door thereof towards the temple. . . ." (Mos. 2:6.) This, then, was a festival of the "booths". Throughout the ancient world, whether among the Greeks, Romans, Celts, Germans, Slavs, Egyptians, Babylonians, Persians, Indians, Arabs, Hebrews, etc., the people must spend the time of the great national festival of the New Year living in tents or booths, which everywhere have taken on a ritual significance.[7]

In theory, these people should all have met "within the walls of the temple," but because of the size of the crowd the king had to teach them from the top of (11) a specially erected tower. (Mos. 2:7.)[8] Even so, "they could not all hear his words," which the king accordingly had circulated among them in writing. (Mos. 2:8.)[9]

King Benjamin's Address Explains All: This formal discourse begins with (12) a *silentium,* that is, an exhortation to the people to "open your ears that ye may hear, and your hearts that ye may understand, and your minds that the mysteries of God may be unfolded to your view." (Mos. 2:9.)[10] The people were there for (13) a particularly vivid and dramatic form of instruction "unfolding to view" the mysteries of God. Then Benjamin launches into his discourse with a remarkable discussion

of the old institution of divine kingship. (14) Throughout the pagan world the main purpose of the Great Assembly, as has long been recognized, is to hail the king
as a god on earth;[11] Benjamin is aware of this, and he will
have none of it:

> I have not commanded you to come up hither that ye should
> fear me, or that ye should think that I of myself am more than
> a mortal man. But I am like as yourselves, subject to all manner
> of infirmities in body and mind; yet I have (15) been chosen
> by this people, and consecrated by my father, and was suffered
> by the hand of the Lord, that I should be a ruler and a king over
> this people . . . (Mos. 2:10-11.)

So far he will go in the traditional claim to divine
rule, but no farther: he has been elected by acclamation
of the people, as the king always must at the Great
Assembly,[12] and the Lord has "suffered" him to be a
ruler and a king. In all this part of his speech concerning
his own status, Benjamin is plainly aware of the *conventional* claims of kingship, which he is consciously re-
nouncing:

> I say unto you that as I have been suffered to spend my
> days in your service . . . and have not sought gold nor silver nor
> any manner of riches of you. (Mos. 2:12.)

This is a reminder that (16) the king at the Great
Assembly everywhere requires all who come into his
presence to bring his rich gifts as a sign of submission.[13]
Benjamin leans over backwards to give just the opposite
teaching: "Neither have I suffered that ye should be
confined in dungeons, nor that ye should make slaves
one of another. . . . And even I, myself, have labored
with mine own hands that I might serve you, and that
ye should not be laden with taxes. . . ." (Mos. 2:13-14.)
Here again he deliberately and pointedly reverses the
conventional role of kings: ". . . and of all these things
(17) . . . ye yourselves are witnesses *this day* . . . I tell
you these things that ye may know that I can answer a
clear conscience before God *this day*." (Mos. 2:14-15.)
"This day" is the formally appointed time for settling
all accounts between the king and the people, as it is for

making and concluding all business contracts—not only the New Year, but specifically the Great Assembly of the New Year in the presence of the king is everywhere the proper time to enter and seal covenants, while restating the fundamental principles on which the corporate life of the society depends.[14] Benjamin states these principles with great clarity, "that ye may learn that when ye are in the service of your fellow beings ye are only in the service of your God. Behold, ye have called me your king; and if I, whom ye call your king, do labor to serve you, then ought not ye to labor to serve one another? . . . and if I . . . merit any thanks from you, O how much you ought to thank your heavenly King!" (Mos. 2:16-19.)

Here King Benjamin tells the people that they are there not to acclaim (18) "the divine king," but rather "your heavenly King . . . that God who has created you, and has kept and preserved you, and caused that ye should rejoice, and . . . live in peace one with another . . . Who has created you from the beginning, and is preserving you from day to day . . . even supporting you from one moment to another." (Mos. 2:20-21.) Fifteen years ago in an article on the Year Rite the author described how the king on that occasion would scatter gifts to the people "in a manner to simulate the sowing of the race itself on the day of creation, with all the blessings and omens that rightly accompany such a begetting and amid acclamations that joyfully recognize the divine providence and miraculous power of the giver."[15] These are the very two motifs (we will call them 18 and 19) emphasized by Benjamin in the sentences just quoted. He continues in this vein, reminding his people that they are completely dependent on one source for all the blessings of life and for life itself, that in and of themselves men are entirely without power, "And I, even I, whom ye call your king, am no better than ye yourselves are; for I also am of the dust." (Mos. 2:25-26.) Then comes (20) the king's farewell, when he declares that he is "about to yield up this mortal frame to its mother earth.

... (Mos. 2:26), to go down to my grave, that I might
go down in peace, and my immortal spirit may join the
choirs above in singing the praises of a just God."
(Mos. 2:28.) "... I have caused that ye should assemble
yourselves together, that I might declare unto you that
I can no longer be your teacher, nor your king."
(Mos. 2:29.) Now one of the best-known aspects of the
Year-drama, is the ritual descent of the King to the
underworld—he is ritually overcome by death, and then
ritually resurrected or (as in the Egyptian *Sed* festival)
revived in the person of his son and successor, while his
soul goes to join the blessed ones above.[16] All this, we
believe, is clearly indicated in King Benjamin's farewell.
The "heavenly choir" is a conspicuous feature of the
Year Rite, in which choral contests have a very prominent place, these choruses representing the earthly
counterpart of "the choirs above."[17] (21)

And now comes the main business of the meeting:
the succession to the throne. Benjamin introduces his son
to the people and promises them that if they "shall keep
the commandments of my son, or the commandments of
God which shall be delivered unto you by him" (22, 23)
prosperity and *victory* shall attend them, as it always did
when they kept the commandments of the king. (Mos.
2:30-31.) In this passage Benjamin shows very plainly
how he is shifting from the conventional formulae—"ye
have kept my commandments, and also the commandments of my father ... keep the commandments of my
son"—to a humbler restatement and correction: they are
really the commandments of God. The people will have
prosperity and victory (the two blessings that every ancient king *must* provide if he would keep his office) provided they remember "that ye are eternally indebted to
your heavenly Father," and (24) preserve the records
and traditions of the fathers. (Mos. 2:34-35.) If they
do that they will be "blessed, prospered, and preserved,"
(Mos. 2:36) "... blessed in all things, both temporal
and spiritual; and if they hold out faithful to the end
they are received into heaven, that thereby they may

dwell with God in a state of never-ending happiness.
O remember, remember that these things are true. . . .''
(Mos. 2:41.) Also they should keep a remembrance of
the awful situation of those that have fallen into transgression." (Mos. 2:40.)

After this (25) blissful foretaste of "never-ending
happiness" which is always part of the Year Rite,[18] King
Benjamin proceeds to look into the future, reporting a
vision shown him by an angel in a dream. (Mos. 3:1-2.)
(26) Divination of the future is an essential and unfailing part of the Year Rite and royal succession everywhere and always in the Old World,[19] but again Benjamin gives it a spiritualized turn, and what he prophecies
is the earthly mission of the Savior, the signs and wonders shown the ancients being according to him "types
and shadows showed . . . unto them, concerning his
coming." (Mos. 3:15.) The whole purport of Benjamin's
message for the future is that men should be found
blameless before the Great King, who will sit in judgment (Mos. 3:21), exactly as the King sat in judgment
at the New Year.[20] (27)

On the theme of eternity, (28) the closing sound
of every royal *acclamatio*,[21] King Benjamin ended his address, which so overpowered the people that they "had
fallen to the earth, for the fear of the Lord had come
upon them." (Mos. 4:1.) This was the kind of *proskynesis* at which Benjamin aimed! (28) The *proskynesis*
was the falling to the earth (literally, "kissing the
ground") in the presence of the king by which all the
human race on the day of the coronation demonstrated
its submission to divine authority; it was an unfailing
part of the Old World New Year's rites as of any royal
audience.[22] A flat prostration upon the earth was the
proper act of obeisance in the presence of the ruler of
all the universe. So on this occasion King Benjamin
congratulated the people on having "awakened . . . to
a sense of your nothingness . . . and come to a knowledge
of the goodness of God, and his matchless power . . .
and also the atonement which has been prepared from

the foundation of the world . . . for all mankind, which ever were since the fall of Adam, or who are, or who ever shall be, even unto the end of the world." (Mos. 4:5-7.) The King then discourses on man's nothingness in the presence of "the greatness of God" (Mos. 4:11), and the great importance of realizing the equality of all men in the presence of each other. This is (29) a very important aspect of the Year Rites, which are everywhere supposed to rehearse and recall the condition of man in the Golden Age before the fall, when all were brothers and equals.[23] Benjamin does not mince matters: "For behold, are we not all beggars? Do we not all depend upon the same Being, even God, for all the substance which we have. . . . And now, if God, who has created you . . . doth grant unto you whatsoever ye ask that is right. . . . O then, how ye ought to impart of the substance that ye have one to another. . . ." (Mos. 4:19-21.) The second half of the 4th chapter is taken up entirely with the theme of how the whole population can be secured in the necessities of life.

When this speech was finished the people approved it by (30) a great *acclamatio,* when they "all cried with one voice," declaring, when the king put the question to them, that they firmly believed what he had told them, and that they "have great views of that which is to come." (Mos. 5:1-3)[24] Then they took a significant step, declaring, "we are willing (31) to enter into a covenant with our God to do his will, and to be obedient to his commandments in all things . . . all the remainder of our days. . . ." (Mos. 5:5.) To which the king replied: "Ye have spoken the words that I desired; and the covenants which ye have made is a righteous covenant." (Mos. 5:6.) Then he gave them (32) a new name, as he promised his son he would:

And now, because of the covenant which ye have made ye shall be called the children of Christ, his sons, and his daughters; for behold, THIS DAY HE HATH SPIRITUALLY BEGOTTEN YOU . . . And I would that ye should take upon you the name of Christ, all you that have entered into the covenant

with God that ye should be obedient unto the end of your lives.
(Mos. 5:7-8.)

As we noted above, the Year Rite everywhere is the
ritual begetting of the human race by a divine parent.[25]

Next Benjamin makes the interesting remark that
whoever complies "shall be found at the right hand of
God, for he shall know the name by which he is called,"
(Mos. 5:9), all others standing "on the left hand of
God." (Mos. 5:10.) At the Great Assembly when all
living things must appear in the presence of the King to
acclaim him, (32) every individual must be in his proper
place, at the right hand or left hand of God.[26] "Retain
the name," Benjamin continues, "written always in your
hearts, that ye are not found on the left hand of God,
but that ye hear and know the voice by which ye shall
be called, and also the name by which he shall call you."
(Mos. 5:12.) "If ye know not the name by which ye
are called," he warns them, they shall be "cast out," as
a strange animal is cast out of a flock to whose owner it
does not belong. (Mos. 5:14.) To avoid this, the king
"would that . . . (33) the Lord God Omnipotent, may
seal you his." (Mos. 5:15.)[27]

All this talk of naming and sealing was more than
figurative speech, for upon finishing the above words
"king Benjamin thought it was expedient . . . that he
should take the names of all those who had entered into
a covenant with God to keep his commandments."
(Mos. 6:1.) And (34) the entire nation gladly regis-
tered. (Mos. 6:2.) Some form of registering in the
"Book of Life" is found at every yearly assembly.[28] Having completed these preliminaries, the king "consecrated
his son to be a ruler and a king over his people . . . and
also had appointed priests to teach the people . . . and
(35) to stir them up in remembrance of the oath which
they had made."[29] Then he (36) "dismissed the multitude, and they returned, everyone according to their
families, to their own houses." (Mos. 6:3.)

Other Assemblies in the Book of Mormon: At this time among the people of Lehi-Nephi, who happened to be in bondage to the Lamanites, "king Limhi sent a proclamation among all his people, that thereby they might gather themselves together to the temple to hear the words which he should speak unto them." (Mos. 7:17.) Apparently such assemblies were a general practice and not invented by Benjamin. A year later Benjamin's son Mosiah again "caused that all the people should be gathered together" (Mos. 25:1) in a national assembly of a political nature in which the people of Nephi and the people of Zarahemla "were gathered together in two bodies." (Mos. 25:4.) One of the tribes attending this meeting "took upon themselves the name of Nephi, that they might be called the children of Nephi and be numbered among those who were called Nephites" (Mos. 25:12), while at the same time "all the people of Zarahemla were numbered with the Nephites," in a general census and reshuffling of tribes. (Mos. 25: 13.) This assembly was organized "in large bodies," and the priest Alma went from one to another speaking to them the same things that Benjamin had taught his people. (Mos. 25:14-16.) Then the king "and all his people" asked to enter the covenant of baptism" (Mos. 25:17), and so Alma was able to establish his church among them.

Over a generation later when one Amlici was able to exert great political pressure to get himself elected king, "the people assembled themselves together throughout all the land . . . in separate bodies, having much dispute and wonderful contentions one with another." (Alma 2:5.) Here the system is abused by an illegal claimant to the throne who insists on holding his own coronation assembly. When a vote was taken "the voice of the people came against Amlici, that he was not made king" (Alma 2:7), that is, he failed to receive the acclamation that every ancient king had to have, and so his followers "gathered themselves together, and did consecrate Amlici to be their king." (Alma 2:9.) It was illegal, yet all recognized that the claim to the kingship had to have an assembly and a consecration.

In another land, King Lamoni was chided by his father: "Why did ye not come to the feast on that great day when I made feast unto my sons, and unto my people?" (Alma 20:9.) From which it is apparent that such royal public feasts were the rule. Over a hundred years later the Nephite governor Lachoneus "sent a proclamation among all the people, that they should gather together their women, and their children, their flocks and their herds, and all their substance, save it were their land, unto one place." (3 Ne. 3:13.) The order was quickly and efficiently carried out with incredible speed, the people "coming forth by thousands and by tens of thousands . . . to the place which had been appointed." (3 Ne. 3:22.) The people were used to such gatherings. Particularly significant is it that they brought with them "provisions . . . of every kind, that they might subsist for the space of SEVEN YEARS. . . ." (3 Ne. 4:4), since as Dr. Gordon has shown, the purpose of the Great Assembly in ancient Palestine had always been to insure a seven-year food-supply, rather than an annual prosperity.[30]

A New Discovery: Years ago the author of these lessons in the ignorance of youth wrote a "doctoral dissertation" on the religious background and origin of the great Roman games. Starting from the well-known fact that all Roman festivals are but the repetition of a single great central rite, he was able to show that the same great central rite and the same typical national festival was to be discovered among half a dozen widely scattered cultures of the ancient world. He has developed this theme through the years in a number of articles and papers read to yawning societies. And all the time it never occurred to him for a moment that the subject had any bearing whatsoever on the Book of Mormon! Yet there can be no doubt at all that in the Book of Mosiah we have a long and complete description of a typical national assembly in the antique pattern. The King who ordered the rites was steeped in the lore of the Old World king-cult, and as he takes up each aspect of the rites of the Great Assembly point by point he gives it a new slant, a genuinely religious interpretation, but with all due respect to established forms. Our own suspicion is that this is not a new slant at all, but the genuine and original meaning of a vast and complex ritual cycle whose origin has never been explained—it all goes back in the beginning to the gospel of redemption. Were it not for the remarkable commentaries of Benjamin, we would never have known about the great Year Rites among the Nephites where, as in the rest of the world, they were taken for granted.

The knowledge of the Year Drama and the Great Assembly has been brought forth piece by piece in the present generation. One by one the thirty-odd details noted in the course of our discussion have been brought to light and associated in a single grandiose institution of the royal assembly or coronation at the New Year, an institution now attested in every country of the ancient world.[31] There is no better description of the event in any single ritual text than is found in the Book of Mosiah.

Questions

1. What is a "sacral" society?

2. How could King Benjamin have produced Old World ritual practices in detail without knowing about them? How could he have known about them?

3. What indication is there that he did know about them?

4. What in Benjamin's address indicates that he is commenting on familiar and established practices?

5. What indication is there in the Book of Mormon that the great gathering was not King Benjamin's original idea?

6. What did Benjamin wish to do by way of reforming the ancient practices?

7. Is the Great Assembly in other parts of the world a spiritual or a purely secular event? Is a king a religious or a civil officer?

8. Where does the idea and practice of a universal assembly survive in the world today?

9. What is a possible origin of the Great Assembly at the New Year found throughout the world?

10. By what method can question 9 be answered?

Lesson 24

EZEKIEL 37:15-23 AS EVIDENCE FOR THE BOOK OF MORMON

Prospectus of Lesson 24: The Latter-day Saint claim that Ezekiel's account of the Stick of Joseph and the Stick of Judah is a clear reference to the Book of Mormon has, of course, been challenged. There is no agreement among scholars today as to what the prophet was talking about, and so no competing explanation carries very great authority. The ancient commentators certainly believed that Ezekiel was talking about books of scripture, which they also identify with a staff or rod. As scepters and rods of identification the Two Sticks refer to Judah and Israel or else to the Old Testament and the New. But in this lesson we present the obvious objections to such an argument. The only alternative is that the Stick of Joseph is something like the Book of Mormon. But did the ancient Jews know about the Lord's people in this hemisphere? The Book of Mormon says they did not, but in so doing specifies that it was the wicked from whom that knowledge was withheld. Hence it is quite possible that it was had secretly among the righteous, and there is actually some evidence that this was so.

Can the Claim be Proven?: The Latter-day Saints have always cited Ezekiel's prophecy concerning the Stick of Joseph and the Stick of Judah (Ez. 37:15-23), as confirmation of the divine provenance of the Book of Mormon. But while these verses may bear the greatest conviction for *them,* before they can be called proof by an unbiased observer a number of propositions regarding them must be established beyond doubt. A few years ago the writer of these lessons was convinced that he had established these propositions, but apparently his evidence was so recondite and his arguments so involved that they defeated their purpose. Since then, however, a number of important studies by "outsiders" who know nothing of the Book of Mormon, have repeated our own labors and put the stamp of Gentile respectability on our conclusions. The preliminary work for determining whether or not Ezekiel was speaking of the Book of Mormon has now been done by unprejudiced scholars,

and we are free to go ahead and demonstrate just why
we are now firmly convinced that the Prophet *was* speaking of the Book of Mormon when he spoke of the Stick
of Joseph.

The preliminary questions are: 1) Is there any obvious interpretation for the passage? 2) If not, does
any existing interpretation, no matter how involved, meet
all the conditions? 3) What could Ezekiel have meant
by "wood"? 4) Did the ancients actually think of a book
as a staff and *vice versa?* 5) How could the sticks "become one"? 6) To what tribal separation and reuniting
can Ezekiel be referring? 7) Could anyone in the Old
World have known about Lehi's secret departure? An
unfavorable answer to any one of these questions would
be enough to refute the claim that the prophet Ezekiel
was thinking of the Book of Mormon when he spoke of
the sticks. Let us consider them briefly one by one.

Ezekiel 37 is not Obvious: 1. The usual clerical rebut-
tal to the claim that Ezekiel's vision refers to the Book of
Mormon is that Ezekiel cannot possibly be referring to
the Book of Mormon because he was "obviously" referring to something else.[1] But whatever obviousness there
is in the reference resides in the will and mind of the
critic and is anything but obvious to the rest of the world.
If no book in the world has been the subject of more dispute than the Bible, certainly no book in the Bible is
more argued about today than Ezekiel; and no passage
in Ezekiel is more variously and more fancifully explained than the mysterious account of the Stick of
Joseph and the Stick of Judah. (Ez. 37:16-23.) To whom
shall we turn for an authoritative explanation of this or
any other part of Ezekiel? Quite recently the retired
dean of one of the greatest American divinity schools,
after a thorough examination of all the scholarly writings
on Ezekiel produced between 1943 and 1953, came to
a significant conclusion: "Not a single scholar has succeeded in convincing his colleagues of the finality of his
analysis of so much as one passage" in that much-

studied book; "They give only opinions," says the dean, "when the situation cries aloud for evidence. . . . Every scholar goes his own way and according to his private predilection chooses what is genuine and what is secondary in the book; and the figure and work of Ezekiel still dwell in thick darkness."[2]

In view of that verdict, how can we accept any man's judgment as final or announce that the Mormons can't be right because, forsooth, Dr. So-and-so thinks otherwise?

Ezekiel 37 Now Given up As Hopeless: 2. But not only is there no "obvious" interpretation to put up against the Mormon one, not even the long and ingenious labors of scholarship have been able to present a convincing interpretation of the passage. Of recent years there has been a strong move among the learned to throw out the passage entirely! "In despair," writes a Jewish Ezekiel scholar, "some will always resort to force: if the puzzling passage cannot be explained, it can be expunged."[3] The astuteness and vanity of scholars do not easily give up the stimulating and challenging game of speculation. When they call, as they now do, for the deletion of a passage of scripture it is truly a sign of "despair," and an admission that the Ezekiel passage as it stands is beyond them.

A more pleasing alternative to expunging the offending verses is of course to rewrite them, and the fact that the leading Ezekiel scholars now insist that they cannot understand the verses about the sticks unless *they* rewrite them, carefully removing as spurious all puzzling and complicating parts, is evidence enough in itself that Ezekiel is speaking of something quite unfamiliar to their training or experience. The wild and contradictory guesses of the ablest scholars on this passage demonstrate beyond a doubt that *Ezekiel is here talking about a matter which, however familiar it may have been to his ancient audience, lies wholly outside the scope of conventional Bible scholarship.*

What is an " 'etz"?: 3. Since it is claimed that Ezekiel's "sticks" stood for books, the questions arise, a) could they have done so? and b) did they? The first thing to consider is that the prophet does not speak of "sticks" at all, but only of "wood," in the singular and plural. The word he uses is 'etz, which in itself simply means "wood," and can only be taken to indicate this or that wooden object or implement when we know the specific use to which it is put. Thus in the Bible one plays music on an 'etz, and then it is not just wood but a harp; one writes with an 'etz, and then it is a stylus or a pen; one ploughs with an 'etz, and then it is more than wood—it is a plough; fruit grows on an 'etz, and then it is a tree; or a tree itself can have an 'etz, which is a branch; when it resembles a person an 'etz is an image; when as such it is worshipped, then it is an idol; as an instrument of execution it is a gallows; as building material it is a beam; as a weapon, it is a spear, etc.[4] As Gregory the Great observed long ago, the Hebrew word 'etz as used in the Old Testament can mean almost anything, depending entirely on the context in which it is used.[5] So before we can translate Ezekiel's 'etz, or even guess at what kind of a thing it was, we must consider the specific uses to which he put it.

It is a Written Text: First of all, the prophet is ordered to *write* upon the "woods". It is not surprising, therefore, that the oldest Jewish commentators on Ezekiel, men who knew far more about Hebrew language, customs and symbols than any modern seminarist ever can, insisted that Ezekiel's "woods" were writing-tablets or books.[6] Recent important discoveries have shown that the board or tablet form of book is exceedingly old—much older than had formerly been supposed, and that "from the Old Babylonian period onwards" a single word was used to designate board, tablet and written documents.[7] The earliest of all surviving Ezekiel commentaries, those of Eusebius and Jerome—the ablest scholars of their time and both trained in Hebrew—maintained that the "woods" of Ezekiel were actually *books*, specifically, books of Scripture.[8] Dr. Keil, in the foremost modern Jewish commentary on Ezekiel, finds it most significant that though the "woods" are definitely rods or staves in some connections, Ezekiel deliberately avoids calling them such, since he does not wish in presenting the complex symbolism of the sticks in any way to obscure the priority of the idea of the "woods" as written documents.[9]

The Word of God as a Staff: 4. Two recent studies give full confirmation to this interpretation. According to Widengren, "the heavenly tablets in the literature of early Judaism play a considerable role," appearing as the Book of Life, Books of Remembrance, records of laws, records of contemporary events, and records of prophecy.[10] "That the various aspects of these tablets in early Judaism can be explained only from the original conception of them as oracles of lots," the same authority continues, "is so obvious that no commentary is needed." Since everything to happen is decided by them, and then written upon them, we hereby gain all the meanings attached to them in Jewish writings.[11] The lots referred to were originally sticks, shaken or drawn from a bag, and the lots and the tablets always went together because originally they were one and the same.[13] In Babylon the King would determine the fates or judgments in imitation of the king of the gods, "who casts the lots by means of the tablets of destiny. . . . These tablets express the law of the whole world, they contain supreme wisdom, and they are truly the mystery of heaven and earth."[12] Studying the Egyptian practices, W. B. Kristensen asks, "What have the staff and the serpent and the Word of Jahwe to do with each other?" He quotes Nöldeke and others who have shown that in Egypt as among the Hebrews the staff was specifically the Word of God, and the Word of God was the *Matteh ha-elohim* or Staff of God.[13] Spiegelberg has shown that the priestly staves were a physical representation of the

presence of God among men, both in Egyptian and
Jewish practice.[14] And while Widengren demonstrates
that such a staff was "a symbol of the Tree of Life,"
Kristensen notes that it also in many instances symbo-
lizes the resurrection.[15]

The Staff As a Book: But the staff symbolized the
Word of God in no abstract sense, it was specifically
the word of God as written down in a *Book*. Hence the
constant identification of the staff with the tablets. The
ancient book took two forms, the tablet form and the
scroll. Both originated with the marked sticks or scepters and always retain marks of their origin. Culin
traces the tablet or sheet book-form to "the bundle of
engraved or painted arrow-derived slips used in divination."[16] To this day our word "book" (and even more
clearly German *Buch-Stabe*, "boxwood-staff" and O.
Slav. *bukva*) recalls the box or beechwood stick scratched
with runic symbols by our Norse ancestors and used exactly as the Hebrews used their rods of identification at
the great public feasts.[17] Even the Latin *codex* and *liber*
refer to the wooden origin of books.[18] Books and staves
are everywhere identified, but what most concerns us here
is the Jewish tradition. Ginzberg has shown that the
tablets of the Law and the *rod* of Moses were in Hebrew
tradition identical.[19] As with other ancient people, inscribed rods were among the oldest forms of written
communication among the Hebrews—the first books, in
fact, and Freeman actually compares the "woods" of
Ezekiel 37 with the tablets and sticks (*axones*) on which
the oldest laws of the Greeks and Romans were kept.[20]

Origin of the Scroll: Even without the abundant
evidence available to prove it, it should be easy to see
how the scroll type of book grew out of the stick-type.
When a lengthy communication was desired, a single
message-stick did not offer enough writing-surface, and
so a piece of leather or cloth was attached to the staff
to hold more writing. For convenience this was wrapped
around the stick when it was not being read. The prac-

tice is found throughout the ancient world.[21] Its antiquity among the Hebrews may be seen in the fact that not parchment (first introduced in the Achemenian period) but leather is the official material for scrolls of the law, and that cannot be ordinary leather, but must be the skins of *wild* animals.[22] This implies "primitive" origins indeed.

In the usage of the Synagogue the sticks around which the scrolls of the law were rolled were always regarded as holy and treated as *scepters*. It should be noted in passing that commentators often point out that the sticks of Ezekiel are plainly meant to represent scepters. The scrolls of the law were used by the king of Judah as other kings used scepters, being "kept near his throne and carried into battle."[25] "The scroll itself," we are told, "is girded with a strip of silk and robed in a Mantle of the Law," while the wooden rod has a crown on its upper end, like the scepter of a king. "Some scrolls," says the *Jewish Encyclopedia,* "have two crowns, one for each upper end."[22] These honors shown the Jewish scrolls of the Law are the same as those accorded to the royal herald's-staff or scepter in other parts of the world.[23]

Rods of Identification: But if the "woods" were written texts, as such they were put to peculiar uses. For the nature of the inscription put upon them—"for Joseph," "for Judah"—shows plainly that they are to serve as rods of identification.[24] When the people ask the prophet what the marked rods signify, he is to explain to them that they stand for the tribes whose names they bear; and when he formally joins the two sticks "before their eyes" it is with the explanation that this represents the joining of the nations represented by the rods. In joining the two sticks, the nations are joined. (Ezek. 37:18-21.)

Such staves or rods of identification enjoyed a prominent place in the public economy of the ancient Hebrews, as of other early peoples. Individuals carried such rods on formal occasions, and tribes as well as individuals were identified by and with their "staves" or "sceptres." Every man who came to the great gathering of the nation at the New Year was required to bring with him a staff with his name on it.[25] For the same occasion the leader of every tribe had to present a tribal staff with official marks of identification on it; the twelve tribal staves were then bound together in a ritual bundle and laid up in the Ark of the Covenant as representing the united force of the nation.[26] The tribe itself on this occasion was called a *"shevet—*staff", the word being cognate with the Greek *skeptron* (cf. Lat. *scipio*) whence our own "sceptre." Indeed, in the crucial 19th verse of our text the Septuagint does not say "sticks" at all, but only "tribes." Commenators on Ezekiel point to parallel passages in the Old Testament which show the "woods" of Ezekiel to be scepters, and suggest that they were "the two parts of a broken sceptre,"[27] "two pieces of what was probably a broken, scepter-shaped stick,"[28] "sticks probably shaped like scepters,"[29] etc.

For the ancients it was quite possible for a piece of wood to be at one and the same time a scepter, a rod of identification (which was only a private scepter), and a book (which was a message written on or attached to the sender's staff). Jewish legend is full of wonderful staffs. The rods of Adam, Enoch, Elijah, Moses, Aaron, David, Judah, etc., were actually thought of as one and the same scepter, loaned by God to his earthly representative from time to time as a badge of authority, and an instrument of miracles, proving to the world that its holder was God's messenger.[30] But such a thing is also the law, and the Rabbis spoke of the law as God's staff, to lead and discipline his people.[31]

How the Sticks Become One: 5. How could the sticks become one? To judge by the commentaries, that is just about the toughest problem in all Ezekiel. All sorts of ingenious explanations have been devised by the experts to describe in what manner the sticks of

Ezekiel could have been put together to "make them one stick."[32] The thing is so totally foreign to any modern experience that even Professor Driver had decided that the passage must be a mistake.[33] But the long experience of scholarship has shown that it is just such oddities as this one, which completely baffle the critics, that give the stamp of authenticity to a record and usually hold the key to the whole business.

The Tally Sticks: Ezekiel is in all probability here referring to an institution which flourished among the ancient Hebrews but was completely lost sight of after the Middle Ages until its rediscovery in the last century. That is the institution of the tally-sticks. A tally is "a stick notched and split through the notches, so that both parties to a transaction may have a part of the record."[34] That is, when a contract was made certain official marks were placed upon a stick of wood in the presence of a notary representing the king. The marks indicated the nature of the contract, what goods and payments were involved, and the names of the contracting parties. Then the stick was split down the middle, and each of the parties kept half as his claim-token (hence our word "stock" from "stick") and his check upon the other party (hence called a "foil").[35] Now both parties possessed a sure means of identification and an authoritative claim upon each other no matter how many miles or how many years might separate them. For the tally-stick was fool-proof. When the time for settlement came and the king's magistrate placed the two sticks side by side to see that all was in order, the two would only fit together perfectly mark for mark and grain for grain to "become one" in the King's hand if they had been one originally—no two other halves in the world would match without a flaw; and if either of the parties had attempted to add or efface any item of the bill ("bill" means originally also a stick of wood), by putting any new marks or "indentures" upon it the fraud would become at once apparent.[36] So when the final payment was made and all the terms of the contract fulfilled, the two pieces of wood were joined by the King's magistrate at the exchequer, tied as one, and laid up forever in the royal vaults, becoming as it were "one in the king's hand."[37]

The announcement in verse 19 that the sticks "shall be one in *mine* hand," has puzzled the commentators no end. They want to substitute in its place, "the hand of Judah,"—an impossible and meaningless arrangement, as the Cambridge Bible points out, showing a complete miscomprehension of the ordinance here described.[38] Ezekiel tells us that the reuniting of the sticks signifies the re-establishment of bonds of brotherhood. In Zechariah 11:10, 14 we read: "And I took my staff, even Beauty, and cut it asunder, that I might break my covenant which I had made with all the people. . . . Then I cut asunder mine other staff, even Bands, that I might break the brotherhood between Judah and Israel." When the two halves of the rod are "cut asunder" that breaks the covenant or bond that binds Judah and Israel together (that is the meaning of the strange name *Bands*), and the two go their separate ways. As we know, this was not to be a permanent separation. As the sticks and nations can be separated, so they can be joined together again, and that is exactly what happens in the case of Joseph and Judah, for the Lord explains that Ezekiel shall "make them one stick" to show that he ". . . will make them one nation in the land. . . ." (Ezek. 37:22.) The Jewish doctors taught that the twelve tribal staves of Israel were originally cut from one staff, and that the rods naturally belong together, since they were all shoots from a single stock.[39]

The use of tally-sticks is very ancient and widespread, and no people of antiquity seem to have made more constant use of them than the Jews.[40] Everywhere the proper time and place for bringing the sticks together as well as for cutting new contracts is the great national assembly at the New Year, the yearly gathering of the nation in the presence of the king—still commemorated by the Jews in the three "pilgrimage festivals." On that occasion, as we have said, each tribe and individual was expected to bring a staff or rod with the proper marks of identification on it. And just as the tribal staves would be bound together and put in the Ark, so the rods of in-dividuals—of every male in Israel—were tied together in the so-called Bundle of Life, which is often mentioned in Rabinnical Writings and is a concept of great antiq-uity.[41] Unless a man's name was included—"bound up" —in the Bundle of Life, he had no place in the Kingdom. Here again we see the tie between sticks and books, for this Bundle can be easily identified with "the Book of Life" which contained the names of all citizens of the holy nation.[42]

Thus the joining of the sticks by Ezekiel does not want for ancient parallels in Israel. The prophet knew what he was doing, and so did his hearers. There are rods many, as there are tribes many, and when Ezekiel shows us the rod of Joseph, he is speaking of that tribe specifically.

Joseph, not Israel: 6. But to what tribal separation and reuniting can Ezekiel be referring? Judah and Israel, some have said, Judaism and Christianity, others maintain. These are the two explanations that spring most readily to mind, but on second thought both fall through completely. As to the first, Herntrich finds it "exceedingly surprising" that Ezekiel should suddenly start talking about the irrelevant separation of Israel and Judah, though he can think of no other explanation for the prophecy.[43] "The book of Ezekiel," writes Spiegel, "spans the years of his captivity, 593-568 B.C., includ-ing perhaps a few earlier oracles, spoken while the prophet was still in Palestine."[44] Yet instead of writing about the scattering and captivity of his own time, he is supposed to be referring indirectly to those occurring 400 years earlier. That is indeed surprising and puzzling, but there is a more serious objection.

Everybody knows that Judah and Israel were two nations that had once been one nation, so what could be more natural than to conclude that their reuniting is the subject of the story? Well, if Ezekiel had meant it that way, he would have said so, and there an end. And that is just what the commentators find so annoying about the whole thing: Ezekiel does *not* say so. He speaks instead of Judah and *Joseph,* a combination which calls forth entirely different associations. Nor does he speak of a simple joining together of two symbolic sticks. He takes one stick and writes upon it: ". . . For Judah and for the children of Israel his companions: . . ." (Ezek. 37:16.) placing both Judah and Israel on a single stick. Then he takes another piece of wood and writes on it. " . . . For Joseph; the stick of Ephraim, and for all the house of Israel *his* companions." (Ezek. 37:16.) It is not Israel over against Judah at all, but Judah and such of Israel as are with him, as against Joseph and such of Israel as are with him. We are dealing with two clearly marked but composite branches of Israel which together make up "the whole house of Israel." The text says literally: "I will take the wood of Joseph, which is in the hand of Ephraim *and* the staves of Israel his associates, and I shall place them alongside the wood of Judah, and I shall take them for one wood, and they shall be one in my hand." This is no simple joining of two sticks: the wood of Joseph goes along with other sticks of Israel—those of Israel "associated with him"—and these are fitted to the wood of Judah.

How much simpler to have Ezekiel speak directly of the joining of Judah and Israel! Impatient of the prophet's refusal to cooperate, the experts have taken it upon themselves either to reject or rewrite the passage entirely.

Joseph and Judah not Old Testament and New Testament: When one thinks of two covenant books, one naturally thinks of the Old and New Testaments, and that is exactly what the two most famous Bible critics of all time — Eusebius and Jerome — thought of. The former says the two sticks must have been the Old and

New Testaments respectively,[45] and Jerome projects the symbolism farther: it is not only the Old and New Testament, according to him; it is likewise the Synagogue and the Church, the Jews and the Gentiles, the old covenant and the new one that followed and replaced it.[46] But it is only too easy to see why this ingratiating interpretation was not accepted by their successors, ancient or modern. To point out but a few of the more obvious objections, 1) the New Testament is no more Joseph's book than it is Judah's; 2) in Ezekiel's account the perfect equality of the two is stressed; Judah does not absorb Joseph, nor Joseph absorb Judah, as the Church is supposed by the fathers to absorb the Synagogue; 3) nor in Ezekiel does one covenant follow after and supplant the other in time; they are strictly contemporary, brought together and placed side by side to become one; 4) the Old Testament and New Testament were brought together almost immediately, and at that time neither of the two parties were scattered, smashed, dead,—"Dry bones,"—as both should have been if the prophecy refers to them; 5) but, most significant, the two nations are described by Ezekiel as being reunited after a long separation (*dudum separata*, says Jerome); they once shared a common covenant and brotherhood which is here simply being renewed. This entirely disqualifies any claims of the Gentiles to hold the stick of Joseph, coming in as they do as outsiders who have never known the covenant.

Did Ezekiel Know?:   7. The most interesting question of all is whether Lehi's departure could have been "leaked out" to the Jews at Jerusalem. We receive solemn assurance in the Book of Mormon that that did not happen:

> . . . because of their iniquity that they know not of you. And . . . other tribes hath the Father separated from them; and it is because of their iniquity that they know not of them. (3 Ne. 15:19-20.)

> And not at any time hath the Father given me commandment that I should tell it unto your brethren at Jerusalem. Neither . . .

that I should tell unto them concerning the other tribes . . . whom the Father hath led away. . . . (3 Ne. 15:14-15.)

Yet Ezekiel knew about them. But the Lord is speaking of his communications to those at Jerusalem during his earthly mission among them when he says: ". . . because of stiffneckedness and unbelief they understood not my word; therefore I was commanded to say no more . . . concerning this thing unto them." (3 Ne. 15:18.) "They" in this case are "the Jews at Jerusalem," from whom precious things are withheld specifically "because of their iniquity." Ezekiel does not come under such a head, and neither do Peter, James and John. When the multitude gathered to hear Jesus he did *not* tell them "the mysteries of the kingdom of heaven"; "Because," he explained to his disciples, "it is given unto you to know the mysteries of the kingdom of heaven, but to them it is not given." (Matt. 13:11.) But nowhere does the Book of Mormon say or imply that *no* one was ever told about the other sheep, indeed the opposite is indicated by the repeated explanation that it is only because of iniquity that people are denied the knowledge, and the ignorant ones are always designated specifically as they at Jerusalem.

Hidden Knowledge: An interesting confirmation of the deliberate withholding of knowledge from the unworthy is the statement of Irenaeus, who is in many things our last link with the Primitive Church, that the meaning of Ezekiel's prophecy about the sticks of Joseph and Judah "is hidden from *us*, for since by the wood we rejected him, by the wood his greatness shall be made visible to everyone, and as one of our predecessors has said, by the holy reaching out of the hands the two people are led to one God. For there are two hands and two nations scattered to the ends of the earth."[47]

Who the "predecessor" was in the Early Church who made that statement we do not know, but his words certainly recall those of Nephi:

... Know ye not that the testimony of two nations is a witness unto you that I am God, that I remember one nation like unto another? Wherefore, I speak the same words unto one nation like unto another. And when the two nations shall run together the testimony of the two nations shall run together also. ... and I shall also speak unto all nations of the earth and they shall write it. ... And ... my people ... shall be gathered home ... and my word also shall be gathered in one. (2 Ne. 29:8-14.)

These words suggest nothing so powerful as the ancient technique of the tallies—totally unknown to the world in Joseph Smith's day, but the fact that Irenaeus is quoting an early Christian disciple on Ezekiel and admitting his own ignorance is significant. While the later doctors of the Church had glib or ingenious explanations for Ezekiel's sticks, the celebrated editor of the *Patrologia* has observed that for the *earliest* Christians that prophecy held immense significance, the real meaning of which they deliberately concealed from the world.[48] Even more interesting is a hint dropped by Origen:

Clement, the disciple of the Apostles, recalls those whom the Greeks designate as *antichthonians* (dwellers on the other side of the earth), and other parts of the earth's sphere (or circuit) which cannot be reached by anyone from our regions, and from which none of the inhabitants dwelling there is able to get to us; he calls these areas "worlds" when he says: "The Ocean is not to be crossed by men, but those worlds which lie on the other side of it are governed by the same ordinances (lit. dispositions) of a guiding and directing God as these."[49]

Here is a clear statement that the *earliest* Christians taught that there were people living on the other side of the world who enjoyed the guidance of God in complete isolation from the rest of the world. Origen knows of mysterious knowledge that was had among the leaders of the Primitive Church but was neither divulged by them to the general public nor passed on to the general membership, and this includes the assurance that there were people living on the other side of the world who enjoyed the same divine guidance as themselves in a state of complete isolation.

The Rejected Key: While it may be clear that the *Jews* were not told of Lehi's departure, it seems likely that Ezekiel did know of it. Yet, the knowledge he possessed was conveyed in such form that only those who held the key were able to recognize it. Even the ablest scholars being without that key are at a loss to say what Ezekiel is getting at. The message was meant only for those who had "ears to hear" it, and in the time of Lehi, the time of Christ, and our own day, only they have heard it, though the documents have at all times been accessible to the public! So it has always been with the mysteries of the kingdom and the preaching of the Gospel: set forth in all plainness to the eye of faith, sealed with seven seals to those that are lost, "that seeing they might not see." So it has been in modern times when the message has been rejected. "I told you," Christ told his contemporaries, "and you would not believe me." Ezekiel when he was asked ". . . Wilt thou not show us what thou meanest by these?" (Ezek. 37:18ff) was ordered to give them a full explanation—which nobody has understood to this day! Why not? Because the Jews were a stiffnecked people; and they

despised the words of plainness, . . . and sought for things that they could not understand. Wherefore, because of their blindness, which blindness came by looking beyond the mark, they must needs fall; for God hath taken away his plainness from them. . . . And because they desired it God hath done it, that they may stumble. (Jac. 4:14.)

". . . because of stiffneckedness and unbelief," the Lord told the Nephites, "they understood not my word; therefore I was commanded to say no more . . . concerning this thing unto them." (3 Ne. 15:18.) That is why the plain testimony of the sticks has been by-passed by the learned in favor of "things that they could not understand." By speaking in a parable, even as the Lord spoke in parables, Ezekiel could give the whole world the opportunity of learning about chosen people in other lands and yet not run the risk of divulging the

Lord's secrets to the unrighteous. "Who has ears to hear let him hear!"

Questions

1. Why is there no agreement among experts on the interpretation of Ezekiel 37:15-23?

2. Why did the ancient Bible commentators insist that Ezekiel's "woods" were books or tablets of scripture?

3. How was the Word of God anciently identified with a staff?

4. How can a stick or staff be a book?

5. How are staff and book identical in the rites of the synagogue?

6. What indication is there in Ezekiel that the sticks of Joseph and Judah were tribal staves, scepters, or identification rods?

7. How could the sticks "become one"?

8. What evidence is there that Ezekiel may have been speaking of tally sticks?

9. Why cannot the two sticks be taken to refer to Judah and Israel?

10. Why can they not symbolize the Church and the Synagogue?

11. Why was all knowledge of the Book of Mormon people kept from the Jews at Jerusalem?

12. How could Ezekiel give the righteous a chance to hear the message without the risk of divulging it to the unrighteous? Does the Lord follow the same policy in the New Testament? What method does he use to spread the gospel while guarding the mysteries?

Lesson 25

SOME TEST CASES FROM THE BOOK OF ETHER

Prospectus of Lesson 25: In this lesson we pick out some peculiar items in the Book of Ether to show how they vindicate its claim to go back to the very dawn of history. First, the account of the great dispersion has been remarkably confirmed by independent investigators in many fields. Ether like the Bible tells of the Great Dispersion, but it goes much further than the Bible in describing accompanying phenomena, especially the driving of cattle and the raging of terrible winds. This part of the picture can now be confirmed from many sources. In Ether the reign and exploits of King Lib exactly parallel the doings of the first kings of Egypt (entirely unknown, of course, in the time of Joseph Smith) even in the oddest particulars. The story of Jared's barges can be matched by the earliest Babylonian descriptions of the ark, point by point as to all peculiar features. There is even ample evidence to attest the lighting of Jared's ships by shining stones, a tradition which in the present century has been traced back to the oldest versions of the Babylonian Flood Story.

Was There a Great Dispersion?: The test of the Epic Milieu is a rigorous and convincing one, (See *The Improvement Era*, Jan. 1956 to Feb. 1957!) but there is a great deal of detail in the Book of Ether that can now be checked against new evidence. Let us consider a few conspicuous examples of this.

Since the idea of the scattering of the nations from the great tower is not original to Ether we need not discuss it here, but there are some peculiar aspects of the event which deserve a word. The tower of the dispersion is never called the Tower of Babel in the Book of Mormon; it is never referred to as anything but "the great tower." Where it stood we do not know; the expression "land of Shinar" in Gen. 11:2 is a vague and general designation for all of Babylonia,[1] and the orientation of the wandering "down into the valley which is northward" (Ether 1:42 — all following references are from Ether) and the long migration that followed with "flocks both male and female of every kind" (Ether 1:41) certainly looks towards the steppes. The great philologist

Hrozny has recently concluded that "we must now seek the Hamito-Semitic home only in the region of the original Indo-European home," that is to say, all the great languages of the earth, ancient and modern, spring from a single center! This center Hrozny finds "north of the Black Sea, Caucasus, and Caspian. "It seems altogether likely," Hrozny continues, "that the earth was populated from Central Asia." It was drought that caused the people to scatter with their herds, he surmises, seeking grass "in a centrifugal emigration . . . that moved out in all directions."[2]

Hrozny's evidence for this is philological, and it merely confirms what is being concluded on other grounds, but the interesting thing is that the principal philological key to the problem is the name *Kish*, which is both an Old World and a Jaredite name. Now this name—Kish, Kash, Kush—is, according to Hrozny, the most widespread proper name in the ancient world, yet it can be traced back "to a definite point of diffusion in the Caspian area."[3] This is what the present writer has always referred to as "Jaredite country." It was our guess that the Caspian was "the sea in the wilderness" that the Jaredites had to cross. (Ether 2:7.) Whatever the specific aspects of the thing, the point to note is that the idea of the diffusion of all the great languages of the world and of civilization itself from a single area in Asia and at a single time is now being seriously considered by the greatest scholars.

Another aspect of the thing to notice is the suggestion that the people had to scatter in all directions to find grass for their herds. This is not a whim of Hrozny's— there is a great deal of evidence to support the claim that the scattering was attended by very unpleasant weather conditions.[4] As cattlemen know, a disastrous year does not have to be one of spectacularly violent meteorological displays: grazing is a marginal business and a few dry years can mean ruin. Nevertheless there is much to indicate that the violent winds on which the book of Ether insists (Ether 6:5, 6, 8), were a reality.

To the Asiatic materials we gave in *The World of the Jaredites*[5] may be added some very old documentary evidence from Egypt and Babylonia.

The Great Winds: Egyptian Traditions: In the Pyramid Texts, "the oldest large body of written material in the world," the first Pharaoh is described as coming into Egypt in a terrible storm, and often the king is depicted as accompanied by a fierce wind, as moving with the North Wind, etc.[6] In one interesting text God is described as "letting loose an inundation over the Ancients," as "letting go a tempest on those who did wrong," and as pushing over "the wall on which thou leanest."[7] Can this be a reference to the flood, the great wind and the fall of the tower? It is possible: the legend persisted in Egypt, that after the waters of the Flood had subsided to the level of the present seashores, a great wind came and piled sand over the idols of the ancients, thus forever concealing their abominations from view.[8] The first king to rule in Egypt after Noah, according to another account, built a great wooden castle on the banks of the Nile (it is interesting that the oldest royal structure known in Egypt *was* a massive wooden edifice!) in which the constellations were depicted, and while the king sat there surrounded by beautiful women before a table loaded with drink, a great and terrible wind arose, dashing the waters against the palace until it collapsed and all in it were drowned.[9] The parallel to the great house of Lehi's dream is interesting. The grandson of that wicked king devised an apparatus by which he "caused the winds to blow against all the lands, until the inhabitants thereof came and submitted to him."[9]

Babylonian Traditions: Haldar has made a study of the wind in the oldest Babylonian texts. According to these, when the divine presence is withdrawn from man "the raging storm blows in over the country, bringing with it locusts and other accompaniments of the desert wind, whereby the country is laid waste and becomes the desert," the "pasturage of cattle" being destroyed.[10]

"The sheep-fold is delivered to the wind," says one text in which "the wind is clearly described as the destructive power."[10] In another text the gods decree the destruction of the city of men by a great wind, the "evil wind" under which "the land trembles, the people are killed, and the dead bodies are lying in the gates of the city."[11] In a Sumerian epic hymn the god departs from the city like a flying bird while the Great Wind comes and the people "perish through hunger, the mother leaves her daughter, the father turns away from his son, the wife is abandoned, the child is abandoned, the possessions are scattered about—an excellent description of the state of chaos . . ."[12] When God leaves the earth, the enemy moves into his place and then "turns the *edin* into a desert by the hurricane," which destroys people and cattle, while the land becomes prey to "the hordes from the 'desert.' "[14] Being expelled from her city by the wind, the Lady Ishtar "wanders among the 'bedouin sheikhs' . . . the pastures and fields have become a desert . . ."[13] In Sumerian and Babylonian ritual texts "the 'word' is very often compared to a raging wind, or an overflowing flood . . . the 'word' (of Enlil) is said to be a storm that destroys the 'stable' and the 'fold', that fells the wood, that causes the Anunnakis to abandon the temples, and locusts to plunder the grove of the goddess."[14]

Haldar cannot avoid the conclusion that all these references to the winds that ruin the grazing and destroy civilization are no mere ritual inventions but are actually "describing historic events in the terms of religious language," even though they may not refer to one "specific historic situation."[15] In one of the oldest of all historic monuments the king compares himself with "an evil storm-wind," in explanation of which Haldar notes that "It may be easy to imagine that in an early period . . . historical experience may have influenced the development of religious worship," since the "storm-wind" epithet seems to be a kind of formula in the earliest Egyptian as well as the earliest Sumerian religion.[16]

A very interesting Jewish apocryphal writing tells

how in the last days "God will bring a strong wind . . . and from the midst of that wind the Holy One . . . will scatter the tribes in every town, and men will find no bread until the Holy One turns sand into flour."[17]

Hebrew Traditions: Eisler has examined the Jewish tradition that tells of how the baptism of the earth by water in the days of Noah, purging it of its wickedness, was later followed by a baptism of wind, to be followed in turn at the end of the world by a baptism of fire. The baptism of winds, we are told, took place at the time of the tower.[18] According to the Book of Jubilees (called the "Little Genesis"), "The Lord sent a mighty wind against the tower and overthrew it upon the earth, and behold it was between Asshur and Babylon in the land of Shinar, and they called its name 'Overthrow'."[19] Of these traditions by far the most interesting is the Mandaean teaching that when the world was purged at the time of the great wind the human race was broken up into many languages, but there were two men whose language was not changed: they were Ram and his brother Rud.[20] The names are contractions, the second from Jared, the first from some unknown name. This Jared may be confused with the son of Mahalaleel in the Book of Jubilees, who was given a vision of "what was and what will be . . . as it will happen to the children of men throughout their generations until the day of judgment." This Jared "testified to the Watchers, who had sinned with the daughters of men, (at the time of the tower, according to the usual calculation) . . . And he was taken from amongst the children of men, and we conducted him into the Garden of Eden . . . and behold there he writes down the condemnation . . . and all the wickedness of the children of men."[21] Since Jared, unlike Lehi, widely publicized his departure, attempting to gather recruits wherever he could (Ether 1:41), it is quite conceivable that some memories of him and his strange departure should have lingered.

Ether makes it very clear that Jared's migration was

but a small part of a great world movement in which "the people" were "scattered upon all the face of the earth," (Ether 1:33); Jared himself hoped to be a lone exception, but in vain. (Ether 1:38.) And so when we find among the oldest traditions of the oldest civilizations that their first kings came into their various lands as wanderers in the beginning in a time of terrible winds we have a confirmation of a clear historical pattern.[22] What is most interesting about this is that in the oldest and best documented of all these instances the royal symbol is the bee, and the word for royalty is Deseret. We have treated this subject elsewhere at considerable length; what we would reiterate here is the easily demonstrable fact that in the Egyptian symbolism the Bee may be substituted for the Deseret crown in any operation.[23]

Lib a Typical "Predynastic" King: The organization of the land of Egypt under the first Pharaoh presents a remarkable parallel to the reorganization of the Jaredite land under King Lib. Let us briefly summarize our longer study of the subject.

Story of the Snakes: There had been a great drought, so severe that it permanently affected conditions of life: the population was terribly reduced by famine; the country began to swarm with snakes; the cattle started a mass movement of drifting towards the south, where there was better grazing; in desperation "the people did follow the course of the beasts, and did devour the carcasses of them which fell by the way . . ." (Ether 9:34.) When the drought finally ended things got better, but the snakes were still so bad towards the south as to shut off attempts at migration and colonization in that direction for at least two hundred years to come. Then came the heroic Lib, who "did that which was good in the sight of the Lord," and in whose days, and apparently under whose leadership, "the poisonous serpents were destroyed." They did not just vanish or cease to annoy, they "were destroyed." Consequently the coveted southland was again open to exploitation, and the first step was a great national hunt; "they did go into the land southward, to hunt food for the people of the land, for the land was covered with animals of the forest." In this King Lib himself would have taken the lead, for "Lib also himself became a great hunter." (Ether 10:19.)

Instead of colonizing the forested land to the south, however, it was set aside as a game preserve: "And they did preserve the land southward for a wilderness, to get game. And the whole face of the land northward was covered with inhabitants." (Ether 10:21.) Exactly at the point of meeting between these two zones, "they built a great city by the narrow neck of land, by the place where the sea divides the land." (Ether 10:20.) Then follows a description of a great economic boom and expansion period, marking King Lib as the founder of a new age. (Ether 10:22-29.)

Turning to Egypt, we note that whoever the first Pharaoh and chief author of Egyptian civilization may have been, it is apparent from the texts we quoted in the *Era* that he opened vast new tracts of land to settlement by a systematic destruction of serpents and crocodiles which hitherto had barred settlement and even passage throughout the area.[24] The serpents are always associated with a drought. It was also he who having come in and settled with his people, "the followers of Horus," established the system of the Two Lands, the double organization of Egypt, building a great city in the narrow neck just at the point of the Delta at a place called "the balance of the two lands."[24] It is also known that the whole Delta with its lush meadows and dense thickets, was preserved down to a late period as a hunting grounds for the nobility, and that Pharaoh himself enjoyed the ritual position of chief hunter.[25] All this information is gathered from ritual texts, and it is folly to try to distinguish too sharply between religious institutions and the secular elements in them, since at all times, as Kees has shown, the Egyptian state itself was a huge religious institution while the king's office was from first to last a sacred one and everything he did was a religious ritual.[26] The great and prolonged drought that marked a new phase in Jaredite history may have been the same world-wide weather disturbance that sent the Horus people into Egypt; at any rate there is to say the least a remarkable resemblance in the way things are done in the two worlds, that puts a clear stamp of authenticity of Ether's claim to be telling a tale of archaic times.

Jared's Ships: Since the story of Jared's barges and the shining stones with which he illuminated them has been the subject of much mockery and fun among the critics of the Book of Mormon, they are all the more convincing evidence if they can be shown to have a genuine archaic background.   The key to the barges is found in the declaration that they were built on conventional lines and yet in their peculiarities patterned after Noah's Ark.[27] The discovery of a number of Babylonian texts has given rise to a good deal of speculation as to just what the ark of Noah may have been like.   According to Babylonian versions of great antiquity which add some important items to the brief Biblical account without in any way contradicting it, Noah's ark must have had certain peculiar features which had never been noted by Biblical scholars, even though the Bible hints at some of them.   These peculiar features are precisely those that have beguiled and amused the critics of the Jared story.   Both Noah's and Jared's boats were designed from conventional lines, but, "according to instructions of the Lord," both were made water tight above as well as below, were peaked at the ends, had a door that could be sealed tight, had a special kind of air-hole, were designed to go under the water, containing all sorts of animals as well as men, were driven by the wind without the use of sails, and were designed to resist the force of unusually violent weather, especially hurricane winds.[28]

The Luminous Stones: But the Babylonian texts do not tell us how the Ark was lighted and the Bible mentions only a *tsohar*, about the nature of which the

Rabbis could never agree.[29] Jared's shining stones have been held up to ridicule as a remarkable piece of effrontery and the invention of a diseased imagination. Yet it can now be shown beyond any dispute:[30]

1) That there existed throughout the world in ancient and medieval times the report of a certain stone, the *Pyrophilus,* that would shine in the dark. This stone, it was believed was a pure crystal and could only be produced and made luminous by the application of terrific heat. It had the miraculous quality of enabling its possessor to pass unharmed through the depths of the water.

2) The story is not a folk-tale but is found only in the recondite writings of the most celebrated scholars in the East and West, who passed the tale around among them. The wonderful shining stone is found only in the possession of a Cosmocrator, like Solomon, its most famous owner being Alexander the Great.

3) The Alexander accounts of the stone are actually much older than Alexander, and have easily been traced back to the Babylonian Gilgamesh Epic, in which the stone appears as the Plant of Life which Gilgamesh seeks from Utnapishtim, the Babylonian Noah. The Pyrophilus legend wherever it is found has accordingly been traced back ultimately in every case to the story of Noah.

4) The most wonderful object in the inmost shrine of the great cult center of Aphek, in Syria, where the deeds of Noah and the story of the flood were celebrated in word and ritual, was a stone that shone in the dark.

5) One of the explanations of the *Zohar* given by the ancient Rabbis was that it was a polished jewel which Noah hung up in the ark so that he could tell night from day; the source of this seems to be a very brief, obscure, and little-known remark in the Palestinian Talmud and attributed to R. Ahia ben Zeira, to the effect that "in the midst of the darkness of the Ark Noah distinguished day from night by the aid of pearls and precious stones, whose lustre turned pale in the daylight and glittered at

night."[31] This is far from the Ether account, which could hardly have been inspired by it, even if the writer of the Book of Mormon had known of this still untranslated passage from the *Talmud Jerushalmi*. But it is obviously an echo of the old account of the shining stones, the association of which with Noah no one suspected until the discovery of the Gilgamesh Epic. It was that discovery which put scholars on its trail at the end of the last century.

Now whether the ark of Noah was actually lit by shining stones or not is beside the point, which is that the idea of stones shining in the darkness of the ark was not invented by Joseph Smith or anybody else in the 19th century, but was known to the ancient Rabbis in an obscure and garbled version, was clearly indicated in the properties of a very ancient shrine dedicated to the Syrian Noah, and was mixed in among the legends of the very ancient Alexander cycle by means of which scholars quickly and easily ran it down to its oldest visible source, namely the old Sumerian Epic of the Babylonian Noah. However, ridiculous the story of the shining stones may sound to modern ears, there is no doubt that it is genuine old stuff, going back to the proper sources as far as Ether is concerned.

Questions

1. On what grounds does Hrozny defend the thesis of the diffusion of all civilization from a single point?

2. What evidence is there that the great winds mentioned in Ether really occurred?

3. How do winds cause people to scatter and wander?

4. Compare conditions described in the Sumerian temple texts with those described in the Book of Ether. Is there any connection between them?

5. How does the story of King Lib's administration resemble that of the first Pharaoh? How do you explain the coincidence?

6. Where could Joseph Smith have got the story of the shining stones?

7. Is it conceivable that some record of Jared's departure might have been left behind?

8. How do Egyptian and Hebrew traditions of the Great Wind match the report of Ether?

9. Is the story of the plague of serpents historically plausible?

10. In what ancient records do we find remarkable parallels to the peculiar ships of the Jaredites?

Lesson 26

THE WAY OF THE "INTELLECTUALS"

Prospectus of Lesson 26: The discovery of the Dead Sea Scrolls has brought to light the dual nature of ancient Judaism, in which "the official and urban Judaism" is pitted against the more pious Jews "intent on going back to the most authentic sources of Jewish religion . . . in contrast to the rest of backsliding Israel." (Moscati.) The official Judaism is the work of "intellectuals" who are not, however, what they say they are, namely seekers after truth, but rather ambitious men eager to gain influence and followers. The Book of Mormon presents a searching study of these people and their ways. There is the devout Sherem, loudly proclaiming his loyalty to the Church and his desire to save it from those who believe without intellectual proof. There is Alma, who represents the rebellion of youth against the teachings of the fathers. There is Nehor, the Great Liberal, proclaiming that the Church should be popular and democratic, but insisting that he as an intellectual be given special respect and remuneration. There is Amlici, whose motive was power and whose tool was intellectual appeal. There is Korihor, the typical Sophist. There is Gadianton whose criminal ambitions where masked by intellectual respectability. For the Old World an exceedingly enlightening tract on the ways of the intellectuals is Justin Martyr's debate with Trypho, and also an interesting commentary on the Book of Mormon intellectuals whose origin is traced directly back to the "Jews at Jerusalem."

Two Views: How does it come about that the most devout and disciplined segment of the believers in every age always appear as a despised and persecuted minority, regarded by the society as a whole as religious renegades and at best as a lunatic fringe? For one thing, those believers themselves have always fully appreciated their uncomfortable position, which can readily be explained by any number of scriptural declarations. The world's ways are NOT God's ways; they do not get along well together, for each is a standing rebuke to the other—"in the world ye shall have tribulation."

In this conflict between two different views of religion, the opposition and overwhelming majority is as unchanging in its methods and attitudes as the saints themselves. It is hard to believe that the Book of Mormon was published 125 years ago when one reads its account of the smart, sophisticated, and scientific arguments put forward by those who would cast discredit on the whole Plan of Salvation. It is as modern as today's newspaper; the situations it describes are those characteristic of our own generation, and quite different from those of Joseph Smith's day, when one could still be a fundamentalist Christian and an intellectual.

The Book of Mormon Explains the Opposition: At the outset of the Book of Mormon Nephi states a clear-cut case for the whole thing—"O that cunning plan of the evil one! O the vainness, and the frailties, and foolishness of men! When they are learned they think they are wise, and they hearken not unto the counsel of God, for they set it aside, supposing they know of themselves, wherefore, their wisdom is foolishness and it profiteth them not. And they shall perish." (2 Ne. 9:28.) Here is the devil's plan, and it is devilishly clever, the best possible way to turn men's minds against the plan of salvation being the appeal to their vanity. The two things people want are to be successful and to be smart —The Elite: ". . . and the wise and the learned, and they that are rich, who are puffed up because of their learning, and their wisdom, and their riches, . . ." are the ones who think they are putting God, in his place, while it is He who is rejecting them: ". . . yea, they are they whom he despiseth; and save they shall cast these things away, and consider themselves fools before God, and come down in the depths of humility, he will not open unto them." (2 Ne. 9:42.) Nephi goes on to speak of conditions in these latter days:

And they shall contend one with another . . . and they shall teach with their learning, and deny the Holy Ghost (2 Ne. 28: 4) . . . they have all gone astray save it be a few . . . nevertheless . . . in many instances they do err because they are taught by the precepts of men. (2 Ne. 28:14) . . . others he (the devil) flattereth away, and telleth them there is no hell; and he saith unto them: I am no devil, for there is none—and thus he whispereth in their ears. . . . (2 Ne. 14:22.)

Since humility is one of the rarest of human qualities, the most direct and effective appeal is to vanity:

. . . priestcrafts are that men preach and set themselves up for a light unto the world, that they may get gain and praise of the world; but they seek not the welfare of Zion. (2 Ne. 26:29.)

The search for knowledge is only a pretext: ". . . for they will not search knowledge, nor understand great knowledge, when it is given unto them in plainness, even as plain as word can be." (2 Ne. 32:7.) There is only one way to know the answers: ". . . And no man knoweth of his ways save it be revealed unto him, . . ." (Jac. 4:8); yet men will not humble themselves to pray for revelation. (See 2 Ne. 32:8.) ". . . How blind and impenetrable are the understandings of the children of men; for they will not seek wisdom, neither do they desire that he should rule over them!" (Mos. 8:20.) When they say they are asking God, men prefer to tell him; rather than "taking counsel from the Lord," they "seek to counsel the Lord." (Jac. 4:10.) They are invincibly reluctant to ". . . believe that man doth not comprehend all things which the Lord can comprehend," (Mos. 4:9), and firmly opposed to consider for a moment their own nothingness and the greatness of God. (Mos. 4:11.)

Highlights in the History of Intellectual Pride: Lehi's people inherited a tradition of intellectual arrogance from their forebears. "The Jews . . ." says Jacob, in a searching passage, ". . . were a stiffnecked people; and they despised the words of plainness, and killed the prophets, and sought for things that they could not understand. Wherefore, because of their blindness, which blindness came by looking beyond the mark, they must needs fall; for God hath taken away his plainness from them, and delivered unto them many things which they cannot understand, because they desired it. . . ." (Jac. 4:14.)

Sherem: Early in Nephite history an ambitious intellectual by the name of Sherem who was a master of smooth talk and rhetorical tricks and made a great show of being a good and devout church-member, set himself to the task of outshining all others as a Great Mind.

> And he labored diligently that he might lead away the hearts of the people . . . (Jac. 7:3) . . . And he preached many things which were flattering unto the people; and this he did that he might overthrow the doctrine of Christ (Jac. 7:2) . . . And he was learned, that he had a perfect knowledge of the language of the people; wherefore he could use much flattery, and much power of speech. . . . (Jac. 7:4)

This man remonstrated sanctimoniously with "Brother Jacob" against "perverting the right way of God," in a way which he said he found quite shocking to his religious sensibilities—it was blasphemy, no less, he declared, to go around teaching people that anyone could know of things to come—such a thing is simply against reason! (Jac. 7:7.) While brushing aside Jacob's testimony, which could tell of visitations of angels and hearing the voice of the Lord (Jac. 7:6) because *he* had not seen or heard, Sherem could none the less bear his own testimony: ". . . but I *know* that there is no Christ, neither has been, nor ever will be." (Jac. 7:9.) Yet after this resounding declaration he asked for a sign! The interesting thing about Sherem is his convincing performance as a devout and active churchman who is not attacking the Gospel but defending it: no wonder he got a large following! In the same spirit the priests who put Abinadi to death did so in a spirit of righteous indignation, (Mos. 17:12), just as the Jews and Gentiles in killing the Apostles were to "think they do God a favor."

Alma: The next intellectual who meets us is the great Alma, who grew up in a time when "the rising generation . . . did not believe the traditions of their fathers. They did not believe what had been said concerning the resurrection of the dead, neither did they believe concerning the coming of Christ." (Mos. 26:1-2.)

True to form, Alma ". . . was a man of many words, and did speak much flattery to the people . . . stealing away the hearts of the people; causing much dissension among the people. . . ." (Mos. 27:8-9.) Why would a man do that? we may ask, but it is experience, not reason, that so richly substantiates the truth of these stories, however implausible they may seem to the rational mind. Alma was one of the smart young men. It took an angel to convert him, yet he was made of the right stuff, as our intellectuals often are![1]

Nehor: Next comes Nehor, the Great Liberal, ". . . declaring unto the people that every priest and teacher ought to become popular; and they . . . ought to be supported by the people." (Alma 1:3) This is a familiar "liberal" paradox. The liberal is unpretentious and open-minded, just like everybody else—yet he forms a jealously guarded clique for the exploitation of the general public, and distinguishes sharply between the intellectual class to which he belongs as a special elite and the layman, who is expected to support him and to seek instruction at his feet. Of course Nehor preaches ". . . that all mankind should be saved at the last day, and that they need not fear nor tremble . . . for the Lord had created all men . . . and, in the end, all men should have eternal life." (Alma 1:4) In a discussion with a very old man named Gideon, who had been a great hero in his day, Nehor the Great Liberal and lover of mankind lost his temper and killed him. (Alma 1:7-9) The crime Alma charged him with at the trial was priestcraft. Nehor's teaching caught on and years later we find one of his followers, a judge, using peculiarly brutal and cruel methods against those guilty of preaching the old faith. (Alma 14:15-18) It is significant that the most violent and inhuman mass persecutions in history—those of the Church in the 4th and 5th centuries, the Mutazilites in Islam, and the Inquisition—were initiated and carried out by idealists and intellectuals. Churches of Nehor's persuasion dotted the land as evidence of the popularity of his teaching, ". . . that God will save all men," as well as his common sense rejection of ". . . foolish traditions, . . ." and the belief in such things as angels or the possibility of prophesy. (Alma 21:6-8) It was simply not scientific to believe such stuff! To remonstrate with these open-minded believers was to incur both their wrath and their mockery. (Alma 21:10) Now let us recall that it was the "priestcrafts" of the Jews at Jerusalem that made things hard for Lehi in the beginning, when he tried to tell his fellow citizens in simple straightforward terms that he had seen a vision, ". . . they did mock him, . . ." and planned to put him to death. (1 Ne. 1:19-20.)

Amlici: Amlici was a man much like Nehor, we are told (Alma 2:1), and extremely clever, ". . . a very cunning man, yea, a wise man as to the wisdom of the world, . . ." who got such a huge following that he finally succeeded in getting himself crowned king (Alma 2:2-9), and caused an immense lot of trouble. In the years of turmoil that followed his rise to power a new type of intellectual becomes conspicuous, men "who were lawyers," holding public office:

> . . . Now these lawyers were learned in all the arts and cunning of the people; and this was to enable them that they might be skillful in their profession. (Alma 10:15)

It was the same old type, only clothed with public office and authority. The essence of their activity and success was still the clever manipulation of words, especially in questioning the prophets of the church, ". . . that by their cunning devices they might catch them in their words, that they might find witness against them . . ." (Alma 10:19.) They would lay their legal traps, and if they failed to work became righteously indignant. ". . . This man doth revile against . . . our wise lawyers whom we have selected . . . (Alma 10:24) . . . this man is a child of the devil, for . . . he hath spoken against our law. . . . And again he has reviled against our lawyers and our judges." (Alma 10:28-29.) Such men are dangerous enough on their own, but when their position becomes official (either in education or government) they have a powerful lever for achieving their aims by force, as Amulek observes: ". . . the foundation of the destruction of this people is beginning to be laid by the unrighteousness of your lawyers and your judges." (Alma 10:27.)

Korihor: Korihor in the Old World would be classed as a Sophist, though his arguments are precisely those that had such an immense vogue among the liberals of the 1920's. He remarked, ". . . Why do ye look for a Christ? For no man can know of anything which is to come. Behold, these things which ye call prophecies . . . they are foolish traditions of your fathers . . . ye cannot know of things which ye do not see. . . ." (Alma 30:13-15.) All this crazy stuff about remission of sins, he says, ". . . is the effect of a frenzied mind; and this derangement of your minds comes because of the tradition of your fathers . . ." (Alma 30:16:) Taking up one of H. L. Mencken's favorite refrains, he went about ". . . telling them that when a man was dead, that was the end thereof," (Alma 30:18), and drawing the inevitable moral corollary that it makes precious little difference how one behaves in life, just so one gets on with people, since ". . . every man fared in this life according to the management of the creature; Therefore every man prospered according to his genius, and that every man conquered according to his strength; and whatsoever a man did was no crime." (Alma 30:17.) Such was the morality of the early Sophists, followed with such fatal effect by Plato's relative Critias. Korihor was out to free the human mind from ". . . foolish traditions of your father, . . ." and from the ". . . foolish ordinances and performances which are laid down by ancient priests, to usurp power and authority over them, to keep them in ignorance. . . ." (Alma 30:23.) His method was to subject all the claims of prophetic religion to a rigorous examination based on his *own* experience of things: ". . . I say that *ye* do not know that there shall be a Christ. . . ." (Alma 30:26.) The motive for this rule of ignorance, he says, is to keep people down, so that their leaders "may glut yourselves with the labors of their hands . . . and that they durst not enjoy their rights and privileges. Yea, they durst not make use of that which is their own," being kept in line by the priests with "their traditions and their dreams and their whims and their visions and their pretended mysteries, that they should, if they did not do according to their words, offend some unknown God—a being who never has been seen or known, who never was nor ever will be." (Alma 30:27-31.) When this was written 19th century liberalism was still to be born—the Book of Mormon in fact leaves virtually nothing for the liberals to say, for all their perennial claims to bold and original thinking. On the other hand, the whole case for their opponents is summed up in Alma's answer to Korihor, including the challenge: "And now what evidence have ye that there is no God, or that Christ cometh not? . . ." (Alma 30:40.) Korihor gave the inevitable reply to this. His critical mind had not been satisfied, ". . . If thou wilt show me a sign, . . ." he said, ". . . then will I be convinced of the truth of thy words." (Alma 30:43.) ". . . I do not deny the existence of a God, . . ." he explained, ". . . but I do not believe that there is a God; and I say also, that ye do not know that there is a God; and except ye show me a sign, I will not believe." (Alma 30:48.)

Gadianton: When Nephite missionaries came among the Zoramites, a general assembly was held to discuss the threat to vested interests, ". . . for it did destroy their craft. . . ." (Alma 35:3.) Finally in Gadianton we find an out-and-out criminal using the intellectual appeal and garb of reason as an instrument to achieve his ends. This Gadianton ". . . was exceeding expert in many words, . . ." (Hel. 2:4) and in the end he ". . . did prove the overthrow, yea, almost the entire destruction of the people of Nephi." (Hel. 2:13.) And it all began with perfectly reasonable and plausible talk.

Faced with such a power what is one to do? The

answer is simple, says Helaman: ". . . whosoever will
lay hold upon the word of God . . ." will have that ". . .
which shall divide asunder all the cunning the snares
and the wiles of the devil. : . ." (Hel. 3:29.) When in
his day ". . . angels did appear unto men, wise men, and
did declare unto them glad tidings of great joy, . . ."
only ". . . the most believing part of the people . . ."
were even interested, while the vast majority

. . . began to depend upon their own strength and upon their own
wisdom, saying: Some things they may have guessed right, among
so many; but behold, we KNOW that all these great and marvelous works cannot come to pass. . . . And they began to reason
and to contend among themselves saying: That is not reasonable
that such a being as a Christ shall come. . . . (Hel. 16:14-21.)

Their main objection was that Christ was to come in
Jerusalem, according to the teachings of the fathers,
". . . therefore they can keep us in ignorance, for we
cannot witness with our own eyes that they are true. . . ."
(Hel. 16:20.)

Dangerous Passions: It was the overwhelming majority of unbelievers who actually set a date for a general massacre of those who expected the coming of
Christ (3 Ne. 1:9, 16.) Fantastic as this may seem, it
has many parallels in history. The slaughter of the Magi
in Lehi's day, the Sicilian Vespers, the liquidation of the
Mamlukes, St. Bartholomew's, the slaughter of the Do-
natists, the Bloodbath of Stralsund, etc., most of them
attempts at the complete wiping out of large unorthodox
minorities, and most of them engineered by devout intellectuals.[2] It is a grim and authentic psychological
touch in the Book of Mormon. When events proved the
believers justified, the others were confounded—but not
for long. In the *Clementine Recognitions,* Peter says
that after the terrible upheavals of nature that accompanied the crucifixion the sun came out again, people
went about their daily tasks, and quickly and efficiently
forgot everything that had happened.[3] So it was in the
New World, where ". . . the people began to forget those

signs and wonders . . . and began to be less and less astonished at a sign or a wonder from heaven . . . and began to disbelieve all which they had heard and seen—

Imagining up some vain thing in their hearts, that it was wrought by men and by the power of the devil. . . . (3 Ne. 2:1-2.)

When later on ". . . there began to be men inspired from heaven and sent forth, . . ." they met with anger and resentment among the people, and especially among ". . . the chief judges, and they who had been high priests and lawyers. . . ." (3 Ne. 6:20-21.) In this case the defenders of rational theology, holding high office, were able to put the offenders out of the way secretly (3 Ne. 6:23), in cynical disregard of the laws which they were supposed to be administering. (3 Ne. 6:24.) When complaints were made to the governor of the land, the offenders formed a solid front in opposition, family and social ties confirming their common interests, and finally got afoot a scheme to overthrow the government and set up a king. (3 Ne. 6:24-30.) Such people, though they ask for miracles, actually hate miracles: "And again, there was another church which denied the Christ; and they did persecute the true church of Christ . . . and they did despise them because of the many miracles which were wrought among them." (4 Ne. 29.) Finally, Mormon speaking of our own day, calls it ". . . a day when it shall be said that miracles are done away . . ." (Morm. 8:26) and he warns those who set themselves up as critics of God's ways that they are playing a dangerous game, "For behold, the same that judgeth rashly shall be judged rashly against . . . man shall not smite, neither shall be judge. . . ." (Morm. 8:19-20.)

It is not pleasant to dwell on this melancholy theme, nevertheless the Book of Mormon places great emphasis upon it, and not without reason. In 1830 there were very few universities in the world, and they were very small. Modern science as we know it was yet to be born, scholarship even at Oxford, did not, according to Mark Pattison's important essay on the subject, include the reading of the Classics; what higher education there was was old-fashioned and religious. It was after the middle of the 19th Century that the illusion of critical objectivity and scientific detachment took over in all fields bringing forth a vast outpouring of literary, philosophical, and scientific panegyrics to the gospel of "science" and reason. "Learning" is the knowledge that men take from each other. It cannot rise above its human source. "But today we have *science!*" the student cries. That is one of the oldest of illusions. We find it in the Book of Mormon, in the Sophists and among the Doctors of the Jews and Christians. The smart people of every age have thought they were being peculiarly "scientific" in their thinking. The "Modern Predicament" is as old as history. The present-day cry in liberal religion is that eschatology and the miraculous belong to another age than ours and that they are hopelessly ancient and foreign to our thought patterns. Meaningless to the "modern mind."[4] Yet that is *exactly* the argument that Korihor puts forward in the Book of Mormon. A bit of research will quickly reveal that it is precisely the charge made against the preaching of the gospel in the Old World. The words and doctrines of the ancient Apostles were just as queer and as distasteful to the people of their *own* day as they are to the modern existentialist, who quite wrongly blames his predicament on to modern science and the differentness of the modern world.[5] Every major "scientific" argument against the Gospel may be found in the Book of Mormon passages we have quoted above.

The Situation at Jerusalem: One of the first, and certainly the greatest, of Christian Apologists was Justin Martyr. In his famous dialogue with the Jew Trypho, he charges "the teachers and leaders of the Jews" with having deliberately defaced and, where possible, removed from the scripture every trace of the true Messianic Gospel which the Jews themselves once taught. He makes it very clear that Christianity is strictly an "eschatological" religion, that stands or falls on its apocalyptic claims. They are the same claims, he insists again and again, that the real inspired Jews of old used to make, the very things that the prophets always taught. The Christians alone, the dialogue insists, are in direct line with the ancient patriarchs and prophets (Dial. 52); the Christians preach an eternal and unchanging gospel (Dial. 29-30), the very same which was taught by the Patriarchs in the beginning. It was Christ whom Abraham saw and talked with (Dial. 56); it was not an angel but the Lord himself who wrestled with Jacob. (Dial. 58-60.) As Elias came anciently, so he came in John the Baptist to announce the Christ, and so he will come to herald Him when he comes again. (Dial. 49.) When Trypho declares this paradoxical, Justin points out that while Moses was still alive God caused the spirit of Moses to descend upon Joshua, who was thereby both a Moses and a Joshua. Circumcision began with Abraham, and sabbaths and sacrifices with Moses; but behind these was an eternal law that had no such beginning, and that is the law brought by Jesus Christ, withheld in other ages because of the wickedness of men and hardness of their hearts, but known to the patriarchs in the beginning none the less (Dial. 43.).

We are really in the same Tradition of teaching that you are, Justin tells Trypho the orthodox Jew (Dial. 11), but we look behind all tentative and provisional rules to the one eternal plan; behind all this passing show is the real thing, ageless and changeless (Dial. 45.).

However much they may quarrel about other things, there are two basic doctrines, say Justin, in which all Christians *must* believe. The *resurrection* and the *millennium*. (Dial. 80.) Why don't the Jews believe in them? Because, says he, they have been led astray by their "teachers" (*Didaskaloi*) and "leaders" (*archontes*). It is they who make and control the official doctrines, and because they happen to sit in Moses's seat and enjoy the support of the government and the control of the schools, it does not follow for a moment that their "official" doctrine is the true patriarchal tradition they claim it is. Indeed, they fight that tradition tooth and nail. "You know very well that your teachers whenever they detect anything in your scriptures that might refer to Christ, diligently efface it." (Dial. 120.) "Your teachers not only undertake their own interpretations in preference to the Septuagint (once their official Bible), but have also removed many passages from the text entirely." To this the indignant Trypho replies: "Do you mean to charge us with completely rewriting the scriptures?" And in answer Justin cites three important passages—all strong evidence for the gospel of Christ—that have been deliberately removed from the scriptures by "the leaders of the people." (Dial. 71-72.) "The teachers of the Jews have shut their minds to the great possibilities of the scripture," he continues,—and are determined to fix things so that no one else will see them either. Motivated by love of wealth, glory, and ease, they have always persecuted the true Church in every age. (Dial. 82.) Justin repeatedly notes that the principal foes of the Savior were always the Scribes and the Pharisees. (Dial. 51.) "It is not surprising that they hate *us*," he says, "since they have *always* killed the prophets," (Dial. 39), thus placing Christianity in the prophetic line. His most serious charge against the doctors is, indeed, that they no longer have prophets among them. (Dial. 51, 52, 87.)

In an enlightening passage, Justin tells how "the leaders of the Jews" went about combating what they regarded as the fanatical sects. "You select special men for the job, and send them out from Jerusalem to every region, warning all against the atheistic of the Christians and making all sorts of unsubstantiated charges against us." (Dial. 17.) The thing is done officially and systematically. One can get an idea of the sort of misinformation that went out by evesdropping on a moment of learned gossip. "Rabbi Eleazer spoke to the scholars (*Hakhimim*). The son of Sotedas brought magic arts out of Egypt tattooed on his body! They answered: "He was a fool, and you can't get reliable evidence from a fool. Son of Sotedas, you say? He was the son of Pandera!" Rabbi Hisda said: "The man's (mother was) Sateda, and her paramour was Pandera; her husband was Paphos ben Jehuda! His mother was called Sateda? No, it was Mary; she was a ladies' hairdresser." In Pumbadetha they explain (the nickname) thus: "Satath-da, meaning she was false to her husband."[6] This passes as first-hand evidence about Jesus. The method of research is that employed by the average "scholarly" investigator of the Mormons.

An Old, Old Story: But how can the doctors of the Law, devout men that they were, have so fallen from grace? Justin explains that as part of the pattern; it did not begin with Christianity. As Israel has rejected the Messiah, so anciently it rejected the higher law which Moses would have given. (Dial. 114.) Enoch found no place in the world and left it to its own darkness, a darkness which is to characterize this world until the "eternal and indissoluble kingdom" and the final resurrection. (Dial. 117.) Justin reviews the great dispensations—Adam, Abel, Enoch, Noah, Abraham-Melchizedek, Moses, David—and duly notes that after each there was an immediate falling-away. (Dial. 19-20.) In the place of *living waters,* he says, the schoolmen in every age busy themselves digging out "puddles that can hold no water." The figure is a powerful one. We see the doctors diligently scraping out holes in the earth in which they hope to preserve the precious water which has ceased to flow from its source. But though they no longer have living water, continually flowing as living water must, the standing pool is not without its uses. "After they fell," says Justin, "They still kept a permanent memory about God, and a questioning in their hearts." He admits that the Jews still have no small "*reminder* of piety," and he wonders just how much of the Old Law is still valid for Christians. (Dial. 46-47.) But in refusing to recognize and accept the truth, men lose their capacity for doing so, and the knowledge of the Son is deliberately withheld from them: ". . . these things seem strange to you, because God has hidden from you the power of recognizing the truth, and that because of your wickedness." (Dial. 55.)

One thing the Book of Mormon illustrates and that is that there is no compromise possible with those who attack the Gospel on what they call intellectual grounds. The church flourished mightily when it got rid of them, but suffered gravely while they were in its midst. No men spent more time with Jesus than the Scribes and Pharisees; they questioned him constantly, and he always answered them—yet there is no instance of his ever converting one of them. The doctors talked his language, they studied the scriptures day and night, they heard him preach, and they held long discussions with him, yet though he converted dockworkers and bankers, farmers and women of the streets, tax-collectors and soldiers, he never converted the doctors. It was they who planned his death.

After all, no man can learn enough in a lifetime to count for very much, and no one knows that better than the man who diligently seeks knowledge—that is the lesson of *Faust*. How then can any *honest* man believe that his modicum of knowledge can supersede revelation and supplant the authority of the priesthood?

Questions

1. According to the ancient Apostles, did the greater danger to the Church come from the outside or the inside? Explain.

2. How does human vanity oppose the teachings of the gospel? Why?

3. What was the intellectual orientation of the Jews at the time of Lehi?

4. Plato says that the man who calls himself an intellectual cannot really be one. Do you agree?

5. What was Sherem's motive for stirring things up? What did he *say* was his real motive and concern? Was he sincere?

6. What does the case of Alma teach us with regard to making hasty judgments?

7. Are those who talk most about broadmindedness and toleration always the most broadminded and tolerant of people?

8. What was the position of Korihor? Were his arguments really scientific?

9. Do people who ask for signs really want to be converted? Illustrate from the Book of Mormon.

10. Is the "Modern Predicament" really modern? Is science a peculiar product of the modern age, unknown to earlier periods?

11. What was Justin's grave charge against the doctors of the Jews? How does it explain the loss of many precious things?

Lesson 27

THE WAY OF THE WICKED

Prospectus of Lesson 27: Crime has a conspicuous place in the Book of Mormon. It is organized crime and for the most part singularly respectable. Here we trace the general course of criminal doings in the Book of Mormon, showing that the separate events and periods are not disconnected but represent a single great tradition. Petty crime is no concern of the Book of Mormon, but rather wickedness in high places. The Book of Mormon tells us how such comes into existence and how it operates, and how it manages to surround itself with an aura of intense respectability and in time to legalize its evil practices. Finally, the whole history of crime in the Book of Mormon is directed to our own age, which is described at the end of the book in unmistakable terms.

Accent on Crime: To the casual reader it might seem that the Book of Mormon refers too much to evil-doing and "all manner of iniquity." But the reasons for this emphasis on the ways of the wicked are fully explained by the book itself. They are meant as a warning and example to that peculiarly wicked age for which the Book of Mormon message has been preserved and to which it is addressed. Nothing marks the Book of Mormon more distinctively as a special message for the New World, or gives it a more convincing ring of authenticity, than the emphasis it puts on the subject of crime and the peculiar type of crime it describes.

Respectable Crime: The pattern of crime in the Book of Mormon is clearly established in the very first chapter, where we read of a plot among the Jews at Jerusalem to put Lehi out of the way. It was no excited street-rabble or quick impulse of a city mob that threatened his life; certain parties "sought his life," (1 Ne. 1:20) with purpose and design: ". . . behold, they seek to take away thy life," said the warning voice of the Lord in a dream (1 Ne. 2:1), and his awareness of the danger gave Lehi time to plan and execute an escape. (1 Ne.

2:4.) In the same way Laman and Lemuel ". . . also . . . sought to take away his life, . . ." in one of their evil plots. (1 Ne. 17:44.) The most significant thing about both these plots is that their authors, "murderers in their hearts" (*Idem*), had themselves convinced that they were doing the right thing; they believed that Lehi was a dangerous and irresponsible trouble maker and, in view of the international situation, treasonable and subversive to the bargain, while they themselves were defenders of respectability and the status quo. ". . . We know," say Laman and Lemuel, "that the people who were in the land of Jerusalem were a righteous people; for they kept the statutes and judgments of the Lord, and all his commandments, according to the law of Moses; wherefore, we *know* that they are a righteous people; and our father hath judged them . . ." (1 Ne. 17:22.) These words deserve careful consideration. Laman, Lemuel and the Jews at Jerusalem were defenders not only of common sense against a man ". . . led away by the foolish imaginations of his heart; . . ." to exchange the comforts of gracious living for years of misery in the desert (1 Ne. 17:20), but they had solid conservative arguments of respectability and religion on their side. In daring to criticize them and to predict awful things about them, Lehi had set himself up as a judge.

How could Nephi answer that? He does so by reminding his brothers that this is simply the old story of the fleshpots of Egypt. It was the Lord who commanded the people to give up all that sort of thing and saved his people in the desert while the Egyptians were destroyed; and what did the people do then? ". . . they hardened their hearts and blinded their minds, and reviled against Moses and against the true and living God." (1 Ne. 17:30.) They took exactly the same position as Laman and Lemuel. And what about their vaunted common sense and righteousness? Forget that pious cant about Chosen People, Nephi tells his brothers. If the Canaanites had been righteous they would have been as "choice" to God as the Hebrews, (1 Ne. 17:34),—

"... the Lord esteemeth all flesh in one; he that is right-eous is favored of God ..." (1 Nephi 17:35) Trust God to destroy the wicked and ". . . lead away the righteous into precious lands . . ." (1 Ne. 17:38), says Nephi, who then reminds his brothers that the Lord has probably already destroyed the Jews at Jerusalem (1 Ne. 17:43), whom they believed to be both righteous and secure.

This first episode in the Book of Mormon sets the stage for all that follows. The criminal element is almost always large and usually predominant in the Book of Mormon, and it is always consciously and vocally on the side of virtue. There is a ring of righteous indignation in Laban's charge against Laman: ". . . Behold thou art a robber, and I will slay thee." (1 Ne. 3:13), and a strong case might be made to show that Laban at all times was acting within his rights.

There are two great treatises on crime in the Book of Mormon, the one in the book of Helaman, describing the doings of the ancient Americans, the other in Mormon, describing the doings of modern Americans. Let us consider them in that order.

Crime under the Judges—The First Phase: The story opens with three of the sons of the great judge Pahoran contending after his death for the vacant judgment-seat, thereby causing ". . . three divisions among the people." (Hel. 1:2-4) The prize went to the eldest brother, but the youngest, Paanchi, continued to make trouble and when he was condemned to death for treason his sup-porters got Pahoran assassinated as he sat on the judg-ment-seat. (Hel. 1:5-9) The man who in disguise committed the crime, one Kishkumen, went back to the Paanchi people and told them that they were now all in it together, so they all took a vow "by their everlasting Maker" not to divulge Kishkumen's secret. (Hel. 1:11) Then having taken this pious religious oath (not by the devil but by the Creator!) the defenders of Paanchi (who was only trying to save his own life) went about their business unrecognized as perfectly respectable citizens. (Hel. 1:12) Soon after, a Nephite dissenter named Coriantumr led a Lamanite army in a surprise attack right into Zarahemla, the capital, and took the city. (Hel. 1:15-20.) The skill and energy of a Nephite commander in charge of defenses in another city, however, trapped and destroyed the invading army. (Hel. 1:28-34.)

Peace being restored a successor was appointed to the chief-judge, who had been killed in the war. But Kishkumen the old judge-killer was back in business, and the old supporters of Paanchi were now a loyal band. This group was taken over and trained to a high state of efficiency by one Gadianton, a smart and competent gentleman ". . . expert in many words, and also in his craft, . . ." which was ". . . the secret work of murder and of robbery. . . ." (Hel. 2:4) Gadianton's object was to become chief-judge himself, and he promised to remunerate his faithful followers by putting them into key positions if he were elected: ". . . they should be placed in power and authority among the people; . . ." (Hel. 2:5) But first of all the ruling judge, Helaman, had to be gotten out of the way, so Kishkumen went to work. Counter-espionage was also at work, however, and a servant of Helaman killed Kishkumen in Kishkumen's attempt to assassinate the judge. (Hel. 2:8-9) Their plans to gain power having been discovered, the gang, under the leadership of Gadianton, ". . . took their flight out of the land, by a secret way, into the wilderness; . . ." and thus escaped the police. (Hel. 2:10-11) Thus we have the negative side of the flight into the wilderness, and Gadianton and his band were now outcasts. How then, could ". . . this Gadianton . . . prove the overthrow, yea, almost the entire destruction of the people of Nephi?" (Hel. 2:13) How could an exposed and discredited criminal bring a whole nation to ruin? That question deserves the closest consideration.

The Second Phase: Twenty-four years after Gadi-

anton's forced retirement things began stirring again.
The chief judge ". . . Cezoram was murdered by an
unknown hand as he sat upon the judgment-seat. And
. . . his son, who had been appointed by the people in
his stead, was also murdered. . . ." (Hel. 6:15.) Such
atrocities were but the reflection of the general moral
depravity, for ". . . the people began to grow exceedingly wicked again." (Hel. 6:16) And of what did such
exceeding wickedness consist? It is important to know,
and the Book of Mormon gives as a clear and frightening answer:

> For behold, the Lord had blessed them so long with the riches
> of the world that they had not been stirred up to anger, to wars,
> nor to bloodshed; therefore they began to set their hearts upon
> their riches; yea, they began to seek to get gain that they might
> be lifted up *one above another*: therefore they began to commit
> secret murders, and to rob and to plunder, that they might get
> gain. (Hel. 6:17)

In a long period of peace and prosperity the people
had come to direct all their energies into economic chan-
nels; the one thing that counted was to get rich and
thereby mount in the world: ". . . to get gain that they
might be lifted up one above another . . ." Wealth became the standard measure of human values and as inevitably happens, people became less and less particular
as to how a man got money, just so he had it—the business of getting gain became utterly sordid and unscrupulous. Before long the more part of the Nephites began
to join up with the Gadianton crowd for protection of
their businesses both against investigation by the government and against the strong-arm methods of competitors:

> . . . the more part of the Nephites did unite with those bands of
> robbers, and did enter into their covenants and oaths, that they
> would protect and preserve one another in whatsoever difficult
> circumstances they should be placed, that they should not suffer
> for their murders, and their plunderings, and their stealings.
> (Hel. 6:21)

The Gadianton Protective Association soon became

the biggest business in America! Card-carrying members (those who knew the secret signs and words (Hel.
6:22) could do about anything they wanted ". . . contrary to the laws of their country and also the laws of
their God," (Hel. 6:23), and thus acquire unlimited
wealth and power. Nevertheless we must not think of
the protective association as a lawless outfit. Far from
it! They operated with great integrity, instructing their
members in all the company rules and disciplining them
in accordance with those rules. (Hel. 6:24) For them
the laws of the land were supplanted by this new code
of laws.

The Criminal Tradition: Helaman gives us a significant account of the history and background of this law
code. He explains that it was not handed down in the
official records of the nation which were transmitted by
Alma to his son but came from another source, having
been ". . . put into the heart of Gadianton by that same
being who did entice our first parents to partake of the
forbidden fruit—. . . who did plot with Cain . . . and . . .
who led on the people who came from that tower into
this land; . . ." (Hel. 6:25-28) And by what means does
the devil put these things into men's hearts? ". . . He
. . . doth hand down their plots, . . . and their plans of
awful wickedness, from generation to generation according as he can get hold upon the hearts of the children of
men." (Hel. 6:30) He does not give men direct revelation but rather he sees to it that the records are there
whenever men fall low enough to be interested in them.
Helaman traces the record here as far back as the Jaredites. These oaths and techniques were given to the
Jaredites ". . . by the power of the devil . . . to help such
[as sought power to gain power . . ."] (Ether 8:16), yet
specifically they were imparted through the consultation
of ". . . the records which our fathers brought across
the great deep. . . ." (Ether 8:9.) When in time the
Gadianton band became extinct, they ". . . concealed
their secret plans in the earth," (Hel. 11:10) and a few

years later when men were again far gone in wickedness
". . . they did search out all the secret plans of Gadianton; and thus they became robbers of Gadianton."
(Hel. 11:26) Thus the devil puts things into men's
hearts by a system of tangible transmission. Since Gadianton's plans were had by the Jaredites and since Gadianton's name is pure Jaredite, as we have pointed out
elsewhere, this would seem to be another of the many
cultural hold-overs of Jaredite civilization among the
Nephites. Certainly the tradition was an unbroken one,
stretching ". . . from the beginning of man even down
to this time." (Hel. 6:29)

Crime Sets the Tone: It is important to understand
that Gadianton's phenomenal success was due to the fact
that the *majority* of the whole Nephite nation submitted
to his plan of operation and his philosophy ". . . and did
build up unto themselves idols of their gold and their
silver. And it came to pass that all these iniquities did
come unto them in the space of not many years . . ."
(Hel. 6:31-32) But while the Nephites sank lower and
lower in their cycle of producing and acquiring goods
as the measure and purpose of man's existence, the Lamanites set about to exterminate the Gadianton society
among their own nations, and succeeded in a most note-
worthy fashion. What were their weapons? No strong-
arm methods were employed; no knives and poison, tear-
gas and sawed-off shot-guns, or the usual arsenal of
crime-bursting futility: they simply ". . . did preach the
word of God among the more wicked part of them, . . ."
and that ended the crime-wave! (Hel. 6:37) If that
sounds a little too idealistic, we must remember that we
are dealing here not with the small and peculiar band of
professional or congenital criminals, but with the general
public gone mad after money—people not really criminal
at heart, but unable to resist the appeal of wealth and
the things it could buy. Among the Nephites these things
actually ". . . seduced the more part of the *righteous*
until they had come down to believe . . ." in the system

of the Gadiantons and "... partake of their spoils, ..."
(Hel. 6:38) Why not? they said, everybody is doing
it! And everybody was: soon Gadianton's Protective
Association "... did obtain the *sole management of the
government*. ..." (Hel. 6:39.)

If the reader has imagined to himself the Gadianton
band as abandoned wretches or street Arabs lurking in
dark alleys and fleeing from the light of day in dingy
and noisome hideouts let him disabuse his mind of such
a concept. They were a highly respected concern that
made their handsome profits by operating strictly within
the letter of the law, as they interpreted and controlled
it. They were the government, the well-to-do, the respectable, and the law-abiding citizens. There *was* a
dangerous and irresponsible element in the society,
namely those improvident and negatively inclined fanatics who called themselves the "followers of God," whose
leaders constantly predicted the worst for society; but
public opinion and common sense were strongly against
such characters and made things pretty hot for them.
They were the anti-social prophets of doom and gloom,
the real criminal element. (Hel. 6:39)

"And thus we see," Helaman concludes, "that they
were in an awful state, and ripening for an everlasting
destruction." (Hel. 6:40) And thus we also see what
Helaman meant when he made the paradoxical statement
that the disreputable Gadianton "... did prove the overthrow, yea, almost the entire destruction of the people of
Nephi." (Hel. 2:13) He did it not as a criminal and
bandit but as one of the most able and successful men
of his time, and entirely with the public's consent.

Corruption Breeds Corruption: Being in control of the
government, we find "... those Gadianton robbers filling
the judgment-seats, ..." (Hel. 7:4) and employing
their office very profitably indeed, "... letting the guilty
and the wicked go unpunished because of their money;
..." and using their positions "... in office at the head
of government ... to get gain and glory ..." (Hel. 7:5)

When the righteous Nephi gave a sermon to a crowd of outraged citizens gathered in his garden (outraged against him, not the government!) he told them some home truths. ". . . How could you have forgotten your God . . .?" he asks, and gives the answer:

> . . . it is to get gain, to be praised of men, yea, and that ye might get gold and silver. And ye have set your hearts upon the riches and the vain things of this world, for the which ye do . . . all manner of iniquity. (Hel. 7:21)

Like Helaman, Nephi puts his finger on the spot: drugs, sex, gambling, anything that comes under the heading of iniquity are all the inevitable adjuncts of national depravity, but they are passed by every time— almost completely ignored—to put the spotlight on the real culprit of which they are but the faithful attendants, the seat of infection and the root of evil being the desire to be rich and successful: "to get gain, to be praised of men. . . ."

Nephi's Crime: Nephi's little sermon received more than a cool reception. Some judges who happened to be card-holding members of the Protective Association were in the crowd and they immediately demanded that Nephi be brought into court and charged with the crime of ". . . reviling against this people and against our law." (Hel. 8:2.) And indeed if contempt of institutions was a crime, Nephi was guilty, for he ". . . had spoken unto them concerning the corruptness of their law . . ." (Hel. 8:3) Still, the judges had to proceed with some care, since they were supposed to be administering justice (Hel. 8:4), and could not be too crude and obvious in their attack, for even among the exceedingly wicked and depraved Nephites the feeling of civic virtue was perhaps as alive as it is in America today; instead of trying to lynch Nephi in fact, the crowd actually protected him from the treatment the judges would liked to have given him. (Hel. 8:4) The latter therefore harangued the people on the monstrousness of Nephi's treasonable behavior in telling them ". . . that . . . our

great cities shall be taken from us. . . . And now we
know that this is impossible, for behold, we are powerful,
and our cities great, therefore our enemies can have no
power over us." (Hel. 8:5-6) Still, even among the
wicked Nephites, there were those in the crowd who
had the courage and fairness to cry out: ". . . Let this
man alone, for he is a good man . . . for . . . he has testified aright unto us concerning our iniquities. . . ." (Hel.
8:7-8) Fair play prevailed, and Nephi continued his
preaching and revealed by inspiration that destruction
was at the doors and that even at that moment the chief
judge had been murdered, ". . . and he lieth in his blood;
. . ." (Hel. 8:27)

At the big public funeral that took place the next
day, the judges who had tried to stir the crowd up against
Nephi declared that his knowledge of the murder showed
he was in on it, and though there were protests he was
bound and brought to formal trial. The trial was held
publicly, ". . . before the multitude, . . ." (in the absence
of television) and the judges were at their best, questioning Nephi "in divers ways that they might cross
him, . . ." slyly offering him bribes and immunity if he
would tell about the murder and his connection with it.
(Hel. 9:19-20) Nephi told them more than they bar-
gained for, advising them to question the brother of the
murdered judge, taking care to inspect the skirts of his
cloak and to accuse him of the murder. Under such
treatment the culprit confessed and in so doing cleared
Nephi, who next went about on a preaching tour through
the whole country, going ". . . from multitude to multitude, . . ." while his assistants did the same. (Hel.
10:17) This alarmed the Protective Association, the
"secret band of robbers" who sat in high places and
whose real motives and methods were concealed from
the public, and to counteract the effect of Nephi's preaching they systematically stirred up contentions everywhere. (Hel. 10:18, 11:2 makes this clear) Nephi's
message was rejected everywhere but the fighting that
had been stirred up got entirely out of hand and devel-

oped into a civil war, or rather a series of ". . . wars throughout all the land among all the people. . . ." (Hel. 11:1)

Now the Lord had promised Nephi that he would grant him whatsoever he asked of him, for he knew that Nephi could be trusted to ask for the right things. (Hel. 10:5.) So to put an end to the terrible state of strife in the nation after it had gone on for two years Nephi prayed for a famine to afflict the land. The prayer was heard and the ensuing famine was so severe that in the end the people gave up fighting and went down on their knees. (Hel. 11:3-7) By the time the famine ended, at the request of Nephi, the Gadianton band had become extinct. (Hel. 11:10)

Third Phase: The end of the famine saw a great improvement in spiritual matters, the more part of the people, both the Lamanites and Nephites belonging to the church. (Hel. 11:18-21) A period of economic expansion and much building also followed, and yet within a scant three years ". . . there began to be much strife . . ." again, certain groups of dissenters taking to murder and plunder in the old style, building up great strength in the mountains and the wilderness by ". . . receiving daily an addition to their numbers. . . ." As they had learned nothing these people ". . . did search out all the secret plans of Gadianton; and thus they became robbers of Gadianton." (Hel. 11:23-26) Within a year the mountains and the wilderness became so infested with the robbers as to be closed entirely to Nephite occupation. (Hel. 11:31) The bands were well organized and defied both Nephite and Lamanite military power, making themselves an object of terror to the whole land by their raids and onslaughts. (Hel. 11:32-33) Still the people continued to forget the Lord and to ripen again for destruction for another five years. (Hel. 11:36-37)

Commenting on this, Helaman observes that ". . . we may see at the very time when he doth prosper his people . . . then is the time that they do harden their hearts . . . and this because of their ease, and their exceedingly great prosperity." (Hel. 12:2) It was at this time that Samuel the Lamanite ". . . came into the land of Zarahemla, and began to preach unto the people. . . ." (Hel. 13:2), telling them that the only reason they had been spared so long was ". . . for the righteous' sake, . . ." and when they should finally cast out the righteous it would be all over with them. (Hel. 13:14) He discoursed on the futility of attempting to achieve security by hiding up one's treasures in the earth, a practice of those who ". . . have set their hearts upon riches; and because they have set their hearts upon their riches, I will hide up their treasures when they shall flee before their enemies . . . cursed be they and also their treasures; . . . Hearken unto the words which the Lord saith; for behold, he saith that ye are cursed because of your riches, and also are your riches cursed because ye have set your hearts upon them . . . unto boasting, and unto great swelling, envyings, strifes, malice, persecutions and murders, and all manner of iniquities." (Hel. 13:18-23) "*All* manner of iniquity," covers every type and variety of crime, but the cause for all of them is always the same.

Next Samuel comments significantly on the suffocating air of respectability and the sanctimonious talk that appear as one of the normal signs of that decadence which according to the Book of Mormon follows upon the enjoyment of great wealth and prosperity:

> And now when ye talk, ye say: If our days had been in the days of our fathers of old, we would not have slain the prophets. . . . Behold ye are worse than they, for . . . if a prophet come among you . . . you will say . . . that he is a sinner, and of the devil . . . But behold, if a man shall come among you and say: Do this, and there is no iniquity . . . do whatsoever your heart desireth . . . ye will receive him and say that he is a prophet. (Hel. 13:25-27)

Their piety was plainly of that brand which styles itself broad-minded, liberal, and understanding. These smart, up-to-date, prosperous, intensely respectable people were in no mood to be told: ". . . the time cometh that he curseth your riches, that they become slippery. . . . And then shall ye lament and say . . . O that we had remembered the Lord our God in the day that he gave us our riches . . . for behold, our riches are gone from us—" (Hel. 13:31-33) After he had told them many wonderful things that converted many, the general public, full of outraged virtue, accused Samuel of being possessed with a devil and tried every means to kill him, but he escaped and "was never heard of more among the Nephites." (Hel. 16:8) After Samuel's departure all the emphasis in the buzz of talk that his preaching and mission had stirred up in the country was on the absurdly unscientific nature of the things he had predicted, and so, with Satan continually going about "spreading rumors and contentions," the book of Helaman ends.

A Typical Deal: In the opening chapter of the book that follows we learn that the revived Gadianton institution was gaining great hold over the imagination of the *young,* who were easily flattered into joining up in large numbers. (3 Ne. 1:29) A letter from the leader of the society to the governor of the Nephite land gives remarkable insight into their psychology. The chief who signs himself the governor of the Society (3 Ne. 3:9) begins by expressing warm admiration for the Nephite governor's firmness "in maintaining that which ye suppose to be your right and liberty," (3 Ne. 3:2) showing himself to be a fair-minded and sporting type. In the next verse he is very patronizing—every inch the "bigshot." "And it seemeth a pity to me, most noble Lachoneus, that ye should be so foolish and vain as to suppose that ye can stand against so many brave men who are at my command, . . ." (3 Ne. 3:3) So, big hearted as he is, the chief proposes a deal, but not until he has first given a little sermon which burns with righteous indignation for the wrongs he and his people have suffered. (3 Ne. 3:4) The deal is that Lachoneus, for whose genuine talent and courage the chief again ex-

presses his sincere admiration, is to be taken into the
Society, and in return for bringing with him all the
property over which his authority extends, he is to be
received on a 50-50 basis—"not as our slaves, but our
brethren and partners of all our substance." (3 Ne. 3:6-
7) It was all very high-minded and idealistic. The chief
was speaking only in the name of virtue; he was simply
giving the other side a break, "feeling for your welfare,"
as he so nicely put it. (3 Ne. 3:5) If the deal was refused, it would be curtains ["mob talk"] ". . . ye shall become extinct." (3 Ne. 3:8) All he is asking for, Giddianhi concludes, is "that this my people may recover their
rights and government, who have dissented away from
you because of your wickedness in retaining from them
their rights of government, . . ." (3 Ne. 3:10.) And let
no one suppose that his followers did not sincerely believe that they were the righteous and offended ones, and
their opponents just too wicked to live with.

A General Strike: In reply to this challenge Lachoneus did a most interesting thing. All the people who
had been producing for the benefit of the predatory half
of society, following instructions from Lachoneus simply
"left their lands desolate, and . . . gathered all their substance, and they were in one body . . . having reserved
for themselves provisions . . . that they might subsist for
seven years. . . ." (3 Ne. 4:3-4) They simply sat tight
and starved out their exploiters. The question has often
been asked, "what would happen if the farmers went on
a strike?" What Lachoneus did was to call a general
strike. Such things had been attempted in the Old World
all through ancient times and especially during the Middle Ages, from the revolt of the Bagaudi at the beginning to the Peasants Revolt at the end of them, and in
every case the robber barons, the "folk-devouring Lords,"
reacted exactly as the Gadianton robbers did. They
decked themselves out most terribly and swooped down
upon the peasants and the cities, sword in hand, to claim
their rights and discipline those who dared defy them.

(3 Ne. 4:7-8) At the sight of these avenging bands the opposition was supposed to fall helpless "with fear because of the terror of their armies." (3 Ne. 4:9) This behavior of the robbers was exactly what Lachoneus was counting on, and by applying hunger as his secret weapon he was able to draw out the oppressors into open battle again and again, until they were virtually exterminated. Of course an alternative of the bands would have been to go to work and make food for themselves, but that is strictly against the heroic code of honor according to which "there was no way they could subsist save it were to plunder and rob and murder." (3 Ne. 4:5)

Fourth Phase: In the years that followed there developed among the Nephites a centralized bureaucracy of businessmen, officials, and lawyers that reminds one strongly of certain periods of the later Roman and Byzantine Empires. (3 Ne. 6:11) Among other things "the people began to be distinguished by ranks, according to their riches and their chance for learning," (3 Ne. 6:12), as under some Byzantine rulers and especially under the Caliphs. That is a sure sign of decadence. "And thus there became a great *inequality* in all the land, insomuch that the church began to be broken up." (3 Ne. 6:14) Economic inequality is a deadly danger to the Church in every age. Again the usual explanation is given for the increasing iniquity of the society. It is nothing but the desire "for power, and authority, and riches, and the vain things of the world." (3 Ne. 6:15) In a word, it is what we all want! This led in a very short time to what Nephi calls "a state of awful wickedness." (3 Ne. 6:17) When inspired men began to oppose the trend, they were met with fierce indignation, especially on the part of the governing classes, "the judges, and they who had been high priests and lawyers; yea, all those who were lawyers were angry with those who testified . . ." (3 Ne. 6:20-21)

These lawyers and judges had one annoying check on their power—the "Federal Government." All orders

of capital punishment had to be signed by the governor
of the whole land. (3 Ne. 6:22) To evade the galling
restrictions of centralized government, these men of
affairs accordingly developed skillful techniques of putting people out of the way before the governor could
hear about it. (3 Ne. 6:23) When news of this leaked
out and they were brought to trial, the friends and families of the judges rallied to the cause of regional rights,
while all the bureaucracy of lawyers and high-priests
closed ranks, came together—"and did . . . unite with
the kindreds of those judges . . ." (3 Ne. 6:27) This is
a clear and vivid picture of class government and how
it worked. All these people, who were the rulers and
masters of the country, holding high office and keeping
the power in their family and their class, then covenanted "to destroy the governor, and to establish a king over
the land . . ." (3 Ne. 6:28-30) The next step is the
breakup of the Nephite state "into tribes, every man
according to his family and his kindred and friends; and
thus did destroy the government of the land." (3 Ne.
7:2) The hated central government with its intolerable
restraints on the great families and the great fortunes
was no more. They formed very great tribes (3 Ne.
7:3-4), and "their leaders did establish their laws, every
one according to his tribe." (3 Ne. 7:11.) The victory
of partisan Nephites over centralized government was
complete. This was the state of things when the great
destructions occurred at the time of the crucifixion.

Fifth Phase: Hundreds of years later we again read
of the usual crimes and abominations, including the revival of the Gadianton society. The first two chapters
of Mormon give a wonderful description of the complete
breakdown of a civilization. ". . . And it was one complete revolution throughout all the face of the land. . . ."
(Morm. 2:8.) Recent studies have shown that when the
Roman Empire collapsed all of a sudden, just such vast
roving and plundering bands filled the earth as those
described in the Book of Mormon. Insecurity was com-

plete (Mormon 1:18); people took refuge in "sorceries, and witchcrafts, and magics." (Mormon 1:19) The Dark Ages were upon them. "No man could keep that which was his own, for the thieves, and the robbers, and the murderers, and the magic art, and the witchcraft which was in the land." (Mormon 2:10) Everywhere, as in the Old World in the days of Salvian, there was a feeling of pathological frustration, men sorrowing "not unto repentance . . . but it was rather the sorrowing of the damned, because the Lord would not always suffer them to take happiness in sin . . . they did curse God and wish to die. Nevertheless, they would struggle with the sword for their lives . . . and I saw that the day of grace was passed with them, both temporally and spiritually, . . ." (Mormon 2:13-15) ". . . A continual scene of wickedness and abominations has been before mine eyes, . . ." writes Mormon, "ever since I have been sufficient to behold the ways of man." (Mormon 2:18) The end of all is the lone survivor, Moroni. ". . . I even remain alone to write the sad tale of the destruction of my people. . . ." (Mormon 8:3)

A Tract for Our Times: And how is it with us? Speaking to our own society, the Book of Mormon does not mince matters, but goes right to the point. The power of God has been denied, the churches have become defiled, there are "great pollutions upon the face of the earth . . . murders and robbing, and lying, and deceivings, and whoredoms, and all manner of abominations," and all for one cause. (Mormon 8:31) "For behold, ye do love money, and your substance, and your fine apparel, and the adorning of your churches, more than ye love the poor: . . . Why do ye adorn yourself with that which hath no life, and yet suffer the hungry, and the needy, and the naked and the sick and the afflicted to pass by you, and notice them not?" (Mormon 8:37-39.) The final warning of the Book of Mormon is that the people of the land have been destroyed because of their concern for the vain things of the world, and al-

ways their destruction has come through the same in-
strumentality, ". . . secret combinations, to get power
and gain, . . ." (Ether 8:22) We are warned that such
combinations, built up to get power and gain, will again
be the overthrow and destruction of America if they are
allowed to get the upper hand. (Ether 8:21-22)

And they do not gain the upper hand by any genius
or skill of their own, but only with the active consent of
the people who ". . . suffer these things to be" (Ether 8:
23) yielding to fair promises because they themselves
love and admire power and gain. (Ether 9:17) This is
the message of the Book of Mormon to the Gentiles
(Ether 8:23), and its message to the Church is like unto
it:

> And if ye seek the riches which it is the will of the Father
> to give unto you, ye shall be the richest of all people, for ye
> shall have the riches of eternity; and it must needs be that the
> riches of the earth are mine to give; but beware of pride, lest ye
> become as the Nephites of old. (D. & C. 38:39)

Here the Lord tells us what the riches are that *he*
wants us to seek; but if we seek the other riches they are
also his to give. God has no objection to man's enjoyment of the good things of the earth. What he condemns
in the strongest and clearest language is the *unequal*
enjoyment of them.

> . . . that which cometh of the earth, is ordained for the use of
> man for food and for raiment, and that he might have in abun-
> dance. But it is not given that one man should possess that
> which is above another, wherefore the world lieth in sin.
> (D. & C. 49:19-20)

This was the lesson the Nephites would not learn,
though their great King Benjamin pleaded with them to
remember, ". . . Behold, are we not all beggars? . . ."
(Mos. 4:19) Wo unto us if we judge a man for his im-
providence, however, real it might be, (Mos. 4:22), or
withhold our substance from those who have brought
poverty on themselves. (Mos. 4:17) The man who
argues that he has a right to more of this world's goods
than another because he has worked harder ". . . hath

great cause to repent; . . ." (Mos. 4:17-18.) The fact a
man has greater gifts, more intelligence, and more
knowledge than others, or that he has worked
harder and sacrificed more, does not give him the
right to coerce even the meanest of his fellow-
men through the command of goods and services.
Jesus made this clear when he laid down the principle
that ". . . he that is greatest among you shall be your
servant. . ." (Mt. 23:11, John 13:16), but not as a seller
of service. (John 10:12-13.) God has given us our gifts
and talents to be placed freely at the disposal of our fel-
lowmen (Jac. 2:19), and not as a means of placing our
fellow men at our disposal. Few men have ever had
greater talent, energy, or devotion to a cause than Gadianton, but since his objective was "power and gain" his
genius was only as that of the brilliant and ambitious
Lucifer, the Prince of this world. Gadianton, too, became top man in his society.

"Money Answereth All Things": The beginning of
the end for the Nephites came when they changed their
pattern of life "And from that time forth they did have
their goods and their substance no more common among
them." (4 Ne. 25) Now the interesting thing about this
change was that it was economically wise, leading immediately into a long period of unparalleled prosperity,
a business civilization in which ". . . they lay up in store
in abundance, and did traffic in all manner of traffic."
(4 Ne. 46) The unfortunate thing was that the Gadianton outfit got complete control of the economic life again.
And the economic life was all that counted. The whole
society was divided into economic classes (4 Ne. 26);
the only righteous people in the land were ". . . the disciples of Jesus . . ." (4 Ne. 46), and they were given a
very bad time. (4 Ne. 34.) It was as in the days of Alma
when anybody could get rich who really wanted to, and
those who were not rich were accordingly ". . . despised
of all men because of their poverty, yea, and more especially by our priests; . . ." (Alma 32:5) Yet only these, the

poor class of people, were willing to embrace the gospel. (Alma 32:2) Such an economic order in which everyone was busy trafficking and getting rich was not, according to 4 Nephi a free society. It was only under the old system, he tells us, that ". . . they had all things in common among them; therefore there were not rich and poor, bond and free, but they were all made free, and partakers of the heavenly gift." (4 Ne. 3.)

This sad tale as we have given it is but a skeleton outline or one aspect of history contained in one section of the Book of Mormon. Nothing can do justice to the power and impact of the Book of Mormon account itself. And still there are those who maintain that a flippant and ignorant youth (so regarded) of twenty-three composes this vast and intricate history, this deep and searching epic of the past, this chastening and sobering tract on the ways of the wicked, in the spirit of sly roguery and jaunty exhibitionism. Those who can continue to make such a claim are not merely mistaken or deluded, they are, by Book of Mormon standards, actually in a state of awful wickedness, and will have terrible things to answer for.

In Joseph Smith's day whole nations were not controlled as they are now by secret combinations to get power and gain. In his day such a thing as a general strike was unknown. Big bosses did not write smooth and flattering letters to competitors making deals and offering protection. The selling of protection by huge gangs operating in high places was unknown. The arts of manipulating public opinion as practiced by the Gadianton society have not been discovered until our own day. This is no picture of the rustic America of the 1820's, but of the world of the Nephites and of Twentieth Century America.

Questions:

1. Why does the Book of Mormon, a religious record, have so much to say about crime?

2. Did Laman, Lemuel, and the Jews at Jerusalem really believe they were righteous?

3. How did Gadianton rise from the status of a discredited outcast to the position of the most influential man in Nephite society?

4. In what ways are the histories given in Helaman and 3 Nephi a sermon for Americans?

5. Is it possible for men to tell when a society as a whole is righteous or wicked?

6. Why will those who love money never admit that they do? By what signs, according to the Book of Mormon do we know who loves money?

7. What was the social status of the wicked, as a rule, among the Nephites? Of the righteous?

8. In what did the "awful wickedness" of the Nephites consist? What was the main cause of it?

9. What reveals Giddianhi to be a typical "big-shot"?

10. What according to the Book of Mormon are the most effective ways of dealing with a crime-wave?

THE NATURE OF BOOK OF MORMON SOCIETY

Prospectus of Lesson 28: The long summary at the end of this chapter tells what it is about. It is a general picture of Nephite culture, which turns out to be a very different sort of thing from what is commonly imagined. The Nephites were a small party of migrants laden with a very heavy and complete cultural baggage. Theirs was a mixed culture. In America they continued their nomadic ways and lived always close to the wilderness, while at the same time building cities and cultivating the soil. Along with much local migration attending their colonization of the new lands, these people were involved in a major population drift towards the north. Their society was organized along hierarchical lines, expressed in every phase of their social activity.

An Unfamiliar Picture: Most of the disagreement and controversy about evidence for the Book of Mormon springs from a complete unawareness of the true nature of Nephite life. If the Book of Mormon merely reflected, in however imaginative a form, the experience and learning of an American of the 1820's, the sociological problem of the book would be a simple one indeed. But the ways of the Nephites and Jaredites are in many things peculiar, and it can be shown now, though it was not known in Joseph Smith's day, that those peculiar ways are historic realities among many ancient peoples.

Transplanted Cultures: In the first place, both the Jaredites and Lehi's people were *small* migrating societies laden with a very heavy and complete cultural baggage. History, surprisingly enough, is full of such groups, of which we have already mentioned the Phoenician and Greek colonizers of Lehi's day. The flight of the Parsees to India presents many parallels to the story of Lehi's people. In American history we have many parallels: the Pilgrim Fathers brought with them a whole civilization in one small boat; Elizabethan gentlemen brought their vigorous and advanced civilization to the wilderness of Virginia, where it perished with them; the Huguenots transplanted a very rich and sophisticated brand of European civilization to the wilds of Prussia and the Carolinas; Mormon pioneers to the Virgin River country brought a bit of New England complete and intact into a region more barren and fantastic than the Gobi Desert. But for that matter small groups of Buddhist monks long ago established islands of a rich and ancient culture in the Gobi itself, just as Christian monks at the other end of the world brought the learning and the ways of Egypt and Syria to the bleak shores and islands of the North Atlantic.

Contrary to what one might expect, small groups that carry cultures to remote and lonely places do not revert to primitive and simple ways, but become fiercely and increasingly loyal to their original culture, leaning over backwards to achieve a maximum of sophistication and smartness. Hence this cultural uprooting and transplanting often leads to a surprising efflorescence of the old culture in the new home, where it often shows astonishing energy and originality.

As we have seen, the cultural baggage of our Book of Mormon emigrants was a mixed heritage in which more than one linguistic, racial, and cultural tradition is apparent from the first. Among other things they brought with them and continued to foster the typically Near Eastern combination of urban, agrarian, and hunting life. Keenly aware of their isolation, they did all they could in the way of education and record keeping to remind themselves of the Old Country, as cultural "wanderers in a strange land" are wont to do. The people who settled Greenland in the Middle Ages continued in complete isolation (for ships soon ceased to visit them from Europe) on the fringe of the New World to cling tenaciously to the pitifully impractical fashions of dress and architecture that prevailed in Europe at the time of their settlement.[1] So it was with the Nephites whose cultural equipment, even had they not been determined at all cost to preserve it, was in itself of such an ancient, tested, and stable nature that it has endured in some parts of the world to this day.

The Desert Tradition: First there is the desert or steppe tradition.   Lehi's whole party had been steeped in it for at least eight years before they set foot in America, where they forthwith continued it.   The grumbling brothers who refused to help Nephi build a ship out of pure laziness (1 Ne. 17:18), continued to grumble all the way across the water, and had barely landed in the New World before they resumed operations true to form.   They took their tents and their people and continued to hunt and rob their brethren in the old accepted fashion of the East, and their descendants after them never gave up that exceedingly attractive way of life. (Alma 18:6, 22:28.)   Theirs was the Bedouin creed: "As long as we live we shall plunder and raid." ". . . *it was the practice of the Lamanites*," according to Alma (18:7), "to stand by the waters of Sebus (an oasis) to scatter the flocks of the people, that thereby they might drive away many that were scattered unto their own land, it being a practice of plunder among them."

But the Nephites as well as the Lamanites continued their desert ways.   Shortly after landing in America Nephi himself took his tents and all who would follow him and continued his wanderings in the new land as in the old. (2 Ne. 5:5.)   The great man in his old age still speaks the language of the desert as we have already seen.[2]

Among the Nephites even after cities were built, uncomfortable or insecure minorities could always flee into the wilderness with their tents as Nephi had done in the beginning. (e.g., Omni 12, 27; Mos. 10:13-16.) Not only individuals like Nephi the son of Helaman or Samuel the Lamanite, but entire populations would depart into the wilderness and disappear. (Mos. 22:2.) These people always seem to have tents at hand, and indeed they were required to, for at the great national assembly every man was expected not to build a booth of green boughs or of rugs or blankets, as the later Jews did for the great *Hag* at the temple of Jerusalem, but to come with his tent, and to pitch his tent near the temple and live in it during the conference. (Mos. 2:6.)   In one and the same Nephite community we find the people dwelling ". . . in tents *and* in houses of cement . . ." (Hel. 3:9.) This sounds like a makeshift sort of pioneer community, and strongly reminds one of the strange combination of tents and buildings in the oldest cities of the Near East. When Alma's people were fleeing from the oppressive Amulon, at the end of the first day's march, they "pitched their tents in a valley, and they called the valley Alma, because he led their way in the wilderness." In spite of the danger of their position, Alma had some difficulty getting them to move again, for an Arab's first camp, we are told, is always a long affair. (Alma 24: 20.)   We seem to be right back in the desert again with Lehi! Again, we seem to be reading from a typical old Arabic inscription when Zeniff (Ar. *ZNB*, Zainab) reports that ". . . after many days' wandering in the wilderness we pitched our tents in the place where our brethren were slain, . . ." (Mos. 9:4.) The fact, often noted above, that the Nephites insisted on thinking of themselves throughout their history as wanderers in a strange land can only mean that they *were* wanderers, and that they did feel themselves lost in a land which was far more sparsely populated than their original home.

The Proximity of the Wilderness: And even more conspicuously than in the old country, these people always had the wilderness right next door. Amulek, calling upon the people to remember to pray to the Lord in every activity and department of daily life, gives us a revealing summing-up of the normal scenes of Nephite existence, just as Homer in describing the shield of Achilles gives us a thumb-nail sketch of Mycenaean society. "Cry unto him," Amulek admonishes his fellows, ". . . in your fields . . . over your flocks . . . in your houses . . . in your closets, and your secret places, and in your wilderness." (Alma 34:20 ff.)

Incidentally, the mention of "closets and secret places" is a clear reference to the recently discovered custom of the ancient Hebrew of having special shrines or prayer-rooms in their houses: ". . . when we could show that this was a private chapel and that the ordinary householder of the time (Abraham's time) had a special room in his house set apart for domestic worship," writes Woolley of his discovery, "we had really learned something about him which, as a matter of fact, literature did not tell us and we should never have guessed."[3] Yet the Book of Mormon tells us about it not only in this passage but in the story of Nephi, who built himself a private tower resembling the public towers of some religious sects of the Nephites (Alma 32:31), and put it to the same purpose in a private capacity: ". . . I have got upon my tower that I might pour out my soul unto my God, . . ." (Hel. 7:14, 10.)[4]

But what we wish especially to notice here is that "your wilderness" is a normal and natural part of the Nephite scene, with people going into the wilderness on regular business, where they are admonished to pray as in other places. It was in fact considered vital to the welfare of a community to have an adjacent wilderness, ". . . that they might have a country whither they might flee, according to their desires." (Alma 22:34.) When we read that not only dogs but "the wild beasts of the wilderness" as well mangled the remains of the inhabitants of the great city of Ammonihah before those remains had time to decay, it is apparent that the city and the wilderness were next door to each other, just as in the Old World.

Open Country: And as in the Old World the "wilderness" in question was not jungle, for when Gideon chased the wicked king to the top of the tower, the two could see from there that "the army of the Lamanites were within the borders of the land," (Mos. 19:6),

which means that the invading host had only the poorest
sort of cover. There were forests, indeed, but they were
scattered woodlands, for while Limhi ". . . had discovered them from the tower . . . all their preparations for
war," he and his people were more clever and ". . . laid
wait for them in the fields and in the forests." (Mos. 20:
8.) But such advantageous visibility from a tower could
only mean that the land and especially the wilderness on
the borders were largely open country. Alma's hideout
at the waters of Mormon was in open country, as we
have seen: ". . . a fountain of pure water, . . . a thicket of
small trees, where he did hide himself in the daytime,"
and where he baptized ". . . in the forest that was near
the waters . . ." (Mos. 18:5, 30.) Streams in arid countries, as we all know, are usually bordered by extensive
"thickets of small trees," like willows or mesquite,
that provide excellent concealment. The Jordan itself
is a classic illustration, and who in Utah has not camped
in the green seclusion of the willow and cottonwood
groves along our streams?

One would expect a land called "Bountiful" to be
an agricultural paradise, yet late in Nephite history
Bountiful was still a wilderness, so named because it
was ". . . filled with all manner of wild animals of every
kind; . . ." (Alma 22:31.) Plainly these people never
ceased thinking in terms of hunting as well as farming
and trading, as did their relatives in the Old World.

Wilderness Everywhere: A surprising part of the
Book of Mormon history takes place in the wilderness.
Of the first generation we have already said enough. In
the second generation we find the righteous Enos hearing the words of the Lord as he "went to hunt beasts in
the forests; . . ." (Enos 3.) Centuries later King Mosiah sent an expedition ". . . go up to the land of Lehi-
Nephi to inquire concerning their brethren," and this
group, having no idea which way to go, wandered forty
days in the wilderness. (Mos. 7:2-4.) At the same time
King Limhi's expedition of forty-three people ". . . were

lost in the wilderness for the space of many days, yet they were diligent, and found not the land of Zarahemla but returned to this land, having traveled in a land among many waters, having . . . discovered a land which had been peopled with a people who were as numerous as the hosts of Israel." (Mos. 8:8.)   In their wars with the Lamanites at this time Nephite forces would lurk in the wilderness (Mos. 9:1), and one army "going forth from Zarahemla to inherit the land of our fathers," was ". . . smitten with famine and sore afflictions;" in the wilderness (Mos. 9:33), from which it is amply clear that though they had not yet contacted the Lamanites they were a great distance indeed from Zarahemla; it was not until "after many days' wandering in the wilderness we pitched our tents in the place where our brethren were slain," that being their objective. (Mos. 9:4.)   This is not a case of getting lost, for a large number of survivors from the earlier expedition certainly knew the way; this party knew exactly where they were going—it was the immense length of the journey that made it so time-consuming and exhausting.

After all that wilderness the party finally came to a city with a king in it, who allowed them to settle in the land, where they repaired the walls of the city of Lehi-Nephi and occupied the land of the same name. (Mos. 9:4-9.)   Meantime, in another region the people of Limhi were put under constant guard ". . . that they might not depart into the wilderness" (Mos. 19: 28), which was obviously not far off and constantly invited flight.   Limhi's people actually made their getaway and ". . . did depart by night into the wilderness with their flocks and their herds." (Mos. 22:11-12.)   Though a Lamanite army immediately gave chase, ". . . after they had pursued them two days, they could no longer follow their tracks; therefore they were lost in the wilderness." (Mos. 22:16.) Now elephants or gorillas, we are told in travel books, can be very easily tracked through the densest tropical jungle—and the denser the better, since they are best trailed by broken twigs, branches and oth-

THE NATURE OF BOOK OF MORMON SOCIETY   343

er wreckage. But a large host of humans driving flocks and herds (of all things) with them would leave a far more obvious trail. Whence it is plain, as it also is from the enormous distances involved, that our story does not take place in the jungles of Central America. How could their tracks have become lost to the swift and clever Lamanite trackers right behind them? Very easily in arid country, by winds laden with sand and dust, which have rendered many an army invisible and effaced its tracks. But never in a jungle.

In these few connected instances, as all through the Book of Mormon, the picture is one of widely dispersed settlements in oasis-like tracts of farm and woodlands, with a central city as a strong point for defense and administrative headquarters, that almost invariably bears the same name as the "land." Such suggests strongly a colonial type of expansion, and we see how it operates in the case of Alma's society, which fled eight days into the wilderness and came to ". . . a very beautiful and pleasant land, a land of pure water," and quite unoccupied, where ". . . they pitched their tents, and began to till the ground, and began to build buildings." (Mos. 23:1-5.)

The Lamanite armies that had pursued Limhi's people in the episode mentioned above ended up getting ". . . lost in the wilderness for many days" (Mos. 23: 30), and the same armies after joining up with another lost company, a band of refugee priests under Amulon, finally came upon Alma's people and begged them to ". . . show the way which led to the land of Nephi . . ." (Mos. 23:36.) Such ignorance of the country by whole "armies" that had been moving about in it for a long time can only mean that the Lamanites own stamping grounds were far, far away. The Lamanites forced Alma's community to accept Amulon, Alma's bitter rival, as their chief, and so there was nothing for it but to make another break. Accordingly they spent the whole night gathering their flocks together, and while the Lord drugged their oppressors with sleep ". . . Alma and his

people departed into the wilderness." (Mos. 24:18-20.)
After one day's journey they felt they were safe, which
means they must have put considerable distance between
themselves and the enemy; yet Alma induced them to
hasten on and after twelve more days they got to the
land of Zarahemla. (Mos. 24:23-25.) From city to
city, farmland to farmland, it was wilderness all the way.

And it was dry wilderness for the most part: During fourteen years of missionary labors among the Lamanites, the sons of Mosiah ". . . in their journeyings . . .
did suffer much, both in body and mind, such as hunger,
thirst and fatigue." (Alma 17:5.) Men who journey
carry water with them, and if thirst was one of their main
afflictions it can only have been because these men were
journeying in very dry regions indeed. For they were
well provided for long journeys, taking with them every type of weapon ". . . that they might provide food for
themselves while in the wilderness." (Alma 17:7.) To
contact the Lamanites after leaving Zarahemla "they
journeyed many days in the wilderness" (Alma 17:
9.) When they at last got to Lamanite country, Ammon,
their leader, got a job tending the flocks of King Lamoni.
This included driving the beasts to the water of Sebus,
". . . and all the Lamanites drive their flocks hither, that
they may have water." (Alma 17:26.) One watering
place for a whole nation, even if it were a long river or
lake, as Sebus apparently was not, certainly implies a
very dry country.

Migrations in the Wilderness: We have already
mentioned some of the migrations in the Book of Mormon. Some were local, as when the Gadianton robbers
would fall back ". . . into the mountains, and into the
wilderness and secret places, . . . receiving daily an addition to their numbers" (Hel. 11:25), or when the people
of Ammon evacuated the land of Jershon so as to leave
a zone of open country for purposes of mobile military
defense, the evacuated area later being occupied by an
influx from the land of Jershon. (Alma 35:13-14.) When

the Amalikites, being frustrated in their attacks on the Nephites, tried to take out their wrath on the people of anti-Nephi-Lehi, the latter "gathered together all their people . . . all their flocks and herds, and . . . came into the wilderness" under the leadership of Ammon. (Alma 27:14.) Years later, the people of Morianton, fearing reprisals for certain acts of violence committed by them in a territorial dispute, decided to ". . . flee to the land which was northward, which was covered with large bodies of water," a project which Moroni was able to defeat by a short and prompt counter-march. (Alma 50:25-35.)

The Great Migration: It is quite another case with the *great* northern migration, a massive drift of population, Nephite and Lamanite alike (Hel. 6:6), to lands far to the north.   In the same year in which Hagoth sent off his first great ship to the north (Alma 63:8), a company of ". . . 5,400 men with their wives and their children, departed out of the land of Zarahemla into the land which was northward." (Alma 63:4.) This was but the beginning of a continuing trend of large-scale migration into the north countries.   Because of troubles and dissension a really great movement took place a few years later when ". . . an exceeding great many . . . went forth unto the land northward to inherit the land.   And they did travel to an exceeding great distance, insomuch that they came to large bodies of water and many rivers." (Hel. 3:3-4.)   This is obviously not to be confused with the northern land of lakes from which Moroni barred access to the people of Morianton in a relatively small-scale military action. (Alma 50:25-35.) When distance is described as "exceeding great" by a people to whom long marches and strenuous campaigns in the wilderness were the established rule, we can be sure that it was at least the equivalent of the migrations of some of our Indian tribes in modern times, which sometimes ran to thousands of miles.   Once the Book of Mormon people break out of the land of Zarahemla, there is no telling how far

they go: since they have all the time in the world we
have no right to limit their wanderings and settlements
by our own standards of foot-travel.

Artificial Desolation: One of the most significant
advances in modern study is the rather sudden realization that the great barren stretches of the Near East and
even of the Sahara may have been in no small measure
the result of human depredations — deforestation and
overgrazing.[5] Dustbowls of enormous extent we now
know, can be formed very rapidly, and such ruin need
not be the work of large populations. Some western
states with very small populations are already dangerously overgrazed, while resources described but a generation ago as "inexhaustible" have suddenly shown signs
of running out.[6] The disastrous effect of human erosion,
now noticed on every side, is the discovery of our own
day, and yet it is clearly set forth in the Book of Mormon. In the great northern migration the people ". . .
did spread forth unto all parts of the land, into whatever
parts it had not been rendered desolate and without
timber, because of the many inhabitants who had before
inherited the land." (Hel. 3:5-10.) The Book of Mormon instructs us not to underestimate the importance of
artificial desolation both in the Book of Mormon terrain and in the land of today.

Sudden Cities: The most significant fact about
both Jaredite and Nephite cities is not that they were
great or fortified or rich or proud, but that they were
built. A city would be planned and built all at one time,
like a house. Cities were not the product of a slow
gradual accretion from hamlet to village to town to city
to metropolis as Fustel de Coulanges and the other
evolutionists once had everybody believing; but if we
believe the Book of Mormon, they were built up all at
once. Thus we read that ". . . the Nephites began the
foundations of a city, and they called the name of the city
Moroni; . . . And they also began a foundation for a city
between the city of Moroni and the city of Aaron; . . .

and they called the name of the city, *or the land,* Nephihah." (Alma 50:13-14.) The Book of Mormon method is the correct one historically. The German evolutionary school brushed aside all the accounts and legends of the founding of ancient cities everywhere as hopelessly unscientific, since cities had to evolve, like everything else.[7] But now we know they were wrong, and countless cases may be supplied of cities that were actually founded in ancient times (over a hundred Alexandrias alone!), while in no case can an ancient city be shown to have evolved, even though some of them might have.

"And they also began in that same year to build many cities on the north, one in a particular manner which they called Lehi." (Alma 50:15.) That one city deserves mention because it was built "in a particular manner" certainly implies that the normal city was built according to a conventional plan, like Greek colonial and later Hellenistic cities. During a time of revival and boom ". . . there were many cities built anew," in a mass operation, "and there were many old cities repaired. And there were many highways cast up, and many roads made, which led from city to city, and from land to land, and from place to place." (3 Ne. 6:7-8.) Again there is definite indication of a regular system and something like a planned network of roads. The clearest picture of city life in the Book of Mormon is a little candid camera shot by Helaman, in which we see a tower in a garden by a highway which leads to the chief market, which is in the capital city of Zarahemla. (Hel. 7:10.) As in the Old World, the city was the market center, the surrounding land bore the name of the city, and all was bound together by a system of roads.[8] The first settlers in a land would begin their occupation by building a city, and city, land and people would have the same name, which was usually that of the founder. Such is the established order in both hemispheres. Bear in mind that we described Lehi at the beginning of this book as a typical colonist of his time, fully acquainted with the methods of the Old World, which we everywhere find faithfully carried out in the New.

Building Materials: The Nephites vastly preferred wood to any other building material, and only worked in cement when they were forced to by shortage of timber.   Indeed, they refused to settle otherwise good lands in the north if timber for building was lacking. (Hel. 3: 5.)   Where they reluctantly settled in unforested areas they continued to ". . . dwell in tents, and in houses of cement," while they patiently waited for the trees to grow. (Hel. 3:9.)   Since cement must be made of limestone, there was no lack of stone for building in the north.   Why then did they not simply build of stone and forget about the cement and wood? Because, surprising as it may seem, ancient people almost never built of stone.[9]   Even when the magnificent, ". . . King Noah built many elegant and spacious buildings," their splendor was that of carved wood and precious metal, like the palace of any great lord of Europe or Asia, with no mention of stone. (Mos. 11:8-9.)   The Book of Mormon boom cities went up rapidly (Mos. 23:5, 27:6), while the builders were living in tents.   And these were not stone cities: Nephite society was even more dependent on forests than is our own.

A Convincing Picture: Let us summarize what has been said so far as to the peacetime nature of Nephite society.   First, there is evidence in the Book of Mormon that we are dealing with a rather small population (this will be made especially clear in the next lesson), with a rich cultural heritage which they are anxious to foster and preserve in their new land.   Their activities are spread over a vast geographical area, in which they preserve the semi-nomadic traditions of their homeland as hunters, warriors, and cattle-raisers.   To contact each others settlements the Book of Mormon people must often move through large tracts of wilderness in which even armies get lost.   This wilderness is not all jungle or forest but seems to be for the most part open country and rather dry. At the same time the Nephites were city builders and farmers as well as hunters and stock raisers. One of the significant discoveries of our time is the realization that these seemingly conflicting economies not only can but normally do exist side by side in ancient times, as depicted in the Book of Mormon.

Each geographic area bore the name of its central city, a fortified market and administration center which in most cases came into being not gradually but as a deliberate act of founding, being often named after its founder. Such cities sprang up quickly, and were built of wood along accepted and conventional architectural lines. We have seen that Lehi started out as a colonizer, and the Nephite system plainly is the projection of the colonial system in operation in the Old World in Lehi's day. The various lands were knit into economic and political units by planned road systems.

Everywhere the organization of society followed a hierarchical principle. For example, the capital city of each region had daughter cities depending on it, as in the Near East;[10] in time of war from local strong places one could flee to fortified towns, and from them to more important fortified cities, and so on, until in the case of a national emergency the entire society would take refuge in the main center of the land. In peacetime the system was reflected in local, regional and national assemblies; politically we find a corresponding hierarchy of judges, from the local petty judges (who made so much trouble) on up to "the chief judge over all the land"; in religion such a hierarchy runs from local priests to the chief high priest over all the land, and even in the sects and churches Alma and Moroni appointed various priests to function under them at various levels. In this world of "island" societies, isolated from each other often by immense stretches of wilderness, we find the same system everywhere faithfully reproduced, and it is identical with that which was flourishing in the Near East in the time that Lehi left Jerusalem.

Just as the normal movement of American population throughout our own history has been a massive and gradual drift from east to west, drawing off the crowded populations of the Atlantic seaboard into the relatively empty spaces inland, so throughout Nephite history we find a constant population drift from the crowded lands of the south to the vast empty regions of the north. There are thus two main areas and settings for Book of Mormon history, the land of Zarahemla, and the land northward, and it is important not to confuse them.

The whole picture of Nephite society convinces us the more we study it 1) that we are dealing with real people and institutions, and 2) that we have here a faithful mirror of Near Eastern society and institutions of the time of Lehi.

Questions:

1. Why did the Nephites not forget their old culture and revert to primitive ways in the wilderness of the New World? Would that not have been natural?

2. Are there any other instances in history in which small bodies of people have transplanted advanced cultures in wild and distant places? Permanently?

3. What is the three-fold cultural heritage of Lehi's people?

4. What important aspects of Nephite society distinguish it from modern society?

5. Describe a Nephite city.

6. What are the indications in the Book of Mormon of small populations?

7. What are the indications that Book of Mormon history takes place over a vast area?

8. What are the indications that much of Book of Mormon history takes place in relatively dry country?

9. What are the indications of a hierarchical organization of Nephite society — economic, political, religious?

10. What important considerations arise from the evidence that the Nephites built almost exclusively of wood?

Lesson 29

STRATEGY FOR SURVIVAL

Prospectus of Lesson 29: Beginning with a mobile defense, the Nephites soon adopted the classic system of fortified cities and strong places, their earth-and-wood defenses resembling those found all over the Old World. Settled areas with farms, towns, and a capital city were separated from each other by considerable stretches of uninhabited country. The greatest military operation described in the Book of Mormon is the long retreat in which the Nephites moved from one place to another in the attempt to make a stand against the overwhelmingly superior hereditary enemy. This great retreat is not a freak in history but has many parallels among the wars and migrations of nations. There is nothing improbable or even unusual in a movement that began in Central America and after many years ended at Cumorah.

Methods of Defense: At the beginning of their history the Nephites put up a mobile defense against their enemies, making skillful use of the wilderness ". . . to fortify against them with their armies. . . ." (Jac. 7:25.) This method was never given up, as we can see in the ordering of the evacuation of the land of Jershon which ". . . gave place in the land . . . for the armies of the Nephites, that they might contend with the armies of the Lamanites" (Alma 35:13.) But in the third generation the Nephites ". . . began to fortify our cities, or whatsoever places of our inheritance," a project rendered necessary and possible by the great increase of population. (Jarom 7-8.) From this time on the strategy of fortified cities and "places of security" becomes the rule, though the fighting is still mostly done in the wilderness. Of recent years students have come to realize that the earthen mounds, circles, walls, and hill-forts that are virtually the only surviving remains of many an Old World civilization actually represent the normal and typical life of ancient people, and from them they have reconstructed a manner of living and warfare that exactly correspond to those described in the Book of Mormon.[1]

The System of Strong Points: The Nephites tended their flocks and tilled their fields within safe distance of some fortified place, either a walled town or a specially prepared "place of resort" to which they could flee at a moments notice in case of a raid by the fierce and predatory Lamanites. In time of general alarm we see all the people converging on the central city and principal national stronghold. "And they (the Lamanites) are upon our brethren in that land; and they are fleeing before them with their flocks, and their wives, and their children towards our city . . ." (Alma 2:25-26.) In this particular case the amazing speed with which the people were able to round up their flocks and flee to the city shows that we are dealing with a standardized type of thing. Nephite cities were used both as defense places for armies to fall back on (Mor. 21:12), and when necessary as regular castles of defense (Mos. 21:19), while the enemy might ". . . come into the land . . . by night, and carry off their grain and many of their precious things. . . ." (Mos. 21:21.) There came a time when every Nephite city had the appearance of a fort, and then the casual visitor would have had a hard time telling whether he was in the Old World or the New, for the fortifications of the Nephites seem to have resembled those of Europe and the Near East in all particulars.[2] Moroni set his armies to

. . . digging up heaps of earth round about all the cities . . . And upon the top of these ridges he caused that there should be timbers, yea, works of timbers built up to the height of a man, round about the cities. And . . . upon those works of timbers there should be a frame of pickets built upon the timbers round about. . . . And he caused towers to be erected that overlooked those works of pickets, and he caused places of security to be built upon those towers. . . . (Alma 50:1-5.)

Alma tells of other fortifications of earth and wood, dirt banks and ditches (Alma 52:6) lined by ". . . a strong wall of timbers. . . ." (Alma 53:4.) Only once is stone mentioned, and that is as an added re-enforcement rather than the normal defense. Moroni erected "... small forts, or places of resort; throwing up banks of earth round about to enclose his armies, and also building walls of stone to encircle them about, round about their cities and the borders of their lands; yea all round about the land." (Alma 48:8.) These, the only stone structures mentioned in the Book of Mormon, seem to have been emergency works of rubble, hastily thrown up for a particular operation; they were certainly not buildings of stone. Towers were built in the New World for the same purposes as in the Old World, but again, while we are told of wooden towers, nothing is said of stone.

In a good description of a typical Nephite fortification (Alma 49:17-20) we are told that elevation was an important element of defense, the enemy being forced to climb up to the fort, which was surrounded by a high bank and a deep ditch; an important feature was the "place of entrance" where assailants were let into a trap and there cut down by the swords and slings of the most expert fighters in the place. (Alma 49:20.) This is the typical arrangement of hundreds of old earthworks scattered all over the Old World, some of which, like the Roman camp on the Taunus, have recently been reconstructed. Typical also is the use of hilltop forts or camps in Book of Mormon strategy. When Amalickiah caused serious trouble between the Nephites and the Lamanites living in the land of Nephi, "... all the Lamanites ... fled to Onidah, to the place of arms, ..." where they "... gathered themselves together upon the top of the mount which was called Antipas, in preparation to battle." (Alma 47:5-7.) The hill was fortified and had a camp on top. (Alma 47:10-14.) Cumorah was another such rallying place.

This type of fortification is taken everywhere to signify a normal warfare of raids and counter-raids rather than of pitched battles, and such we find to be the case in the Book of Mormon, where we see the people "... watering and feeding their flocks, and tilling their lands, . . ." and one day the Lamanite hosts come to raid their lands, ". . . and began to slay them, and to take off their flocks, and the corn of their fields." (Mos. 9:14.) In the conventional manner the people flee to the city for protection. (Mos. 9:15.) In this case their army counterattacked and in a single day drove the raiders out of the land, killing over 3000 of them in the process. (Mos. 9:18.) It all happened within a few hours.

A Small Population: Everything about the military picture in the Book of Mormon gives evidence of a very small population, scattered in little states (originally colonies) separated from one another by wide expanses of wilderness. The land of Zarahemla would be the only exception. The Nephites were greatly impressed by the signs of former habitation in the lands to the far north, ". . . a land which had been peopled with a people who were as numerous as the hosts of Israel," they said with wonder. (Mos. 8:8.) Yet by modern standards the hosts of Israel were never very numerous, though by Nephite standards they were fabulous. For them their New World population was nothing at all to what they remembered or had recorded of the Old. The greatest military slaughter except that at Cumorah was that which quelled the Amlicite uprising with 12,532 Amlikite and 6,562 Nephite casualties. (Alma 2:18-20.) That is a stiff day's loss for any army, but in terms of a war it is tiny by modern standards. Yet we are told that the Amlicites were ". . . so numerous that they could not be numbered," (Alma 2:35), and that their Lamanite allies were ". . . as numerous, almost, as it were, as the sands of the sea. . . ." (Alma 2:27.) The "as it were" is a reminder that such statements are not to be taken literally. The routed host sought safety, as ever, in the wilderness, and ended up in Hermounts, ". . . that part of the wilderness which was infested by wild and ravenous beasts," where the beasts and the vultures finished off the wounded. (Alma 2:37.) All this shows a military operation taking place in great stretches of empty and desolate territory. Where were the inhabitants?

The calamities of the Amlicite war brought the people back to a remembrance of God, and the Church throve mightily, ". . . and many were baptized in the waters of Sidon and were joined to the Church of God . . ." (Alma 4:4.) After Alma's enthusiastic account, which calls up images of thousands and tens of thousands flocking to the waters of the mighty Sidon,[3] it comes as a shock to learn that the record increase of the church in the seventh year of the judges was just 3,500 souls. This is another reminder that terms like "great," "mighty," "numerous," etc., are purely relative and cannot for a moment be taken to indicate population on a modern scale. We are told, for example, that the people of the great northern migration ". . . began to cover the face of the whole earth, . . ." (Hel. 3:8.) What does Helaman mean by "cover"? In case one thinks of something like greater Los Angeles one need only read a few verses farther to learn that the Gadianton robbers established their cells ". . . in the more settled parts of the land, . . ." (Hel. 3:23), which makes it clear that "covering the face of the whole earth" does not mean a dense and uniform occupation but can signify the thinnest possible settlement.

This is implied in Mormon's impression of the land of Zarahemla when he came as a boy from the north country with his father: "The whole face of the land had become covered with buildings, and the people were as numerous almost, as it were the sands of the sea." (Morm. 1:7.) The "as it were" again bids us be cautious, but it is clear that compared with his native north country the land of Zarahemla seemed to the youthful Mormon to be fairly bursting with people. Yet in the very year he made his visit a war broke out in the Zarahemla country ". . . by the waters of Sidon," for which ". . . the Nephites had gathered together a great number of men, even to exceed the number of thirty thousand. . . ." (Morm. 1:11.) That is, the whole Nephite army

gathered from a nation "as numerous, almost as it were
the sands of the sea," amounted to hardly more than a
single modern infantry division! The overwhelmingly
superior enemy host was only 50,000—less than two
infantry divisions.

To starve out the Gadiantons the Nephites on one
occasion joined ". . . in one body . . . having reserved
for themselves provisions, and horses and cattle, and
flocks of every kind, that they might subsist for the space
of seven years. . . ." (3 Ne. 4:4.) Since flocks and cattle
of every kind have to be fed for seven years, and since
horses are only necessary where there is a demand for
transportation, it is plain that the Nephites were not all
shut up in one city, but united within one land. The
area was not enough to support such a host indefinitely
but it must have been considerable. The gathering out
of the surrounding lands went forward slowly and
systematically, for we read that the robbers ". . . began
to take possession of all the lands which had been deserted by the Nephites, and the cities which had been
left desolate (3 Ne. 4:1) ". . . for the Nephites had left
their lands desolate, and had gathered their flocks and
their herds and all their substance, and they were in one
body." (3 Ne. 4:3.) Heretofore they had NOT been in
one body, but settled in a number of "lands".

Concentration and Dispersion: A good deal of Nephite history takes place in a land so small that its whole
expanse can be surveyed from the top of a high tower.
(Mos. 11:12.) Yet we read of Nephite communities so
far apart that parties trying to get from one to the other
get lost in the wilderness for weeks. There is nothing
contradictory about that. As the history of France is
largely the history of the city of Paris and its environs,
and the history of Rome and Athens and Jerusalem, etc.,
rarely looks beyond those territories (old Latium, Attica,
"the land of Jerusalem," etc.) which can be seen in their
entirety from the high place and seat of dominion—the
Capitol, the Acropolis, the Rock of David,[4] even so the

history of the Nephites is centered in Zarahemla with only occasional references to the provinces. Yet the provinces were there. When Coriantumr in a surprise raid actually got possession of Zarahemla he thought the whole land was his, ". . . supposing that their great strength was in the center of the land. . . ." (Hel. 1:24), whereas actually their strength was in ". . . the cities around about the borders. . . ." (Hel. 1:26.) So while the invaders ". . . had come into the center of the land, and had taken the capital city . . . and were marching through *the most capital parts* of the land . . . taking possession of many cities and of many strongholds" (Hel. 1:27), they were really playing right into Moroni's hands. For the most part the scenes of Book of Mormon history are laid "in the most capital parts of the land," as is the case with most ancient histories. In times of danger, as we have seen, it was the practice for the people to seek refuge in their cities, walled towns, and "places of security," driving their cattle with them. That many of them were so far from towns that special strong places had to be set up for them is an indication of how thinly settled much of the land must have been. In time of national emergency, as in the days of Lachoneus, the people would bypass the local centers and fall back on the big ones or even leave all the rest deserted to unite themselves in one body in the capital. From Rome to China this is exactly the way the ancients did everywhere.

The Great Retreat: In the days of Mormon the greatest national emergency of all occurred. The Nephite armies under Mormon being outnumbered and the land having become completely insecure, the people lost their nerve, ". . . they would not fight, and they began to retreat towards the north countries." (Morm. 2:3.) This was simply the old system of falling back to stronger positions, as the Greeks did before the Persians or the Great King did before Alexander's advance. In this case the armies of Mormon occupied the city of Angola

and did "make preparations to defend ourselves against
the Lamanites. And . . . did fortify the city with our
might." (Morm. 2:4.) But they lost the city and fell back
again, being next driven ". . . forth out of the land of
David." (Morm. 2:5.) So next there was a great rallying and gathering in the land of Joshua. ". . . we did
gather in our people as fast as it were possible, that we
might get them together in one body." (Morm. 2:7)
It was the old system faithfully and mechanically followed. But here the whole population was wicked and
extensively infiltrated with Gadianton members, so that
there was nothing but trouble, "one complete revolution
throughout all the face of the land." Here the Lamanites attacked with an army of 44,000 (tiny by modern
standards) and were beaten back by a Nephite army of
42,000 (the same size as the little army that Alexander
led all over Asia). But fifteen years later the Lamanites
again got the best of them and they were driven out of
the land and pursued clear ". . . to the land of Jashon,
before it was *possible to stop them* in their retreat."
(Morm. 2:16.) By this time, unless they had been going
in circles, they were years away from Zarahemla. Near
the city of Jashon in the land of Jashon was the land of
Ammaron, where Mormon picked up some record-plates
which had been deposited earlier for safe keeping.
(Morm. 2:17.) But the people could not stay in Jashon
either, but were driven ever farther northward, until they
came to the land of Shem, where they "did fortify the
city of Shem, and we did gather in our people as much
as it were possible, that perhaps we might save them
from destruction." (Morm. 3:21.) Notice that the whole
operation is strictly defensive—the whole problem is one
of survival, and every move is made with great reluctance. In the city and land of Shem Mormon made a
passionate appeal to his people to ". . . fight for their
. . . houses and their homes," (Morm. 2:23), though
they had only been occupying the place for less than a
year! Plainly the Nephite community was established in
peace as rapidly as it was abandoned in war; semi-nomad

is not too strong a term for such a society. Here the
Nephite hosts, though numbering only 30,000, stood off
a Lamanite army of 50,000 (Morm. 2:25), and within
three years had won back ". . . the lands of our inheritance." (Morm. 2:27) The lands were divided up in a
treaty made with the Lamanites in the following year, and
the share allotted to Mormon's people was all the land
north of ". . . the narrow passage. . . ." (Morm. 2:29.)

Mormon's Account only a Sampling: In all this account Mormon has only been dealing with the hosts
under his command, "my armies" (Morm. 2:2-3.) Here
he makes a deal with the Lamanites for "lands of inheritance". We have seen above (Lesson VI) that any
land settled by a Nephite group was called by that group
"the land of its inheritance," following the Old World
practice of Israel, meaning that the land taken was now
the legitimate property of the family to hand on to its
heirs. Here "the lands of our inheritance" are not to be
confused with the "first inheritance" of the Nephites,
which was far to the south. Nor is the "narrow passage" the same thing as the much-mentioned "narrow
neck of land." A passage is a way through, "an entrance or exit," says the dictionary—a pass. Here it is
specifically stated to be such: ". . . the narrow passage
which *led* into the land southward. . . ." Now the Isthmus
of Panama, never less than thirty miles wide, is *not* "a
narrow passage" for an army of less than two divisions.
Or will anyone maintain that after years of constantly
being bested by the Lamanites in steady ". . . retreat
towards the north countries" (Morm. 2:3) the Nephites
were in a position to contain all the Lamanites not only
south of Zarahemla, where the long retreat began, but
even south of Panama? (Morm. 2:29.) It is quite another
feature of the land to which Mormon here refers, and it
is far, far from Zarahemla. Unless we are prepared to
grant that the Lamanites willingly gave up all their gains
clear back to Zarahemla and far to the south of it, yielding up to the defeated Nephites territories that had

never belonged to them, we cannot identify the narrow passage here mentioned with the Isthmus of Panama. To call the Isthmus of Tehuantepec, one hundred and thirty miles wide, a "narrow passage" is of course out of the question.

During the ten years that followed, the Nephites made great preparations for defense, at the end of which, on receipt of a letter from the king of the Lamanites formally declaring war, Mormon ordered the people "to gather themselves together" again, this time at their southernmost city "at the land Desolation . . . by the narrow pass which led into the land southward, . . ." where they ". . . did fortify against them with all our force," (Morm. 3:6), hoping to stop them at the pass. This strategy, which was successful, shows that the narrow passage was a pass and not one of the Isthmuses, 30 to 150 miles wide, which of course could not be blocked by any little city or a few battalions of troops. Like Marathon, the pass was near the sea. (Morm. 3:8.) Two years later the Nephites foolishly took the offensive and as a result lost both the land and the city of Desolation, "And the remainder did flee and join the inhabitants of the city of Teancum. . . ." (Morm. 4:3) This makes it clear that we are still reading only of Mormon's band of Nephites, and not a history of the whole nation, for the people of Teancum, which was ". . . in the borders by the seashore . . . near the city Desolation" (Morm. 4:3) had up to then taken no part in the fighting. It must always be borne in mind that by this time the Nephite people had become broken up into "tribes," each living by itself and following its own tribal laws. (Hel. 7:2-4, 11.) So what Mormon gives us is only a sampling of the sort of thing that was going on.

The Great Evacuation: The Nephites retook the city of Desolation in the following year, only to lose both it and Teancum three years later (Morm. 4:14), and regain them again. But in 375 A.D. came the turning point. The Nephites lost their strong places and were never again able to make a successful rally and defense, ". . . but began to be swept off by them (the Lamanites) even as a dew before the sun." (Morm. 4:18.) They fled to the city of Boza only to be driven out of it ". . . and slaughtered with an exceedingly great slaughter. . . ." (Morm. 4:21.) So they took to headlong flight ". . . taking all the inhabitants with them, both in town and villages." (Morm. 4:22.) Then it was that Mormon went to the hill Shim and got the records. (Morm. 4:23.) After that evacuation they fled to another land and city, the city of Jordan, where they held their own for a while. (Morm. 5:3) At the same time the same sort of thing was going on in the rest of the scattered and disintegrating Nephite world. ". . . And there were also other cities which were maintained by the Nephites, which strongholds did cut them (the Lamanites) off. . . ." (Morm. 5:4.)

The next verse is very revealing. "And it came to pass that whatsoever lands we had *passed by,* and the inhabitants thereof were *not* gathered in, were destroyed by the Lamanites, and their towns, and villages, and cities were burned with fire. . . ." (Morm. 5:5.) Here you have a clear picture of Nephite society. Separate "lands" living their own lives, now in this last crisis terribly reluctant to move and join the swelling host in the retreat to the north. Those who refused to pull up stakes were one by one completely wiped out by the Lamanites. This was no planned migration but a forced evacuation, like dozens of such we read about in the grim and terrible times of the "Invasion of the Barbarians" that destroyed the classic civilizations of the Old World. In this case Mormon's people were only part of the general and gradual evacuation of the whole land. The Nephites lost a general battle in the next year and resumed their headlong flight, "and those whose flight was swifter than the Lamanites' did escape," says Mormon, not mincing words, while the rest "were swept down and destroyed." The fitful but continual falling back of the Nephites towards the north, which had now

been going on for *fifty-three years*, became something
like a route, with speed the only hope of survival. So,
says Mormon, ". . . we did march before the Lamanites,
. . ." and finally received permission to ". . . gather together our people unto the land of Cumorah, by a hill
which was called Cumorah, and there we could give
them battle." (Morm. 6:2.) To the very last they followed the usual custom of assembling the hosts around
some fortified hill-camp for a formal show down.

The Last Stand: By this time, we have seen, Mormon's migration was fused with the general migration
of the nation, and as it had been the practice in the past
for the whole nation in times of extreme danger to fall
back on a single point of defense, so now they all by
special arrangement and permission, gathered for the
last time at Cumorah, ". . . in a land of many waters,
rivers, and fountains. . . ." (Morm. 6:4.) Such a description of the country can only come from people who are
used to a relatively dry terrain and who are strange
enough in the new setting to be impressed by it. It was
four years after their last ". . . marching before the Lamanites . . ." before the Nephites had completed their
final gathering — a long march, and a long gathering!
In the last assembly, which ". . . gathered in all the remainder of our people unto the land of Cumorah, . . ."
the tribal order was still observed, the host being organized into independent armies of about ten thousand each.
(Morm. 6:10ff.) All told they numbered 230,000, as
against the largest Nephite army mentioned earlier,
42,000. Plainly Mormon has been showing us only one
typical episode in Nephite history; here all the strands
are drawn together for the last time.

The Way to Cumorah: It is often claimed that it is
quite unthinkable that the Nephites should have met a
military threat in Central America by fleeing to western
New York. Such hasty pronouncements are typical of
much Book of Mormon criticism, building impetuous
conclusions on first impressions and never bothering to

find out what the Book of Mormon says actually happened. Any schoolboy of another generation, raised on Xenophon and Caesar, would brush such objections aside with a laugh—apparently these self-appointed archaeologists have no idea of what ancient armies and nations could do and did in the way of marching and retreating. But what does Mormon tell us? That Operation Cumorah was only the culminating phase of many years of desperate shifts and devices to escape a steadily growing Lamanite pressure. The movement that ended at distant Cumorah was not a single project but the last of innumerable and agonizing hopes and setbacks, a bungling, peacemeal process of retreat that lasted for two generations. In the histories of the tribes many a nation after being uprooted from its homeland wandered thousands of miles in desperate search of escape and survival, fighting all the way, only to be eventually exterminated in some last great epic battle. We need only think of the tragic fate of the Visgoths, Burgundians or any number of Celtic or Asiatic nations (including the Torguts in our own day) to realize that there is nothing incredible or even improbable about the last days of the Nephites.[5] The Kirghiz, almost the same size as the Nephite nations, migrated just as fast and as far as the Nephites in attempting to escape their Chinese oppressors through the years—and they never knew just where they were going next.

The strategy of survival is a strategy of expedience in which a move cannot be planned far ahead. You move when and where you must. Chief Joseph, trying to escape the U. S. Army, took his people over 3,000 miles, always into the most remote and inaccessible regions possible. For the same reason the Nephites found themselves moving into uninviting regions—their motive was flight; they left their homes with great reluctance, they did not *want* to go anywhere, but they had to get away. (Morm. 5:5.) As long as a relentless hereditary foe pursued them, they had to keep moving. And the enemy was not to be appeased, as we see in the brutal and systematically thorough mopping-up operations which went right on after the Nephite nation had been destroyed in battle. (Morm. 8:2.)

Once one gets a mobile situation such as we have in the Book of Mormon from 375 A.D. on, distance takes on a wholly new aspect—the dimensions of mobile warfare (as against that of prepared lines) are unlimited. The battalions of Napoleon within the short space of fifteen years fought on the plains of Italy, on the banks of the Nile, in the high Swiss Alps, at the gates of Copenhagen and Vienna, all over the rocky uplands of Spain, and across the Russian steppes to Moscow. And many a trooper, present at all these operations, covered all that distance (except, of course, for the trip to Egypt) on foot. Yet over 2,000 years earlier Alexander performed far swifter and longer marches through hostile and unknown regions many of which remained unexplored and unknown to western man down to our own day. There is no reason for supposing that ancient people could not walk or ride just as far as moderns. On the contrary, they constantly negotiated distances on foot that would appall us. There were Indians with Lewis and Clark who knew the continent all the way from the lower Mississippi to Puget Sound—why should the Nephites have been any less informed than they? The movement of the Nephites along the Gulf Coast to the Mississippi and hence up the valley to the eastern headwaters is an ordinary, even a typical, performance by ancient standards.

Questions:

1. Why did the Nephites in their early days confine their military operations to mobile defense?

2. What was the nature of Nephite fortifications?

3. Why is it difficult to date ancient mounds?

4. How large must a "great city" be to be great? How numerous must a "numerous" population be?

5. Describe the normal Nephite strategy for defense. How does it compare with that in the Old World?

6. What indication is there that Mormon's account is not a history of the whole Nephite nation as such? What had already happened to the nation?

7. Is it conceivable that the Lamanites would actually give permission to the Nephites to gather their forces in order to oppose them?

8. Why does Central America seem so far away to us?

9. How far is far? Why is it best to avoid speculation on Book of Mormon geography?

10. What difference does it make whether the Hill Cumorah is in Central America or in New York state?

Appendix 1

THE ARCHAEOLOGICAL PROBLEM

Prospectus of Lesson: The Book of Mormon is so often taken to task by those calling themselves archaeologists that it is well to know just what an archaeologist is and does. Book of Mormon archaeologists have often been disappointed in the past because they have consistently looked for the wrong things. We should not be surprised at the lack of ruins in America in general. Actually the scarcity of identifiable remains in the Old World is even more impressive. In view of the nature of their civilization one should not be puzzled if the Nephites had left us no ruins at all. People underestimate the capacity of things to disappear, and do not realize that the ancients almost never built of stone. Many a great civilization which has left a notable mark in history and literature has left behind not a single recognizable trace of itself. We must stop looking for the wrong things.

Impressive and Misleading Names: Ever since the Book of Mormon first appeared its claims have been both challenged and defended in the name of "archaeology." The writer frequently receives letters from people calling themselves archaeologists proposing to discredit the Book of Mormon, and other letters from those who have been upset by such claims, not daring to question the authority of "archaeology." But what is an archaeologist? To quote from a recent study which is as near to an "official" statement as we can get, he is simply an "expert in the cultural history of a particular part of the world."[1] He is strictly a specialist, not in "archaeology" but in the ways of a particular society: "specialization in archaeology is necessarily by area, as in the humanities, rather than by subject matter, as in the natural sciences." That is, there is no "subject matter" of archaeology as a single discipline, but only a lot of widely separated fields in which "the program of training for each area is different."[2] As any archaeologist will tell you, "the actual techniques of archaeological excavation and recording can be learned only by field experience," and not by reading books or taking courses.

Anyone who wants to be an archaeologist must "choose an area of specialization early and stick to it," receiving his degree not in "archaeology" but in that area. Proficiency in one area (usually Classical Languages, Near Eastern Languages, Far Eastern Languages, or American Anthropology)[3] does not in any way qualify the student in any of the others; there is no "general archaeology." If after centuries of diligent archaeological study and the outpouring of vast sums of money in archaeological projects the world's great universities are still without archaeology departments, it is not because the idea has never occurred to them, but simply because archaeology cannot be studied as a single discipline.

Advice to Book of Mormon Archaeologists: "It cannot be too strongly emphasized," a leading archaeologist writes, "that archaeological finds in themselves mean nothing; they have to be *interpreted*."[4] And for that, as Braidwood says, "no tool may be ignored," the most important tool by far being that which enables the archaeologist to examine the written records of the culture he is studying.[5] The careful critical study of original texts is the principal activity of every competent archaeologist, who "uses the evidence of written history, and the material remains of human activities" together. For this he must "learn the historian's techniques and . . . acquire an intimate familiarity with the historical literature. . . . This procedure involves learning the languages . . . so that the archaeologist will not have to depend on other people's interpretations of these materials in his work."[6] Today, we are told, an archaeologist's "training must be wider and more intensive than it has ever been. The day has long passed when it was sufficient for a student of the Near East to know Hebrew and have a nodding acquaintance with one or two of the cognate languages. One must have a working knowledge of all if he is to be really competent."[7] The archaeologist, according to the director of the Oriental Institute of Chicago, "needs, for example, enough of the modern local languages to steer the physical work . . . and to gain that traditional setting of his site which persists through long ages. He needs enough of the ancient local languages to exercise a judicial, topical control on the pronouncements of the professional linguists."[8] In other words, he must at least speak the modern languages of the area in which he works, and read the ancient ones. "To recreate the past, we need . . . a great deal more than a dog-Latin transcription of observed data," said R. E. M. Wheeler in his presidential address to the Council for British Archaeology, ". . . it is not enough that we archaeologists shall be a variety of natural scientist . . . man's recorder . . . must be a good deal more than a rather superior laboratory assistant; what is needed," he concludes, is "something equivalent to a classical education," with its rigorous training in language, "to save archaeology from the technicians."[9]

Limitations of Archaeology: J. De Laet, a Belgian archaeologist of wide experience in Europe and the Near East, has just written a monograph on the limitations of archaeology. He begins by pointing out the great amount of jealousy and tension that always exists among archaeologists, and the conflicting definitions of archaeology that are still being put forward. Archaeology in its proper function of "auxiliary of history" is at present falling down, he claims, due to "the encroachment of techniques on ideas," a trend which is dangerously far advanced in America.[10] Because of faulty concepts and practices "we do not hesitate," says De Laet, "to affirm that at least fifty percent of all archaeological material gathered in the course of the past century in almost every country of the ancient world is actually of more than questionable value."[11] As to the rest, "the archaeological documents of undoubted validity to which one can accord complete confidence . . . are still insufficiently numerous to be used as a foundation for systematic historical and philological study." "Historians and philologists," he concludes, "have attempted much too soon to utilize the offerings of archaeology in the attempt to solve problems of a historical or philological order."[12] Half the material is useless and the other half can't be used! If such can be seriously described as the state of archaeology in the Old World, where the study is ancient and established, the documents numerous and detailed, and the workers many and zealous, what can we expect of archaeology in the New World, or how can we seriously attempt at this state of the game to apply archaeological evidence to prove the Book of Mormon?

The archaeologists are no more to blame for this state of things than is the nature of the material they work with. The eminent Orientalist Samuel Kramer, director of one of the greatest archaeological museums in the world, notes that material remains unaccompanied by written texts are necessarily in themselves "highly ambiguous material," and always the object of "unavoidably subjective interpretation." As a result, while one group of archaeologists reaches one conclusion, "another group of archaeologists, after analyzing practically identical archaeological data, arrives at an exactly opposite conclusion."[13] "The excavator," writes Woolley, "is constantly subject to impressions too subjective and too intangible to be communicated, and out of these, by no exact logical process, there arise theories which he can state, can perhaps support, but cannot prove."[14] "To illuminate the distant past," Henry Breuil has written recently, "nothing remains but anonymous debris, worked stones, sharpened bones, skeletons or scanty and scattered remains of ancient men lost in the floors of caves, the sands of beaches and dunes, or mixed with the alluvial wash of rivers,"—all quite anonymous and dateless.[15] No wonder Kramer deems it "fortunate" that the evidence for understanding Sumerian early history "has nothing to do with the highly ambiguous material remains . . . (but) is of a purely literary and historical character."[16] All these warnings and instructions the Book of Mormon student should take to heart when questions of archaeology are raised.

Proceed with Caution!: There is certainly no shortage of ruins on this continent, but until some one object has been definitely identified as either Nephite or Jaredite it is dangerous to start drawing any conclusions. There was no Hittite archaeology, for example, until some object was definitely proven to be Hittite, yet men were perfectly justified in searching for such objects long before they discovered them. The search must go on, but conclusions should wait. We are asking for trouble when we describe any object as Nephite or Jaredite, since, as Woolley says, "no record is ever exhaustive," and at any moment something might turn up (and often does!) to require a complete reversal of established views. Aside from the danger of building faith on the "highly ambiguous materials" of archaeology and the "unavoidable subjective" and personal interpretations of the same, we should remember that archaeology at its best is a game of surprises.

A Disappointing Picture: People often ask, if the Book of Mormon is true, why do we not find this continent littered with mighty ruins? In the popular view the normal legacy of any great civilization is at least some majestic piles in the moonlight. Where are your Jaredite and Nephite splendors of the past? A reading of previous lessons should answer that question. In the Nephites we have a small and mobile population dispersed over a great land area, living in quickly-built wooden cities, their most ambitious structures being fortifications of earth and timbers occasionally reinforced with stones. This small nation lasted less than a thousand years. Their far more numerous and enduring contemporaries, the Lamanites and their associates including Jaredite remnants (which we believe were quite extensive)[17] had a type of culture that leaves little if anything behind it. Speaking of the "Heroic" cultures of Greece, Nilsson writes: "Some archaeologists have tried to find the ceramics of the invading Greeks. I greatly fear that even this hope is liable to be disappointed, for migrating and nomadic tribes do not use vessels of a material which is likely to be broken, as will be proved by a survey of the vessels used by modern nomadic tribes."[18] Neither do they build houses or cities of stone.

The vast majority of Book of Mormon people, almost all of them in fact, are eligible for the title of "migrating and nomadic" peoples. We have seen that the Lamanites were a slothful predatory lot on the whole, and that even the Nephites were always "wanderers in a strange land." A great deal of Epic literature deals with mighty nations whose deeds are not only recorded in Heroic verses but in chronicles and annals as well— that they existed there is not the slightest doubt, yet some of the greatest have left not so much as a bead or a button than can be definitely identified! "Archaeological evidence is abundant," writes Chadwick of the remains of Heroic Ages in Europe, "though not as a rule entirely satisfactory. Great numbers of raths or earthen fortresses, usually more or less circular, still exist . . . ."[19] But such remains look so much alike that English archaeologists are always confusing Neolithic, British, Roman, Saxon and Norman ruins.[20] And this is the typical kind of ruins one would expect from Book of Mormon peoples.

Scarcity of Stone: The surprising thing in the Old World is that so little seems to have been built of stone, except in a few brief periods such as the late Middle Ages or the early Roman Empire. Welsh heroic literature, for example, is full of great castles, yet long and careful searching failed to reveal a single stone ruin earlier than the time of the invader Edward I, who learned about stone castles while crusading in the Near East.[21] An official list of Roman castles from the time of Justinian enumerates 500 imperial strongholds and gives their locations; yet while the stone temples and amphitheatres built at the same time and places still stand, not a scrap of any of those castles are to be found.[22] Though a great civilization flourished in Britain before Caesar, generations of searching has failed to produce in all England a single stone from pre-Roman times "on which the marks of a chisel appear, nor any kind of masonry, by which we can determine with certainty, what sort of materials were used by them before the arrival of the Romans."[23] Scandinavian bogs have brought forth objects of great refinement and sophistication in leather, metal, wool and wood. But where are the mighty buildings that should go with this obviously dense population and advanced civilization? They are not there.[24]

Like the Nephites, the ancients in general built of wood whenever they could. Even in Egypt the chambers of the first kings at Nagadah when not actually built of boards and beams were built in careful imitation of them in clay and stone.[25] The few surviving temples of the Greeks are of course of stone, yet they still carefully preserve in marble all the boards, logs, pegs, and joinings of the normal Greek temple.[26] In ranging afoot over the length of Greece, the writer was impressed by the strange lack of ruins in a country whose richest natural resource is its building stone. Except for a few famous landmarks, one might as well be wandering in Scotland or Wales. It is hard to believe as one travels about the upper reaches of the Rhine and Danube, as the author did for several years by foot, bicycle, and jeep, even if one visits the local museums and excavations conscientiously, that this can have been the mustering area of countless invading hordes. There are plain enough indications that somebody was there, but in what numbers? for how long? and who were they? Only the wildest guesses are possible. The history of the great migrations is a solid and imposing structure, "clearly perceptible to the linguist," but until now completely evading the search of the archaeologist.[27]

Vanished Worlds: In the center of every great Epic poem looms a mighty fortress and city, yet how few of these have ever been located! Schliemann thought he had found Troy, but, as every schoolboy knows, he was wrong. He thought he had found the tomb of Priam and the Treasury of Atreus—wrong again! What he did discover was a type of civilization that Homer talked about, but to this day Hissarlik is still referred to as "the presumed site of Troy." We have no description of any Book of Mormon city to compare with Homer's description of Troy. How shall we recognize a Nephite city when we find it? The most we can hope for are general indications of a Book of Mormon type of civilization— anything more specific than that we have no right to expect. From reliable Egyptian lists we know of scores of cities in Palestine whose very existence the archaeologist would never suspect.[28] Northern Germany was rich in megalithic monuments at the beginning of the 19th century, but now they have vanished. In every civilized country societies were founded in the 19th century to stem the tide of destruction that swept away monuments of the past with the increase of population, the opening of new lands to cultivation by new methods, the ceaseless depredations of treasure and souvenir hunters. But the antiquities went right on disappearing.[29]

The same thing happened in America. We too easily forget what a wealth of imposing ruins of the Heroic type once dotted the eastern parts of the country. "Not content with having almost entirely exterminated the natives of this continent," an observer wrote at the beginning of this century, "unsatisfied with the tremendous fact that we have violated covenant engagements and treaty pledges with the Indians a hundred times over, we seem to be intent on erasing the last vestige of aboriginal occupation of cur land."[30] This was written in an appeal to save some of the great mounds of Ohio: "There are numbers of structures of earth and stone scattered throughout our state. . . . All such earthworks are, of course, placed on the summits of high hills, or on plateaus overlooking river valleys. At Fort Miami it seems as if blockhouses or bastions had been burned down when once protecting the gateway."[31] This is not only an excellent description of Book of Mormon strong places, but it also suits exactly the picture of the standard fortified places of the Old World. Hundreds of such hill forts have been located all over Europe and the British Isles, where they seem to represent the normal life of the people over long periods of time.

Standard Structures: These hill forts are now held to represent "the setting up of a fortified centre of tribal life by every little autonomous group at some capital point of its block of usually upland territory. Politically, the hill fort . . . was the Celtic version of the earlier Greek *polis*."[32] That is, we find this type of structure and society standard throughout the ancient world, where it persists in many places right down to the Middle Ages.[33] It is certainly typically "Book of Mormon," and throughout ancient times was also at home throughout Palestine and the Near East.[34] In Europe these communal strong-points "appear at intervals in large numbers, from which we can readily trace their erection to political causes," while "the sparsity of cultural remains would tend to show that they were not permanently occupied."[35] It is a strange picture presented to us here, of great fortified communal structures built in large numbers at one time only to be soon deserted in a land that reverts to nomad-ism, devoid of cultural remains. And it is valid throughout the whole ancient world. The best illustration, in fact, of this peculiar but universal type of civilization and building, is to be found in modern times among the Maoris:

> The average Maori *pa* was a place of permanent occupation. . . . It is as the home of the people, the center of their social and economic life, no less than their defensive stronghold and focus of their military activity that the Maori *pa* has its peculiar interest for the archaeologist, and anthropologist and the pre-historian.[36]

This is the typical old Greek, Celtic, Hittite and Maori community, and it is typically Nephite as well—but it will give you no spectacular ruins.

This peculiar order of society is usually explained

as the normal result of a sparse population occupying large areas of land. The dense world-population of our own day is a unique—and an alarming—phenomenon. On the other hand, populations can be too small: "The Roman Empire had an exceedingly small population," writes Collingwood, ". . . the fall of the Western Empire . . . depended on the fact that it neither possessed enough men to cultivate its own soil, nor invented methods of cultivating its soil so . . . as to stimulate an increase of population." And so it broke up, exactly as Nephite society did, "into a congeries of barbarian states," living in a semi-nomadic manner.[37]

Looking for the Wrong Things: Blinded by the gold of the Pharaohs and the mighty ruins of Babylon, Book of Mormon students have declared themselves "not interested" in the drab and commonplace remains of our lowly Indians. But in all the Book of Mormon we look in vain for anything that promises majestic ruins. They come only with the empires of another and a later day, and its great restraint and conservatism in this matter is a strong proof that the Book of Mormon was not composed by any imaginative fakir, who could easily have fallen into the vices of our archaeologists and treasure-hunters. Always there is a ruinous temptation to judge things in the light of one's own reading and experience—and indeed, how else can one judge? Two hundred years ago an English archaeologist wisely observed:

. . . our ideas are apt to be contracted ("conditioned", we would say today) by the constant contemplation of the manners of the age in which we ourselves live, and we are apt to consider *them* as the standard whereby to judge of, and to explain, the history of past times; than which there can be no more delusive error; nor indeed is there any more effective method to prevent our understanding the truth of things.[38]

Yet we still persist in judging the ability of the ancients to cross the Pacific or move across the continent without automobiles in the light of our own inability to do such things. We as gravely underestimate the Book of

Mormon people on one side as we overestimate them on the other. If they did not build cities like ours, neither were they as helpless in their bodies as we are. More than anything else, as Paul Herrmann has recently shown, modern man underestimates the ability of the ancients to get around: "Manifestly," he writes, "the world has been since early times as great and wide as in our own day. And clearly nothing hindered early man from setting sail from his European or Asiatic homeland to regions as remote as America and Australia."[39]

Above all, we must be on guard against taking the argument of silence too seriously. The fact that we don't find a thing in a place need not be taken to prove that it was not there. "Since the record is never complete," Woolley reminds us, "the archaeologist . . . never has the last word." "The Islamic people," for example, "made no use of the wheel and the cart," but that does not prove that wheels and carts were unknown to them, for they were in constant contact with people who used them.[40]

But what of the mighty ruins of Central America? It is for those who know them to speak of them, not for us. It is our conviction that proof of the Book of Mormon *does* lie in Central America, but until the people who study that area can come to some agreement among themselves as to what they have found, the rest of us cannot very well start drawing conclusions. The Old World approach used in these lessons has certain advantages. The Near Eastern specialists are agreed on many important points that concern the Book of Mormon, and the written records of that area are very ancient, voluminous, and in languages that can be read. It is our belief that the decisive evidence for the Book of Mormon will in the end come from the New World; the documents may be already reposing unread in our libraries and archives, awaiting the student with sufficient industry to learn how to use them.

Questions

1. What is an archaeologist? What is he not? Do you know one? Could you tell one if you saw him?

2. Can "archaeology" prove or disprove the Book of Mormon?

3. Why are there so few competent archaeologists? Why do so many people take a try at archaeology?

4. What are the limitations of archaeology? Why does the archaeologist "never have the final word"?

5. Why are there so few "Book of Mormon" ruins?

6. How would you know a Book of Mormon ruin if you found one?

7. What are some of the preconceptions that have doomed seekers for Nephite and Jaredite ruins to disappointment and failure?

8. Does the scarcity of ruins in North America disprove the Book of Mormon?

9. Are earthen and wooden structures necessarily the sign of a primitive or backward population?

10. How can archaeology support the Book of Mormon in the Old World? in the New World?

11. What are the advantages of an "Old World" approach to the Book of Mormon? Of a "New World" approach? Why cannot the two approaches be combined?

Footnotes

Lesson 1 Notes

[1]H. Torczyner, "Das Literarische Problem der Bibel," *Zeitschr. der Deut. Morgenland. Ges.*, 85 (1931), 287-8.

[2]This is discussed by H. H. Rowley, *The Zadokite Fragments and the Dead Sea Scrolls* (Oxford, 1952), pp. 1ff.

[3]H. Nibley, "Controlling the Past," in *The Improvement Era* 58 (May, 1955), pp. 306ff, (June, 1955), pp. 384ff.

[4]See our discussion, "New Approaches to Book of Mormon Study," *Ibid.*, 56 (Nov., 1953), pp. 830ff, (Dec., 1953), 919ff.

[5]W. R. Cross, *The Burned-over District* (Ithaca: Cornell Univ. Press, 1950), p. 145f.

[6]Francis W. Kirkham, *A New Witness for Christ in America, the Book of Mormon* (Independence: Zion's Printing, 1951), pp. 39-40.

[7]See our discussion in *The Improvement Era* 58 (Dec., 1955), pp. 902ff.

[8]*Loc. cit.*, and *The World and the Prophets* (Salt Lake: Deseret, 1954), pp. 178-180, for sources.

[9]Ernst Percy, *Die Botschaft Jesu* (Lund Univ. Aarsskrift, N. F. I, Bd. 45, No. 5, 1953), p. 1.

[10]S. G. F. Brandon, "The Historical Element in Primitive Christianity," in *Numen* II (1955), pp. 156-7.

[11]The expression is Brandon's, *op. cit.*, p. 157.

[12]H. J. Paton, *The Modern Predicament* (Gifford Lectures, London: Allen & Unwin, 1955), p. 374. "Modern humanity is very much of the same opinion as Pliny (*Nat. Hist.* VII, 55) in regarding rebirth of life after death as merely a sop for children," writes P. Pucha with approval (*Archiv Orientalni*, XX, 162).

[13]In *The Improvement Era,* Dec. 1955, pp. 903ff, we quoted at length from a Catholic article of this type, and from recent Protestant writings in *The World and the Prophets,* pp. 180-2. Recently in "The Crisis of Civilization," *Hibbert Journal* LIV (1956), p. 168, Hugh Sellin writes of Toynbee: ". . . (he) believes that a new orientation, a new development of Christianity, will give to the old cultural foundations of Western civilization a new life to vitalize the coming change in our Society. Yet he declares himself a Christian. Surely some confusion enters here. It is of the very nature of Christianity that it claims to be a final revelation, and . . . it does seem to mark the end of the religious road which Western Man has trod during his recorded history."

[14]Charles S. Braden, *The Scriptures of Mankind, An Introduction* (New York: Macmillan, 1952), p. 482.

[15]*Ibid.*, p. 481. Braden's own uncertainty is apparent from the fact that while treating Joseph Smith's Inspired Translation of the Bible at considerable length, he has almost nothing to say about the Book of Mormon, an infinitely more ambitious and significant work. In the same spirit, Henry J. Forman, *The Story of Prophecy* (New York: Farrar & Rinehart, 1936), while dealing with prophecy and fulfillment especially in modern times, makes no mention of Joseph Smith at all!

[16]Braden, *loc. cit.*, mentions with approval the theory that the Book of Mormon manuscript passed through other hands as stolen goods before it reached Joseph Smith. This absurd theory is discussed in the last lesson of this series. Even if it were true, it merely tells us who is supposed to have handled the manuscript, with never a word as to how it was actually produced.

Lesson 2 Notes

[1]" 'We are thankful,' wrote Schweitzer years ago, 'that we have handed down to us only gospels, not biographies, of Jesus.' The scholars have shown by word and deed that they do not want to know any more about Christ than

they do; instead of joyfully embracing the priceless discoveries which from the *Didache* to the Dead Sea Scrolls have brought us step by step nearer to a knowledge of the true Church of Jesus Christ, they have fought those documents at every step. If the resurrected Jesus were to walk among them they would waste no time in beseeching him 'to depart from their coasts' — they have the only Jesus they want, and they will thank you not to complicate things by introducing new evidence." Thus we wrote in the *Era,* December 1955, pp. 902 ff., following Eisler, whose remarks on the subject have been confirmed since he wrote them by the rise of the "existentialist" theology, which rejects as myth anything the individual does not feel is in line with the complex of experiences and emotions that makes up his own existence.

[2]Quoted in Egon Friedell, *Kulturgeschichte Aegyptens und des Alten Orients* (Munich: Beck, 1953), pp. 78-79.

[3]*Ibid.,* p. 130.

[4]Walter Otto, "Zur Universalgeschichte des Altertums," *Historische Zeitschrift,* 146 (1932), p. 205. The author of these lines is the fortunate possessor of Otto's own copy of Meyer's great work, extensively annotated with his own pencil markings.

[5]*Ibid.,* pp. 205-6.

[6]The quote is from R. J. Braidwood, *"The Near East and the Foundations of Civilization* (Condon Lectures, Eugene, Ore.: 1952), p. 5.

[7]J. Paterson, in C. J. M. Weir, Ed., *Studia Semitica et Orientalia* (Glasgow Univ., 1945), II, 95.

[8]Ed. Meyer, *Gesch. des Altertums,* I, i (1913), p. 131: "Genuine historical literature arose only among the Israelites and Greeks, and among them independently. Among the Israelites (who for that reason enjoy a unique distinction among all the peoples of the Ancient East) this literature took its rise at an astoundingly early period, and brought forth from the first highly significant productions, such as the purely historical accounts in Judges and Samuel."

[9]Edward Koenig, "Ist die jetzt herrschende Einschatzung der hebraischen Geschichtsquellen berechtigt?" *Historische Zeitschrift* 132 (1925), 289-302, treats the subject in a study that deserves to be summarized here. He tells how all the scholars brushed aside the account in Gen. 23 of Abraham's dealings with the Hittites as a fabrication or a mistake—until the Amarna discoveries proved that the Bible was right and they were wrong. The account of Judah's seal-ring in Gen. 38:18 was treated as a clumsy anachronism until around 1913 the use of seals in early Palestine was proven by excavation. The favorite creed that the early history of Israel rested entirely on oral tradition was blasted by discoveries proving widespread literacy in the earliest days of Israel. The universal belief that Israel had no interest in real history is disproven by the care with which memorial stones, trees, etc., were designated, and by the fullness and detail of early accounts. It was taken for granted that the early histories of Israel did not reflect the ancient times they purported to describe, but depicted actually the much later periods in which they were written; yet archaeological, ethnological, and philological findings in and around Israel show that these texts do *not* depict the Aramaic times but give an authentic picture of a much earlier world. Naturally it was assumed that the early historians of Israel knew nothing about the correct use of sources and evidence; yet they are careful to cite their sources (often now lost), have a keen eye for historical changes and often include comments and sidelights from various related sources. The prevailing conviction that Israelite history was a "harmonizing and rationalizing" piece of free composition is disproven by the very scholars who make the charges when they claim they are able to detect a great variety of styles and levels of composition—i. e. that the texts have *not* been harmonized. The very common claim that the history of Israel was all painted over and prettied up so as to quite conceal the original runs contrary to the many unsavory and uncomplimentary things said about Israel and her founders throughout these writings; the weaknesses of Israel's heroes are not concealed, as such things are in other ancient histories, and the actions of the nation are certainly not "bathed in a golden light," as the scholars claimed.

[10]Ed. Meyer, "Die Bedeutung der Erschliessung des alten Orients für die Geschichtl. Methode," *Berlin Akademie Sitzungsbericht,* Hist-Phil. Kl. 1908, p. 653. The italics are ours.

¹⁰First in 1886 came Meyer's own discovery of the name Jakob-el in a document of Pharaoh Thutmosis III. Then came the Amarna Tablets in 1887—a whole library. Then in 1896 the inscription of Merneptah (1240 B. C.) showing there were actually Israelites in Palestine. In 1906 came the sensational discovery of the great Hittite record hordes, and in 1907 the wonderful Elephantine finds. Tell Halaf in 1911, Kirkuk (Nuzu) and the Hurrians in 1925, Ras Shamra in 1929, Tepe Gawra in 1931, Mari in 1933, the Lachish Letters in 1938, and in our own day the Dead Sea Scrolls. Documents casting the most direct light on Lehi's world would be the Gezer Calendar, the Samarian ostraca, the Siloam Inscription, the Ophel ostracon, numerous seals, inscribed jar-handles and potsherd both private and royal, wieths and measure, inscriptions, the Samarian ivories, etc. These are all mentioned below. See S. Moscati, "L'Epigrafia Hebraica Antica 1935-1950," in *Biblica et Orientalia* N. 15, 1951.

¹¹P. Meinhold, *op. cit.,* p. 86, n. 35.

¹²E. I. Mittwoch, in *Monatsschr. f. Gesch. u. Wiss. d. Judent.* 83 (1939), 93-100; S. Birch, "Some Leather Rolls," *Aegypt. Ztschr.* 19 (1871), 103f, 117f.

¹³D. W. Thomas, in *Pal. Expl. Quart.,* 1950, p. 5. "In 1942 there was discovered at Saqqarah a letter written in Aramaic upon papyrus, belonging to the Jeremian period." It was from King Adon to Pharaoh, asking for help against the invading Babylonians. *Ibid.,* p. 8.

¹⁴*Bull. Am. Sch. Or. Res.* 73, 9ff; cf. J. Obermann, "An Early Phoenician Political Document," *Jnl. Bibl. Lit.* 58 (1939), p. 229; it was "engraved on a metal tablet of copper or bronze..."

¹⁵A. E. Cowley, *Aramic Papyri of the Fifth Century B. C.* (Oxford: Clarendon Press, 1932).

¹⁶An excellent photograph of these plates and their box is given in the Frontispiece of S. B. Sperry, *Ancient Records Testify* (M.I.A. Study-Course, 1938-9). For a general survey of writing on plates in antiquity, see F. S. Harris, Jr., *The Book of Mormon, Messages and Evidences* (Salt Lake City: Deseret, 1953), Ch. 10.

¹⁷J. Bothero, "Deux tablettes de fondation, en or et argent, d'Assurnasirpal II," *Semitica* I (1948), 25-32.

¹⁸F. Thureau-Dangin, "Une tablette en Or provenant d'Umma," *Revue d'Assyriologie,* 34 (1937), 177-183.

¹⁹Jawad Ali, *Tarikh al-Arab qubl al-Islam* (Baghdad, 1951), I, 14.

²⁰Eusebius, *Chronicon* I, 19 ff. (*Frag. Hist. Graec.* II, 125).

²¹H. Ranke, "Eine Bleitafel mit hierogl. Inschrift," *Aegypt. Ztschr.* 74 (1938), 49-51. Ranke declares himself completely mystified by this document.

²²M. Anstock-Darga, "Semitische Inschriften auf Silbertäfelchen aus dem 'Bertiz'-Tal," *Jahrb. f. Kleinasiat. Forschung* I (1950), 199f.

²³A. Dupont-Sommer, "Deux lamelles d'argent a inscription hebreo-araméenne," in *Jahrb. f. Kleinasiat. Forschung* I (1950), 201-217.

²⁴Inscribed tablets play an important roll in the Greek mystery cults. Beside the golden tablets, whose texts are reproduced by A. Olivieri, *Lamellae Aureae Orphicae,* in *Kleine Texte,* No. 133, 1915, were those tablets which were inscribed by the initiates: "All who have gone down to Trophonius are obliged to set up a tablet containing a record of all they heard or saw." Pausanius, *Graeciae Descriptio,* IX, 39; cf. VII, 25, 6. When the celebrated traveling seer Apollonius visited Trophonius, he emerged from the underground passages bearing a holy book, which caused a great sensation and drew many sight-seers to Antium, where it was put on display. Philostratus, *Life of Apollonius of Tyana* VIII, 19.

²⁵J. S. Morrison, in *Jnl. of Hellenic Studies,* 75, p. 66.

²⁶Plato, *Gorgias* 524A. See M. Rostovtzeff, *Mystic Italy,* p. 74.

²⁷See below, pp. 173f.

²⁸See the *Improvement Era* 56 (April, 1953), pp. 250f.

²⁹A. von Gall, *Basileia tou Theou,* pp. 77 ff.

³⁰Sten Konow, "Kalawan Copper-plate Inscription of the Year 134," *Jnl. Royal Asiat. Soc.,* 1932, pp. 950, 965.

³¹The fullest account to date is in the *Chemical and Engineering News,* Sept. 3, 1956, pp. 425 ff.

³²E. Schreder, "A Phoenician Alphabet on Sumatra," *Jnl. Am. Or. Soc.* 47 (1927), 25-35.

[33]H. Bossert, in *Orientalia,* 20 (1951), 70-77; W. Andrae, *Hittitische Inschriften auf Bleistreifen aus Assur* (Leipzig: Hinrichs, 1924).

[34]D. J. Wiseman, "Assyrian Writing-Boards," in *Iraq,* 17 (1955), 14-20.

[35]*Ibid.,* p. 13.

[36]*Ibid.,* p. 3; cf. M. Howard, "Technical Description of the Ivory Writing-boards from Nimrud," *Iraq* 17 (1955), 14-20.

[37]V. Krackovskaya, *Publications of the Asiatic Museum, Ancient Oriental Studies* (Acad. of Sciences, USSR, Vol. V, 1930, 109-118. [in Russian].

[38]*Lehi in the Desert,* etc., pp. 119ff.

[39]A. Bunker, in *Jnl. Am. Or. Soc.* 10 (1872), 173, who also notes (p. 175), that a gold and copper plate was "the talisman by which the chief held his power over the people."

[40]See below, pp. 255ff.

[41]A. H. Sayce, "The Libraries of David and Solomon," *Jnl. of the Royal Asiat. Soc.,* 1931, p. 789. On Meyer's contribution, Ed. König, in *Hist. Ztschr.* 132:289-302.

[42]F. E. Pargiter, in *Jnl. Royal Asiat. Soc.,* 1913, 152f.

Lesson 3 Notes

[1]The latter part of the 5th Book of Lucretius' *De rerum natura* contains a discussion of the evolution of human institutions that is hardly to be distinguished from what might be heard in the halls of our western universities today. It must be admitted, however, that the teachings of said universities are a good thirty years behind the thinking of the more advanced centers of thought abroad. The intellectuals of the 18th Century regarded all other ages as "elegant and refined" in direct proportion to their proximity to them in time—a strictly evolutionary pattern. Typical is Gibbon's observation at the beginning of the 26th chapter of the *Decline and Fall,* that "the savage tribes of mankind, as they approach nearer to the condition of animals, preserve a stronger resemblance to themselves and each other . . ."

[2]Two recent and readable discussions of the world-wide diffusion of the earliest civilizations are Paul Herrmann, *Conquest by Man* (Trsl. M. Bullock, New York: Harpers, 1954), and Carleton S. Coon, *The Story of Man* (New York: Alf. Knopf, 1954).

[3]This is treated in Lessons 28 and 29 below.

[4]In the 3rd ed. of Eb. Schrader, *Die Kleinschriften und das Alte Testament* (Berlin, 1903), p. 169.

[5]H. C. Gordon, "The Patriarchal Narratives," *Journal of Near Eastern Studies,* XIII (1954), pp. 58-59.

[6]Herrmann, *op. cit.,* Part iv, pp. 85ff.

[7]T. Watek-Czerniecki, "La Population de l'Egypte a l'Epoque Saite," in *Bulletin de l'Institut de l'Egypte,* No. 33 (1940-1), p. 60.

[8]*Ibid.,* pp. 37-62, where the population of Egypt in 600 B.C. is placed at 20 to 35 millions as a conservative estimate, other estimates exceeding 30 million. Less than a century later, in 525 B.C., the population stood on good evidence at only 16.5 million, and in 1800 A.D. Egypt had only 2.4 million inhabitants! In 1937, on the other hand, it had 15.9 million. Such astonishing fluctuations in population should be kept in mind in reading Book of Mormon history.

[9]Thus Lehi's great contemporary and friend Jeremiah denounced the loud boasts of peace: "For they have healed the hurt of my people slightly (lit. lightly, superficially), saying, Peace, peace; when there is no peace." (Jer. 6:14, 8:11). Lehi's son denounces the same complacency in strong terms: ". . . they will say: All is well in Zion; yea, Zion prospereth, all is well." (2 Ne. 28:21). So, says Nephi, Satan "will . . . pacify, and lull them away into carnal security."

[10]For the complete text and discussion, U. Wilcken, in *Ztschr. für Aegyptische Sprache,* 60, pp. 90-102.

[11]See below, Lesson 29, Note 5.

[12]Georg Ebers, *Aegyptische Studien and Verwandtes* (Stuttgart-Leipzig, 1900), p. 315.

[13]See the discussion by J. L. Myers, "The Colonial Expansion of Greece," Ch. xxv, Vol. III, *Cambridge Ancient History*, pp. 631-684.

[14]P. Bosch-Gimpera, "Phoeniciens et Grecs dans l'Extreme-Occident," *Nouvelle Clio* III (1950), 269-296, emphasizes the intense competition between the two.

[15]Ed. Meyer, *Gesch. d. Altertums*, III, i, 106-9, reporting that the Greeks in Lehi's day were getting their gold from Tibet.

[16]Herodotus, History IV, 42, discussed by P. Herrmann, *op. cit.*, pp. 73-76, 79-93.

[17]For a recent reconstruction of Hanno's itinerary, G. Marcy, in *Journal Asiatique*, Vol. 234 (1947), pp. 1-57.

[18]Herrmann, *op. cit.*, pp. 120, 130.

[19]*Ibid.*, p. 36; Paul Haupt, *The Babylonian Noah*, p. 22, thinks that even the prehistoric sea epics of Babylonia and Greece "both go back to the same source, viz. the yarns of early Tartessian mariners."

[20]Herrmann, *op. cit.*, p. 83; cf Ebers, *op. cit.*, pp. 311-338.

[21]J. Partsch, *Die Grenzen der Menschheit* (Königl. Sächs. Ges. d. Wiss., 68 (1916), ii, p. 62. J. M. A. Janssen, "Notes on the Geographical Horizon of the Ancient Egyptians," *Bibliotheca Orientalia* VIII (1951), 213-7. P. Bolchert, *Aristoteles Erdkunde von Asien u. Libyen* (Berlin, Heft 15 of *Quellen u. Forschungen zu alt. Geschichte u. Geographie*, 1908), p. 3. For the world-map of Lehi's contemporary Hecataeus, John Ball, *Egypt in the Classical Geographers* (Cairo: Govt. Press, 1942), p. 9. For a general survey, A. Scharff & Anton Moortgat, *Aegypten und Vorderasien im Altertum* (Munich: R. Brickmann, 1951).

Lesson 4 Notes

[1]See below, Lesson 6, Note 1.

[2]See below, pp. 74-75.

[3]"Is it not remarkable," asks P. Herrmann (*Conquest by Man*, p. 27), "that the New World, apart from Peru, in spite of its plentiful supplies of copper, never succeeded in discovering bronze on its own account?" It has been noted with wonder that many typical Near Eastern objects, such as bells, are found in the New World, but instead of being of bronze, as they are in the Old World, they are invariably of copper. This, we believe, is a dead give-away of the true nature of the cultural transmission, which must have been by a small group, unacquainted with the secret of making bronze (a *very* closely-guarded secret, strictly the property of certain nations and groups of specialists), but familiar with the design and use of all sorts of things made from bronze. The form they could imitate, the substance they could not duplicate, for its formula was secret. And so we have Nephi carefully copying the bronze or brass plates he brought with him from Jerusalem, not in bronze, however, but in *ore* (I Ne. 19:1). Herrmann's book contains a good deal of information on the subject of the extreme secrecy with which ancient traders merchants, and manufacturers guarded all their knowledge, technical and geographical.

[4]Herrmann, *op. cit.*, p. 21.

[5]H. Winckler, in E. Schrader, *Die Keilinschriten und das Alte Testament* (3rd Ed., Berlin, 1903), pp. 169ff.

[6]One of the best-known tales of antiquity is the story of Solon's visit to Croesus, the richest man in the world, as told in Herodotus, *Hist.* I, 30ff, one of the greatest sermons on moderation and humility. Cf. Arist. *Const. Ath.*, V.

[7]"No precise date is known for any event in Solon's life. Even the year of his archonship cannot be fixed, and we can only say that it fell within the period between 594 and 590 B.C." I. M. Linforth, *Solon the Athenian* (Berkeley: U. C. Press, 1919), p. 27. This does mean, however, that Solon reached the peak of his career within ten years of the fall of Jerusalem, which makes him strictly contemporary with Lehi.

[8]Contacts between Greece and Palestine were quite close, F. M. Heichelheim, "Ezra's Palestine and Periklean Athens," in *Ztschr. f. Religion u.*

Geistesgeschichte III (1951), 251-3. Plutarch's *Life of Solon* and Book 2 of Herodotus tell of the great man's wanderings, and are excellent background reading for the world of Lehi.

⁹Linforth, *op. cit.,* p. 37.

¹⁰Plutarch, *Solon,* VIII, 2.

¹¹The quotation is from one of Solon's own poems, quoted by Aristotle, *Const. Athen.,* IX, 25. Thirty-two years after Solon had given Athens its model constitution, his old friend Peisistratus overthrew the government and made himself dictator. The aged Solon alone stood out against him, and in the end, thanks to him, democracy triumphed. "The marvellous thing," writes Linforth (*op. cit.,* p. 101), "is that at so early a day, in the midst of the corruption of a declining aristocracy and the ignorance of an unintelligent populace, Solon should have discerned with such clear insight and maintained with such resolute faith the true principle of equality before the law."

¹²Thales can be dated by an eclipse which he predicted in 585 B.C., that is, within a year or two of the destruction of Jerusalem. (Herodot., *Hist.* I, 74). Diogenes Laertius in the *Lives of the Philosophers* I, 22, says his mother was a Phoenician, while Herodotus (I, 170) simply says he was of Phoenician descent. His Egyptian education is mentioned by Euclid (Sect. 19), who says he first brought the knowledge of geometry from Egypt to Greece.

¹³"When they made fun of him because of his poverty, as showing how useless his philosophy was to him, it is said that he made a study of weather conditions (lit. "astrology" in the broad sense) and estimated what the olive crop would be for the coming season; and while it was still winter he borrowed a little money and bought up all the olive presses used in oil manufacture in Miletus and Chios, getting them for a song, since nobody thought they were worth very much out of season. But when a bumper crop came along there was a sudden and overwhelming demand for olive-presses, and Thales was able to get whatever he asked for his. In this way Thales was said to have shown the value of *sophia* (intellectual application) in action, and indeed, as we have said, the achievement of such a monopoly is a triumph of business intelligence." (Aristotle, *Politics,* 1259a). This is the earliest known use of the word "monopoly". "That, my dear Theodore, is like the case of Thales," says Socrates (Plato, *Theatitus* 174a), "who once when he was looking up into the heavens thinking about the stars walked right into a well. A smart Thracian servant-girl saw it and made a joke about the man who would sound the depths of the sky when he didn't even see what was at his feet. That's the way philosophers seem to everybody." That is certainly the way Lehi seemed to his family, who called him a dreamer and even a fool, but still, like Thales, he seems by the accumulation of his "exceeding great wealth" to have given quite adequate evidence of an astute and practical nature when that was necessary.

¹⁴Herodotus, *Hist.* I, 170. The plan seems to have been a good one, worked out on the basis of wide experience. It might have saved the Greeks tragic centuries of senseless wars had it been followed out.

¹⁵The sources for the study of the Seven Wise Men have been gathered by Barkowski in Paul Wissow's *Real-Encyclopädie der class. Altertumswiss.,* II Reihe, ii, 2242-4. Actually the concept of the Seven Sages is very ancient, being clearly indicated in early Sumerian temple texts (Alf. Jeremias, *Handbuch des Altorientalischen Geisteskultur* (Leipzig, 1913), p. 81). Beneath the pavement of a building in Ur were found two clay boxes, each containing seven figurines representing the Seven Sages (Bab. *ummerni*) and certainly "connected with the antediluvian kings . . . called the 'Seven Ancients' (*apquallu*) of the seven earliest cities; to them was attributed the editing of all the secrets of divination, magic, and wisdom." Thus G. Contenau, *Le Deluge,* p. 46. These seven were thought of as constantly wandering through the world as bearers of wisdom, observing and instructing the ways of mankind. They have often been compared with the seven planets and certainly suggest the Seventy wise men of the Jews, who were wandering missionaries to the seventy nations and seventy tongues of mankind. Cf. W. H. Roscher, *Die Sieben—und Neunzahl im Kultus u. Mythus der Griechen,* Bd. 24, of *Abh. d. Kgl. Sächs. Ges. d. Wiss.,* No. 1, 1904.

¹⁶See H. Nibley, Victoriosa Loquacitas," *Western Speech* XX (1956), p. 60.

¹⁷C. Niebuhr, "Einflüsse orientalischer Politik auf Griechenland im 6. u. 5. Jh." in *Mitt. d. Vorderasiat. Ges.* IV (1899), No. 3. For the general picture, see all of Vol. III of *Cambridge Anc. Hist.*, especially pp. 609-701, 548-558.

¹⁷C. Niebuhr, "Einflüsse orientalischer Politik auf Griechenland im 6. u. 5. Jh." in *Mitt d. Vorderasiat. Ges.* IV (1889), No. 3. For the general picture, see all of Vol. III of *Cambridge Anc. Hist.*, especially pp. 699-701, 548-558.

¹⁸A. Jeremias, *Das Alte Testament im Lichte des Alten Orients* (Leipzig, 1916), pp. 542f, 605-7.

¹⁹A. Moret, *Histoire de l'Orient* (Paris: Presses Universitaries, 1944) II, 411f, comparing Zoroaster's political reforms with Solon's. See especially J. L. Myres, "Persia, Greece and Israel," *Palest. Explor. Quart.*, 1953, pp. 8-22.

²⁰The only serious dispute is about the date of Zarathustra. Ed. Meyer, Andreas, Carl Clemen and other put him between 1000 and 900 B. C., but more recently West, Jackson, and others have put him between 660 and 583 B.C., with an alternative dating of 625 to 548 B.C. (J. Charpentier, "The Date of Zoroaster," *Bull. of the School of Oriental Studies*, London Institute, III (1923-5), pp. 747-755. Still more recently F. Altheim and R. Stiehl, "Das Jahr Zarathustras," *Ztschr. f. Relig. u. Geistesgesch.* VIII (1956), 1-14, put his birth in 599 or 589 B.C. The *traditional* date of his death by violence is 582, which makes him about the same age as Lehi.

²¹Quoted in Stobaeus, *Eclogues,* IV, 34 (Linforth, Frg. 51).

²²Plutarch, *Solon* II, 2. The long quote is in Strobaens, *op. cit.*, III, 9, 23. For the other Wise Men, Barkowski, *op. cit.*, 2260ff.

Lesson 5 Notes

¹A. Moret, *Histoire de l'Orient*, II, 727f.

²Al-Hariri, *Maqama of Ramleh*, these are the opening lines.

³Thus Sir Leonard Woolley writes in *Digging Up the Past* (Penguin Books, 1950), p. 116 ". . . At once there is called up the astonishing picture of antediluvian man engaged in a commerce which sent its caravans across a thousand miles of mountain and desert from the Mesopotamian valley into the heart of India." Cf. A. F. Oppenheim, in *Jnl. Am. Or. Soc.* 74 (1954), p. 6; S. N. Kramer, *Israel Explor. Jnl.* III, 228ff.

⁴This view is described by Ed. Meyer, *Kleine Schriften,* I, 82, 90ff.

⁵Herbert H. Gowen, "Hebrew Trade and Trade in Old Testament Times," *Jul. Soc. Or. Research,* VI (1922), p. 1, quoting Josephus, *Contra Apionem* I: "We do not dwell in a land by the sea and do not therefore indulge in commerce whether by sea or otherwise."

⁶Meyer, *op. cit.*, I, 90-91.

⁷G. Ebers, *Aegyptische Studien,* etc., p. 315.

⁸Meyer, *op. cit.*, I, 92.

⁹Ebers, *op. cit.*, p. 316.

¹⁰J. Gray, in *Hibberts Journal,* 53 (1956), p. 115.

¹¹Gowen, *op. cit.*, pp. 2-3.

¹²Alf. Bertholet, *Die Stellung der Israeliten und der Juden zu den Fremden* (Frieburg i/B and Leipzig: Mohr, 1896), p. 7.

¹³*Ibid.*, pp. 22, quoting Is. 21:13ff, Jer. 31:21, Num. 20:19, Ex. 21:8, 14:21, 2 Kings 12:5, Gen. 3:16.

¹⁴Ibid., pp. 43, 45ff. cf. I Kings 20:34

¹⁵For many years the debate has continued about the location of Ophir. One of the main purposes of Bertram Thomas' famous expedition that crossed the Empty Quarter of Arabia in 1930 was to seek for Ophir in the Hadramaut. The decisive factor, according to the latest conclusions, is that not only gold but antimony were brought from Ophir, which fact, along with others, points to the Zambesi mines near the Great Zimbabwe. See Herrmann, *Conquest by Man*, pp. 67-70. Ebers, *op. cit.*, p. 315 puts it at the mouth of the Indus.

¹⁶H. Gowen, *op. cit.*, p. 4. Cf. J. Lewy, "Old Assyrian Caravan Roads," *Orientalia,* 21 (1952), 265-292 and 393-425.

¹⁷Ed. Meyer, *Kleine Schriften,* I, 91; cf. Ed. Glaser, in *Mitt. d. Vorderas. Ges.* IV, 1899, p. 2.

[18]This was the greatest trade-route for luxury goods in the world, according to Herrmann, *op. cit.*, p. 55, and was of prehistoric antiquity. "It is quite certain," writes Ebers, *op. cit.*, p. 315, "that Sidonian and Tyrian travelling merchants reached south Arabia to fetch their incense, spices, ivory, and ebony."

[19]P. Wechter, "Israel in Arabia," *Jewish Quarterly Review*, 38 (1947), 476.

[20]*Ibid.*, p. 473-4.

[21]Fritz Hommel, *Ethnologie und Geographie des alten Orients* (Munich: Beck, 1926), pp. 720, 734.

[22]J. Pirenne, "Grece et Saba," *Acad. d. Inscrs. et Belles Lettres, Comptes Rendus*, 1954, pp. 120-5.

[23]Gust Hoelscher, *Palastina in der persischen und hellenistrschen Zet.* Heft 5 of *Quellen und Forschungen* (Berlin, 1903), p. 18, citing numerous sources.

[24]De Lacy O'Leary, *Arabia Before Mohammed* (London: Trubner, 1927), pp 172-3.

[25]P. Wechter, *op. cit.*, p. 473.

[26]Holscher, *op. cit.*, p. 17.

[27]Meyer, *Kl. Schr.*, I, 91.

[28]See note 14 above.

[29]The background of this institution is discussed by the writer in "The Arrow, the Hunter, and the State," in *Western Political Quarterly* II (1949), 335ff.

[30]*Corp. Inscr. Graec.*, 2271, cited by Bertholet, *op- cit.*, p. 75.

[31]Al-Hariri, *Maqamah of Alexandria*, 11, 14 ff. (after Preston).

[32]Gust. Dalman, in *Ztschr. der dt. Palestina Vereins*, 62, pp. 61ff.

[33]Hariri, *Maqamah of Singar*, beginning.

[34]Hariri, *Maqamah of Denar*, 11ff.

[35]Woolley, *Digging Up the Past*, p. 66.

[36]Wechter, *op. cit.*, pp. 473-4

[37]Gowen, *op. cit.*, p. 16. On the ardent missionary activity of these Jewish merchants, Bertholet, *op. cit., pp.* 76, 78.

[38]P. Wechter, *op. cit.*, p. 476.

[39]Stade, *Geschichte Israels*, I, 376, quoted by Bertholet *op. cit.*, p. 75.

[40]Wechter, *op. cit.*, p. 478.

[41]Xenophon, *Anabasis* V, 6, 17.

[42]Israel Friedlander, "The Jews of Arabia and the Rekhabites," *Jew. Quart. Rev.*, I (1910), p. 252.

[43]Gowen, *loc. cit.*, of W. W. Tarn in *Jnl. of Egypt. Archaeol*, XV, 16f 21.

Lesson 6 Notes

[1]A. Bergman, "Half-Manasseh," *Jnl. Pal. Or. Soc.* XVI (1936), pp. 225, 228, 249; M. H. Segal, "The Settlement of Manasseh East of the Jordan," *Pal. Explor. Fund Quart.*, 1918, pp. 125-131.

[2]W. F. Albright, *Archaeology and the Religion of Israel* (Baltimore: Johns Hopkins Press, 1942), p. 171.

[3]D. S. Margoliouth, *The Relations between Arabs and Israelites Prior to the Rise of Islam* (Schweich Lectures, London, 1924), p. 29; A Guillaume, "The Habiru, the Hebrews, and the Arabs," *Pal. Expl. Fund Quart.*, 1946, p. 80.

[4]Ed. Meyer, *Die Israeliten und Ihre Nachbarstämme* (Halle, 1906), p. 302.

[5]Gen. 16:12. J. Zeller, "The Bedawin," *Pal. Expl. Fund Quart (PEFQ)*, 1901, p. 198.

[6]J. Burckhardt, *Notes*, I, 113: "A man has the exclusive right to the hand of his cousin; he is not obliged to marry her, but she cannot without his consent, become the wife of another person." R. Burton, *Pilg. to al-Nadinah*, etc., II, 84: "Every Bedawi has a right to marry his father's brother's daughter before she is given to a stranger; hence 'cousin' (*Bint Amn*) is polite phrase signifies 'a wife.'"

[7]The retention of tribal identity throughout the Book of Mormon is a typically desert trait and a remarkably authentic touch. Early in their history the people were divided into "Nephites, Jacobites, Josephites, Zoramites, Lamanites, Lemuelites, and Ishmaelites," (Jac. 1:13). Where are the Samites? Why

are no groups named after Ishmael's sons as they are after Lehi's? The Jews, like other ancient peoples, thought of the human race as divided like the universe itself into seven zones or nations, a concept reflected in certain aspects of their own religious and social organization. Can this seven-fold division of Lehi's people, which was certainly conscious and deliberate, have had that pattern in mind? At the end of Book of Mormon history we read that the Nephites, Jacobites, Josephites, and Zoramites were all called Nephites for convenience, while the "Lamanites and the Lemuelites and the Ishmaelites were called Lamanites, and the two parties were Nephites and Lamanites." (Mor. I, 8-9). Still, it will be noted that there were actually seven tribes, strictly speaking, rather than two nations.

⁸Thos. Harmer, *Observations on Divers Passages of Scripture . . . in Books of Voyages and Travels into the East* (London, 1797), I, 117.

⁹R. Burton, *op. cit.*, II, 118f. Today when striking resemblances turn up between peoples no matter how far removed from each other in space and time, scholars are much more ready to consider the possibility of a common origin than they have ever been before. Actual lines of contact have now been proven between so many cultures formerly thought to have been absolutely independent and inaccessible to each other that it is no longer safe to say that cultural transmission even between the remotest parts of the globe and in the earliest times is out of the question. For an interesting treatment of this subject, see Lord Raglan, *The Origins of Religion* (London, The Thinker's Library, 1949), Ch. V.

¹⁰Ed. Meyer, *op. cit.*, pp. 322f.

¹¹P. Haupt, "Heb. Lehi, cheek . . ." *Jnl. Bibl. Lit.*, 33 (1914), 290-5.

¹²N. Glueck, in *Bull. of Am. Schools of Or. Res.* 80 (1940), 5-6, fig. 2.

¹³*Survey of Western Palestine* (E. H. Palmer's commentary, London, 1881), p. 358.

¹⁴E. ben Yahuda, "The Edomite Language," *Jnl. Pal. Or. Soc.* I (1921). 113-5; J. A. Montgomery, *Arabia and the Bible* (Univ. of Penna., 1934), p. 171, notes that there was an Arabic Massa tribe, but "no Hebrew king Lemuel."

¹⁵Yahuda, *loc. cit.*

¹⁶Below, pp. 247f.

¹⁷In *Surv. of Wstn. Palest.*, Special Papers, p. 272.

¹⁸*Ibid., Name Lists*, pp. 40, 17, 66; see below, Lesson XXII.

¹⁹J. A. Montgomery, *Arabia & the Bible*, p. 5.

²⁰See above, pp. 49-55. Of the ties between the Bedouins, the merchants, and the farmers of Palestine and Egypt, Baldensperger says: ". . . anybody who takes the trouble to investigate and understand these relationships will find it comparatively easy to make arrangements with tribes in the desert, however far they may be." *Pal. Expl. Fund Quart.*, 1897, p. 45.

²¹A Reifenberg, in *PEFQ*, 1943, pp. 102f; S. E. Cook, *Ibid.*, 1907, 68f.

²²Cowley, *Aramaic Papyri*, col. xiv.1.208.

²³Montgomery, *op. cit.*, pp. 52, 18.

²⁴H. Nibley, in *Improvement Era* 59 (Jan. 1956), 30-31; cf. D. Barrington, "Observations on Patriarchal Customs and manners," *Archaeologia* V (1785), 318ff.

²⁵J. Benzinger, *Hebräische Archäologie* (Freiburg, 1894), p. 11.

²⁶H. Winckler, in *Keilinschr. u. das A.T.* (3 Ed.), p. 136.

²⁷Thos. Harmer, *Observations on Divers Passages of Scripture* (1797), I, Ch. 2. It was Harmer who first fully appreciated and demonstrated the possibility of using the unchanging customs of the East as a check on the authenticity of the Bible, a method which we extended to the Book of Mormon in *Lehi in the Desert*, etc.

²⁸G. Hölscher, *Palästina*, p. 17, citing Jer. 3:1, I Kings 10:15, II Chron. 9:14. Job has long been considered an Arabic book, J. Reider, in *Jnl. Bibl. Lit.* 38 (1919), pp. 60-65.

²⁹Above, p. 40.

³⁰In the great Schick relief map of the Holy Land in the Peabody Museum at Harvard, all the country east of the Jordan and the Dead Sea is marked UNEXPLORED—and the map was made in 1925! Within the last five years priceless manuscript treasures have been found in what F. M. Cross calls "the howling wilderness of Ta'amireh," but a scant twelve miles from Jerusalem.

[31]Margoliouth, *op. cit.,* p. 25; Montgomery, *op. cit.,* p. 186.
[32]P. Baldensperger, in *PEFQ,* 1923, p. 176.
[33]W. F. Albright, "Recent Progress in North Canaanite Research," *BASOR* 70 (1938), p. 21.
[34]Margoliouth, *op.cit.,* p. 8, 5; Noeldeke, *Die Semitischen Sprachen,* pp. 52, 57; Ed. Meyer, *Israeliten u. ihre Nachbarstämme,* pp. 305, 307.
[35]D. B. Macdonald, *The Hebrew Literary Genius* (Princeton, 1933), cit. Montgomery, *op. cit.,* p. 53.
[36]Montgomery, p. 47.
[37]W. F. Albright, *The Vocalization of Egyptian Syllabic Orthography* (New Haven: Am.Or.Soc., 1934), x, 12.
[38]Jennings-Bramley, in *PEFQ,* 1908, p. 257.
[39]T. Canaan, in *Jnl. Pal. Or. Soc.* II (1922), 139; cf. Hogarth, *Penetration of Arabia,* p. 162.
[40]T. Canaan, "Studies in the Topography and Folklore of Petra," *Jnl. Pal. Or. Soc.,* IX (1929), 140.
[41]L. Woolley and T. E. Lawrence, *Wilderness of Zin* (London: Cape, 1936) pp. 86f; cf. Conder, in PEFQ, 1875, p. 126.
[42]Bertram Thomas, *Arabia Felix,* p. 50.
[43]A. Guillaume, "The Habiru, the Hebrews, and the Arabs," *PEFQ,* 1946, 65f, 67: "I do not think that there is much doubt that the Hebrews were what we should call Arabs, using the term in its widest sense."
[44]In *Bull. Am. Schools of Or. Res.,* 70, p. 21; cf. Guillaume, *op. cit.,* p. 77; S. L. Caiger, *Bible and Spade,* p. 84.

Lesson 7 Notes

[1]J. W. Jack, "The Lachish Letters, their Date and Import," *PEFQ,* 1938, p. 178.
[2]Sir Arthur Keith, "The Men of Lachish," *PEFQ,* 1940, pp. 7 f.
[3]For sources, see *Lehi in the Desert,* p. 9, notes 20 and 21.
[4]A. H. Sayce, "The Jerusalem Sealings on Jar Handles," *PEFQ,* 1927, 216 f; J. G. Duncan, in *PEFQ,* 1925, pp. 19 f.
[5]A. S. Yahuda, *The Accuracy of the Bible* (London: Heinemann, 1934), p. xxv; see especially by the same author *The Language of the Pentateuch in its Relation to Egyptian* (Oxford, 1933), I, xxxii-xxxv.
[6]W. F. Albright, in *Jnl. Palest. Or. Society* VIII (1928), 226 f, 223 ff; and II, 110-138.
[7]D. G. Hogarth, *"Egyptian Empire in Asia,"* Jnl. of Egypt. Archaeol., I (1914), pp. 9, 12-13. Cf. *Camb. Anc. Hist.,* III, 250, 256f, 261, 295-9.
[8]For the first quotation, H. Frankfort in *Jnl. Egypt, Archaeol,* XII (1926), 96; for the second Alex. Moret, *Histoire de l'Orient* (Paris Presses Universitaires, 1936), II 787.
[9]Ed. Meyer, *G. d. A.* II, i, 132; Hogarth, *op. cit.,* I, 12.
[10]W. Wreszinski, *Photographische Expedition,* Taf. 38; p. 80. *Aegypt. Ztschr.* XIII, 5-6; H. Winckler, "Musri, Meluhha, Ma'in," in *Mitt. d Vorderasiat. Ges.,* 1898, No. 1.
[11]The old Egyptian gold standard was that used by the Athenians, H. Brugsch, in *Aegypt. Ztschr.,* 27 (1889), p. 95; 27 (1889), pp. 4-28, in which the identity of Egyptian and Babylonian weights is fully demonstrated. From this same system the Hebrews derived their basic weight, the ephah, K. Sethe, in *Aegypt Ztschr.* 62 (1927), p. 61.
[12]A. F. L. Beeston, in *Jnl. Royal Asiat. Soc.,* 1937, p. 61.
[13]For the text, W. Wolf, in *Aegypt Ztschr.* 69 (1933), pp. 39-45.
[14]Ed Meyer, *Kleine Schriften,* I, 97; M. Ebers, *Aegyptische Studien* p. 314. Gowen. *Jnl. Soc. Or. Res.* VI (1922); pp. 1-2.
[15]Herrmann, *Conquest, etc.,* pp. 68-69; Gowen, *op. cit.,* p. 6, attributes Israel's dependence on others for ships to the "absence of harbors on the Syrian coast."
[16]C. H. Gordon, *Ugaritic Lit.,* p. 3, citing Ed. Meyer, *G. d. A.* II, ii, 63.
[17]G. Hoelscher, *Palaestina,* p. 13, citing Ezek. 27:8-9.
[18]*Ibid.,* pp. 13-14.

[19]Albright, in *Jnl. Bibl. Lit.*, 51 (1932), pp. 94f.

[20]N. de. G. Davies & R. O. Faulkner, "A Syrian Trading Venture to Egypt," *Jnl. Egypt. Archaeol;* 33 (1947), pp. 40ff.

[21]J. Breasted, *History of Egypt*, (1909), p. 577.

[22]Davies & Faulkner, *op. cit.*, pp. 45-46.

[23]Gowan, *op. cit.*, p. 4.

[24]Hoelscher, *Palaestina*, p. 13.

[25]U. Wilcken, in *Aegypt. Ztschr.*, 60 (1925), p. 101.

[26]Davies & Faulkner, *op. cit.*, p. 45.

[27]N. de G. Davies, in *Jnl. of Egypt. Archaeol.*, 27 (1941), pp. 97ff, and *Jnl. Eg. Arch.*, 28 (1942), 50-52.

[28]Davies, in *Jnl. Eg. Arch*, 33 (1947), p. 45.

[29]1 Ne. 17:17, 18:2.

Lesson 8 Notes

[1]Wilhelm Nowack, *Lehrbuch der Hebräischen Archaeologie* (Freiburg i/B, 1894), p. 300ff.

[2]H. Torczyner, *The Lachish Letters* (London: Oxford Univ. Press, 1938).

[3]J. W. Jack, in *Palestine Exploration Fund Quarterly*, 1938, pp. 175ff. Cf. W. F. Albright, "A Brief History of Judah from the Days of Josiah to Alexander the Great," *The Biblical Archaeologist*, IX (Feb. 1946), p. 4. The title *sar*, of which *sarim* is the plural is obviously the Egyptian *sr*, and is probably related to German Herr.

[4]H. Graetz, "Die Zeit des Konigs Chizkija und der zeitgenössischen Propheten," *Monatsschrift für Geschichte und Wissenschaft des Judentums*, N. F. II (1870), pp. 49ff.

[5]Graetz, *op. cit.*, p. 66.

[6]Winckler (Schrader), *Keilinschr. u. d. A. T.*, p. 170.

[7]Graetz, *op. cit.*, p. 13.

[8]*Ibid.*, p. 14.

[9]S. Zeitlin, in *Jewish Quarterly Review* XLIII (1953), 369ff., discussed in *The Improvement Era*, May, 1954, pp. 309ff.

[10]Graetz, *op. cit.*, p. 15.

[11]Kurt Galling, *Die Israelitische Stastsverfassung in ihrer Vorderorientalischen Umwelt*, in *Der Alte Orient*, No. 28, Heft 3/4, 1929, p. 8, 10-11. A. Alt. *Die Landnabme der Israeliten* (1925), 59 (Jan. 1956ff.).

[12]"There Were Jaredites," in *The Improvement Era*, 59, (Jan. through Dec., 1956). In the October issue pp. 710ff. the "heroic" beginnings of Israel are treated.

[13]Ed. Meyer, *Die Israeliten and ihre Nachbarstämme*, pp. 428ff. Cf. Galling, *op. cit.*, p. 11.

[14]Galling, *op. cit.*, pp. 9, 11, 24. Cf. Jud. 11:26.

[15]*Ibid.*, pp. 12-24.

[16]J. A. Knudtzon, *Die El-Amarna-Tafeln* (Leipzig, 1915), II, 876-877. The Armarna Letters are the actual documents of the official correspondence between the Egyptian Government and the rulers of the various principalities of Palestine and Syria about 1400 B.C., at the very time the Hebrews were entering Palestine. They were found on clay tablets at El-Amarna on the middle Nile in 1887.

[17]*Ibid.*, I, pp. 864-867.

[18]As a matter of fact, there is "a striking disagreement between the canon and the apocryphal literature" regarding the exact birthplace of Jesus, the latter sources, which are often very old, placing it at a point half-way between Jerusalem and Bethlehem. W. Foerster, "Bemerkunger und Fragen zur Statte der Geburt Jesu," *Ztschr. d. Dt. Palestine Vereins*, 57 (1934), 1-7. Foerster thinks that the disagreements are so clear, so persistent and so old that the misunderstanding on the subject goes right back to the beginning, e.g. some sources favor a cave, others a stall. The only thing that sources agree on is that the birth took place "in the land of Jerusalem." So serious are the differences on the subject that they have been the subject of at least one entire (and quite shallow) book, W. J. Ramsay, *Was Christ Born at Bethlehem?*

(London, 3rd Ed., 1905), which defends the credibility of the Gospel of Luke.

[19]Galling, op. cit., pp. 12ff.; 27-28; Cf. 2 Kings 23:1. K. Sethe, "Der Titel 'Richter' als allgemeiner Ehrentitel." Aeg. Ztschr. 38 (1900), pp. 54f.

[20]From the eleventh century on "the high priest of Amon . . . could and constantly did reduce the king to a position of subservience" in Egypt. (Cab. Anc. Hist., III, p. 268). For the rise of the priests to power, see C.A.H., III, 253f. and A. Moret, Histoire de l'Orient, II, p. 569. The divine patron of the priests was the god Ammon, who "continually intervened directly in the affairs of the government by specific oracles," which put the state completely under priestly control. (J. Breasted, History of Egypt, p. 538). Some striking illustrations of what he calls the "versatility in wickedness" of the Egyptian priests are given by T. E. Peet, "A Historical Document of the Ramasside Age," Jhl. Egypt. Archaeol., X, 116ff. Egypt under the priests "was not only externally exhausted but internally rotten, and simply collapsed on itself," according to Ed. Meyer, G.L.A., II, i, p. 420, who notes that the attempts of the priests to lead the country back to ancient virtues and old-fashioned ways was a complete failure. This was the Egypt of Lehi, confident that it had restored the glories of the past. Cf. F. K. Kienitz, Die Politische Geschichte Aegyptens vom 7 bis 4 Jh. vor der Zeitwende (Berlin: Akad. Verlag, 1953) and H. Kees, Das Priestertum im Aegyptischen Staat von Neuen Reich bis zur Spätzeit (Leiden-Köln: Brill, 1953).

[21]H. M. Weiner, "The Relations of Egypt to Israel and Judah in the Age of Isaiah," Ancient Egypt, 1926, pp. 52 ff.

[22]Ibid., p. 70. A good summary of the international picture is by C. Virolleaud, in L'Ethnographie, N. S. 48, pp. 6-7. S. A. B. Mercer, Extra-Biblical Sources for Hebrew and Jewish History (N. Y. Longmans Green, 1913), p. 57ff. John Bright, in the Biblical Archaeologist, 12 (May, 1949) p. 46ff., Pfeiffer, Jnl. Bible Lit. LVI (1937).

[23]Virolleaud, op. cit., p. 7. After the fall of Jerusalem only two independent states remained in all the world to defy Nebuchadnezzar! A. Wiedemann, "Der Zug Nebucadnezars gegen Aegypten," Aeg. Ztschr. 16 (1878), p. 2.

[24]Wiedemann, op. cit., pp. 2-3, 6, and "Nebucadnezar und Aegypten,"

[25]W. F. Albright, in The Bible Archaeologist, IX (1946), p. 4.

[26]Albright, "The Seal of Eliakim, etc." Jnl. of Bibl. Lit., 51 (1932), 94ff. Wiedemann for example, in the earlier study, op. cit., p. 2, does not believe that Nebuchadnezzar ever took Tyre.

[27]Gust. Holscher, Palastina in der persischen und hellenistischen Zeit, Heft 5 of Quelle u. Forschungen (Berling, 1903), p. 21.

[28]J. W. Jack, in PEFQ 1938, pp. 177-179.

[29]Albright, Bibl. Archaeologist, IX (1946), pp. 2-4 and notes 15-16.

[30]Virolleaud, op. cit., p. 6.

[31]G. R. Tabouis, Nebuchadnezzar (N. Y.: Whittlesey, 1931), pp. 135-133.

[32]Ibid., p. 146.

Lesson 9 Notes

[1]J. Dissard, "Les Migrations et les Vicissitudes de la Tribu des 'Amer," Revue Biblique, N. S. II (1905), 411-6.

[2]Kitab Taghrib Bani Hilal (Damascus: Moh. Hashim, Undated), pp. 13-15.

[3]Jawad Ali, Tarikh al-Arab quabl al-Islam (Baghdad, 1951), I, 6, 13.

[4]See below, p. 232.

[5]See below, p. 111.

[6]C. Brockelmann, Geschichte der Arabischen Litteratur (Leipzig, 1909), p. 34.

[7]A. Mez, Die Renaissance des Islams (Heidelberg, 1922), p. 190.

[8]"Just as I came to the gate of Dionysus, I saw a lot of men come out of the Odeion and go over to the Orchestra. Being alarmed at the sight, I drew back into the shadow between a pillar and the side of the wall of the

gate, where the bronze statue of the general stands. I saw there must be at least three hundred men, standing around in groups of five and ten, a few maybe of twenty. I recognized most of them, since they faced the moonlight..." Deposition given in Andocides, *Oration on the Mysteries*, c. 38-39. Though a good lawyer could make hash of this witness's testimony, it is plain that there was no downtown lighting in Athens.

[9]Juvenal, Satire iii, 268ff. Particularly interesting is the *proseucha* of line 296, which is usually taken to be a Jewish synagogue, since the satirists like to make fun of the Jews in Rome. At any rate, it brings us a step nearer to Lehi's Jerusalem.

[10]1 Ne. 4:31. It was Nephi who supervised the making of swords after the manner of Laban's sword, which he so admired, 2 Ne. 5:14.

[11]Sir Rich. Burton, *Personal Narrative of a Pilgrimage to al-Madinah and Maccah* (London, 1893), I, 11, 19, and throughout Vol. II.

Lesson 10 Notes

[1]J. W. Jack, "The Lachish Letters," *Pal. Expl. Fund Quarterly*, 1938, p. 168.

[2]H. Graetz, in *Monatschr. f. Gesch. u. Wiss. d. Judentums*, XIX, 16.

[3]Ed. Meyer, *Gesch. d. Altert.*, II, i, 137.

[4]These remarks are based on the instructive essay by Richard J. H. Gottheil, in the Introduction to his edition of Al-Kindi's *History of the Egyptian Cadis* (Paris: Geuthner, 1908), pp. iii-xvii; the quotations are from pages vii, xvi, and xiv-xv, respectively.

[5]The Wenamon story is told in J. Breasted, *History of Egypt* (1905), pp. 513-518; James Bakie, *The History of the Pharaohs* (London, 1908), pp. 285-7; and in *Camb. Anc. Hist.*, II, 193. The original text, the Moscow Papyrus, is reproduced in the *Aegypt. Zeitschr.*, Vol. 38, pp. 1ff.

[6]J. Offord, "Archaeological Notes on Jewish Antiquities," *PEFQ*, 1916,

[7]W. F. Albright, "The Seal of Eliakim, etc." *Jnl. Bibl. Lit.*, 51 (1932), pp. 79-83, shows that the title "servant" in Jerusalem at this particular time meant something like "official representative," and was an honorable rather than a degrading designation.

[8]W. Ewing, in *PEFQ*, 1895, p. 172f.

[9]A. Jaussen, "Judgments," *Revue Biblique* XII, 259. Cf. *Survey of Western Palestine*, p. 327.

[10]Leo Haefeli, *Die Beduinen von Beersheba* (Lucerne: Räber, 1938), p. 44.

[11]*Surv. of Wstn. Palest.*, Spec. Papers, p. 326; P. Baldenspreger, in *PEFQ*, 1910, p. 261. See especially G. Dalman, in *Ztschr. d. dt. Pal. Ver.*, 62, pp. 59-61.

[12]Ch. Daughty, *Arabia Deserta* (1. Ed.), II, 27.

[13]S. Rosenblatt, "The Relations between Jewish & Muslim Laws Concerning Oaths and Vows," *Am. Acad. of Jewish Research*, 1936, pp. 231, 238. Cf. Joh. Pedersen *Der Deid bei den Semiten in seinem Verhälnie zu verwandten Erscheinungen*, etc. (Strassburg, 1914).

Lesson 12 Notes

[1]See above, pp. 114-115.

[2]G. Molin, *Sohne des Lichtes*, (Vienna-Munich: Herold, 1954) p. 140.

[3]D. Daube, "Concerning Methods of Bible-Criticism, Late Law in Early Narratives," *Archiv Orientalni* XVII (1949), p. 88.

[4]Alf. Halder, *The Notion of the Desert in Sumero-Accadian and West-Semitic Religions* (Uppsala Univ. Aarskrift, 1950:3), p. 5.

[5]*Ibid.*, pp. 7-9, 14.

[6]*Ibid.*, pp. 25-26.

[7]*Ibid.*, p 68.

[8]See the *Improvement Era*, Sept. 1956. Herbert Braun, "Der Fahrende Oidipous Planetes . . . Vergleich mit Hosea 9:15-17 LXX," *Zeitscher. f. Theologie and Kirche* 48 (1951), 32-37, comparing the Greek with the

Scriptural wandering hero. For a wide scope of comparisons, V. Vikentiev, in *Bulletin de l'Institut d'Egypte*, XXIX, 189ff.

The reader may wonder why we cite pagan rituals and legends to illustrate Jewish, Christian, and Book of Mormon teaching. In this case it is the great and undoubted antiquity of the sources that makes them significant. We do not pretend for a moment that these people had the true Gospel but we do believe, as Eusebius maintained long ago in the opening sections of his *Church History*, that all the ancients possessed fragmentary bits and distant memories of the true Gospel. This teaching is brought out by President John Taylor in *The Mediation and Atonement* (Salt Lake: Stevens and Wallis, 1950). Today scholars everywhere realize for the first time that the scriptures must be read along with all the other old sources. Thus Cyrus Gordon tells us that the Old Testament must be studied "in the light of parallel literatures from the pagan forerunners and contemporaries of the Hebrews, in Bible lands," if it is to be rightly understood. (C. H. Gordon, Ugaritic Literature (Rome: *Pontif. Inst. Bibl.*, 1949), (p. 7.) "The Bible strikes root into every ancient Near Eastern Culture," writes Albright, "and it cannot be historically understood until we see its relationship to its source in true perspective." (*Jnl. Am. Or. Soc.*, 64 (1944), p. 148). Today, says another scholar, "The Old Testament horizon must be expanded and its history interpreted against this larger background." (J. Paterson, *Studia Orientalia*, I. 97). T. Haering (in *Ztschr. f. Neutest. Wiss.* 17., p. 222) goes so far as to suggest that all ancient literature, sacred and profane, Jew and Gentile, may be regarded and should be read as a single book. All this should give great impetus to Book of Mormon study. In Lessons 16 and 23 below we make extensive use of pagan sources as evidence for the Book of Mormon. Just as we find in the writings of many churches today much that is of value in illustrating and proving the true Gospel, which they do *not* possess, so the pagans of old can teach us a great deal.

[9]Burckhardt, *Notes*, I, 360.

[10]*Ibid.*, pp. 367, 363.

[11]Victor Muller, *En Syrie avec les Bedouins* (Paris: Leroux, 1931), p. 182.

[12]Hariri, *Maqamat of the Bedouin*: These are the opening lines.

[13]Claude R. Conder, *Tent Work in Palestine* (London, 1879), I, 272.

[14]T. Harmer, *Observations*, I, 101: "When the Arabs have drawn upon themselves such a *general* resentment of the more fixed inhabitants of those countries, that they think themselves unable to stand against them, they withdraw into the depths of the great wilderness. . . ."

[15]*Ibid.*, p. 102, quoting Jer. 49:8, 30; Jud. 6:2; I Sam. 13:6; Jer. 41:7,9; Is. 31:6; Ez. 3:5-6; and noting confirmatory passages from writers in the time of the Crusades.

[16]De Lacy O'Leary, *Arabia Before Mohammed* (London: Trubner, 1927), p. 3.

[17]The city people knew the desert from personal contact—and loathed it. The thought of one living his whole life there was simply unendurable. A famous Egyptian text, the *Teaching of Merekaure* says (Sect. 21): "Behold the wretched Amu (desert-dweller, Asiatic), toilsome is the land wherein he is. . . . He dwells not in a single place, but his legs are ever driven wandering (?) . . ." cited by Gardiner in *Jnl. Eg. Archaeol.* I, p. 30. Cf, L. Keimer, "L'horreur des Egyptiens pour les demons du desert," *Bull de l'Inst. d'Egypte*, 26 1943-4), pp. 135-147. The attitude of Lehi's family on the subject is very plainly stated. See below, pp. 211ff.

[18]H. Gressman, in *Archiv fur Orientforschung*, III, 12, citing IV Ezra 13:40ff and Deut. 29:27.

[19]R. Eisler, *Iesous Basileus* . . . I, 14, 479ff, 512ff, for the meaning of the words; II, 267, 493, 571, 575, 787, for the charges against them.

[20]Exactly as in other cases "the king's men" spied on them and his armies tried to exterminate them, *Ib.*, 2:30f; cf. Mos. 18:32ff, and below, p. 156.

[21]H. Graetz, "Die Ebioniten des Alten Testaments," *Monatsschr. f. Gesch. u. Wissensch, des Judentums*, 18 (1869), 1-20, 49-71, 115ff. He identifies the Ebionites with the Levites, p. 13, and even the Prophets, p. 71.

[22]Molin, *Sohne des Lichtes*, p. 144. The Nasirite vows and ways of

life have been the subject of much investigation. The identity of the word with Nazarene has often been insisted on. The Nazarenes were strictly speaking those who had taken secret holy vows and entered into sacred covenants.

[23]E. Käsemann, *Das Wandernde Gottesvolk,* pp. 137-138.

[24]Doctrine & Covenants 1:36. Idumea was both the classic land of rebellion (Josephus, *Bel. Jud.* II, 55; Eisler, *Op. Cit.,* I, 512f), and the home of false priests and royal pretenders, the most notable of whom was Herod the Great. "The Idumeans were not originally Jews, says an ancient fragment (quoted by Eisler, I, 343, Note 1), "but were Phoenicians and Syrians who had been overcome by the Jews and forced to accept circumcision." Cf. L. Iktonen, "Edom und Moab in den Psalmen," in *Studia Orientalia,* I (1925), 78-83; F. Hommel, *Ethnologie u. Geographie Les Alton Orients,* pp. 182-3, 594, on Idumea as the wicked world.

[25]Kasemann, *op. cit.,* pp. 5ff.

[26]*Ibid.,* pp. 11, 15, 24.

[27]Thus *Serek* II, 1; Barnabas, *Ep.* c. 18.

[28]Kasemann, *Op. cit.,* pp. 27ff, 45ff.

[29]*Ibid.,* pp. 51, on wandering as an education device, 141, 147: the greatest of all these High Priests was Jesus, of whom Adam was a type, 156.

[30]*Ibid.,* p. 156, cf. 37.

[31]A. Dupont-Somner, *The Dead Sea Scrolls* (N. Y.: Macmillan, 1952,) pp. 61ff. A. Rubinstein, "Urban Halashah and Camp Rules . . ." *Sefared* XII (1952) 283-296.

[32]Below, Lesson XVI, Note 12. Henri de Contenson, "In the Footsteps of St. John the Baptist, "Notes on the Rolls of the Dead Sea," in *Antiquity and Survival* I (May 1955), 37-56 for some wonderful photos. M. Gaster, *Studies,* I, 370.

[33]P. Sabatier, *Les Religions d'Autorite et la Religion de l'Esprit* (Paris, 1904,) pp. 60-61.

[34]The avoidance of the theme is very noticeable in the indices of the Latin *Patrologia* Vol. 219, Col.s 233, 673. The idea of the Church still looking for its heavenly home was repugnant to the fathers after Augustine, who first established the doctrine that the Church on earth *is* the Kingdom of God and the heavenly home of the saints. Methodius, *Conviv.* (In *Patrol. Graec.* 18:152-157) Claims that the woman who flees to the desert is the Church in Paradise!

[35]"The Church of Constantine drove into solitude and the desert those who wished to devote themselves to religion," says A. von Harnack, *Saint Augustine and Monasticism,* p. 43.

[36]Bern. Lotting, *Peregrinatio Religiosa. Wallfahrten in der Antike und das Pilgerwesen in der alten Kirche.* (Munster-Regensburg: Forschungen sur Volkskunde, Heft 33-35, 1950), deals with the pagan background of the Christian pilgrimage, which was not a continuation of ancient Jewish or Christian practices.

[37]Nibley, *The World and The Prophets,* pp. 214f.

[38]Thus 1 Nephi Chapters 19 to 22, quoting various prophets.

Lesson 14 Notes

[1]The most comprehensive treatment of the controversies and perplexities of the doctors on these subjects is Olaf Linton, *Das Problem der Urkirche in her Neueren Forschung* (Uppsala: Almquist & Wiksell, 1932). See our discussion, "Two Views of Church History," in *The Improvement Era,* Vol. 58, July through October, 1955, and "Controlling the Past," *Ibid.,* Jan., 1955, pp. 20 ff.

[2]On the perplexities of Eusebius, see *The Improvement Era,* Jan. 1955, p. 22.

[3]Space will not allow another retelling of the story of the finding of the Dead Sea Scrolls. The most readily available accounts are Millar Burrows, *The Dead Sea Scrolls* (New York, Viking Press, 1955), which contains an extensive bibliography, and Edmund Wilson, *Scrolls from the Dead Sea* (New

York, Oxford University Press, 1956). The latter book is available in install-
ment form in the *New Yorker Magazine*, beginning May 14, 1955.

[4]G. Lankester Harding, in D. Barthelemy and J. T. Milik, *Discoveries in
the Judean Desert* I, *Qumran Cave* I (Oxford, Clarendon Press, 1955) p. 4.

[5]The 300 written fragments found in Cave Four in 1952 "range (in date)
from the late fourth century to the first half of the second century B.C. . . ."
F. M. Cross, "The Oldest Manuscripts from Qumran," *Jnl. of Biblical Lit.*,
74 (1955), p. 164. The coins run from 125 B. C. to 135 A. D., but the manuscripts "cannot be later than A. D. 68," and there is clear evidence that the
main buildings of the community were destroyed for good by the earthquake
of 31 B.C., according to G. L. Harding, in *The Illustrated London News*, Sept.
3, 1955, pp. 379 f. See below, Note 33, for the possible age of the community.

[6]The quote is from A. Dupont-Sommer, 'Les Mss. de la Mer Morte; leur
Importance pour l'Histoire des Religions," *Numen* 11/3 (1955), 168 ff., who
notes, p. 189, that the study of the scrolls has just begun. See our article,
"More Voices from the Dust," in *The Instructor*, March, 1956, pp. 71 ff.

[7]C. Clemen, *Die Himmelfahrt des Mose* (1904), Kl. Texte, No. 10, from
a Latin Poliopsest of the early 7th century.

[8]H. Nibley, in *The Improvement Era* 57 (Feb. 1954), p. 89.

[9]G. L. Harding, in Barthelemy and Milik, *op. cit.*, p. 4.

[10]Mrs. C. M. Crowfoot, in Barthelemy and Milik, *op. cit.*, p. 25. We
emphasized the importance of the Genizahs in the article cited above in note 4,
pp. 88 ff. The assumption of Moses is one of the works actually found among
the fragments of the scrolls, thus proving that the people who hid the scrolls
were aware of the practices described and may have been consciously imitat-
ing them.

[11]In *The Instructor*, Mar. 1956, p. 72, citing the study of Peter Meinhold
in *Saeculum* V (1954), p. 86 where he taxes the Book of Mormon with being
a fraud and a forgery because it attributes New Testament practices and
terminology to people who lived hundreds of years before New Testament
times. This is exactly what the Scrolls do, and for that reason were so
vigorously opposed. "The battle over the date of the scrolls is decided," says
Cross, placing their production between 200 B.C. and 70 A.D. This is
"disputed only by a few, who like Southern politicians, still think that an
ancient defeat can be reversed by bombastic oratory." See his article in *The
Christian Century*, August 3, 1955, p. 85. The bombast and the fury still continue in the ill tempered discourses of Prof. S. Zeitlin, the latest to date being
"The Dead Sea Scrolls," in *Jewish Quarterly Review* 46 (1956), 389 ff.

[12]On the sale of the scrolls, S. Zeitlin, "The Hebrew Scrolls," *Jew. Quart.
Rev.* 46 (1956), 257 ff. This article is perhaps the longest and most furious
attack yet launched by Zeitlin against the scrolls, which he regards as an
utterly worthless piece of Medieval illiteracy.

[13]C. M. Cross, in *Christian Century*, Aug. 24, 1955, p. 970.

[14]G. L. Harding, "Where Christ Himself May have Studied, an Essene
Monastery at Khirbet Qumran," *Illust. London News*, Sept. 3, 1955, pp. 379-
381. The quote is from p. 379.

[15]Thus *Time Magazine*, Sept. 5, 1955, p. 34.

[16]F. M. Cross, in *Christian Century*, Aug. 10, 1955, p. 920.

[17]*Ibid.*, p. 921.

[18]*Time Magazine*, ibid., p. 33.

[19]Cross, *loc. cit.*; a distinct undertone of alarm is discernable in such protests as those of A. Metzinger, a Catholic, who writes in *Biblica*, 1955, p. 481:
"Christianity and the Church have nothing to fear from such comparisons (between the New Testament and the Scrolls), if they are carried out with
scientific conscientiousness; their peculiar value is in no wise diminished, the
unique and original quality of the New Testament is made only the clearer:
'Christianity as a new experience.' Insight into the Jewish and Christian
contacts. If any man be in Christ, he is a new creature . . .' (II Cor. 5:17)."
F. F. Bruce, "Qumran and Early Christianity," in *New Testament Studies*
II, 3 (1956), 190, thinks to dispel misgivings with the irrelevant declaration
that Christianity "contained all that was of value in Qumran—and much be-
sides." Who would deny that?

[20]G. Graystone in *The Catholic World*, April, 1956, p. 11.

²¹See above Note 11. Meinhold's recent attack (1954) is particularly ferocious. Even the anti-Mormon literature of the last century cannot surpass it for spine-chilling savagery of language.

²²F. M. Cross (*Christ. Cent.* Aug. 24, 1955, p. 971).

²³J. Teicher, "The Habakkuk Scroll," *Jnl. of Jewish Studies*, V. 2, 1954, 47-59, quote is from p. 53.

²⁴F.M. Cross, *Biblical Archaeologists*, Feb. 1954, p. 3.

²⁵S. Zeitlin, *Jew. Quart. Rev.*, 46 (1956), p. 390, 392.

²⁶H. Nibley, *The Improvement Era*, 58 (June, 1955), p. 384. In this series we treated the subject of translation at considerable length in the issues for May, 1955, pp. 307 ff, and June, 1955, 84 ff.

²⁷Zeitlin, *op. cit.*, p. 390.

²⁸This has been especially studied by Oscar Cullmann, "The Significance of the Qumran Texts for Research into the Beginning of Christianity," *Jnl. Bibl. Lit.*, 74 (1955), pp. 213-226. Equally available is Lucetta Mowry, "The Dead Sea Scrolls and the Gospel of John," *Biblical Archaeologist*, 17 (Dec. 1954), pp. 78-97, who would read John as part of one big book to which the Scrolls belong, along with other widely scattered writings, especially of Iranian origin. Another attempt to explain certain exact parallels between passages in the Scrolls and New Testament is by W. D. Davies in *Harvard Theological Review*, 46 (1955), p. 139.

²⁹A list is given in George Molin, *Die Sohne des Lichtes Zeit and Stellung der Handschriften vom Toten Meer*, pp. 102-166.

³⁰Cullmann, "Die neuentdeckten Qumran-Texte und das Judentum des Pseudo-Clementinen," in *Neutest. Studien fur Rud. Bultmann*, Beiheft zur *Zeitschrift f. Neutestaementliche Wissenschaft* 21 (1954), pp. 25-51.

³¹Teicher, in *Jnl. Jew. Stud.*, V. 2, p. 47. Special code signs are treated by R. Coossens, "L'enigme du signe 'nun' dans le Manuel de Discipline," *La Nouvelle Clio*, VI (1954), pp. 5-39; cf. A. Dupont, Commer, "La Doctrine Gnostique de la Lettre "Wa'" *Bibl. Archaeol. et Hist.*, XLI (Paris, Geunther, 1946); F. M. Cross, *Biblical Archaeologist*, Feb. 1954, pp. 3, 14.

³²*Biblical Archaeologist*, Feb. 1954, p. 16.

Lesson 15 Notes

¹It has recently been maintained that the name Christians did not originate, as has always been supposed, as a mocking nickname, but was actually first applied by the followers of Christ to themselves, "not as 'worshipers' of Christ," but as 'the supporter and servants of the King,'" i.e., those who willingly "took his name" upon them. J. Moreau, "Le Nom des Chretiens," *Nouvelle Clio*, I-II (1949-1950), 190-2.

²The weekly observance of another day beside the Jewish Sabbath as a day of religious worship is one of the authentic marks of Alma's Church. Throughout history those Jewish priests who were determined to live the Old Law in its perfection as far as possible insisted on the pre-eminent holiness of the *first* day as well as the seventh. The observance of this day in the very earliest times of the Christian Church is not, therefore, to be attributed to innovating practices of the Apostate Church—it is there from the beginning. Seven days represent the life-span of this world, but the eighth or the first is the new age to follow, "it is the beginning of another world," writes Barnabas (Epist. 15:5), "wherefore we also celebrate with gladness the eighth day." Many examples are given by O. Cullmann, Urchristentun und Gottesidienst (Zurich: Zwingli-Verlag, 1950), pp. 14-15, and H. Gunkel, *Zum Religions-verstandniss des N.T.*, pp. 75-76. The Talmud, *Sabbath* IX, iii-lv, gives ten reasons for regarding the first day of the week rather than the seventh as the most holy.

³The great public readings in the Book of Mormon, such as those given by Abinadi and King Mosiah, were in the old established Hebrew tradition. When the High Priest read the law to the people every seven years, all, in-

cluding women, children, and servants, were expected and required to listen, according to Josephus, *Antiquities* IV, 8, 12.

⁴The term "united order" is a most literal translation of the expression *etseth ha-yahad*, which Burrows, *op. cit.*, p. 377 renders "council of the community." No word in the scrolls has caused more debate and speculation than *yahad*; its basic meaning is oneness or unity, while an *etseth* is a body of people organized as a council or the pattern of organization by which a council is formed. It is a closed body or corporation met together to discuss policy. Hence "united order" is as near as one can get to a literal translation of the term. These and related terms having to do with organization have been recently made the object of special study by Robert North, "Qumran 'Serek a' and Related Fragments," *Orientalia*, XXV (1956), 90-99. North notes that the terms *eda* and *Yahad* are not synonymous at all. "The Eda includes wives and children; and its structure is more warlike," p. 91. Bathelemy says it is identical with the *Hasidim* of I Macc. 2:42, while *Yahad* refers specifically to the more peaceful Essenes. (*Loc. cit.*) North commenting on the expression *etseth ha-yahad* mentions Dupont-Sommer's theory that *eda* and *etsah* are the same, the latter being the sources of the Greek word Essene; North himself prefers but does not insist on viewing *etseth* as "an act of counsel" rather than the meeting itself. (p. 92.) At this time the matter is completely up in the air. The expression "Sons of Zadok" gives rise to many problems "clustering around the relation between the Qumran community and the name "Sadducee." (p. 92.) Schurer claims "that the SDWQ (of the Scrolls) after whom the Sadducees are named in unquestionably a proper name, Sadeq, which in the late Old Testament period began to be *pronounced* sadduq." (*loc. cit.*) Of course frequent attempts have already been made to link this with the name and priesthood of Melchizedek, but to date, to quote North again, "Our only conclusion is that we must face honestly and reflectively the Sadducee-links of the Qumran documents, even while granting that the probabilities are far greater in favor of the Essenes." (p. 93.) He is speaking of the latest period, of course. What the name signifies for earlier times remains to be discovered.

⁵G. Molin, *Die Söhne des Lichtes*, pp. 140, 146.

⁶"Several passages in the Manual of Discipline indicate that the sect practiced community of goods. At the same time it is said that one who has inadvertently destroyed the property of the order shall repay it in full. One naturally wonders how a member who had turned over his private possessions to the order would have anything left with which to pay for such damage . . . The Damascus Document puts some restrictions on the ownership of property but does not deny the right of private possession. Members of the group who work for wages pay . . . for community purposes the wages of two days out of each month . . ." Burrows, *Dead Sea Scrolls*, pp. 233 ff. The one thing that is clear that these people had a claim to their own property from which they contributed "of their own free will"; a person who left the community could take his property with him. It was not communism. Everyone had "his own substance" but was expected to impart of it freely for the good of others.

⁷Dr. Cross comments interestingly on this organization, noting with surprise the presence of a presidency of three, a council of twelve, and a general assembly who must vote on all important matters (*Christian Century*, Aug. 24, 1955), p. 968. He notes also in the Scrolls the practice of *correptio fraterna*, "otherwise unparalleled in Judaism" but found in Matthew 18:15-17: "a brother is to be reproved in private first of all, then before witnesses, then before the church, after which he is to be excommunicated." (p. 968.)

⁸The "waters of *NDH*" may be read either *nedeh*, "a liberal gift, Grace", or *niddah*, "removal, purifying of uncleanness," from the Heb. root *NADAH*, Cross, *op. cit.*, p. 969, notes that they "seem to have practiced continual lustrations as well as baptism or initiation into the covenanted community." G. Harding (*ILN*, Sept. 3, 1955, p. 379) believes that John the Baptist "undoubtedly derived the idea of ritual immersion, or baptism" from Qumran.

⁹The Qumran sacramental meal looks to the future, exactly as the Early Christian sacrament looked both to the past ('in memory . . .') and to the future, according to O. Cullmann, *Unchristentum und Gottesdienst* (Zurich: Zwingly Verlag, 1950), pp. 39 ff. For a good treatment of the anticipation motif, Cross, *op. cit.*, pp. 969-970, the following is quoted: "The life of the

sect is understood as life in anticipation of the Kingdom of God." Their sacrament is "the litrugical anticipation of the messianic banquet." They "partake in the Kingdom proleptically, anticipating the coming day when the ambiguity will end. . . ." The theme of anticipation receives its fullest treatment in the Book of Mormon.
[10]Molin, op. cit., pp. 162-166.
[11]Ibid., p. 140; J. S. Kelso, "The Archaeology of Qumran," in Jnl. Bibl. Lit. 74 (1955), p. 145.

Lesson 16 Notes

[1]The Apocrypha originally got their name of "hidden" writings from the fact that they were considered too sacred to be divulged to the general public. The name does not designate, as it later came to, books of dubious authenticity, but rather scripture of very special importance and holiness, according to W. O. E. Oesterley, An Introduction to the Books of the Apocrypha (London: S. P. C. K., 1953), p. 1.
[2]Thus the Book of Enoch while it "influenced the thought and diction" of "nearly all the writers of the New Testament," and "is quoted as a genuine production of Enoch by St. Jude, and as scripture by St. Barnabas," and while "with the earlier Fathers and Apologists it had all the weight of a canonical book," was none the less disdained and rejected by the schoolmen of the fourth century, "and under the ban of such authorities as Hilary, Jerome, and Augustine, it gradually passed out of circulation and became lost to the knowledge of Western Christendom." R. H. Charles, The Book of Enoch (Oxford, 1912), pp. ix-x. It is interesting that President John Taylor frequently quotes from this work, and recognizes its authority in his book The Mediation and Atonement.
[3]Irenaeus, Centra Haereses II, 27 (Migne, Patrol Graec. VII, 803.)
[4]M. Caster, Studies (1925), I, 280.
[5]The most significant recent study of this much-treated theme is by F. Ebrard, in Archiv Orientalni, XVIII, pp. 18ff. See Note 2 above.
[6]G. Molin, Söhne des Lichtes, pp. 158, 164-6. Typical is the statement in the Clementine Recognitions I, 52 (Patrol. Graec. I, 1236), that "Christ, who was always from the beginning, has visited the righteous of every generation (albeit secretly), and especially those who have looked forward to his coming, to whom he often appeared." This reads like a sermon out of the Book of Mormon, but the fact that this is a genuine teaching of the earliest Christian Church has only recently been appreciated. See Robt. M. Grant, Second-Century Christianity (London: S. P. C. K., 1946), p. 10.
[7]Of recent years many studies have shown that the name Nasorene by which the earliest Christians were designated was actually a very ancient technical term meaning "keeper of secrets," the secrets in question being "the mysteries of the kingdom." R. Eisler, Iesous Basileus, etc., II, 21f. See above, Lesson XVI, Note
[8]R. H. Charles, in Encyclopedia Britannica (xi Ed.), I, 171, s. v. "Apocalyptic Literature."
[9]Ibid., I, 169.
[10]Serek Scroll (Manual of Discipline), iii, 15.
[11]Charles, op. cit., I, 170.
[12]D. Fjusser, in Israel Exploration Journal, III (1953), 30-47.
[13]Sirach (Ecclesiasticus) 44:16ff; 49:14f.
[14]W. H. Brownlee, "Biblical Interpretation among the Secretaries of the Dead Sea Scrolls," Biblical Archaeologist xiv (Sept. 1951), 54ff.
[15]Babylonian Talmud (Goldschmidt, I, 464), Sab. VI, iv, quoting R. Hiya b. Abba.
[16]H. Gunkel, Zum religionsgeschichtlichen Verständnis des Neuen Testaments (Göttingen, 1930), passim.
[17]All this is clearly set forth in Serek IV, 15-16.
[18]Serek III, 9-10.
[19]Ibid., III, 13ff.

[20]W. H. Brownlee, in *Supplementary Studies,* Nos. 10-12. *Bull. Am. Schools of Oriental Research* (New Haven, 1951), p. 16. *Serek* IV, 17-18.

[21]One can find the doctrine of the Two Ways in almost any of the *early* apocrypha, e. g., IV Ezr. IV, 3; I Clement 36; Justin, *Apol.,* II, 7, 11; II Clem. vi; *Apostol. Constitutions* VII, 1; Ignatius, *Ep. ad Ephes.,* xi; Barnabas *Epist.,* 18; Enoch 94:1, 92:18, and in numerous Logia of Jesus. It also turns up in the Classical writers, e. g., Zeonophon, *Memorab.,* II, i, 21ff; Dio Chrysost., *Orat.* I 66f.

[22]For a discourse on the Way of Light, *Serek* IV, 2-8. See Sverre Aalen, *Der Begriff 'Licht' und 'Finternis im A. T.,* in *Spätjudentum und im Rabbinismus* (Oslo: Videnskaps-Akad. II, Hist-Phil., 1951, No. 1).

[23]*Serek* V, 4-5.

[24]*Ibid.,* III, 21ff.

[25]*Ibid.,* IV, 19.

[26]*Ibid.,* V, 6-7.

[27]*Ibid.,* VIII, 10.

[28]*Ibid.,* V, 10ff.

[29]*Tal, Sabbath* II, vi.

[30]*Ibid.,* V, iv.

[31]*Ibid.,* IX, iv: "In the hour in which Israel said: We will do it (i. e., keep the Law), and we will obey! sixty myriads of ministering angels descended and wove for every Israelite two crowns, one for 'doing' and the other for 'obeying'. But when the Israelites later sinned, one-hundred-twenty myriads of angels came down and *took the crowns back again!*" Crowns are a familiar property of early Christian imagery, especially apocalyptic. The doctrine of lost glory is much emphasized by all the so-called Apostolic Fathers, who harp on the theme: "If the angels kept not their first estate . . ." how can men expect to be secure?

[32]See F. M. Cross, in *Christian Century,* Aug. 17, 1955, p. 945, and *Serek* IX, 11. A Catholic editor of apocryphal writings notes that "one hardly knows whether the Christ is to come before or after the end of the world. It seems that Jesus must come first to the just alone, for they alone will recognize his token, which the wicked will not recognize. . . . at a later time he come in clouds of glory to judgment." L. Guerrier, in *Patrologia Orientalis* IX, Fasc. 3, p. 151.

[33]*Serek* IV, 19; *Didache* 16:3-6; *Hermae Pastor,* Vis. ii:2-4, Simil 3-4.

[34]All details in Gunkel, *op. cit.,* cf. Charles, in Encl. Brit. (*op. cit.*).

Lesson 17 Notes

[1]Johs. Pedersen, *Israel* (London: Oxford Univ. Press, 1946), I, 227.

[2]A partial translation of the text may be found in M. Burrows, *The Dead Sea Scrolls,* pp. 390-399, and in A. Dupont-Sommer, *That Dead Sea Scrolls,* (1952), pp. 79-84. A. L. Sukenik, *Otsar ha-Megillot ha-Genuzot* (Jerusalem: Heb. Univ., 1954) is the original text with photographs. For complete translation and commentary, J. van der Ploeg, "La Regle de la Guerre," *Vetus Testamentum* V (1955), 373-420.

[3]H. Rowley, *The Zadokite Fragment,* etc., p. 19; Dupont-Somner, *op. cit.,* pp. 79ff. Gerh. von Rad, *Der Heilige Krieg im alten Israel* (Zürich: Zwingli-Verlag, 1951), finds that the ritual practices were used in real war in the period between Deborah and Saul.

[4]These and many other titles may be found in Burrows, *op. cit.,* pp. 392-3.

[5]*Ibid.,* p. 394.

[6]*Ibid.,* pp. 393ff. Dupont-Somner, loc. cit.

[7]The rite is mentioned in Varro, *Ling. Lat.* V, xv, 25; Livy, *Hist,* I, 32,5; IV, 30, 14; Cicero, *Leg.* II, 9.

[8]Burrows, *op. cit.,* p. 395.

[9]Dupont-Sommer, *op. cit.,* p. 79.

[10]*Ibid.,* p. 81.

[11]*Ibid.,* p. 83. Typical "Asiatic" sentiments in the hymn are: "A multitude of cattle in Thine estates, silver and gold and precious stones in Thy palaces! . . . Open ((Thy) gates for ever, to bring the riches of the nations into Thy

dwelling! And may their kings serve Thee, and may all Thine oppressors prostrate themselves before Thee, and may they lick (the dust) from Thy feet! . . ."

[12]Thus L. Mowry, in *The Biblical Archaeologist*, XVII (Dec. 1954), pp. 78-97.

[13]For an extensive bibliography of works dealing with this theme, see Carl Clemen, *Primitive Christianity*, pp. 153ff, 161, 164ff, 124f; W. Bousset, *Hauptprobleme der Gnosia*, pp. 57, 70ff, 114ff, 55-57, 144, 148, 38; and *Religion des Judentums im späthellenistischen Zeitalter* (1926), pp. 202ff; Ed. Meyer,*Ursprung and Anfänge des Christentums*, II, 58, 85, 128ff; III, 161-2; A. Moret, *Hist. de l'Orient*, II, 782-4.

[14]The story is told in C. Huart and L. Delaporte, *L'Iran Antique* (Paris: A. Michel, 1943), pp. 454-5; A. J. Carnoy, *Iranian Mythology* (Boston: 1917), pp. 320f; cf. Edv. Lehmann, in C. de la Saussaye, *Lehrb. der Religionsgesch.*, II, 213ff. The banner is discussed in sources given in Arthur Christensen, *Die Iranier* (Munich: Beck, 1933), p. 277.

[15]If the expression "Title of Liberty" should seem to the casual reader to have a peculiarly modern and even American ring, he should be reminded that the liberty theme is extremely prominent among the ancient Jews. Thus Josephus (*Antiquities* IV, 6 11) describes Zimri as saying to Moses: "Thou deprivest us of the sweetness of life, which consists in acting according to our own wills, and is the right of freemen, and of those who have no lord over them . . ." The Greeks and Romans were constantly harping on the theme of liberty in the strictly modern sense, and indeed we have borrowed the word directly from them. The Ancients actually have a good deal more to say about liberty than we do, and it is from them that our Founding Fathers took many of their political ideas, that of the sweetness of liberty being one among them.

[16]Tha'labi, *Qissas al-Anbiya* (Cairo, A. H. 1337), pp. 80-81.

[17]*Ibid.*, p. 96.

Lesson 18 Notes

[1]G. Ebers, *Aegyptische Studien*, p. 315.

[2]"Behold the wretched Amu, toilsome is the land wherein he is. (A land) troubled with water, made difficult by many trees, its ways made toilsome by reason of the mountains. He dwells not in a single place, but his legs are ever driven wandering (?). He is fighting ever since the time of Horus. He conquers not, nor yet is he conquered . . ." This is No. 21 of the Sayings of Menkaure, given by Alan H. Gardiner in *Jnl. Egypt. Archaeol.* I (1914), p. 30.

[3]This is the East India House Inscription. Sir Richard Burton, *Pilgrimage to al-Madinah*, etc., I, 149, writes: "To the solitary wayfarer there is an interest in the Wilderness unknown to Cape Seas and Alpine glaciers, and even to the rolling Prairie, — the effect of continued excitement on the mind, stimulating its powers to their pitch . . . a haggard land infested with wild beasts, and wilder men,—a region who very fountains murmur the warning words 'Drink and away!' What could be more exciting? What more sublime? Man's heart bounds in his breast at the thought of measuring his puny force with Nature's might, and of emerging triumphant from the trial. This explains the Arab's proverb, 'Voyaging is victory.' In the desert, even more than upon the ocean, there is present death: hardship is there, and piracies, and shipwreck . . ."

[4]Eno Littmann, *Altnordarabische Inschriften*, in *Abh. d. dt. Morgenld. Ges.* 1940, Vol. XXV: i, Thamud & Safa; Safaitic Inscr., No. 1260.

[5]*Ibid.*, Safait. Inscrs., p. 1.

[6]*Ibid.*, No. 701.

[7]*Ibid.*, Thamud Inscr., No. 66.

[8]*Ibid.*, No. 70.

[9]Burckhardt, *Notes*, I, 185.

[10]C. S. Jarvis, in *PEFQ*, 1937, p. 122.

[11]Doughty, *Arabia Deserta* (1st Ed.), I, 259.

[12]R. E. Cheesman, *In Unknown Arabia* (London: Macmillan, 1926), pp. 27, 52.

[13]W. J. Phythian-Adams, in *PEFQ*, 1930, p. 199.

[14]Albright, *Archaeol. & the Relig. of Israel*, p. 97.

[15]W. E. Jennings-Bramley, in *PEFQ*, 1907, p. 284.

[16]P. Baldensperger, in *PEFQ*, 1923, p. 180.

[17]Burckhardt, *op. cit.*, I, 227f.

[18]J. J. Hess, *Von den Beduinen des innern Arabiens* (Zürich & Leipzig: M. Niehaus, 1938), p. 63.

[19]Conder, *Tent Work*, II, 274.

[20]*Ibid.*, II, 288.

[21]Norman Lewis, *Sand and Sea in Arabia* (London: Routledge, 1938), p. 16.

[22]H. Frankfort, in *Jnl. Aegypt. Archaeol.*, XII (1926), p. 81.

[23]C. L. Woolley & T. E. Lawrence, *The Wilderness of Zin* (London, 1936), p. 32, cf. p. 35.

[24]B. Thomas, *Arabia Felix*, p. 141.

[25]Cheesman, *op. cit.*, pp. 338f.

[26]Moritz Mainzer, in *Monatsschr. f. Gesch. u. Wiss. des Judentums* 53 (1909), pp. 179-181.

[27]Hariri, *Maqamah of the Beduins*, line 50.

[28]Burckhardt, *Notes* I, 217-220.

[29]J. J. Hess, *op. cit.*, pp. 57-58.

[30]W. E. Jennings-Bramley, in *PEFQ*, 1900, 369f.

[31]Mainzer, *op. cit.*, pp. 305-7.

[32]*Ibid.*, p. 188. Italics ours.

[33]*Lehi in the Desert*, etc., pp. 66-67.

[34]G. Jakob, *Altarabisches Beduinenleben*, pp. 131f.

[35]Thus Antarah says in the Sixth poem of the *Mu'allaqat*, line 61: "Then I left him a prey for the wild beasts who seize him."

[36]Littman, *op. cit.*, Safait., No. 161.

[37]*Ibid.*, No. 720.

[38]*Ibid.*, Nos. 130ff, the whole section being of this type.

[39]*Ibid.*, No. 732.

[40]At the beginning of the century, in *Mitteilungen des Dt-Palaest. Vereins*, 1905, 27-29; M. Mainzer, *Monatsschr. f. Gesch. u. Wiss. d. Judent.*, 53, 539ff; P. H. Hänsler, in *Ztschr. d. Dt.-Paläst. Ver.*, XXXV (1912), 186ff.

[41]P. Baldensperger, in *PEFQ*, 1925, p. 82. See above, Note 34.

[42]H. St.-J. Philby, *The Empty Quarter*, p. 249.

[43]Burckhardt, *Travels*, II, 297.

[44]J. Euting, *Tagebuch einer Reise in Inner-Arabien* (Leiden, 1892), II, 76-80, 92f.

[45]Burckhardt, *Notes* I, 242.

[46]St. Nilus, in Migne, *Patrol. Graeca*, Vol. 79, col. 612.

[47]See *Improvement Era*, 53 (Sept. 1950), p. 547. For a photograph of the original source, R. S. Williams, *After One Hundred Years* (Zion's Printing, 1951), opposite p. 200.

[48]*Arabia Felix*, pp. 48f. See *Lehi in the Desert*, etc., pp. 125-6.

[49]Burton, *Pilgrimage*, etc., I, 3.

Lesson 19 Notes

[1]B. Thomas, *Arabia Felix*, p. 137.

[2]Cheesman, *Unknown Arabia*, pp. 228f, 234, 240f, 280.

[3]K. Raswan, *Drinkers of the Wind*, p. 200.

[4]Cited by J. Zeller, in PEFQ, 1909, p. 256.

[5]Al-Hariri, *Maqamah of Damascus* 11, 28ff (Preston, p. 188.)

[6]Conder, *Tent Work* II, 274.

[7]Al-Hariri, *Maqamah of the Beduin* (Preston, p. 275).

[8]Burckhardt, *Notes* I, 134.

[9]Conder, *op. cit.*, II, 278.

[10]E. Littmann, *Thamud and Safa*, Inscrs., No. 644.

[11]*Ibid.,* No. 169.
[12]*Ibid.,* No. 306.
[13]*Ibid.,* Safait., p. 21, No. 93.
[14]*Ibid.,* Safait., Inscrs., Nos. 1064ff, most of the 600's and 700's; and Thamud Inscrs., Nos. 138ff.
[15]*Ibid.,* No. 90.
[16]B. Thomas, *op. cit.,* pp. 142, 172f.
[17]In the *Seven Mu'allaqat,* III, 58.
[18]St. Nilus, in *Patrol. Graec.,* Vol. 79, col. 669.
[19]In *PEFQ,* 1952, p. 81.
[20]P. Baldensperger, in *PEFQ,* 1922, pp. 168f.
[21]H. Helfritz, *Land Without Shade* (1936), p. 33.
[22]M. J. Lagrange, in *Revue Biblique* X, 29.
[23]Burckhardt, *Notes* I, 133. 24.
[24]T. Harmer, *Observations* I, 108.
[25]Dupont-Sommer, *The Dead Sea Scrolls,* p. 9.
[26]J. Dissard, in *Revue Biblique,* N.S. II (1905), 411f.
[27]*Ibid.,* p. 416. Cf. Harmer, *op. cit.,* I, 101: ". . . they will be quite ready to decamp upon less than two hours warning, and retiring into the deserts render it impossible to other nations, even the most powerful, to conquer them; they not daring to venture far into the deserts, where the Arabs *alone* know how to steer their course so as to hit upon places of water and forage."
[28]J. Hess, *op. cit.,* p. 96.
[29]*Notes,* I, 157-8.
[30]Harmer, *op. cit.,* I, 96, 126.
[31]Hess, *op. cit.,* p. 57; Burton, *Pilgrimage,* etc., II, 114.
[32]Burton, *op. cit.,* I, 144-5.
[33]*Ibid.,* I, 147; 143, 151.
[34]Leo Haefeli, *Die Beduinen von Beersheba* (Lucerne: Raber, 1938), p. 144.
[35]Interpretations differ, but the general idea is always the same. F. Thornton, *Elementary Arabic* (Cambridge, Univ. Press, 1943), p. 156.
[36]Musil, *Arabia Petraea,* III, 353ff, 130.
[37]This is "the only activity that fills out the time between raiding and hunting expeditions," says Hess, *op. cit.,* p. 111.
[38]Burckhardt, *Notes* I, 185f.
[39]Alb. de Boucheman, "Materiel de la Vie Bedouine" in *Documents d'Etudes Orientales de l'Institut Francais de Damas,* 1934, p. 108. Burckhardt, *op. cit.,* 1, 101: ". . . the tent-posts are torn up immediately after a man has expired, and the tent demolished."
[40]Conder, *op. cit.,* II, 275.
[41]Burckhardt, *Notes* I, 33.
[42]W. Robertson Smith, *The Religion of the Semites* (London, 1907), p. 201.
[43]K. Raswan, *op. cit.,* p. 237.
[44]A. Jaussen, in *Revue Biblique,* N.S. III, 109f.
[45]St. Nilus, in *Patrol. Graec.,* 79:612.
[46]See above, Lesson VI, Note.
[47]Bertholet, *Israel und Fremden,* pp. 70f, 75.
[48]Nowack, *Hebraeische Archaeologis,* p. 152.
[49]H. Philby, *The Empty Quarter,* p. 219.
[50]R. Burton, *Pilgrimage to al-Madinah,* etc., I, 276.
[51]Jennings-Bramley, in *PEFQ,* 1905, p. 213.
[52]C. Doughty, *Arabia Deserta* I, 272, 282f.
[53]Burckhardt, *Notes* I, 353.
[54]Doughty, *op. cit.,* I, 258.
[55]*Ibid.,* I, 114.
[56]Thus one ancient man of the desert boasts how ". . . he flogged a family, their servants together with their master, and he returned to the waters of Rais by grace of (the deity) Dusares." (Littmann, *Safait.,* No. 1135.) Burton records matter-of-factly, "We should have made Yambu (the port) in the evening but for the laziness of the Rais (captain). Having duly beaten him, we anchored on the open coast." (Burton, *op. cit.,* I, 222).
[57]P. Baldensperger, in *PEFQ,* 1901, p. 75
[58]M. von Oppenheim, *Benuinen,* etc., I, 30.

[59]Jennings-Bramley, in *PEGQ*, 1905, p. 217.

[60]"An Arab often leaves the camp of his friends out of caprice or dislike of his companions, and joins another camp of the tribe," says Burckhardt, *Notes* I, 118.

[61]A. Jaussen, in *Revue Biblique*, XII, 109.

[62]L. Haefeli, *Beduinen*, etc., p. 87; V. Mueller, *En Syrie*, etc., p. 188.

[63]Conder, *Tent Work* II, 283.

[64]Burckhardt, *Notes* I, 116f.

[65]*Ibid.*, I, 139.

[66]Burton, *op. cit.*, II, 94, 141f.

[67]K. Budde, "Die Hebraeische Leichenklage," in *Zt. d. Dt. Pal. Ver* VI (1883), 184, 190. The second quote is from Burckhardt, *op. cit.*, I, 101.

[68]Budde, *op. cit.*, pp. 191f Canaan, in *Jnl. Pal. Or. Soc.* XI (1931), 192.

[69]Budde, *op. cit.*, p. 193. Ancient Hebrews and Arabs followed the same burial practices, according to Benzinger, *Hebr. Archaeol.*, p. 163.

Lesson 20 Notes

[1]More than thirty references from the poets are given in *Lehi in the Desert*, etc., p. 74, note 2.

[2]Littmann, *Safait. Inscrs.*, No. 288.

[3]*Ibid.*, Nos. 1260, 306,

[4]Al-Hariri, *Maqamah of Damascus*, lines 43, 75.

[5]Thus Al-Bochtori, cit., C. Brockelmann, *Gesch. der Arab. Lit.* (Leipzig, 1909), p. 88, and Lebid, *Ibid.*, p. 55. The word "maidan" means both "large, spacious field," and "an ample life" in Arabic.

[6]*Pastor Hermae*, Simil. VIII, iii; *Clem. Recog.*, II:23-25 (Patrol. Graec., I, 1260f).

[7]F. Hommel, *Ethol. u. Geog.*, etc., pp. 13ff; H. Dantine, *Arbres Sacres*, pp. 210f; A. Alfoldi, in *Nouvelle Clio* X (1950), pp. 552ff.

[8]G. Jakob, *Altarab. Beduinenleben*, p. 13.

[9]Littmann, *op. cit.*, No. 28.

[10]*Ibid.*, Nos. 152, 156.

[11]*Ibid.*, No. 644.

[12]*Ibid.*, No. 342.

[13]*Ibid.*, No. 233

[14]Montgomery, *Arabia and the Bible*, p. 5.

[15]See our discussion, "A Note on Rivers," in *Lehi in the D.*, etc., pp. 91-95.

[16]For many references, *Lehi in the Desert*, etc., pp. 47f, Notes 2 and 3.

[17]In W. Ahlwardt, *Sammlungen alter arabischer Dichter* (Berlin, 1903), II, No. 1.

[18]F. Wünstenfeld, *Orient und Occident*, I, 336f.

[19]E. J. Byng, *The World of the Arabs* (Boston: Little, Brown, 1944), pp. 64f.

[20]Al-Hamdani, *Al-Iklil, Book* viii (Baghdad, 1931), pp. 15f.

[21]*Ibid.*, p. 16.

[22]Burckhardt, *Notes.*, I, 186.

[23]Van der Ploeg, in *Biblical Orient*, 1949, p. 77.

[24]Conder, *Tent Work*, etc., II, 271.

[25]Littmann, *op. cit.*, No. 407.

[26]Ed. Robinson, *Biblical Researches in Palestine*, etc. (Boston, 1841), I, 259.

[27]Al-Hariri, *Maqamah of Ramleh* (Preston, p. 418).

[28]Littmann, *op. cit.*, No. 1013.

[29]*Ibid.*, No. 206.

[30]*Ibid.*, No 156. There is a large class of inscriptions left by parties describing themselves as "on the lookout" for friends and relatives, e.g., No. 709: "N. was on the lookout for his father . . . So Allat, peace!"

[31]Al-Hariri, *Maqamah of Rye* (Preston, p. 298).

[32]Burton, *Pilgrimage to Al-Madinah*, etc., I, 207. And thus C. R. Conder, in *PEFQ*, 1875, p. 130f: "Farther south the country is absolutely impassable, as huge gorges one thousand to fifteen hundred feet deep and nearly a mile wide in some places are broken by the great torrents flowing in winter over

perpendicular precipices into the sea." The cover of the *Biblical Archaeologist*, Vol. 18, February, 1955, gives a magnificent view of a "great and yawning gulf" in the Negev.

[33]E. A. W. Budge, ed., *Chronography of . . . Bar Hebraeus* (Oxford Univ., 1932), I, 167.

[34]C. Doughty, *Arabia Deserta* (1st Ed.) II, 229.

[35]Montgomery, *op. cit.*, p. 85.

[36]Conder, *Tent Work*, II, 274.

[37]N. Lewis, *Sand & Sea in Arabia*, p. 16.

[38]G. Schumacher, in *Ztschr. d. Dt. Palast. Vereims*, 36 (1913), p. 314.

[39]*Ibid.*, p. 315.

[40]Littmann., *op. cit.*, No. 435.

[41]*Ibid.*, No. 436.

[42]*Ibid.*, No. 438.

[43]*Ibid.*, No. 1291.

[44]In Ahlwardt, *op. cit.*, III, No. 1.

[45]Lucy Mack Smith, *History of Joseph Smith* (Salt Lake: Stevens & Wallis, 1945), pp. 47-50.

Lesson 21 Notes

[1]P. Baldensperger, in *PEFQ*, 1925, p. 81.

[2]Burton, *Pilgrimage to Al-Madinah*, etc., I, 280.

[3]R. Patai, *Man and Temple in Ancient Jewish Myth and Ritual* (London: Thos. Nelson, 1947), p. 27.

[4]Conder, *Tent Work*, II, 287.

[5]Alf. Haldar, *Associations of Cult Prophets among the Ancient Semites* (Uppsala: Almquist & Wiksell, 1945), p. 199.

[6]D. S. Margoliouth, in *Jnl. Royal Asiat. Soc.*, 1925, p. 449.

[7]*Ibid.*, pp. 419-420, cf. 417.

[8]R. A. Nicholson, *A Literary History of the Arabs* (New York, 1907), p. 103.

[9]T. E. Peet, *Comparative Study of the Literature of Egypt, Palestine, and Mesopotamia* (London: Schweich Lects., 1931), pp. 4-6, 12f.

[10]Al-Hariri, *Maqamah of Kufa*, (Preston, p. 222).

[11]*Ibid.*, p. 323.

[12]I. Goldziher, *Abhandlungen zur arab. Philologie* (Leiden, 1896), I, 58.

[13]St. Nilus, in *Patrol. Graec.*, 79: 648.

[14]Abbe Bourdaid, "La Source Divine . . ." *Receuil de Traxaux*, 21 (1899), 177ff.

[15]Ibn Qutaiba, *Maqaddamah Kitab-ish-Shi're* . . . (Ed. Gaudefroy-Demombynes, Paris, 1947), Pt. 15.

[16]B. Thomas, *Arabia Felix*, p. 153.

[17]H. Grapow, *Die Bildlichen Ausdrücke der Aegypten*, p. 63: The Egyptians freely refer to tubs and basins as lakes and pools, and to bodies of water in the wilderness as springs and fountains. For them, "a running spring in the desert is like the cavern of the two fountain orifices at Elephantine." Yet Elephantine was not a fountain place but rather one where the water poured through narrows.

[18]Al-Hariri, *Maqamah of Temise* (about ⅔ of the way through).

[19]Nicholson, *op. cit.*, p. 18.

[20]Thus Hariri, *Maqamah of Kufa* (Preston, p. 216), says: "Long may you live in plenty's vale." Preston explains the use of Khfd (valley) in this case, "because low places generally are well watered and fit for habitation in the East."

[21]In the *Mu'allaqat* iii, 13.

[22]A. Bloch, "Qasida," in *Asiatische Studien*, iii-iv (Bern, 1948), p. 116.

[23]Nicholson, *op. cit.*, p. 74.

[24]Goldziher, *op. cit.*, I, 67-71.

[25]*Ibid.*, pp. 59, 72-75.

[26]Ibn Qutaiba, *op. cit.*, Pt. 23; cf. Goldziher, p. 74.

[27]P. Cersoy, "L'Apologue de la Vigne," *Rev. Biblique*, 1899, 40-47.

²⁸*Op. cit.,* p. 54f, n. 7.
²⁹*Pilg. to Al-Madinah,* etc. II, 99: "I cannot well explain the effect of Arab poetry on one who has not visited the Desert. . . ."
³⁰Gust. Richter, "Zur Entstehungsgeschichte der altarabischen Qaside," *Deutsche Morgenland. Ges. Ztschr.* 92 (1939), 557f. The passage cited is from 'Antar.
³¹*Ibid.,* pp. 563-5.
³²C. Brockelmann, *Gesch. der Arabischen Litteratur* (Weimar, 1898) I, 16.
³³Burton, *op. cit.,* I, 278, n. 3.
³⁴Richter, *op. cit.,* p. 58.
³⁵Brockelmann, *Gesch. d. Arab. Lit.* (Leipzig, 1909), p. 12.
³⁶J. A. Montgomery, *Arabia and the Bible,* p. 21.
³⁷Thus H. Ragaf, in the leading American Yiddish newspaper, *Vorwärts,* April 26, 1953.
³⁸F. Delitzsch, *Das Land ohne Heimkehr. Die Gedanken der Babylonier u. Assyrer über Tod und Jenseits* (Stuttgart, 1911).
³⁹P. Jensen, *Assyrisch-babylonische Mythen and Epen* (Berlin, 1901), p. 50.
⁴⁰Knut Tallquist, "Sumerisch-Akkadische Names der Totenwelt," *Studia Orientalia,* V, iv (Helsingfors, 1934), pp. 3, 15f.
⁴¹E. Ebeling, in *Orientatlia* 18 (1950), p. 37.
⁴²T. E. Peet, *Comparative Study,* etc., p. 58.
⁴³H. Kees, "Ein Klagelied über das Jenseits," Aegypt. Ztschr. 62 (1927), p. 76.

Lesson 22 Notes

¹Walter F. Prince, "Psychological Tests for the Authorship of the Book of Mormon," *American Jnl. of Psychology,* XXVII (July, 1917), 373-395, and XXX (Oct., 1919), 427-28. His findings are accepted as final by W. R. Cross, *The Burned-over District* (Ithaca: Cornell Univ., 1950), p. 144: "Walter F. Prince proved beyond dispute thirty years ago, by a rigorous examination of the proper names and other language in the volume, that even if no other evidence existed, it could have been composed only in Western New York between 1826 and 1834, so markedly did it reflect Anti-masonry and other issues of the day." 250 proper names plus "other language in the volume" rigorously and thoroughly examined in an article of 22 pages! The psychologists of forty years ago must have known just everything.
²If the reader thinks this is too stringent a censure on the "science of linguistics" we would refer him to the latest summary of things in W. J. Entwhistle, *Aspects of Language* (London: Faber & Faber, 1953), especially Chap. iii.
³T. E. Peet, *Egypt and the Old Testament* (1922), p. 169.
⁴H. R. Hall, in *Camb. Anc. Hist.,* III, 268. See above, pp. 86f.
⁵*Improvement Era* 51 (April, 1948), p. 203.
⁶W. F. Albright, *Archaeol. and the Relig. of Israel,* pp. 5f.
⁷D. W. Thomas, *Palest, Explor, Quarterly,* 1950, pp. 5ff.
⁸*Ibid.,* p. 8.
⁹See our lists in *Lehi in the Desert,* etc., pp. 27-30.
¹⁰A. F. L. Beeston, in *Jnl. Royal Asiat. Soc.,* 1952, p. 21, according to Whom the female name Drm.t found recently in a South Arabic inscription "should no doubt be related etymologically to Hebrew *zerem* 'heavy rain'."
¹¹A. Gustavs, in *Zeitschr. des Bt.-Paläst Vereins,* 50 (1927), 1-19, and 51 (1928), pp. 191, 198, 207. In the lists are 9 Subaraean (north Mesopotamian), 5 Hittite-Hurrian, 1 Egyptian, 1 Sumerian, 1 Iranian, 1 Kossaean, 1 Indian, 10 Akkadian (Babylonian), 2 Amorite, 5 Arabic (Aramaic?), and 21 Canaanitish names, including such names as Bi-na-ammi, Zi-im-ri-kha-am-mu (Canaaninte-Phoenician); one Edomite king is called Am-mi-na-ad-bi; Jews in Babylon in the 6th century B.C. bore names like Abu-na-dib, Ammihor, Abi-la-ma, Zi-im-ri-a-bu-um, etc., M Noth, in *Ztschr. der Dt-Morgenl. Ges.,* LXXXI, 17, 24-29.

[12]See *Improvement Era, loc. cit.,* and pp. 202ff.

[13]H. Ranke, *Die aegyptischen Personennamen* (Hamberg, 1934); J. Leiblein, *Dictionnaire de Noms Hieroglyphiques* (Christiania, 1871).

[14]Ranke, *op. cit.,* p. 412, Nos. 8, 9.

[15]A. Jirku, in *Biblica,* 34 (1953), pp. 78-80.

[16]Montgomery, *Arabia & the Bible,* p. 47. Cf. W. Albright, *The Vocalization of Egyptian Syllabic Orthography* (New Haven: Am. Or. Soc., 1934), X, 12.

[17]D. W. Thomas, *op. cit.,* p. 2.

[18]A. Reifenberg, *Ancient Hebrew Seals* (London: East & West Lib., 1950), Nos. 12-25.

[19]E. O. Forrer, in *PEFQ,* 1937, pp. 100f, 114f.

[20]For sources see *Lehi in the Desert,* etc., p. 33, note 2.

[21]*Jnl. Eg. Archaeol.,* XI, 20, 24.

[22]*Lehi in the Des.,* etc., p. 34, note 8.

[23]Ed. Meyer, *Gesch. des Altertums* II, i, 553.

[24]Jud. 15:9, 14, 19. This is Lehai-ro'i, the legendary birthplace and central shrine of Ishmael, which provides an interesting tie-up between Lehi and his friend (and relative) Ishmael—both men of the desert. See Ed. Meyer, *ibid.,* pp. 322f.

[25]N. Glueck, in *Bull. Am. Schools of Or. Res.,* 80 (1940), 5-6, with a reproduction of the potsherd.

[26]Jaussen & Savignac, *Mission Archaeologique in Arabie* (Paris, 1909), No. 336. Other inscriptions containing the name LHI are found on pp. 313 (Minaean), 552, 557, 564, 569, 570, 571, 588, 609 (Thamudian).

[27]*Ibid.,* II, No. 77: "Lamay son of Nafiyah . . ." The first Nabataean inscr., p. 141, No. 1, is the son of one Nafiyu. Other Nafy inscriptions are Nos. 259, 215, 302, 322, 351, 441, 236, 237. No. 80 is by "Ha-Nafy and Maram-law."

[28]Thus in Jaussen, *op. cit.,* No. 277, 'Alim; No. 475 'Alman from 'ALM; No. 622 'Almah (a man's name); Littman, *Safait. Inscrs.,* Nos. 394, 430, 984, 1292, all have the name ALM, also found in the diminutive form 'Ulaim, and in the Greek transliteration Olaimou, 'Allam, "Allum (*ibid.,* p. 335), M. Noth, in *Ztschr. d. Dt.-Morgenl. Ges.,* 81, p. 29, notes from an inscription the Phoenician-Canaanitish form of 'I'm (pronounced Alam).

[29]The name MRM is found also in Nos. 290, 307, 294, 361, 327 of Jaussen, according to whom (p. 450) it is the Arabic *Maram,* "intention, wish, desire," (Cf. Nos. 361, 284), and is certainly cognate with the common Egyptian *Mr-,* which has the same meaning. It is also cognate, Jaussen suggests, with the Hebrew *Marim.* Thus one might seek the root for "Mormin" in either Egyptian, Hebrew, or Arabic, all of which build proper names with *MRM,* meaning "desirable," "Good." An Egyptian doorkeeper of the XX Dynasty has the name of Mrmnu, or Mormon (W. Spiegelbarg, in *Zeitschr. für Assyriologie,* 13 (1898), p. 51. Since the nunated -on ending is highly characteristic of Nephite names, the final -on of Mormon may belong to that class, in which case the root must be the Arab-Heb. *MRM,* a desert name.

[30]P. Haupt, in *Jnl. Bibl. Lit.* 33 (1914), pp. 290-5.

[31]*Survey of Western Palestine,* Name Lists (E. H. Palmer, ed., London, 1881), p. 358.

[32]*Corpus Inscriptionum Semiticarum* II, i, p. 361, No. 498.

[33]H. Grimme, in *Le Museon,* XLVIII, 269.

[34]Jaussen & Savignac, *op. cit.,* No. 77.

[35]C. Clemont-Ganneau, in *Survey of Wstn. Palest.,* Spec. Papers, p. 325. Cf. Conder's remarks in the same volume, p. 272.

[36]See above, p. 62.

[37]S. Spiegel, in *Ginzberg Jubilee Volume,* pp. 349-350.

[38]R. Harris, *Boanerges* (Cambridge, 1913), p. 275f.

[39]*Corp. Inscr. Semit.* II, i, p. 239, No. 207.

[40]J. Offord, in *PEFQ,* 1917, p. 127.

[41]W. F. Albright, *Archaeol. & the Relig. of Israel,* p. 160.

[42]A. Jirku, *Aegyptische Listen,* p. 52; G. Kampfmeyer, in *Ztschr. d. Dt.-Pal. Vereins,* 15 (1892), p. 83.

[43]M. Noth, in *Ztschr. d. Dt. Morgenl, Ges.*, 81 (1927), p. 5,
[44]S. Zeitlin, in *Jewish Qart. Rev.*, 43 (1953), 367ff, discussed in the *Improvement Era*, 57 (May 1954), 309ff.
[45]Ed. Meyer, *Ursprung u. Geschichte der Mormonen* (Berlin, 1904), p. 42.

Lesson 23 Notes

[1]H. Kees, *Aegypten* (Munich; Beck, 1933), p. 176.
[2]For the best general summary, H. Frankfort, "State Festivals in Egypt and Mesopotamia," *Jnl. of the Warburg & Courtauld Institutes* XV (1952), 1-12, and articles by E. Burrows, C. N. Deedes, and A. R. Johnson, in S. H. Hooke (ed.), *The Labyrinth* (London: SPCK, 1935); M. Gaster, *Thespis, Ritual, Myth and Drama in the Near East* (New York: Schuman, 1950), is good for the ritual side, as is H. P. L'Orange, *Apotheosis in Ancient Portraiture* (Oslo: Ashehoug, 1947), Ser. B, No. 44, of Inst. f. Sammenlign. Kulturforsking.
[3]See our study, "The Hierocentric State," *Western Polit. Quart.* 4 (1951) 226-253.
[4]On the royal proclamation which summons all to the Great Assembly in the presence of the king, see our discussion of "summons arrows" in *Wstn. Pol. Quart.* II (1949), 331-4.
[5]The transmission of three royal treasures, symbolizing the sacred origin and miraculous preservation of the nation, is found among such widely separated peoples as the ancient Japanese (the "three jewels" passed from king to king being the mirror, the *tama*, and the sword, R. Grousset, *L'Asie Orientale* . . . (Paris Presses Univs., 1941, p. 448) and the ancient Norse, whose three treasures of royalty (*thria kost gripi*) were a hammer, a belt, and an iron glove, according to the Prose Edda, *Gylfaginning*, c. 19.
[6]In the yearly census at the Assembly, Nibley, *op. cit.*, pp. 334-7.
[7]Thus among our own ancestors, "When Torgin gave the Yule (year) feast the people assembled from all about and lived in booths for half a month." *Erbyggia-saga*, c. 43. Even to modern times people at the great English fairs "universally eat, drink, and sleep in their booths and tents," according to R. W. Muncey, *Our Old English Fairs* (London, 1935), p. 105. When Ariamnus at the time of Christ feasted all the people of Gaul at a great assembly at which they acclaimed him king "he erected booths of vine-props and poles of reed and osiers . . . for the reception of the crowds," Athenaeus, *Deipnos.* IV, 150. In the middle Ages William of Rubruck (*Travels*, c. 21) says of the assembly in the presence of the Great Khan: "As among the people of Israel each man knew on which side of the tabernacle to pitch his tent . . ." Hundreds of examples might be cited from all over the world.
[8]There are many ancient parallels to this, of which the best-known perhaps is the annual sermon delivered by the Caliph to the whole believing world from a high wooden *minbar*. That this usage is pre-Moslem and pre-Christian is indicated by the accounts of addresses being delivered from such towers by Roman Emperors on formal occasions, with the specification that the Roman practice was *Phoenicio ritu*, i. e., in imitation of a Syro-Palestinian practice. (Herodian, *Hist.*, V. 6, 9; Dio, *Hist.* LIX, 25). For some interesting Oriental parallels, H. Nibley, *Class. Jnl.* 40 (1945), 527, n. 78.
[9]See above, pp. 19-20.
[10]Though a Latin word, *silentium* is the proper designation for a solemn assembly in the presence of the Byzantine Emperor; it is taken from the formula with which meetings are formally opened in many Christian churches: "The Lord is in his holy temple: let all the earth keep silence (lit. 'hush') before him." (Hab. 2:20). An impressive description of a silentium in the presence of King Solomon is given in an Arabic account of *The Assembly of Animals and Men in the Presence of the King and the Genies*, ed. F. Dieterici (Leipsig, 1881), p. 52. Others in *Kalilah wa Dimnah.*
[11]A Jeremias, *Handbuch der altorientalischen Geisteskultur* (Leipzig, (1913), pp. 208f, 313ff, 171ff. The idea was completely at home in Palestine, A. F. Silverstone. "God as King," *Jnl. Manchaster Egypt. & Or. Soc.* XVII (1932), 47-49: "The numerous (Hebrew) Hymns which were intoned dur-

ing the services on the New Year invariably lay stress on the role of the King which God assumes on that day." This is the very interpretation that Mosiah puts on the business: not that the King is God, as elsewhere in the East, but that God is the King! Even at Uppsala at the Great Assembly "the king was worshipped in the Oriental manner," C. Clemen, *Religionsgeschichte Europas* (Heidelberg 1926) I 353. If the King failed to preside all the rites were considered null and void and life and property would be withheld from the nation for the coming year; for that reason any king who refused to officiate in the great sacrifice at Uppsala forfeited his throne, according to Adam of Bremen (in *Mon. Hist. Ger.* VII, 379). Even the Welsh *gorseth* seems to have been "but a continuation of a court of which the Celtic Zeus was originally regarded as the spiritual president," according to John Rhys, *Celtic Heathendom* (London, 1898), p. 129.

[12]The best treatment of the *acclamatio*, with hundreds of examples, is by Ferrarius, in the VI Vol. (1697) of J. G. Graevius, *Thesaurus Antiquitatum Romanarum.*

[13]"Thou shalt not come into the presence of the king empty-handed" is the universal and stringent rules. The earliest kings of the east and west "showed themselves to their subjects, when they received presents from them, according to the ancient custom," M. Ducange, *Dissert.* No. IV, 53f, citing many sources.

[14]H. Frankfort, *Kingship and the Gods: A Study of Ancient Near Eastern Religions as the Integration of Society and Nature* (Chicago: Univ. of Chi. Press, 1948) treats this theme at length.

[15]Nibley, *Class. Jnl.,* 40:543.

[16]A Moortgat, *Tammuz. Der Unsterblichkeitsglaube in der Altorientalischen Bildkunst,* (Berlin: De Gruyter, 1949). The theme is also treated in most of the sources mentioned so far in this lesson.

[17]The singing of the heavenly choirs is either the model or the copy of the choral events that figure so prominently at the Year celebrations everywhere. This is clear all through Pindar, e. g., *Pythian Ode* XI, 1-16; cf. G. Weicker, Der *Seelenvogel in der alten Littratur und Kunst* (Leipzig, 1902), pp. 18-19; Joh. Kelle, *Chori Saecularium,* Wien. Akad. Sitzungsber. 161 (1909), No. 2.

[18]It is this fact which furnishes irrefutable proof of the great antiquity of the apocalyptic tradition of the blissful age to come, as S. Mowinckel has recently shown in his study *Religion und Kultus.* (Göttingen, 1953.)

[19]G. Widengren, *Ascensio Isaiae,* pp. 16f, with special emphasis on Israelitic practice.

[20]"The Great Assembly on the Day of Judgment shall be as the day of creation. . . . All things shall be restored on the day of decision," Thus an apocryphal text given in M. R. James, *The Apocryphal New Testament* (Oxford, 1925), p. 512. The scriptures, like the apocrypha, are full of this theme. For a striking pagan parallel, W. Golther gives a most enlightening discussion of the customs of the ancient North in his edition of *Are's Icelandbook* (Halle, 1923), pp. 7ff.

[21]Ferrarius, *loc. cit.,* gives numerous examples: "Forever and forever!" is the closing refrain of almost every ancient acclamation the world over. The walls of royal Egyptian tombs and palaces (e.g. the famous Festival Hall of Osorkon II) are literally covered with it.

[22]This is a constant refrain in Babylonian ritual texts: "At thy word all the Igigi cast themselves upon their faces; at thy word all the Anunnaki kiss the earth. . ." (B. Meissner, *Bab. u. Assyr.,* II, 166). As the Assyrian King mounts the throne at the New Year "all throw themselves upon the earth before him, kiss his feet, and cry out: 'Father of the Fatherland; there is none like unto him!" while the army hails him crying, 'That is our King!" (*Ibid.,* I, 63). *All* subjects had to come "yearly to Nineveh bringing rich gifts, to kiss the feet of their lord," the King. (*Ib.* I, 138). In a cylinder of 536 B.C. King Cyrus boasts: " . . . every king from every region . . . as well as the Bedouin tent-dwellers brought their costly gifts and kissed my feet." (Caiger, *Bible & Spade,* p. 181). Every year at the great "submission assembly" the Hittite king would prostrate himself before the empty throne in the sanctuary, after which he would mount the throne and receive the pros-

trations of his subjects in turn. (A. Goetze, *Kleinasien,* pp. 96, 155). To
refuse the *proskynesis* was an act of rebellion (Zenophon, *Aegesil,* I, 34). The
Byzantine Emperors continued it (St. Theophilus, *Ep. Antioch,* 11, in *Patrol.
Graec.,* VI, 1040-1). J. Balsdon (in *Historia* I (1950), 374), argues that
proskynein means simply "to blow a kiss," yet we are specifically told that
"Sovereigns coming into the presence of the Emperor at Constantinople were
required to kiss his knees." (Ducange, *Dissert.* XXV, p. 201). Even among
the Germanic nations those who came to submit to a king were required to
fall to the earth before him. (*Thithrik af Bern-saga,* Sect. 54).

²³Nibley, *op. cit.,* pp. 516ff.

²⁴"And he will summon all the hosts of the heavens, and all the holy
ones above, and the host of God, and the Cherubim, Seraphim, and Ophannim,
and all the angels of power, and all the angels of principalities, and the Elect
One, and the other powers on earth and over the water. On that day shall
they raise one voice: '. . . Blessed is He, and may the name of the Lord of
Spirits be blessed forever and ever!" All flesh must join in this acclamation.
(Enoch LXI, 10-12). This is exactly the way the Emperor was acclaimed
at Constantinople: "All the people cried out their assent with a single voice,
saying, 'As thou hast lived, so reign, O lord!'" (Cedrenus (Bonn ed.), p.
626). "All the people young and old vied in approval and with a single voice
and single mind . . . crying out: 'Conquer, Justin!'" (Corippus, *Justin,* 11,
345ff). "All the people, as with a single sound, chant hymns to thy divinely
bestowed power." (Georg. Pisid., *Exped. Persica,* II, 76f). In Rome innumerable voices proclaim at once that they acknowledge the Emperor as their
"ruler and sacred lord," Dracontius, *Satisfactio,* 193ff.

²⁵For the broadest treatment of this theme, see S. Hooke, *The Labyrinth,
passim,* and *Myth and Ritual,* pp. 8ff.

²⁶For very ancient instances of this, see the *Pyramid Texts* (trsl. S. A. B.
Mercer (London: Longmans, Green, 1952), I, passion. Characteristic
of the Great Assembly is the strict arrangement by order and rank ob-
served there, Dieterici, *Thier u. Mensch, op. cit.,* pp. 37, 43f, 48ff, 51ff, 69;
Dio Chrysost., *Orat.* xl, 28f, 32-40; for other sources, Nibley, *Wstn. Pol. Quart.*
II (1949), 343, n. 86. Cf. *Pastor Hermae* V, v, 6; VI, 3; IX, i, 8.

²⁷On the importance of everyone's having a seal at the Year Feast, see
Nibley, *op. cit.,* pp. 334ff.

²⁸A. Wensinck, "The Semitic New Year and the Origin of Eschatology,"
in *Acta Orientalia* I (1925), 172; and *Passim. Midrash Jubil.* 19:9; 30:20ff.
Enoch 103:2, Leo Koep, *Das himmlische Buch in Antike u. Christentum* (Bonn:
P. Hanstein, 1952), 46ff, 68ff, 97ff.

²⁹The main purpose of priestly colleges throughout the world is to rehearse the Year Feast at shorter intervals and to keep its significance alive
among the people. This is very clear in the case of the Arval and Salian
colleges at Rome, and in the Asvamedha of India, P. E. Dumont, *L'Asvamedha*
(Paris, 1927), pp. vii, 50, & passim.

³⁰C. Gordon, *Ugaritic Literature,* pp. 4-5.

³¹"We find that the Ras Shamra festivals exhibit that same 'ritual pattern'
which has been detected also in Babylonian and Israelitic cultus, and which
has been postulated, by Professor S. H. Hooke and others, as the common
basis of seasonal ceremonies throughout the ancient Near East. The essential
elements of this pattern are: (a) a battle-royal between two rival powers, each
claiming dominion over the earth; (b) the formal installation of the victor as
King; (c) the erection of a new habitation for him; (d) the celebration of a
seven-day festival." Thus T. H. Gaster, in *Antiquity* XIII, 314. A Catholic
writer has recently tried to disassociate Israel from this pattern, which does
obvious damage to the conventional ideas of the history and religion of Jew
and Christian alike. J. de Fraine, "Les Implications du 'patternism',*" Biblica*
37 (1956), 59-73.

Lesson 24 Notes

[1]For the other interpretations, see H. Gressmann, *Der Ursprung der isra-elitisch-jüdischen Eschatologie* (Göttingen, 1950), pp. 302ff. The classic illustration of this type of argument is to be found throughout Justin Martyr's *Dialogue with Trypho*. Recently the argument was the subject of a special feature article in *Awake!* Jan. 22, 1953. For the fullest treatment of the two sticks, see "The Stick of Judah and the Stick of Joseph," *Improvement Era*, 56 (1953) Jan. through May.

[2]W. A. Irwin, "Ezechiel Research since 1943," *Vetus Testamentium* III (1953), pp. 61f.

[3]V. Hertrich, *"Ezechielprobleme,"* Beiheft 61 of *Ztschr. f. Alt. Test. Wiss.* (Giessen, 1933), p. 118. Attempts at rewriting and deletion are treated by the author in *The Improvement Era*, 56 (Jan. 1953), pp. 16ff.

[4]F. Zorell, *Lexicum Hebraicum et Aramaicum Vetaris Testamenti*, p. 618.

[5]In Migne, *Patrologiae Latinae* LXXV, 394.

[6]C. F. Keil, *Biblical Commentary on the Prophecies of Ezekiel* (Edinburgh), II, 130.

[7]See above, p. 22. D. J. Wiseman, "Assyrian Writingboards," *Iraq* XVII (1955), 3, 11.

[8]See below, pp. 278f.

[9]Keil, *loc. cit.*

[10]G. Widengren, *Ascensio Isaiae*, pp. 38f, 9.

[11]*Ibid.*, pp. 8-12.

[12]*Ibid.*, p. 11.

[13]W. B. Kristensen, *De Slangenstaf en het Sprackvermogen van Mozes en Aäron* (Nederl. Ak. Wet., N. S. 16, No. 14, 1953), pp. 2-3

[14]W. Spiegelberg, "Der Stabkultus bei den Aegyptern," *Recneil de Travaux* 25 (1903), 184-190.

[15]Widengren, *op. cit.*, p. 9; Kristensen, *op. cit.*, pp. 7-8.

[16]S. Culin, in *U. S. National Museum Report*, 1896, p. 887.

[17]H. Nibley, in *Westn. Pol. Quart.*, II, 33-57, for many examples.

[18]Frd. Blass, in I. von Muller's *Handbuch der Altertumswissenschaft* (Munich, 1892), I, 334.

[19]L. Ginzberg, *The Legends of the Jews* (Philadelphia: Jewish Publ. Soc., 1909 ff) VI, 54; cf. III, 19, where the Rod of Moses bears no less than thirty-two separate inscriptions.

[20]J. N. Freeman, *Handbook of Bible Manners and Customs* (New York, 1902), No. 583.

[21]For the ancient North, K. Weinhold, "Beiträge zu den deutschen Kriegs altertümern," *Sitzber. d. Akad. d. Wiss, zu Berlin*, 1891 (Phil-Hist. Kl., No. 29), p. 548 For the general Asiatic practice, G N. Roerich, *Trials to Inmost Asia* (Yale Univ., 1931), p. 352. For Japan, *Japanische Volksmärchen* (Jena; Diederich, 1938), p. 43; among the American Indians, G. Mallery, in *Bureau of Ethnology Reports* X (1889-9), p .367, fig. 375. These are typical instances in which writing space on an original message-stick or arrow was augmented by an attached cloth, skin, or roll of bark.

[22]*Jewish Encyclopedia*, s.v. "Scroll."

[23]F. S. Burnell, "Staves and Sceptres," *Folklore* LIX (Dec. 1948), p. 165.

[24]In a large class of Semitic seals bearing the inscriptional form "*for* So-and-so" (the identical formula employed in Ezekiel), that formula "indicates thereby that the seal belongs to that man whose name is thus presented," and is not, as some have suggested, a dedicatory term. M. de Vogue, *Corpus Inscriptionum Semiticarum*, II, i, 56.

[25]Num. 17:2. A remarkable illustration of this may be found in the *Pastor of Hermas*, Simil. VIII, 1-6. For the same practice among the heathen nations, Nibley, *op. cit.*, pp. 335-7.

[26]Num. 34:13-29. The practice is dramatically described in one of the oldest of all Christian writings, I Clement, *Eaist.*, c. 43. Cf. R. Jamieson et al., *Commentary on the Old and New Testaments* (1878), p. 220.

[27]*The Abingdon Bible Commentary*, C. F. Eiselen, ed. (New York, 1929), p. 740.

[28]Thos. Scott, *Commentary on the Holy Bible* (London, 1850), IV, Ez. 37.

[29]Abingdon Commentary, *loc. cit.*

[30]See our long notes on this subject in *The Improvement Era* 56 (Feb. 1953), pp. 126-127. To these we should add Justin's remark (*Trypho,* c. 86), that "the rod of Aaron bearing blossoms showed him to be the High Priest. A rod from the root of Jesse became the Christ. . . . By the wood God showed himself to Abraham. Moses with a rod went to liberate the people; and holding the rod in his hands as commander of the nation he divided the Red Sea. By its power he struck water from the rock, and by throwing it into the waters of Merra he made them sweet . . . Jacob boasted that he passed through the river on this staff," etc. Innocent III in the thirteenth century rays that the pontifical staff signifies the power of Christ, and quotes Psalms ii and xliv as proof (*Patrol. Graec.* CCIVII, 790). Yet it is well known that the Pope of Rome has no official staff, a peculiarity explained by the legend of Eucherius of Trier (See *Patrol. Lat.* CCL, 600). The Bishop's crozier or staff makes its first appearance in the Christian Church no earlier than the fifth century (E. Power, "The Staff of the Apostles," *Biblica* IV (1923), 266), and by its earliest forms clearly betrays its borrowing from pagan cults. (Nibley, *loc. cit.*)

[31]Ginzberg, *Legends of the Jews,* II, 291; V. 412; VI, 106.

[32]E. g., by joining together the two broken ends (*Abingdon Commentary*); or else "the two sticks are being joined together lengthwise in the hand," (G. A. Cooke, *The Book of Ezekiel* (*Internat. Crit. Comm.,* N. Y.: Scribners, 1937), p. 401; or by simply carrying the sticks together in one hand (H. A. Ironside, *Ezekiel the Prophet* (New York: Loizeaux, 1949), p. 261; or "by a notch, docetail, glue, or some other such method," (A. Clarke, *Holy Bible Commentary and Notes* (New York: Abingdon) IV, 524; or by being tied together with a string, according to the Septuagint and many commentators. J. Skinner, *The Book of Ezekiel* (London, 1895) suggests that "when the rods are put together, they miraculously grow into one." On the other hand, some go so far as to say that "it is no longer necessary to assume that the action was really performed at all! (Thus Skinner, *loc. cit.*, and A. B. Davidson, *Ezekiel* (Cambridge Univ., 1896), s.v. Ch. 37.

[33]G. R. Driver, "Linguistic and Textual Problems: Ezekiel" *Biblica* XIX (1938), p .183.

[34]H. Jenkinson, "Exchequer Tallies," *Archaeologia* LXII (1911), p. 367.

[35]H. Jenkinson, "Medieval Tallies, Public and Private," *Ibid.* LXXIV (1924), pp. 305, 373 f, 370.

[36]*Ibid.,* LXII (1911) 374, and LXXIV (1924), 315, 369. 371. On the meaning of "bill,"*Ibid.,* p. 305.

[37]*Ibid.,* LXII (1911), 374, 371, 369; LXXIV (1924), 315

[38]Kautsch in the *Abingdon Commentary,* and Von Dummelow and Rabbi S. Fisch, *Ezekiel* (London: Soncino Press, 1950), p. 249, all favor Judah; against which the Cambridge Bible notes that the passages lays very heavy stress on the *equality* of the contracting parties, and not on the ascendancy of Judah. Both Davidson and Cooke favor "in *my* hand," though the latter (*Book of Ezekiel,* p. 401), confesses that "it sounds surprising."

[39]Ginzberg, *Legends,* III, 306.

[40]The best known source for the study of private tallies is the Jewish Plea Roll. Moreover, while tallies in England had to be inscribed in Latin, and even English and French were not permitted, *Hebrew* writing was allowed; and this special favor shown to an alien language shows that the Jews already had their own system of tally marking in the Middle Ages. Jenkinson, LII (1911), 378; LXXIV (1924), 313f, 293, 314.

[41]It is mentioned in the colophon of the oldest text of the Pentateuch in existence, the Aleppo Codex (cir. 930 A.D.): ". . . Rab Asher, may his soul be bound in the Bundle of Life with th righteous and wise prophets." (P. Kahle, *Masoreten des Westens* (Stuttgart, 1927) I, 3f); "May their souls be bound in the Bundle of Life in the Garden of Eden beneath the Tree of Life." (*Ibid.,* p. 6). For the great antiquity of the idea, M. A. Murray, "The Bundle of Life," in *Ancient Egypt,* 1930, Sept., Pt. iii, pp. 66ff,

[42]See above, Lesson II.

[43]Herntrich, *Ezechielbrobleme*, p. 118.

[44]S. Spiegel, "Noah, Daniel, and Job," in *Louis Ginzberg Jubilee Volume* (New York: Am. Acad. for Jewish Res., 1945), p. 309.

[45]Eusebius, *Demonstr. Evang.*, in *Patrol. Graec.*, XXII, 745.

[46]Jerome, Epist. 75 "On the Church & the Synagogue," c. 3, in *Patrol. Lat.* XXII, 683; on Jew and Gentile, *Ibid.* XXXV, 518, 168, 786; Comment. in Ezech. xl, c. 37, *Ibid.*, XXV, 350-4; The two sticks are Judah and Israel, who are no longer called Judah and Israel "but called by the single name of Judah: and in the figurative language of the prophet, a type and foreshadowing of our Lord and Savior, are held not in two hands, but in the single hand of Christ." To prove that their descendants shall be brought back to an original state of unity, Jerome then cites the pagan poet Virgil, *Aen.* IV! Morover, this unitl "shall not be after the manner of the flesh but of the spirit, by which the tribe of Ephraim is rejected and that of Judah is chosen, as in Ps. 78;67-68: 'And he rejects the tabernacle of Joseph and chooses not the tribe of Ephraim,' " etc. (Ib. 353). All this is the exact antithesis to what Ezekiel tells us!

[47]Irenaeus, *Contra Haereses* V, xvii, in *Patrol. Graec.* VII, 1171.

[48]Migne's commentary, in *Patrol. Graec.* VI, 681, n. 43.

[49]Origen, *Peri Archon* II, iii, 6, in *Patrol. Graec.* XI, 194.

[50]Irenaeus—Against the heresies. Book 5, Chapter 17 (*Patrol. Graec.* VII, 1171.)

[51]J. P. Migne's comment in *Patrol. Graec.* VI, 681, note 43.

[52]Clement Origen *Peri Achon* II, iii, 6, *Patrol. Graec.* II, 194 F.

Lesson 25 Notes

[1]*Book of Jubilees* 10:25: "For this reason the whole land of Shinar is called Babel, because the Lord did there confound all the languages of the children of men, and from thence they were dispersed into their cities . . ."

[2]B. Hrozny, in *Archiv Orientalni, Monographs*, No. VII, pp. 5-7.

[3]*Ibid.*, pp. 7-8, 22.

[4]An authoritative treatment of the natural forces that caused these migrations is the massive work of C. Schaeffer, *Stratigraphie Comparee et Chronologie de l'Asie Occidentale* (London, 1948). A good popular treatment with chronological charts and maps in Robt. J. Braidwood, *The Near East and the Foundations for Civilization* (Eugene, Ore.: Candon Lects., 1952.)

[5]*Lehi in the Desert*, etc., pp. 167-174. Many studies written since this one, including the two cited in the previous footnote, support our conclusions completely.

[6]See our discussion in *The Improvement Era* 59 (Mar. 1956), p. 152, and H. Grapow, *Die B ildlichen Ausdrüeke des Aegyptischen* (Leipzig, 1924), pp. 38f, 41, 49.

[7]*Pyr. Text.* No. 298 b-c, 299 a-b.

[8]R. Klinke-Rosenberg, "Das Götzenbuch Kitab al-Asnam des Ibn al-Kalbi," in *Samml. Or. Arb*, No 8, 1941, p. 58.

[9]F Wüstenfeld, in *Orient und Occident*, I, 331.

[10]A. Haldar, *The Notion of the Desert in Sumero-Accadian*, etc., pp. 22-23.

[11]*Ibid.*, p. 28.

[12]*Ibid.*, p. 19.

[13]*Ibid*, p. 24.

[14]*Ibid*, pp. 21-22.

[15]*Ib.*, p. 29.

[16]*Ib.*, p. 32

[17]B. Lewis, in *Bull. Or. & Afr. School*, XXIII, 318-320, with much more to the same effect.

[18]R Eisler, *Iesous Basileus*, etc., II, 662, 105, 107-9, 686, 114.

[19]*Jubilees*, 10:26.

[20]Sources in Eisler, *op. cit.*, II, n. 1. Eisler surmises that Ram means "high" and Rud means "wanderer," the same as Jared.

[21]Jubilees, 4:23   Among others, Bar Hebraeus, *Chron.* I, 3-4, reports that this happened in the days of the fall of the Tower.

[22]See *The Improvement Era* 59 (Oct. 1956), 712ff, for a number of cases in which these first kings (Hittite, Greek, Indian, Persian, Roman) always advance to the roar of thunder in the sky, swept along with the storm-wind, like the "raging lords" who first invaded Mesopotamia. (*Ibid.,* July 1956, p. 509), and Egypt (*Ibid.,* March, 1956), p. 152.

[23]Ether 2:3   *The Improvement Era,* April 1956, pp. 244ff; *Lehi in the Desert,* etc., pp. 184ff.

[24]*The Imrovement Era,* June 1956, pp. 390ff.

[25]See *The Improvement Era,* March 1956, p. 152 for sources.

[26]H. Kees, *Aegypten* (Munich: Beck, 1933), pp. 172ff.   This is the most authoritative work to appear so far on Egyptian economy and politics.

[27]Ether 2:16; 6:7. Discussed in *The Imrovement Era,* August 1956, pp. 566ff.

[28]*Ibid.,* p. 566.   A long and valuable Babylonian account of the building of the ark was copied very badly many years ago by George Smith; the original has vanished, but the texts has been carefully studied with an eye to reconstructing the boat, by Paul Haupt, "The Babylonian Noah," in *Beiträge zur Assyriologie* X, ii, 1-30.   All the main features of the prehistoric *Maghur*-boats seem to have survived in some of the huge river-craft still found on the streams of southeast Asia, to judge by the material in Jas. Hornell, "Primitive Types of Water Transport in Asia: Distribution and Origin," *Jnl. Roy. As. Soc.,* 1946, 124-141; especially Pl. XIV, fig. 2, looks like a typical *maghur*-boat. Speaking of the most "primitive" boats, C. S. Coon writes (*The Story of Man,* N. Y.: Knopf, 1954), p. 162: "Dogs howled, pigs grunted, and cocks crowed on these seagoing barnyards. . ." The idea that the oldest boats might have been built for the specific purpose of transporting large numbers of animals strikes any reader as strange at first, yet there is ample evidence now that such was the case!

[29]H. Freedman, *Midrash Rabbah,* I, 244.

[30]Sources for the statements that follow are given in the *Improvement Era* 59, August 1956, pp. 567 ff and September 1956, pp. 630 ff.

[31]Talmud Jerus., *Pesahim* I, i.

Lesson 26 Notes

[1]On the little understood paradox of good men as false prophets, see our *World and the Prophets,* pp. 230-2.

[2]Walter M. Patton, *Ahmed b. Hanbal and the Mihna* (Leiden, 1897), and in the *Ztschr. d. Dt. Morgenl. Ges.* LII, 155ff, has treated this strange theme.   More readily available are the comments of M. Trevor-Roper, *The Last Days of Hitler.*

[3]*Clem. Recog.,* I, 42, in *Patrol. Graec.* I, 1231.

[4]See above, pp. 8-10.

[5]Christ's teachings were utterly strange and hostile to the world into which they were introduced, "a slap in the face" to all conventional thought-forms, as the celebrated Karl Holl puts it, in "Urchristentum und Religions-geschichte," *Ztschr. für systematische Theologie* II (1924), 402; cf. Nibley, *op. cit.,* p. 146.

[6]Tal. Bab. *Sabbath,* XII, 4-5 (Goldschmidt I, 564.)

Lesson 28 Notes

[1]For a full and vivid account of this, see P. Herrmann, *Conquest by Man,* pp. 241-256.

[2]Above, p. 61, cf. pp. 114, 118-9, 135.

[3]L. Woolley, *Digging up the Past,* p. 66.

[4]An almost identical picture is presented in a recently discovered text from Ras Shamra, in which the hero Keret goes up to the top of the tower . . . lifts up his hands to heaven and sacrifices to Tor. his father Il . . .

Then he goes down from the roof and prepares food for the city, wheat for the community." Gordon, *Ugaritic Literature*, p. 71.

[5]"There is clear evidence, in certain well examined sub-areas (of the Near East), for rapid erosion of parts of the land since the end of the last ice age. This could depend either on greater rainfall or on tectonic movement, but another significant factor was undoubtedly deforestation, probably connected with the appearance of settled villages, husbanded sheep and goats, and expanded human population." R. J. Braidwood, *The Near East and the Foundations for Civilization* (Eugene Ore., 1952), p. 13. Man himself may have cause "the existing regime of absolute drought" in the Sahara, says V. G. Childe, "In fact the rock-pictures just demonstrate the survival of the . . . appropriate vegetation to a time when stock-breeders were actually using the latter as pasture." *New Light on the Most Ancient East* (4h ed., N. Y.: F. A. Prager, 1953), p. 17. The reader is especially recommended to Paul B. Sears, *Deserts on the March* (Univ. of Oklahoma, 1947).

[6]E. Ayres, "The Fuel Situation," *Scientific American* 195 (Oct., 1956), pp. 43 ff.

[7]See our discussion in the *Improvement Era*, 60 (Feb., 1957).

[8]Exactly the same picture is given in our apocryphal description of Abraham at home in Beersheba which, since it was written in the Holy Land, reflects actual conditions, not necessarily in Abraham's time but at the time of writing. *Jasher* XXII, 11-12.

[9]See below, pp. 368-9.

[10]See above, pp. 84ff.

Lesson 29 Notes

[1]See below, pp. 371-2.

[2]C. Hawkes, "Hill-Forts," *Antiquity* 5 (1931), 60-97; P. W. Townsend, "*Bur, Bure,* and *Baris* in Ancient North African Place Names," *Jnl. of Near Eastern Studies* 13 (1954), 52-55; K. Galling, in *Ztschr. d. Dt. Palest. Ver.,* 62, 112, all point to a single and uniform type of cummunal fortification throughout Europe and the Near East.

[3]At the end of the fourth century John Chrysostom speaks of 3,000 people joining the Church in one day and 5,000 in another as typical of the growth of the Church once it had been favored by the Emperors. (In *Patrol. Graec.* 55, 483).

[4]From the Tower of Psephinus at Jerusalem one could see Arabia and all the Hebrew territories, right up to the sea, according to Josephus, *Jewish War* V, 159.

[5]For other examples, see *Lehi in the Desert,* etc., pp. 231-8. In our own day the complete extermination of some nationalities has again become if not yet a reality at least a definite part of the program of some governments.

Appendix 1 Notes

[1]J. H. Rowe, "Archaeology as a Career," in *Archaeology* VII (Winter, 1954), p. 234.

[2]*Loc. cit.* The areas are so specialized that "the M.A. degree, which primarily qualifies the holder to teach at the secondary school level, is of no direct value in archaeology." *Ibid.,* p. 231.

[3]These are the conventional approaches to archaeology, which is never taught as an independent major: "Because it is important for archaeologists to have a solid grounding in the ancient languages of the areas where they intend to work, it is convenient to have the archaeology of those areas taught in direct association with the language." *Ibid.,* 230.

[4]T. J. Meek, in *Jnl. Am. Or. Soc.,* 63 (1943), p. 83.

[5]R. J. Braidwood, *Near East & Foundations for Civilization,* pp. 6-7, defining archaeology as "the discipline which reclaims and interprets the material remains of man's past." That pretty well covers everything, since there are

no immaterial remains: the immaterial part is purely a matter of modern reactions to ancient materials, including written documents.

[6]Rowe, op. cit., p. 229.

[7]Meek, op. cit., p. 86.

[8]J. W. Wilson, in Jnl. of Near Eastern Stud., I (1942), p. 6.

[9]R. E. Wheeler, in Antiquity, Sept. 1950, p. 129.

[10]S. J. De Laet, L'Archaeologie et ses Problemes (Berchem-Brussels: Latomus, 1954), pp. 7-9, 93.

[11]Ibid., p. 88.

[12]Ibid., pp. 89-92.

[13]S. N. Kramer, in Am. Jnl. Archaeol., 52 (1948), pp. 156-7.

[14]L. Woolley, Digging up the Past, p. 119.

[15]H. Breuil, in Anthropos 37-40, p. 687. He is speaking of course of prehistoric archaeology, but his study bears out what Woolley says about archaeology in general.

[16]Kramer, op. cit., p. 157.

[17]See Lehi in the Desert, etc., pp. 238-254.

[18]M. P. Nilsson, The Minoan-Mycenaean Religion (Lund: Gleerup, 1950), pp. 6-7.

[19]H. M. Chadwick & N. K. Chadwick, The Growth of Literature, I, 173, 296, 404, 424, 559.

[20]O. G. S. Crawford, in Antiquity, I, 434, and E. C. Curwen, Ibid., IV (1930) 22, for typical confusion of types.

[21]J. Barrington, in Archaeologia, I (1785), 281f, 286f.

[22]Ibid., p. 290.

[23]Essex, in Archaeologia IV, 74; C. Fox & C. A. R. Radford, Ibid., Vol. 83, p. 107, placing "the Prestone period of castle-building in England" between 1106 and 1275 A.D.

[24]Typical is the tremendous Viking border fort of Iborsk, which flourished first from 860 to 900 A.D., yet did not receive its rim of stone reenforcement until 1330 A.D., L. Tudeer, in Antiquity VIII (1734), 310-4.

[25]J. De Morgan, Prehistoire Orientale (Paris, 1926), II, 163-211.

[26]L. Whibley, Companion to Greek Studies (Cambridge, 1931), p. 261.

[27]W. Vycichl, "Notes sur la Prehistoire de la Langue Egyptienne," Orientalia XXIII (1954), 218.

[28]M. Noth, in Ztschr. d. Dt. Pal. Ver., 60 (1937), p. 196.

[29]Old prints show enormous Megalithic ruins such as those of Stonehenge and Avebury standing almost intact as late as the 18th and even mid-19th centuries. Their disappearance in the last hundred years is an astonishing phenomenon. C. Schuchardt, Alteuropa (Berlin: de Gruyter, 1935), has much to say on this theme.

[30]W. K. Moorhead, Fort Ancient, Ohio (Cincinnati, 1890), p. 107.

[31]Ibid., p. 102.

[32]C. Hawkes, in Antiquity V, p. 93.

[33]Ibid., p. 75: "The Dark Ages were in many ways the Early Iron Age restored," with the people moving back again into the old fortifications and reconditioning them for use, exactly as in the Book of Mormon (3 Ne. 6:7-8).

[34]A. A. Kampman, "De historische beteekenis der Hethietische vestingsbouwkunge,' in Kernmomenten, 1947, p. 142.

[35]F. Wagner, in Antiquity II, 43, 55.

[36]R. Firth, "Maori Hill-Forts," Antiquity I, (1927), 78.

[37]R. G. Collingwood, in Antiquity III, 274.

[38]Ed. King, "Observations on Ancient Castles," Archaeologia IV (1777), 365.

[39]Herrmann, Discovery by Man, p. 15.

[40]Ibid., p. 179.